8 Papers Relating to Claims to the Viscountcy of Tracy of Rathcoole

by Parliament Lords, Proc, Will. Iv

Address:
HardPress
8345 NW 66TH ST #2561
MIAMI FL 33166-2626
USA
Email: info@hardpress.net

MINUTES OF EVIDENCE

GIVEN BEFORE

THE COMMITTEE OF PRIVILEGES

TO WHOM

THE PETITION OF JAMES TRACY, ESQUIRE,

CLAIMING, AS OF RIGHT,

To BE VISCOUNT AND BARON TRACY

OF RATHCOOLE,

TOGETHER WITH

HER MAJESTY'S REFERENCE THEREOF TO THIS HOUSE,

WAS REFERRED,

7th May and 18*th June* 1839.

Ordered to be printed 19th March 1841.

Die Martis, 7° *Maii* 1839.

The Earl of SHAFTESBURY in the Chair.

Evidence on the
Tracy Claim of
Peerage.

THE Order of Reference was read.

The Petition of James Tracy, of No. 11, South Street, Grosvenor Square, in the County of Middlesex, Esquire, to His late Majesty, praying that it may be declared and adjudged that the Petitioner is entitled to the Title, Honour, and Dignity of Viscount and Baron Tracy of Rathcoole, together with Her Majesty's Reference thereof to this House, and the Report of Her Majesty's Attorney General thereunto annexed, were read.

The Counsel and Parties were ordered to be called in.

And Sir Frederick Pollock, Mr. Hedley, and Mr. Gibson appearing as Counsel for the Petitioner;

And Mr. Attorney General appearing on behalf of the Crown;

Sir Frederick Pollock stated, That as only a short Time could be given to the Case To-day, he would, with Permission of the House, defer his Opening to another Day, and proceed to examine Two Clergymen, who were very anxious to return as soon as possible to their Homes.

Then the Reverend GEORGE SALE PRIOR was called in; and having been sworn, was examined as follows:

Rev. G. S. Prior.

(*Mr. Hedley.*) Who are you?
I am the Curate of Toddington. I have a Certificate from the Rector of Toddington, who is very old and very infirm, and it would have been impossible for him to have attended without great Inconvenience, and indeed Danger. He is the Incumbent of Didbrooke and Toddington, which are united Parishes.

Do you produce the Parish Registers of Toddington?
I do; here is the Register of the Year 1836.

What is the Book you have in your Hand?
This is the Didbrooke Register, for Hayles and Didbrooke, of the Date of 1686.

(*Mr. Attorney General.*) Is it Toddington cum Didbrooke?
Toddington cum Didbrooke; it is Didbrooke cum Hayles, and Toddington cum Stanway, but the Two are united Parishes, and therefore they are in fact One.

But with separate Registers?
With separate Registers.

(46.1.)　　　　　　　　　A 2　　　　　　　　　Are

Rev. G. S. Prior.

Are you Curate of Didbrooke?
No, I am not Curate of Didbrooke.
Is there a Curate of Didbrooke?
There is.

Mr. Attorney General submitted, That as the Witness was not the Curate of Didbrooke, his Evidence was not sufficient with respect to the Registers of that Parish.

Sir Frederick Pollock stated, That he would confine the Question to this Witness to the Toddington Registers, and that he would upon a future Day produce the Clergyman of Didbrooke.

(*Mr. Attorney General.*) Are you aware that this is the Toddington Register?
Yes.

How long have you been Curate of Toddington?
Half a Year. The Register was passed into my Custody, as Curate; and has been in the joint Custody of myself and the Rector during the Time I have been there.

And this, with other Parts of the Register, was handed over to you?
It was in an Iron Chest that is particularly set aside for the Custody of the Registers.

(*Mr. Hedley.*) Do you find in the Register an Entry of the Burial of Elizabeth Tracy, of the 26th of September 1688?
I do.

The same was read as follows:

No. 1.

" Anno Doñi (88).

" The Right Hoñble the Lady Elizabeth Tracy died September yᵉ 20ᵗʰ, and was buried Septembʳ 26ᵗʰ, Anno p̃edicꞇ."

What is the Year?
Anno Domini 1688.

The only Date in the Entry is 1688, but what is the Date of the preceding Entry?
1687.

Have you the Register of the Year 1686?
Yes.

The same was read as follows:

No. 2.

" Anno Doñii 1686.

" The Right Honʳble John Lord Viscount Tracy died March yᵉ 8ᵗʰ, and was buried March yᵉ 11ᵗʰ, Anno p̃edicꞇ."

Have you the Register of the Year 1684?
I have.

Will you read the Entry you find there?

The same was read as follows:

No. 3.

" Anno Doñii 1684.

" John, the Son of William Tracy, Esq., and Frances his Wife, was baptized April yᵉ 30ᵗʰ, Anno p̃edicto."

In

In the same Year have you another Entry ?
Yes.

The same was read as follows :
" Anno Dom̃ 1684.

No. 4.

" John, the Son of William Tracy, Esq., and Frances his Wife, was buried May the 1ˢᵗ."

Do you find an Entry of a Burial in 1687 ?
I do.

The same was read as follows :
" 1687.

No. 5.

" The Right Hoñble ye Lady Frances Tracy died March yᵉ 20ᵗʰ, and was buried March 23ʳᵈ, Anno p̃edict."

Have you an Entry of Baptism in the Year 1690 ?
I have.

The same was read as follows :
" 1690.

No. 6.

" Thomas Charles, the Son and Heir of yᵉ Rᵗ Hoñable William Lord Viscount Tracy and the Rᵗ Hoñble the Lady Jane Tracy, was born on Sunday yᵉ 27ᵗʰ Day of July, about Halfe an Hour after Seaven in yᵉ Evening, and was baptized Aug. 3."

(Mr. Attorney General.) Did you receive the Entry of Burials at the same Time as the Registry of Baptisms?
It is in the same Book.

(Mr. Hedley.) Do you find an Entry of a Burial in 1707 ?
I do.

The same was read as follows :
" Anno Dom̃ 1707.

No. 7.

" The Right Honorable yᵉ Lady Jane Tracy died Feb. 25, & was buried Feb. 27."

Is it signed ?
It is signed " Samuel Jefferis Vic. de Toddington." It does not form Part of the Entry, I think.

Have you an Entry of a Burial in 1712?
I have.

The same was read as follows :
" Anno Dom̃ 1712.

No. 8.

" The Right Hoñble William Lord Viscᵗ Tracy died Apr. 18, was buried April 19."

Have you an Entry of a Baptism in 1715?
I have.

The same was read as follows :

No. 9.

" William, Son of yᵉ Rᵗ Honᵇˡᵉ Thomas Charles L. Viscount Tracy, was born at Stratford upon Avon, August 25, 1715, and baptized there."

B Do

Do you find an Entry of any Baptism in 1719 ?
I do.

The same was read as follows :

No. 10.

" 1719.

" Thomas Charles, Son of y⁰ R ͭ Hon ᵇˡᵉ Thomas Charles Visc ͭ Tracy, was born June 15, & baptiz'd July 12 ͭʰ."

Do you find an Entry of any Burial in 1752 ?
I do.

The same was read as follows :

No. 11.

" 1752.

" The Hon ᵇˡᵉ William Tracy, Esq ͬ, Son to the Right Hon ᵇˡᵉ Thomas Charles Lord Viscount Tracy by the Lady Elizabeth, was buried April 15 ͭʰ."

Have you an Entry of any Burial in 1719 ?
I have.

The same was read as follows :

No. 12.

" 1719.

" The R ͭ Hon ᵇˡᵉ Elizabeth Viscountess Tracy was buried Nov ᵇʳ 1 ˢᵗ."

Have you an Entry of a Burial in 1756 ?
I have.

The same was read as follows :

No. 13.

" 1756.

" The Right Hon ᵇˡᵉ Thomas Charles Lord Viscount Tracy was buried June 7 ͭʰ."

Do you find an Entry of a Burial in 1792 ?
I do.

The same was read as follows :

No. 14.

" 1792, August 18 ͭʰ.

" The Right Honourable Thomas Charles Leigh Lord Viscount Tracy was buried."

Do you find an Entry of Baptism in 1722 ?
I do.

The same was read as follows :

No. 15.

" 1722.

" John the Son of y ͤ R ͭ Honourable Thomas Charles Lord Viscount Tracy by y ͤ Lady Ffrances was born August 18, and baptiz'd August 26."

Have you an Entry of a Baptism in the Year 1725 ?
I have.

The same was read as follows :

No. 16.

" 1725.

" Robert Pakington, Son of y ͤ R ͭ Hon ᵇˡᵉ Thomas Charles Lord Viscount Tracy by the Lady Frances, was born August 28, and bap- tiz'd September 21, 1725."

Have

Have you an Entry of a Baptism in 1732 ?

I have.

The same was read as follows :

"1732.

" Henry, Son of the R^t Honble the Ld Viscount Tracy by the Lady Frances, was born January 25th, and baptiz'd February 8th."

Do you find an Entry of a Burial in the Year 1751 ?
I do.

The same was read as follows :

"1751.

" The R^t Honble Frances Viscountess Tracy was buried April 26th.

Do you find an Entry of a Burial in 1791 ?
I do, under the Head of Burials in 1793.

The same was read as follows :

"1793, February 10th.

" The Right Honourable and Reverend John Lord Viscount Tracy, D.D., Warden of All Souls College, Oxford."

Have you an Entry of a Burial in 1783 ?
I have.

The same was read as follows :

"1783, Novr 25th.

" Buried the Honble Mrs Susanna Tracy, Wife of the Honble Henry Tracy."

Do you find an Entry of a Burial in 1797 ?
I do.

The same was read as follows :

"1797.

" May 11th. The Right Honourable Henry Leigh Lord Viscount Tracy was buried, Æ. 64."

Have you an Entry of a Burial in the Year 1676 ?
I have.

The same was read as follows :

"1676.

" Mr. Charles Tracey was buried May ye 6th, Anno p̃edicto."

Do you find an Entry of a Burial in 1682 ?
I do.

The same was read as follows :

" Anno Dom̃i 1682.

" Ferdinando, the Son of Ferdinando Tracy, Esqr, & Katherine his Wife, was buried Feb. ye 19th, Anno p̃edict."

The Witness was directed to withdraw.

(46.1.)

Rev. F. E. Witts. Then the Reverend FRANCIS EDWARD WITTS was called in, and having been sworn, was examined as follows:

(*Mr. Hedley.*)   What are you?
I am Incumbent of Stanway ; Vicar of Stanway.

Do you produce the Stanway Registers?
I do.   These are the Register Books of the Parish of Stanway.

Have you an Entry of a Burial in the Year 1761 ?
I have.

The same was read as follows:

No. 24.   " 1761.

" M" Ann Tracy (Relict of John Tracy, Esq°,) was buried October y° 28th."

Do you find a Burial in the Year 1729?
I do.

The same was read as follows:

No. 25.   " 1729.

" Maij — Ferdinando, Filius Johannis Tracy, Armigeri, sepultus, p. iii°."

Have you an Entry of a Burial in 1729?
I have.

The same was read as follows:

No. 26.   " 1729.

" Maij — Gulielmus, Filius Johannis et Annæ Tracy, Armig^r, sepultus, xvii°."

Do you find an Entry of a Baptism in 1721 ?
I do.

The same was read as follows:

No. 27.   " 1721.

" Jan. — Gulielmus, Filius Johannis Tracy, Armigeri, baptizatus, viiii°."

(*Sir Frederick Pollock.*)   Did you know the last Viscount Tracy ?
No.

Or his Family ?
His Family I have known ; his Descendants.

Do you know whether he left any Issue Male ?
I have always understood not.

(*Mr. Attorney General.*)   By his Descendants you mean the Children of Lord Sudely ?
The Children of Lord Sudely.

The Witness was directed to withdraw.

Then

Then **ALFRED HYDE CLARKE** was called in ; and having been *Alfred H. Clarke.*
sworn, was examined as follows :

(*Sir Frederick Pollock.*) Are you Clerk to the Solicitor for the Claimant?
I am.

Have you handed in Copies of the Entries in the Parish Registers which have been read?
I have.

Are they all of them true Copies ?
They are.

In whose Handwriting are they?
The greater Part of them my own.

Have you compared every one of them with the original Entries ?
The whole of them.

They are literally Copies ?
Literally.

The Witness was directed to withdraw.

Proposed to adjourn this Committee *sine Die ;*

Accordingly,

Adjourned *sine Die.*

Die Martis, 18° *Junii* 1839.

The Earl of SHAFTESBURY in the Chair.

THE Order of Adjournment was read.

The Minutes of the last Committee were read.

The Counsel and Parties were ordered to be called in.

Sir Frederick Pollock, Mr. Hedley, and Mr. Gibson appeared as Counsel for the Claimant.

Mr. Attorney General appeared on behalf of the Crown.

Mr. Hedley stated, That he proposed to fill up the Blanks in the former Day's Proceedings, by putting in the Proofs in the First and Second Divisions of the Case. That in the first place he proposed to prove the Grant of the Dignity of Viscount and Baron Tracy of Rathcoole.

Then HENRY GEORGE HOLDEN, Esquire, was called in ; and having been sworn, was examined as follows :

(Mr. Hedley.) What are you?
I am a Clerk in the Record Office in the Rolls Chapel.

What do you produce?
The Inrolment of Letters Patent creating Sir John Tracy to be Baron and Viscount Tracy of Rathcoole in the Kingdom of Ireland, dated 18th of Charles the First.

The same was read as follows :

D coñ honoř Joħi Tracy ⎱ Rex ℔č. archiep̄is ducib₃ marchioñ comitib₃
  miƚ ℔ hered̃.   ⎰   vicecomitib₃ ep̄is baronib₃ militib₃ pre-
positis lib̄is homiñ ac om̄ib₃ officiař ministř ℔ subditis nr̄is quibuscunꝗ,
ad quos p̄sentes lr̄e pveneř salƚm   Regalis nr̄e dignitaƚ fastigiū ornari
℔ augeri censem⁰ cum viri virtuƚ splendore geñis nobilitaƚ ℔ fortuñ
amplitudiñ p̄lucentes hono₃ tiƚlis decorant⁰ ℔ insigniunt⁰ hinc eciam
industř atꝗ, virtutes om̄es eximie excitari comp̄im⁰ ℔ augeri qđ nos
serius ꝑpendeñ regio intuitu inspexim⁰ merita clarissimi viri Joħis
Tracy de Toddington in coñ nr̄o Gloucestř miƚ cujus non solum virtus
spectatissima sed ℔ nataliū splendoř antiqua origiñ ℔ illustriū majo₃
serie p̄celebris satis eciam amplo patrimoñ ad nobilitatis tiƚlos honorifice
sustentandos locupletaƚ ejusmodi eum virum exhibet qui in magnaƚ
nuṁum condigne sit adsciscendus   Ideo equū invenim⁰ et meriƚ tam

(46.2.)   insignis

Side notes:

Evidence on the Tracy Claim of Peerage.

H. G. Holden, Esq.

No. 28.

H. G. Holden, Esq.

insignis viri consentaneũ esse duxim° ut honoris accessioñ nobilitat̃ foret atq̢ eum in statum titl̃m honorem nomen ꝉ dignitatem tam vice-comĩ q°m baroñ in regno nr̃o Hiꞇnie creand̃ censuim° Sciatis igit̃ q̃d nos de gr̃a nr̃a sp̃iat̃ ex ꝭta scienc̃ ꝉ mero motu nr̃is p̃fat̃ Joh̃em Tracy ad statum gradum dignitat̃ ꝉ honoꝛ baronis ꝉ vicecomitis Tracy de Rathcule in comĩ nr̃o Dubliñ infra regnũ nr̃m Hiꞇnie constituim° ordinavim° erexim° p̃fecim° ꝉ creavim° ip̃mq̢ Joh̃em Tracy baroñ ꝉ vicecomitem Tracy de Rathcule in comĩ nr̃o Dubliñ infra regnũ nr̃m Hiꞇnie constituim° p̃ficim° erigim° ordinam° ꝉ cream° p p̃sentes eidemq̢ Joh̃i nomen statum titl̃m dignitat̃ graduum ꝉ honoꝛ baroñ ꝉ vicecomĩ Tracy de Rathcule imposuim° dedim° ꝉ p̃buim° ꝉ p p̃sentes imponim° dam° ꝉ p̃bem° h̃end̃ ꝉ tenend̃ eadem stat̃ grad̃ dignitatem titl̃m nomen ꝉ honoꝛ p̃fat̃ Joh̃i ꝉ hered̃ masculis de corpore suo exeuñ imp̃p̃m voleñ ꝉ p p̃sentes concedeñ p nob̃ hered̃ ꝉ successoꝛ nr̃is q̃d p̃dict̃ Joh̃es ꝉ hered̃ sui masculi de corpore suo exeuñ p̃dict̃ nomen statum gradum stilum titl̃m dignitat̃ ꝉ honorem gerant ꝉ teneant ꝉ quil̃t eoꝛ gerat ꝉ teneat ꝉ p nomen baronis ꝉ vicecomĩ Tracy de Rathcule vocent̃ ꝉ nuncupent̃ ꝉ eoꝛ quil̃t vocet̃ ꝉ nuncupet̃ q̃dq̢ p̃dict̃ Joh̃es ꝉ hered̃ sui masculi successive baroñ ꝉ vicecomĩ Tracy de Rathcule in omĩibꝫ teneant̃ ꝉ ut baroñ ꝉ vicecomĩ t°ctent̃ ꝉ reputent̃ ꝉ eoꝛ quil̃t teneat̃ t°ctet̃ ꝉ reputet̃ q̃dq̢ p̃dict̃ Joh̃es ꝉ hered̃ sui masculi p̃dict̃ ꝉ eoꝛ quil̃t h̃eat teneat ꝉ possideat sedem locum ꝉ vocem in parliameñ publicis comiciis atq̢ conciliis nr̃is hered̃ ꝉ successoꝛ nr̃oꝛ infra regnũ nr̃m Hiꞇnie int̃ alios baroñ ꝉ vicecomĩ ut baroñ ꝉ vicecomĩ parliameñ ꝉ publicoꝛ comicioꝛ ꝉ concilioꝛ Et q̃d p̃dict̃ Joh̃es ꝉ hered̃ sui masculi p̃dict̃ uxꝝes ꝉ libi tam masculi q°m femelli gaudeant ꝉ utant̃ ꝉ eoꝛ quil̃t ꝉ quel̃t gaudeat ꝉ utat̃ omĩibꝫ ꝉ singulis paribꝫ privileg̃ p̃heminenc̃ p̃cedenc̃ ꝉ imũunitat̃ ad statum ꝉ loc̃ baroñ ꝉ vicecomĩ regni nr̃i Hiꞇnie in omñ rite ꝉ de jure p̃tiñ quibꝫ ceꞇi baroñ ꝉ vicecomites d̃c̃i regni nr̃i Hiꞇnie ante hec tempora melius honorificencius ꝉ quietius usi sunt ꝉ gaviš seu in p̃senti gaudent ꝉ utunt̃ Volum° eciam t̃c̃ Absq̢ fine in hanapio t̃c̃ In cujus rei t̃c̃ T. ꞃ. apud Oxoñ duodecimo die Januaꝛ. ꝑ ip̃m Regem.

Have you an Office Copy?
I have; it is examined by myself.

The Counsel being asked whether Search had been made for the original Patent.

Sir Frederick Pollock stated, That the Claimant had no Means of searching in any Direction; that it could not possibly be in any Custody or Possession to which he had Access; that he had inherited no Estate, and was not the personal Representative; and therefore had no Muni-ments to refer to, and had not entitled himself to search for Papers.

The Counsel were informed, That the Evidence might be received de bene esse.

The same was delivered in.

Mr.

Mr. Hedley stated, That he proposed next to prove that Robert Tracy was the Second Viscount, and that John Tracy was his eldest Son and Heir.

Then Mr. GEORGE JAMES MUSSETT was called in; and having been sworn, was examined as follows:

Mr. G. J. Mussett.

(*Mr. Hedley.*)   What are you?
A Clerk in the Prerogative Office, Doctors Commons.

Do you produce a Will?
I produce an official Copy, which was left on the File when the Original was delivered out; the Original having been delivered out.   It is the Will of Sir Robert Tracy of Alderton in the County of Gloucester, Knight, Lord Viscount Tracy of Rathcule in the County of Dublin; it is dated the 3d of May 1662, and proved the 25th of June 1662.

By whom is it executed?
He describes himself as Sir Robert Tracy Lord Viscount Tracy of Rathcule in the County of Dublin.

To whom was the Probate granted?
To the Honourable John Tracy Viscount Tracy of Rathcule, the Son—" filii naturalis," and general Executor.

An Extract was read therefrom as follows:

* * * * And as to for or concerning all and singuler the same lands tenements and hereditaments herein-before in vse lymited vnto the said dame Dorothy my wife from and imediately after my decease and the determinačon of the said estates herein-before lymited vnto the said dame Dorothy concerning the same respectively and also as to for and concerning all and singuler the rest and residue of the said mannors lands tenements and hereditaments whatsoever in the said indenture menčoned and thereby graunted and released or menčoned to bee graunted and released withall and singuler their and every of their appurtenances from and imediately after my decease to the vse and behoofe of John Cocks of the Middle Temple London esq' Henry Cocks of the Middle Temple aforesaid gent and their heyres and assignes for ever vpon speciall trust and confidence nevertheles and to the intent and purpose that they the said John Cocks and Henry Cocks their heyres and assignes or the survivor of them and his heyres shall by and with the rents issues and proffitts of the said mannors lands and premisses or by sale demise or mortgage thereof or of any part or parts parcell or parcells thereof or otherwise as to them in their discrečons shall seeme fitt levy and raise moneys and therewith satisfy all such debts as I shall justly and truely owe vnto any person or persons at the time of my decease and alsoe satisfy and pay vnto each of my three sonnes viz' Thomas William and Henry and to my daughter Frances severally the yearely sume or annuity of threescore pounds apeece dureing their respective lives and vnto my sonnes Robert and Benjamin and vnto my daughter Mary the yearely summe of twenty poundes a peece to be paid vnto my deare wife Dorothy their mother for and towards their maintenance vntill such time as their respective porčons hereafter by me given shall become due and payable if they shall soe long live to bee paid vnto them severally at twoe feasts or dayes of pay-

No. 29.

Mr. G. J. Mussett.

ment that is to say the feast of St Phillip and Jacob and the feast of All Saints yearely in every yeare by equall porçons the first payment to begin at such of the said feasts as shall first and next happen after my decease and alsoe satisfy and pay vnto every of my said three sonnes vizt Thomas William and Henry and my daughter Frances from and after the decease of dame Mary Vere widowe who hath an estate for her life in some part of the said lands and premisses the further yearely summe of forty poundes apeece during their respective lives over and besides the yearely sūme of threescore poundes apeece * * * * And my further will is that in case my said sonne and heyre apparent shall bee willing to take vpon him the management of the premisses and truely to pay and satisfy all the debts annuityes or yearely sums of money or other sūmes of money herein-before appointed to bee paid that then at his request the said John Cocks and Henry Cocks their heyres and assignes shall and may convey all the said lands tenements and hereditaments vnto him the said John Tracy and his heyres soe as in such conveyance soe to be made there be effectually conteyned a provisoe or condiĉon for payment of all the said debts annuityes or yearely sūmes of money or other sūmes of money herein-before appointed to bee paid soe that in case of any default to bee made in payment thereof or of any of them the said John Cocks and Henry Cocks and their heyres may reenter and have againe all the said lands and premisses for the performance of the trusts aforesaid * * * * And I do make and ordaine the said John Cocks and Henry Cocks to bee executors of this my last will and testament and doe give vnto them the sūme of twenty poundes a peece for their paines and care herein provided nevertheles that if my said sonne John Tracy doe within the space of three moneths after my decease take vpon him the management and performance of the trust above menĉoned and shall accept and seale and deliver as his act and deed the counterparte of such a condiĉonall conveyance as is abovemenĉoned that then and from thenceforth hee the said John Tracy shall bee sole executor of this my last will and testament   Item my will is that my wife doe dispose of all my wearing apparrell and doe recommend to her care Alice Stephens my mayd   In witnes whereof I haue herevnto set my hand and seale this third day of May annoq, Dñi 1662 and in the fourteenth yeare of the raigne of our gratious soveraigne lord Charles the second by the grace of God of England Scotland France and Ireland king defender of the faith &c.

The marke of the lord viscount Tracy.

Signed sealed and published to be my last will
and testament in the presence of
ANTHONY IZOD.
RICHARD WILKINS.

Probatum fuit testamentum suprascriptum apud Londoñ coram veñli viro Jacobo Master legum dĉore surrō veñlis viri dñi Guilielmi Mericke militis legum etiam dĉoris curiæ prærogativæ Canͭ maḡri custodis sive com̄issarii ͭtime constituti vicesimo quinto die mensˢ Junii anno Dñi miͭtimo sexcentesimo sexagesimo sĉdo juramento honorandi viri Joħis dñi Tracy modo ᵗñi vicecomiͭe Tracy de Rachcule filii ñralis ͭtimi dĉi defunĉt et executoris generalis in testamento predĉo nominaͭt cui com̄issa fuit administraĉo omnium et singulorum bonorum
jurium

jurium et creditorum dc̄i defuncti de bene et fidelr administrand̄ eadem ad Sancta Dei Evangelia jurat̄ (Johanne Cocks ar̄ et Henrico Cocks generoso executoribus specialibus in testamento pred̄c̄o defunct̄ sub limitac̄onibus in eod̄m testamento expressis nominat̄ onus execut̄onis testament̄ pred̄c̄i in se acceptare penitus et expresse ad huc (et in præsenti etiam) respective recusantibus vt coram judice tempore p̃stac̄onis juramenti predict̄ p eosdem executores speciales etiam in judicio respective presentes extitit allegatum).

Then Mr. ALFRED CLARKE was called in ; and having been sworn, was examined as follows :

(*Mr. Hedley.*) Do you produce an examined Copy of the Will just produced ?
I do.

Did you examine that yourself ?
I did.

It is correct ?
It is.

The same was delivered in.

Mr. Hedley stated, That he proposed next to prove that John the eldest Son of Robert the Second Viscount succeeded, and became the Third Viscount.

Then HENRY GEORGE HOLDEN, Esquire, was further examined, as follows :

(*Mr. Hedley.*) What do you produce ?
I produce the Inrolment of a Commission to Clarencieux King of Arms to visit, in the First of James.

The same was read as follows :

Com̄ sp̄ial Wil̄lo Camden ar̄. } James by the grace of God &c. To oure trustie and welbeloved servaunte William Camden esquier surnamed Clarencieulx kinge of armes of the east west and southe partes of oure realme of Englande from the ryver of Trente southwardes and to all other oure lovynge subject̃ greetinge Forasmuche as God of his greate clemencye and goodnes hathe subjected to oure empyre and governance the nobillitie people and com̄ons of this realme of Englande Wee myndynge of oure royall and absolute power to us com̄ytted to visitte survey and viewe throughout all oure realme of Englande and other domynyons aswell for a due order to be kepte and observed in all things touchinge the office and dueties appteyninge to armes as also for reformac̄on of dyvers and sundrie abuses and disorders daylye arysynge and groweinge for wante of ordynarie vysytac̄ons surveys and viewes in tymes conveniente accordinge to the aunciente forme and laudable custom̄e of the lawes of armes And that the nobillitie of thys realme maye be preserved in everie degree as appperteyneth aswell in honor as in worshippe And that every person and persons bodies politique corporate and others maye be the better knowne in hys and theire estate degree and mys-   terye

(46.2.)

terye without confusion or disorder Have therefore constituted deputed ordayned and appoynted for us and in oure name oure saide welbeloved Svante William Camden esquire alias Clarencieulx kinge of armes in the said easte west and southe partes of oure realme of Englande from the saide river of Trente southwarde to visitte all the saide province and the partes and members thereof apperteynynge to the offyce and charge of the saide Clarencieulx kinge of armes from tyme to tyme as often and when as he shall thinke moste necessarye and conveniente for the same And not onelye to enter into all churches castles howses and other places at hys discrecion to peruse and take knowledge survey and viewe of all manner of armes cognisances creste and other devises of armes of all and singuler oure subjecte aswell bodies pollitique as others within the saide province of what dignitie or degree estate or mysterie soever they be lawfullye aucthorised to have use or beare any suche armes cognizances creste and other like devises with the notes of theire discentes pedegries and marriages And the same to enter of recorde in a regyster booke of armes accordinge to suche order as ys prescrybed and sett forthe in the office charge and oathe taken by oure saide servante at his creaçon and coronaçon but also to correcte controlle and reforme all manner of armes crestes cognysaunces and devices unlawfull or unlawfullie usurped borne or taken by any manner person or persons within the same province cont*rye to the due order of the lawe of armes And the same to reverse pull downe or otherwise deface at his discrecion aswell in cote armes helme standerde pennons and hatchmentes of tentes and pavilions as alsoe in plate jewells paper parchmente wyndowes gravestones and monumentes or elles where wheresoever they be sett or placed whether they be in sheilde scutcheon lozenge square roundell or otherwise howsoever contrary to the antiquitie and aunciente lawes customes rules priviledge and orders of armes And further wee by theise presentes doe give and graunte to the saide Clarencieulx full power and aucthoritie to reprove controlle and make infamous by pclamaçon to be made at the assizes or generall sessions within the same hys province to be had and kepte or at suche other place or places as he or they shall thinke moste meete and conveniente all and all manner of person or persons that unlawfullye and withoute juste aucthoritie vocaçon or due callinge do or have donne or shall usurpe to take uppon hym or them anye manner of tytle of honor or dignitie as esquier gentleman or other And likewyse to reforme and comptrolle all suche as at any funeralle or intermentes shall use or weare anye mourninge apparell as gownes hoodes tippetts or suche like cont*rie to the order lymitted and prescrybed in the tyme of the moste noble prince kynge Henrie of famous memorie the seaventh oure grandfather otherwise or in anye other sorte then to theire estates and degrees dothe or shall appertayne And furthermore by theise presentes wee prohibitte and forbidde that no paynter glasier gouldsmythe graver or any other artyfycer whatsoever he or they be within the saide province of the saide Clarencieulx shall take uppon them to paynte grave glase devise or sett forthe by anye wayes or meanes any manner of armes crestes cognyzaunce pedegrees or other devises appertaynynge to the offyce of armes otherwise or in anye other forme or manner then they maye lawfullie doe and shalbe allowed by the saide Clarencieulx hys deputie or deputies accordinge to the auncyente lawes and statutes of armes And wee forbidde and straightlie comaunde all oure sheriffes comyssyoners archdeacons officialle scryvenors clerks wryters or other

H. G. Holden, Esq.

β
whatsoever

H. G. Holden, Esq.

whatsoever they be to calle name or write in anye assyse sessyons courte or other open place or places or ells to use in any writinge the addicōn of esquire or gentleman unlesse they be able to stande unto and justyfye the same by the lawe of armes of oure realme or ells be ascertened thereof by advertysemente in writinge from the saide Clarencieulx kinge of armes or his deputye or deputies attorney or attorneys And further wee straightlie charge and comaunde that noe other person or persons shall intromytte or meddle with anye thinge or thinges touchinge and concerninge the office of armes within the saide provynce without speciall lycence and aucthoritie of the saide Clarencieulx in writinge under the seale of the said office firste had and obteyned from the saide Clarencieulx All the which said power prehemynence jurisdiccōn and aucthoritie above specified for us oure heires and successors wee doe geve and graunte by theise presentℯ to the saide Willm Camden alias Clarencieulx dueringe his naturall lief in as large and ample manner and forme in everye thinge and thingℯ as anye hys predecessors or anye other bearinge the name or tytle of Clarencieulx have or had did or mighte doe by force of anye ℓres patentes graunted by anye of oure p̄decessors or as of righte he or they oughte or mighte have used to doe and exercysed by force of his saide office with all manner of proffittℯ advantages and emolumentes thereunto belonginge Wherefore wee will and straightlie charge and comaunde all and singuler oure justices sheriffes mayors bailiffs and all other oure officers mynysters and constables and all and everie oure lovinge subjectℯ that in the execucōn of the premysses they effectuallye imploye theire best ayde assistaunce furtheraunce and counsaile to oure saide servante hys deputie or deputies soe often and when as he or anye of them shall requyre the same in all that they convenientlie maye as they tender oure favoure and will answeare the contrarie at theire perrill And further by theise presentes wee doe aucthorise oure saide servante to nomynate and appoynte under the seale of his saide office soe manye deputies or attorneys as shalbe thoughte to hym expediente for the better execucōn of all and singuler the premysses And yf there fortune to falle oute in this visitacōn any manner of scruple doubte questyon or anye mysdemeanor of anye person or persons whatsoever that cannot be convenientlye decided or ended by oure saide servante or by suche deputie or deputyes or attorneys as he under the seale of hys saide offyce shall name and appoynte Then oure mynde and pleasure ys that oure saide servante hys deputye deputies or attorneis named as ys aforesaid shall comaunde suche person or persons whome the saide question scruple or misdeameanor shall concerne under a certayne payne and at a certen daie to appeare before the earle marshall of Englande for the tyme before whome the saide scruple question or misdemeanor shalbe hearde and ordered accordinge to the lawes and custome of armes in that case provided and of auncyente tyme used anye statute lawe p̄clamacōn custome or usage to the contrarie in any wise notwithstandynge In wytnes whereof &c. Wytnes oure selfe at Harfeilde the fyfte daye of Auguste.

p bře de privato sigillo &c.

Have you an Office Copy of that Commission?
Yes; it is examined by me.

The same was delivered in.

T. W. King, Esq.

Then THOMAS WILLIAM KING Esquire was called in; and having been sworn, was examined as follows:

(*Mr. Hedley.*)   What is it you produce?
This is the original Book of Visitation of the County of Gloucester, taken in the Year 1623.

Is that signed?
It is signed by Two Members of the Family.

What are their Names?
It is signed by a John Tracy and Paul Tracy, of Two different Lines.

(*By a Lord.*)   By what Officer does it appear to have been made?
It is made by William Camden, Clarencieux.

Does that appear upon it?
It does not appear upon the Face of the Pedigree.

How do you know that Fact; is there a Title to the Book?
I do not know whether there is any Title to the Book.

(*Mr. Hedley.*)   From whence do you produce it?
From the Heralds College.

Is it kept there among the Muniments?
Yes.

(*By a Lord.*)   How is it described?
There is no Title Page to it.   We receive it as the original Book of Visitation of the County of Gloucester, made in 1623, Camden being the Clarencieux.

How do you connect that with the Commission?
From its Date; the Commission is granted to Camden for Life, and he was living in 1623.

Has it any official Signature?
No; only the Signatures of the Parties.

Are not your Visitation Books generally intituled?
They are.

(*Mr. Hedley.*)   Can you identify that with the Commission?
No further than by the Corroboration of the Dates.

Is it like the other official Books in the Office?
Oh yes, precisely so.

Both before and after?
Oh yes; it is upon the same Principle exactly.

And having the same Appearance?
Yes, the same Appearance in every respect.

It was taken by the same Person who is mentioned in the Commission?
Either taken by him or his Deputy.

Is this the only one you have ever seen without a Title?
No; I believe there are others which are just the same.

Is this a single Book?
It is the Book for the County of Gloucester.

Is it one of a Set?
It is one of a Set, but the other Books are for other Counties.

s

Is

Is it numbered?

It is numbered "17," with a Mark of "C."

Have you the Numbers before and after this?

Oh yes; there are "C. 16." and "C. 18."

Have you another "C. 16." besides this?

No, certainly not.

Is there any Return to the Commission?

No, I believe not.

(*By a Lord.*) What is there which shows you that that Book has Authority belonging to it; that it is compiled under the Authority of a Royal Commission?

That I cannot answer.

What is there by which you can satisfy the House that that Book is the Result of the Labours of a Royal Commission?

The only Evidence is its having the same Appearance, and having consecutive Numbers with the others, and all the others being in the same State.

Mr. Attorney General submitted, That this Book was not Evidence, there being nothing to connect it with the Commission, and there being no Evidence of the Handwriting of the Signatures as being those of Members of the Family.

(*Mr. Hedley.*) Do you find any Reference to the Visitation?

Yes; under the Head of Tewkesbury there is a Reference to the Visitation. It is said, "At this Time of the Visitation."

Is there any Date to it?

Only to each Pedigree.

Are all the Books in the Office intituled?

I cannot speak to that Fact; for the most Part they are, certainly; some may not be; I will not speak to that Fact, not having examined.

Has each Pedigree a Date?

The Date of the Year.

Mr. Attorney General submitted, That this must be withdrawn for the present, without Prejudice to the offering it again, if by Search further Evidence could be given of its Authenticity.

Mr. Hedley withdrew the Evidence for the present, and stated, That he next proposed to prove the Death of John the Third Viscount.

Then Mr. GEORGE JAMES MUSSETT was further examined as follows:

(*Mr. Hedley.*) Do you produce a Will?

I do.

What Will is it?

It is the Will of John Lord Viscount Tracy, dated the 3d of March 1682.

What is the Date of the Probate?

The 11th of June 1687.

The

The same was read as follows :

In the name of God Amen I John lord viscount Tracy being of sound and perfect memory and understanding do make, this my last will and testament in manner following Imprimis I commend my soule into the hands of Almighty God and my body to the earth to be decently buried at the discretion of my executrix hereafter named and as for that worldly estate which it hath pleased God to blesse me withall I dispose of the same as followeth I devise and bequeath those severall closes or inclosed grounds lying in Hayles in the county of Gloucester comonly called or known by the names of the Great Grove-Leys Pages More and Long Meadow with the appurtences unto my dear wife during her life and from and after her decease unto William Tracy my son during his life and after the decease of the said William Tracy to the first son of the said William Tracy and the heires males of the body of such first son lawfully to be begotten and for default of such issue to the second son of the said William Tracy and the heires males of the body of such second son lawfully to be begotten and for default of

such issue to the third fourth fifth sixth and seaventh sons _{& all & every other the son & sons} of the said William Tracy and the respective heires males of the body of every such son and sons lawfully to be begotten the elder of such sons and the heires males of his body being alwaies preferred before the younger of such sons and the heires males of his body according to their priority of birth and seniority of age and for default of such issue I give and devise the said grounds and premises unto John Tracy my grand son and the heires males of the body of the said John Tracy lawfully to be begotten and for default of such issue my will is that the same shall remaine to my right heires for ever Item I do give and bequeath unto my dear wife all my goods chattells money plate jewells rings household stuffe debts and all other personall estate whereto I have any right or title either in law or equity or otherwise howsoever And I do hereby make and constitute my said wife my sole executrix of this my last will and testament In wittnesse whereof I have hereunto sett my hand and seale this third day of March in the five and thirtieth yeare of the raigne of our soveraigne lord king Charles the second &c annoq Dñi 1682.

J. TRACY. (L.S.)

Signed sealed and published in the presence of
R. FREEMAN
THO. WILDING
FRANCIS MYNETT.

Probatū apud Londoñ &c undecimo die Junii anno Dñi miłłimo sexceñmo octogmo septimo coram dño &c juramento prenobilis et honorandæ fœminæ dñæ vicecomitissæ dotissæ Tracy executricis &c cui &c de bene &c vigore comnis jurat.

Then Mr. ALFRED CLARKE was further examined, as follows :

(*Mr. Hedley.*) Do you produce an examined Copy of that Will ? I do.

The same was delivered in.

Mr.

Mr. Hedley stated, That he next proposed to prove that William
Tracy, the eldest Son of John Third Lord Viscount Tracy, succeeded
his Father, and became the Fourth Viscount, the last Will having mentioned " and after her Decease unto William Tracy, my Son, during
his Life."

Then Mr. Mussett was further asked :—

(*Mr. Hedley.*) Do you produce the Will of William the Fourth
Viscount Tracy?
I do, the Will of William Lord Viscount Tracy, dated the Three-
and-twentieth of November, in the Ninth Year of our Sovereign Lady
Anne; it is proved the 2d of July 1712.

By whom was that Will proved ?
By the Honourable Thomas Charles Viscount Tracy, the Son and
Executor.

The same was read as follows :

In the name of God Amen   I William lord viscount Tracy being
under some indisposition of body but of a sound mind and memory
blessed be God for the same doe make my last will and testament this
three and twentyeth day of November in the nineth year of the reigne
of our soüaigne lady Anne by the grace of God of Greate Brittaine
Fraunce and Ireland queene defender of the faith &c. annq̃ Dñi one
thousand seaven hundred and tenn in manner and forme following that
is to say   First and principally I comitt and comend my soule into the
hands of Almighty God hopeing to bee saved by the meritorious death
and passion of Jesus Christ my blessed Saviour and Redeemer and my
body I comitt to the earth to bee decently interred att the discretion of
my exõr herein-after named _{in Toddington Church}   And for my worldly estate whereof God
hath made me a disposer I give and dispose thereof as followeth that
is to say   I give devise and bequeath unto mᵣˢ Susannah Overton widdow
the sume of two hundred pounds of lawfull money of Great Brittaine
to bee payd unto her by my exõr herein-after named within the space of
six moneths next after my decease   Item I give devise and bequeath
unto my servant Thomas Wilding the sum of one hundred pounds of
lawfull mony of Great Brittaine to bee payd unto him within the space
of six monethes next after my decease   Item I give devise and bequeath
unto my sonne Thomas Charles Tracy all and sinğler my plate ready
mony goods chells cattle and all the rest and residue of my psonall
estate and do make constitute and ordaine my sayd sonne Thomas
Charles Tracy sole exõr of this my last will and testament hereby
revoakeing and makeing voyd all former wills by me made and declare
this to bee my last will and testament   In witness whereof I have hereunto putt my hand and seale the day and year first above written.

TRACY (L.S.)

Signed sealed published and declared by the sayd
  Wiḷḷm lord Tracy for his last will and testament
  in the presence of
                  EDW. BULSTRODE   SAMUEL JEFFERIES
                  H. IZOD   SAMˡ BULSTRODE

April 17, 1712   Memorandum that the right hoñble William lord
viscᵗ Tracy did yᵉ day before his decease in yᵉ presence of us whose
names are under written declare it to be his will & desire that one

Mr. G. J. Mussett.
Mr. A. Clarke.

hundred pounds should be given unto Catharina Bishop daughter of Thomas Bishop of Broadway in y° county of Worcester and that y° said hundred pounds to be paid wᵗʰin twelve months after his decease & put into y° hands of her uncle John Horseley of Henley in y° county of Warwick mercer in trust for y° said Catharina Bishop to be paid her when she shall come to be at age and y° use of y° mony to be for her maintenance in y° meantime   Witness oʳ hands

> JOHN BAGLEY.
> SAMUEL JEFFERIES.
> SUSANNA OVERTON.

Probatum Londini cum cod anneẍ coram dño secundo die mensis Julii anno Dñi 1712 jurañito pʳnobilis et hoñdi viri Thomæ Caroli vicecomitis Tracy filii dči defti et eẍris unici &c. cui &c. de bene &c. vigore commiš jurat̃.

Then Mr. Clarke was further asked :—

(*Mr. Hedley.*)   Do you produce an examined Copy of that Will ? I do ; I examined it myself.

The same was delivered in.

Mr. Hedley stated, That the Will just put in proved that William the Fourth Viscount was succeeded by Thomas Charles, who became the Fifth Viscount ; that he now proposed to prove that he had Issue by his Marriage with Lady Elizabeth, his First Wife, Two Sons, William his eldest Son and Thomas Charles.

Mr. T. A. Bulgin.

Then Mr. THOMAS AUGUSTUS BULGIN was called in ; and having been sworn, was examined as follows :

(*Mr. Hedley.*)   What are you ? Clerk to the Masters of the Court of Common Pleas.

What do you produce? An Inrolment of a Bargain and Sale.

From what Custody ? From the Treasury of the Court of Common Pleas.

The same was read as follows :

No. 33.

The rolls of deeds and writings acknowledged and allowed before sir John Willes knight and his associates justices of his majesty's court of Common Bench of the term of the Holy Trinity in the twenty-first and twenty-second years of the reign of George the second by the grace of God of Great Britain France and Ireland king defender of the faith &c.

Thomas Wyld came the seventh day of June in this term before Thomas Burnett one of the justices of his majesties court of Common Pleas at Westminster and acknowledged this writing following to be his deed and required the same to be inrolled in these words   This indenture made the fourth day of April in the twenty-first year of the reign of our sovereign lord George the second by the grace of God of Great Britain France and Ireland king defender of the faith &c. and in

5

the

the year of our lord one thousand seven hundred and forty-eight between the right honourable Thomas Charles lord viscount and baron Tracy of Rathcule in the county of Dublin in the kingdom of Ireland and the honourable William Tracy esquire eldest son and heir apparent of the said Thomas Charles lord viscount Tracy of the first part Thomas Wyld of the Inner Temple London gentleman of the second part and John Hughes of the Inner Temple aforesaid stationer of the third part witnesseth That for the barring and destroying all estates tail heretofore made or limitted of and in the manor messuages lands tenements and hereditaments with the appurtenances herein-after mentioned and all reversions and remainders thereupon depending and expectant and for settling and assuring the same hereditaments and premises to and for the several uses intents and purposes and under and subject to the provisoes herein-after declared and expressed concerning the same and also in consideration of five shillings of lawful money of Great Britain to the said Thomas Charles lord viscount Tracy and William Tracy in hand paid by the said Thomas Wyld at or before the sealing and delivery of these presents the receipt whereof is hereby acknowledged and for divers other good causes and considerations they the said Thomas Charles lord viscount Tracy and William Tracy have and each of them hath granted bargained and sold and by these presents do and each of them doth grant bargain and sell unto the said Thomas Wyld and his heirs all that the mannor of Toddington in the county of Gloucester with its rights members and appurtenances and also all that capital messuage or manor house called Toddington House in Toddington in the said county of Gloucester with the gardens orchards barns stables outhouses and other appurtenances therewith used and enjoyed And also all that park called Toddington Park lying and being in Toddington aforesaid and in Greet and Gretton or elsewhere in the said county of Gloucester or some or one of them And all messuages lands tenements and hereditaments parcel or reputed parcel of the said manor of Toddington or thereto belonging or in anywise appertaining And all that the rectory or parsonage of Toddington aforesaid with the appurtenances and all tythes of corn grain and hay and all other tythes arising growing renewing and increasing within the parish of Toddington aforesaid And all that the advowson or right of patronage of the vicarage of the parish church of Toddington aforesaid And also all that capital messuage or mansion house called Hayles House situate lying and being within the manor or reputed manor of Hayles in the said county of Gloucester together with all orchards gardens barns stables and other outhouses and appurtenances thereunto belonging or therewith used or enjoyed And also all that messuage tenement and farm situate and being within the said manor or reputed manor of Hayles consisting of divers closes or inclosed grounds of arable meadow and pasture land heretofore in the tenure or occupation of John Stiles or his assigns at the yearly rent of one hundred and twenty pounds but now or late of John Crips And also all those closes or grounds inclosed lying and being within the said manor or reputed manor of Hayles consisting of meadow or pasture ground called the Ox Leasou the two Madcrofts and the Great Parks heretofore in the tenure of Dobbins widow and afterwards in the tenure of John Fardon or his assigns at the yearly rent of one hundred and twenty pounds but now or late of Fardon widow And also all that close or ground inclosed of meadow or pasture lying and being within the said manor or reputed manor of Hayles called the Old Orchard heretofore in the tenure of Whittle

Whittle widow at the yearly rent of three pounds but now or late of the said John Crips And also all that close or ground inclosed of meadow or pasture called the Little Park lying and being within the said manor or reputed manor of Hayles heretofore in the tenure of
Sexty widow at the yearly rent of thirteen pounds ten shillings but now or late of William Candle And also all that close or ground inclosed of meadow or pasture lying and being within the said manor or reputed manor of Hayles called Ewe Leasow now or late in the tenure of William Candle at the yearly rent of forty-five pounds And also all that close or ground inclosed of meadow or pasture lying and being within the said manor or reputed manor of Hayles called the Green heretofore in the tenure of the said John Stiles or his assigns at the yearly rent of ten pounds but now of the said John Crips And also all that close or ground inclosed of meadow or pasture lying and being within the said manor or reputed manor of Hayles called Warner's Close now or late in the tenure of William Baylis or his assigns at the yearly rent of five pounds ten shillings And also all those closes of meadow or pasture lying and being within the said manor or reputed manor of Hayles called the New Fields and the Great Breach heretofore in the tenure of Isaac Baylis and afterwards in the tenure of
Baylis his widow at the yearly rent of ninety pounds but now or late of William Baylis And also all that close of meadow or pasture within the said manor or reputed manor of Hayles called the Little Breach heretofore in the tenure of George Reeves or his assigns at the yearly rent of ten pounds but now of Thomas Agge And also all that close of meadow or pasture lying and being within the said manor or reputed manor of Hayles called Paynes Leys heretofore in the tenure of John Cheshire and afterwards of Robert Sexty or his assigns at the yearly rent of four pounds ten shillings but now or late of   Sexty widow And also all that close of meadow or pasture lying and being within the said manor or reputed manor of Hayles called Hayles Lane heretofore in the tenure of the said   Whittle widow or her assigns at the yearly rent of two pounds but now or late of   Fardon widow And also all those closes of meadow or pasture lying and being within the said manor or reputed manor of Hayles called Tobacco Piece and Carlow Furlong heretofore in the tenure of John Hull or his assigns at the yearly rent of twenty-eight pounds but now or late of William Candle Together with all houses outhouses edifices buildings barns stables mills orchards gardens lands tenements rents of tenants as well freeholders as copyholders courts leets views of frankpledge courts baron perquisites and profits of courts and leets woods underwoods meadows pastures commons wast and wast ground feedings waters watercourses free warrens and which to free warrens belong fishing fowling hawking hunting mines quarries liberties royalties fines heriots goods and chattels of fellons and fugitives and felons de se waifs estrays estreats reliefs amerciaments advowsons donations and rights of patronage tenths tythes oblations obventions ways passages emoluments jurisdictions franchises privileges advantages easements and hereditaments whatsoever to the said manor capital messuages and other the premises and to every of them belonging or to or with the same usually occupied or enjoyed accepted reputed or taken as part parcel or member thereof or of any part thereof with their and every of their appurtenances and all other messuages lands tenements woods tyths rents reversions and hereditaments whatsoever of them the said Thomas Charles lord viscount Tracy and William Tracy or either of them
scituate

scituate lying and being within the manor parish precincts liberties or
territories of Toddington aforesaid and the reversion and reversions
remainder and remainders rents and services of all and singular the said
manor hereditaments and premises and all the estate right title interest
use property claim and demand whatsoever of them the said Thomas
Charles lord viscount and William Tracy or either of them of in and
to the same and every part thereof To have and to hold the said
manor messuages lands tenements tyths hereditaments and premises
herein-before mentioned and intended to be hereby granted bargained
and sold and every part and parcel thereof with all and every their appurtenances unto the said Thomas Wyld his heirs and assigns To
the only use and behoof of him the said Thomas Wyld his heirs and
assigns for ever To the intent and purpose that he the said Thomas
Wyld may be and become perfect tenant of the freehold of the same
manor messuages lands tenements tyths hereditaments and premises
with the appurtenances to the end that one or more good and perfect
common recovery or recoveries shall or may be thereof had suffered
and perfected in due form of law for which intent and purpose it is
hereby declared by and between the said parties that it shall and may
be lawful to and for the said John Hughes his heirs at the costs and
charges of the said Thomas Charles lord viscount Tracy to bring sue
forth and prosecute against the said Thomas Wyld or his heirs one or
more writ or writs of entry sur disseisin en le post out of his majesty's
high court of Chancery of and for the said manor messuages lands
tenements tyths hereditaments and premises with the appurtenances by
such apt names quantities qualities and descriptions to ascertain the
same as shall be thought meet the which said writ or writs of entry
shall be made returnable before his majesties justices of the court of
Common Pleas at Westminster as of last Hilary term or by or before
the end of next Easter term And thereby the said John Hughes shall
and may demand against the said Thomas Wyld or his heirs all and
singular the said manor messuages lands tenements tythes hereditamaments and premises with the appurtenances by such apt and convenient
names numbers of acres and such quantities and qualities of land and
other descriptions as shall be thought proper to ascertain the same To
which said writ or writs of entry he the said Thomas Wyld shall appear
gratis in the said court in his proper person or by his attorney lawfully
authorized in that behalf and shall thereupon vouch to warranty the
said several premises the said Thomas Charles lord viscount Tracy who
shall also appear gratis in the said court in his proper person or by his
attorney lawfully authorized in that behalf and enter into the said
warranty and vouch over the said William Tracy who shall thereupon
also appear gratis in the said court in his proper person or by his
attorney lawfully authorized in that behalf and shall enter into the
said warranty and vouch over the common vouchee who shall also appear
gratis in the said court and after imparlance had shall make default and
so demean himself in all things that one or more good and perfect
common recovery or recoveries with treble voucher shall or may be
thereof had suffered and perfected in due form of law according to the
usual course of common recoveries for assurance of lands in such cases
used and accustomed The which said common recovery or recoveries
so as aforesaid or in any other manner or at any other time to be had or
suffered of the said premises or any part thereof and also all and
every other recovery and recoveries fine and fines conveyances and

Mr. T. A. Bulgin.

assurances in the law whatsoever already had made levied and suffered or executed or hereafter to be had made levied suffered or executed of the said manor messuages lands tenements tyths and premises herein-before mentioned and intended to be hereby granted bargained and sold or any of them or any part thereof alone or together with any other lands or tenements by or between the said parties to these presents or any of them or whereunto they or any of them have been are or shall be party or parties or wherein they or any of them shall vouch or be vouched shall be and enure and shall be adjudged construed deemed and taken to be and enure and is and are hereby declared to be meant and intended to be and enure in the first place for corroborating and confirming the estate limitted to the right honorable Frances lady viscountess Tracy wife of the said Thomas Charles lord viscount Tracy for her life of part of the said lands tenements and hereditaments hereby bargained and sold by indenture tripartite of settlement bearing date the thirteenth day of July in the year of our Lord one thousand seven hundred and twenty-one made or mentioned to be made between the said Thomas Charles lord viscount Tracy of the first part sir Thomas Cookes Winford late of Ashtley in the county of Worcester baronet deceased Herbert Perot Packington of Westwood in the county of Worcester esquire and Edward Jefferies alias Winnington late of Holm Castle in the county of Hereford esquire also deceased of the second part and sir John Packington late of Westwood aforesaid baronet deceased and Frances Packington spinster youngest daughter of the said John Packington of the third part and subject thereto and to a term of five hundred years for raising six thousand pounds for the portions of younger children of the said Thomas Charles lord viscount Tracy by Elizabeth lady viscountess Tracy his first wife deceased by indenture tripartite of release and settlement bearing date the eighth day of May in the year of our Lord one thousand seven hundred and eighteen and made or mentioned to be made between the said Thomas Charles lord viscount Tracy and the said Elizabeth lady viscountess Tracy his late wife deceased of the first part sir William Keyt late of Old Stratford in the county of Warwick baronet deceased and sir John Clopton of Clopton in the said county of Warwick knight also deceased of the second part Hugh Clopton of Stratford upon Avon in the said county of Warwick esquire and the reverend William Somerville rector of Wickingam in the county of Norfolk clerk of the third part to and for such estate and estates and to and for such uses upon such trusts and for such intents and purposes and subject to such provisoes limitations and agreements as they the said Thomas Charles lord viscount Tracy and William Tracy shall at any time or times during their joint lives by any deed or writing deeds or writings under both their hands and seals attested by two or more credible witnesses grant convey settle assure limit or appoint and for want of such grant conveyance settlement assurance limitation or appointment and in the mean time until such grant conveyance settlement assurance limitation or appointment shall be made and executed to such and the same uses and upon the same trusts and to and for the same intents and purposes as are mentioned and expressed in and by the aforesaid indenture of release or settlement bearing date the eighth day of May in the said year of our Lord one thousand seven hundred and eighteen and to and for no other use intent or purpose whatsoever In witness whereof the said parties to these presents have hereunto

1

inter-

interchangeably sett their hands and seals the day and year first above written.

> TRACY
> Wᵐ TRACY
> THOˢ WYLD
> JOHN HUGHES

Sealed and delivered by the within named Wᵐ Tracy and Thomas Wyld (being first duly stampt) in the presence of

> NEAL GAHAGAN
> ABRAHAM BANKS
> Clerks to mʳ Pusey

Sealed and delivered by the within named Thomas Charles lord viscount Tracy in the presence of

> Jnᵒ ALLEN PUSEY
> WILLIAM BATTEN servᵗ to mʳ Pusey

Sealed and delivered by the within named John Hughes (being first duly stamped) in the presence of

> NEAL GAHAGAN clerk to mʳ Pusey
> JOHN THOMAS servᵗ to mʳ Pusey.

Then Mr. JOSEPH BARTHOLOMEW was called in; and having been sworn, was examined as follows :

(*Mr. Hedley.*) What do you produce?
An examined Copy of the Enrolment just produced.

Have you examined it with the Original?
I have.

It is a correct Copy?
It is.

The same was delivered in.

Mr. Hedley stated, That the Fact that Thomas Charles the Fifth Viscount married, secondly, Lady Frances, was proved by the Bargain and Sale just put in ; that he next proposed to prove that John Tracy, the eldest Son of Thomas Charles the Fifth Viscount by Lady Frances, his Second Wife, succeeded his Half-brother Thomas Charles the Sixth Viscount, and became the Seventh Viscount.

Then Mr. Mussett was further asked : —

(*Mr. Hedley.*) Do you produce the Will of Thomas Charles Lord Viscount Tracy?
This is the Will of the Right Honourable Thomas Charles Lord Viscount Tracy, dated the 22d of April 1756.

When was that proved?
The 25th of June 1756, by the Oath of the Honourable and Reverend John Tracy, the sole Executor.

(46.2.)   The

The same was read as follows :

This is the last will and testament of me Thomas Charles lord viscount Tracy   Whereas by indenture tripartite bearing date the sixteenth day of September in the year of our Lord one thousand seven hundred and forty eight and made or mentioned to be made between me the said Thomas Charles lord viscount Tracy and the honourable William Tracy my son since deceased of the first part sir Robert Burdet and sir Thomas Charles Keyt baronets of the second part and John Parsons and John Allen Pusey esquires of the third part I am impowered by deed or deeds or by my last will and testament in writing duly executed and attested in the presence of two or more credible witnesses to charge all or any the mannors lands and premisses thereby mentioned to be granted bargained sold released limitted and appointed (except as therein is excepted) with any sume or sumes of money not exceeding three thousand pounds in the whole to be paid to such person or persons for such uses intents and purposes as I shall think fitt   Now I do hereby by virtue and in pursuance of the powers and authoritys in the said recited indenture contained and in part of execution thereof and by virtue of all other powers and authoritys whatsoever in me being charge all and every the mannors lands and premisses in and by the said recited indenture granted bargained sold released limitted and appointed or mentioned so to be (except as therein is excepted) with the full sume of three thousand pounds of lawfull money of Great Britain to be paid to and equally divided amongst my three daughters Frances Anne and Elizabeth to and for their own respective use and benefitt within one month next after my decease   And whereas in and by the said recited indenture I am also impowered by deed or deeds writing or writings or by my last will and testament executed and attested as therein is mentioned to grant limitt and appoint all those messuages or tenements lands hereditaments and premisses lying and being in Hayles in the county of Gloucester called or known by the name of Sheephouse and Sheephouse Closes then and now in the tenure or occupation of William Baylis his undertenants or assigns at the yearly rent of thirty pounds unto or to the use of my son John Tracy for and during the term of his naturall life without impeachment of waste at and under the yearly rent of a pepper corn   And I am likewise thereby impowered by the ways and means last before mentioned or by any of them to grant limitt and appoint all those the tythes of and in Didbrooke in the said county of Gloucester unto and to the use of my said son John Tracy for his life without impeachment of waste in reversion after or expectant upon or subject to the estate for life therein of Catherine Hutchins therein named   And I am likewise thereby impowered by the ways and means aforesaid or any of them to grant limitt and appoint all that messuage or tenement garden orchard lands and premisses called by the name of Gardners Breaches scituate and being in Hayles aforesaid then in the possession or occupation of John Crips but now of Richard Crips at the yearly rent of forty pounds unto my said son John Tracy for and during the naturall life of the said Catherine Hutchins at and under the like rent of a pepper corn to and for his own use and benefitt as in and by the said recited indenture relation being thereunto had may more fully and at large appear   Now I do hereby by virtue and in pursuance of the powers and authoritys in the said recited indenture contained and in

further

further execution thereof and by virtue of all other powers and authoritys whatsoever in me being devise grant limitt and appoint all those
said messuages or tenements lands hereditaments and premisses in
Hayles aforesaid called or known by the names of Sheephouse and
Sheephouse Closes or by whatsoever names or descriptions they or any
of them are now called described or known in the tenure or occupation
of the said William Baylis his undertenants or assigns at the yearly
rent of thirty pounds unto and to the use and benefitt of my said son
John Tracy for and during the term of his naturall life without impeachment of waste he paying for the same to the person or persons intitled
to the immediate reversion or inheritance thereof the yearly rent of a
pepper corn And I do hereby by virtue and in pursuance and further
execution of all and every the powers and authoritys aforesaid devise
grant limitt and appoint all those the tyths of and in Didbrooke aforesaid unto and to the use and benefitt of my said son John Tracy for
his life without impeachment of waste in reversion after or expectant
upon or subject to the estate for life therein of the said Catherine Hutchins he paying in like manner the yearly rent of a pepper corn for
the same And I do hereby by virtue and in pursuance and further
execution of all and every the powers and authoritys aforesaid devise
grant limitt and appoint all that said messuage or tenement garden
orchard lands and premisses called or known by the name of Gardners
Breaches or by whatsoever other names or descriptions they or any of
them are now called described or known scituate lying and being in
Hayles aforesaid then in the possession or occupation of the said John
Crips but now of the said Richard Crips at the yearly rent of forty
pounds unto and to the use and benefitt of my said son John Tracy for
and during the naturall life of the said Catherine Hutchins at and under
the like yearly rent of a pepper corn And whereas in pursuance of the
power given and reserved to me in and by the said recited indenture
of settlement I have by indenture of lease bearing date the fourth day
of December in the year of our Lord one thousand seven hundred and
fifty two demised and leased all that messuage or tenement called the
Middle House with the lands meadows pastures and feedings with the
appurtenances to the same belonging in Toddington in the county of
Gloucester aforesaid now in the occupation of Paul Greening at the
yearly rent of forty two pounds and heretofore were in the tenure
holding or occupation of Jonathan Dobbins but late of   Dobbins
widow to the aforesaid John Parsons and John Allen Pusey for ninety
nine years if my sons John Tracy and Henry Tracy or either of them
shall so long live (subject to the rents therein reserved) And by another
indenture of lease also bearing date the said fourth day of December
one thousand seven hundred and fifty two I have also demised and
leased all that messuage or tenement in Toddington aforesaid wherein
John Curties the elder heretofore dwelt and all that one yard and three
quarters of one yard land and all lands meadows pastures and feedings
with the appurtenances thereto belonging now in the occupation of
John Diston at the yearly rent of forty pounds and heretofore were in
the tenure holding or occupation of John Curtis and afterwards of
Richard Clarke but late of Robert Jennings to the said John Parsons
and John Allen Pusey for the like term of ninety nine years if my said
sons Henry Tracy and John Tracy or either of them shall so long live
(subject to the rents therein reserved) And by another indenture of
lease also bearing date the said fourth day of December one thousand

Mr. J. Bartholomew. seven hundred and fifty two I have likewise demised and leased all that messuage or tenement and all lands meadows and pastures thereunto belonging with the appurtenances heretofore in the tenure holding or occupation of William Mutton and late of Anne Mutton widow and now in the holding of John Boulton and also the scite of all that messuage or tenement heretofore called Anne Willis's with all lands meadows pastures and feedings to the same belonging (except as therein excepted) late in the tenure holding or occupation of Thomas Juggins and Anne his wife formerly Anne Willis which said last mentioned messuage or tenement scite of a messuage or tenement lands and premisses are scituate in Toddington aforesaid and now are in the occupation of the said John Boulton at the yearly rent of sixty two pounds and also all that messuage or tenement called Toddington Inn in Toddington aforesaid and all lands meadows pastures and feedings thereunto belonging now in the occupation of William Hitch at the yearly rent of fifty two pounds and heretofore were in the tenure holding or occupation of   Warren but late of mr.   Serjeant and also all that messuage or tenement and all lands meadows closes pastures feedings commons and appurtenances thereunto belonging in Toddington aforesaid late in the occupation of John Beckett and now in the tenure of Anne Beckett widow and Thomas Beckett her son or one of them at the yearly rent of twenty eight pounds and heretofore were in the tenure holding or occupation of John Read but late of John Stephens to the aforesaid John Parsons and John Allen Pusey for the like term of ninety nine years if my said daughters Frances Tracy Anne Tracy and Elizabeth Tracy or any or either of them shall so long live (subject to the rents therein reserved) all which said severall leases so respectively made as aforesaid are therein and thereby respectively declared to be in trust nevertheless and to the use intent and purpose that the said John Parsons and John Allen Pusey their executors and administrators do and shall permitt and suffer the rents issues and profitts of the premisses thereby demised and leased after deducting thereout the rents thereby reserved and made payable (to be from time to time during the continuance of the said respective demises had received and taken by such person and persons and for such uses intents and purposes as I should at any time thereafter by any deed or writing or by my last will and testament in writing to be by me respectively executed in the presence of two or more witnesses give devise direct limitt and appoint the same and in default thereof by me my executors or administrators   Now I do hereby give devise direct limitt and appoint all and every the rents issues and profitts of the said messuage or tenement called the Middle House with the lands meadows pastures and feedings with the appurtenances to the same belonging in Toddington aforesaid now in the occupation of the said Paul Greening at the yearly rent of forty two pounds comprized in the said lease first above mentioned (after deducting thereout the rents thereby reserved and made payable) unto my said son John Tracy for and during so many years of the said term of ninety-nine years as he shall happen to live to and for his own use and benefitt and from and after his decease I give devise direct limitt and appoint the rents issues and profitts of the aforesaid premisses (after deducting thereout the said rents thereby reserved and made payable) unto my said son Henry Tracy for the residue of the said term of ninety nine years (determinable as aforesaid)   And I do also hereby give devise direct limitt and appoint the rents issues and

profitts

profitts of the said messuage or tenement in Toddington aforesaid wherein John Curtis the elder heretofore dwelt and all that one yard and three quarters of one yard land and all lands meadows pastures and feedings with the appurtenances thereto belonging now in the occupation of the said John Diston at the yearly rent of forty pounds mentioned and comprized in the said second above mentioned lease to be granted as aforesaid (after deducting thereout the rents thereby reserved and made payable) unto my said son Henry Tracy during so many years of the said term of ninety nine years as he shall happen to live and from and after his decease I give devise direct limitt and appoint the rents issues and profitts of the same premisses (after deducting thereout the said rents thereby reserved and made payable) unto my said son John Tracy for the residue of the same term of ninety nine years (determinable as aforesaid) And I do hereby also give devise direct limitt and appoint the rents issues and profitts of the said messuage or tenement and all lands thereunto belonging with the appurtenances heretofore in the tenure holding or occupation of William Mutton and late of Anne Mutton widow and now in the holding of John Boulton and also the scite of all that messuage or tenement heretofore called Anne Willis's with all lands meadows pastures and feedings to the same belonging (except as before excepted) late in the tenure holding or occupation of Thomas Juggins and Anne his wife formerly Anne Willis and now in the occupation of the said John Boulton at the yearly rent of sixty two pounds and also all that messuage or tenement called Toddington Inn in Toddington aforesaid and all lands meadows pastures and feedings thereunto belonging now in the occupation of the said William Hitch at the yearly rent of fifty two pounds and also all that messuage or tenement and all lands meadows closes pastures feedings commons and appurtenances thereunto belonging in Toddington aforesaid late in the occupation of John Beckett and now in the tenure of the said Anne Beckett widow and Thomas Beckett her son or one of them at the yearly rent of twenty eight pounds mentioned and comprized in the lease last above mentioned to be granted as aforesaid (after deducting thereout the rents thereby reserved and made payable) unto my said three daughters Frances Anne and Elizabeth Tracy for and during so many years of the said term of ninety nine years as they shall jointly happen to live to be equally divided amongst them share and share alike And from and after the decease of any or either of my said three daughters I give devise direct limitt and appoint the same rents and profitts (after deducting thereout the said rents in and by the said last mentioned lease reserved and made payable) to the survivors and survivor of them for the residue of the said term of ninety nine years (determinable as aforesaid) And whereas I am likewise impowered in and by the said recited indenture of settlement by deed or deeds or by my last will and testament in writing executed as therein mentioned to charge the said mannor and park of Toddington and all and every the messuages lands tenements hereditaments and premisses scituate within the said mannor and parish of Toddington aforesaid (except the two farms limitted to my said late son William Tracy for his life) and all other the hereditaments and premisses in Hayles aforesaid and elsewhere settled in and by an indenture tripartite bearing date the eighth day of May in the year of our Lord one thousand seven hundred and eighteen with any sume of money not exceeding five hundred pounds

or

or otherwise to borrow the same at interest on security of the said premisses or any part thereof for such purposes and to be paid to such
persons and for such uses and intents as I shall think fitt And whereas
I have (pursuant to the said power) allready borrowed of the said John
Allen Pusey by way of mortgage of the whole or some part of the said
premisses the sume of four hundred pounds now I do hereby by virtue
and in pursuance of the powers and authoritys in the said recited
indenture tripartite of settlement of the sixteenth day of September
one thousand seven hundred and forty eight contained and in performance thereof and by virtue of all other powers and authoritys whatsoever in me being charge all and every the said mannor and park of
Toddington and all and every the messuages lands tenements hereditaments and premisses scituate within the said mannor and parish of
Toddington (except as aforesaid) and all other the hereditaments and
premisses in Hayles aforesaid and elsewhere settled in and by the said
recited indenture tripartite of the eighth day of May one thousand
seven hundred and eighteen with the further full sume of one hundred
pounds of lawfull money of Great Britain to be paid to my executor
hereinafter named within one month next after my decease Provided
allways and my will and meaning is that in case my son Thomas Charles
Tracy his heirs and assignes do and shall permitt and suffer my present
family to live and reside at the capitall messuage tenement or mansion
house wherein I now inhabitt and dwell lying in Toddington aforesaid
and to hold and enjoy the barns stables courts yards backsides and
gardens thereto belonging for and during the space or term of three
kalendar months next after my decease without giving them any sort
of trouble or interruption in the quiett possession thereof or attempting
to live and reside there himself with his family then I direct and order
and my will and meaning is that the said sume of one hundred pounds
shall not be raised or paid but that the bequest hereby made of the
same shall be null and void to all intents and purposes whatsoever any
thing hereinbefore contained to the contrary notwithstanding I give
and bequeath unto my said three daughters Frances Anne and Elizabeth Tracy the sume of fifty pounds a piece to be paid them out of my
personall estate by my executor hereinafter mentioned within three
months next after my decease Also I give and bequeath unto my sister
in law mrs. Agnes Keyt who now lives with me the sume of fifty pounds
of good money as a mark of the esteem and regard I have for her for
her great care of. and tenderness to me the same to be paid her by my
executor hereinafter mentioned out of my personall estate within three
months next after my decease All the rest residue and remainder of
my plate household goods linnen furniture moneys chattells effects and
all other my personall estate of what nature kind or quality soever after
payment of my just debts and funerall charges which I order to be
thereout paid (except such debts as are any ways charged on my reall
estate or any part thereof and which I direct to be paid and born out
of such reall estate) I give and bequeath unto my said son John Tracy
his executors admors and assigns And I desire to be buryed in the
chancell of the parish church of Toddington aforesaid as private and
decency will permit of And I do hereby nominate constitute and
appoint my said son John Tracy sole executor of this my will And I
do hereby revoke all former wills by me at any time heretofore made
and declare this only to be and contain my last will and testament In
witness whereof I the said Thomas Charles lord viscount Tracy have

6   to

Mr. J. Bartholomew
Mr. A. Clarke.
Mr. G. J. Mussett.

to this my last will and testament contained in and wrote upon eight sheets of paper put my hand and seal to each sheet this twenty second day of Aprill in the year of our Lord one thousand seven hundred and fifty six.

TRACY (L.S.)

Signed sealed published and declared by the said Thomas Charles lord viscount Tracy the testator as and for his last will and testament in the presence of us who in his presence and at his request and in the presence of each other have hereunto subscribed our names as witnesses

HEN. WHITAKER.
GEORGE GILBERT JONES.
THOMAS ATTWOOD.

Proved at London before the judge the twenty fifth day of June in the year of our Lord 1756 by the oath of the honourable and reverend John Tracy the sole executor to whom admion was granted he having been first sworn (by commission) duly to administer.

Then Mr. Clarke was further asked :—

(*Mr. Hedley.*)   Have you an examined Copy of that Document? I have.

The same was delivered in.

Then Mr. Mussett was further asked :—

(*Mr. Hedley.*)   What do you next produce?
The Will of the Right Honourable and Reverend John Tracy, formerly Warden of All Souls College in the University of Oxford, and Doctor in Divinity, dated the 19th of January 1792.

When was that proved?
The 6th of March 1793, by the Oath of the Right Honourable Henry Lord Viscount Tracy of the Kingdom of Ireland, formerly the Honourable Henry Tracy, the Brother of the deceased and sole Executor.

The same was read as follows:

I John Tracy warden of All Souls College in the university of Oxford do hereby make and declare this to be my last will and testament in manner following   First I give to the bursars of All Souls College so being at the time of my decease the sum of five hundred pounds for the use of the said college   I also give to my brother the honourable Henry Tracy the sum of one hundred pounds   I also give to my servants Frances Marshall & William Mander if they shall be living with me at the time of my decease one year's wages to each over and above what shall be then due to him or her   All the rest of my personal estate if there be any after my debts and funeral expences are paid I give unto my sister the honourable mrs Frances Tracy   And I desire to be buried in the common place of burial belonging to the place where I shall happen to die in as private a manner as may be   Lastly I appoint my brother the honourable Henry Tracy whole & sole executor of this my last will and

No. 35.

Sic orig.

Sic orig.

I

Mr. G. J. Mussett,
Mr. A. Clarke.

and testament to which I set my hand and seal this nineteenth day of January in the year of our Lord one thousand seven hundred and ninety two.

JOHN (L.S.) TRACY.

Proved at London the 6th day of March 1793 before the worshipful James Henry Arnold doctor of laws and surrogate by the oath of the right honble Henry lord viscount Tracy of the kingdom of Ireland (formerly the honble Henry Tracy) the brother of the deceased and sole executor to whom admion was granted having been first sworn duly to administer.

Then Mr. Clarke was further asked :—

(*Mr. Hedley.*) Do you produce an examined Copy of that Document?
I do.

The same was delivered in.

Mr. Hedley stated, That he put this Will in to prove that John the Seventh Lord Viscount Tracy died without Issue ; that he next proposed to prove that Robert Packington Tracy, Second Son of Thomas Charles the Fifth Viscount by Lady Frances his Second Wife, died unmarried.

Then Mr. Mussett was further asked :—

(*Mr. Hedley.*) Do you produce a Will?
I produce an official Copy which has been proved in our Register as an Original ; it is an official Copy from Bombay of the Will of Robert Packington Tracy.

(*Mr. Attorney General.*) What is the Nature of this Copy of a Will?
It is sent from the official Court of Bombay, and received as the Original, and Probate granted, the Original being deposited at Bombay ; this purports to be signed by William Shaw, the Registrar.

(*Mr. Hedley.*) Are there other Wills sent from Bombay in the same Manner?
Yes ; and from some other Places we receive them, and grant Probate upon them.

Has Probate been granted on that Will?
Yes ; it is dated Bombay Town Hall, 24th August 1748 ; registered and collated with the Original the said Day, Bombay Town Hall, 19th October 1748 ; a true Copy, collated from the Registry, and sealed.

Is that the Seal of the Supreme Court of Bombay?
I do not know the Fact ; but I have great Reason to doubt it.

Where did you find it?
In the Strong Room of the Prerogative Court of Canterbury.

What is the Date of it?
The Date of it is the 29th of July 1748, and it is proved in the Prerogative Court of Canterbury, 15th June 1749.

To whom was Probate granted of that Will?
It is proved by the Oath of the Right Honourable Thomas Charles
5
Lord

Lord Viscount Tracy, the natural and lawful Father of the Deceased and sole Executor.

The Counsel, being asked for what Purpose he produced this Will, stated, That it was to prove the Death of the Party, and that he died without Issue, Administration being granted to his Father.

The same was read as follows:

In the name of God Amen   I Robert Packington Tracy being in an ill state of health but of sound mind and memory do make this my last will and testament   I name and appoint my friend m^r Laurence Sulivan trustee to this my will and my sole executor my dearly beloved father Thomas George Tracy lord Tracy and to my said father I give and bequeath all that I am possessed of or may belong to me in any shape whatsoever   In witness whereof I have set my hand in presence of the witnesses under mention'd   Dated in Bombay this 29th July 1748.
No. 36.

Robt P. Tracy.

Sign'd in the presence of us
  Thomas Satchwell Robert Went.

Bombay Townhall ye 24th Augt 1748 registred & collated with ye original the s^d day

Wm Shaw reg^r (L.S.)

Bombay Townhall the 19th Octr 1748   A true copy   Collated from ye registry & attested by .

Wm Shaw reg^r (L.S.)

Proved at London before the judge on the 15th day of June 1749 by the oath of the right honourable Thomas Charles lord viscount Tracy the natural and lawful father of the deceased and sole executor named in the said will by the names and title of Thomas George Tracy lord Tracy to whom adm͞on was granted being first sworn by commission duly to administer.

The same correction — Then Mr. Clarke was further asked:—

(*Mr. Hedley.*)   Do you produce an examined Copy of that Will?
I do.

The same was delivered in.

Mr. Hedley stated, That he next proposed to prove that Henry Tracy, Third Son of Thomas Charles the Fifth Viscount by Lady Frances his Second Wife, succeeded his Brother John Tracy, Seventh Viscount, and became the Eighth Viscount.

Then Mr. Mussett was further asked:—

(*Mr. Hedley.*)   What do you produce?
This is the Will of the Honourable Henry Tracy of Portman Street in the Parish of St. Mary-le-bone in the County of Middlesex, dated the 3d of December 1783, proved with the Codicil the 3d of June 1797 by the Oath of the Right Honourable Henrietta Susanna, Spinster, the Daughter and sole Executrix.

The same was read as follows:

In

In the name of God Amen   I the honorable Henry Tracy of Portman street in the parish of Saint Marylebone in the county of Middlesex do make this my last will and testament for the sole purpose of leaving my dear daughter Henrietta Susanna Tracy under the care and guardianship of such persons as I can most entirely rely upon for the kindest attention to her during her minority   I do therefore hereby constitute and appoint my dear brother the honorable and reverend John Tracy warden of All Souls college in the university of Oxford and William Strode of Northaw in the county of Hertford esquire guardians of my said dear daughter and I do make it my earnest request to them to accept of and act in such guardianship   And as this my will relates only to the event of my dying during the minority of my daughter I do therefore in that event constitute and appoint the said John Tracy and William Strode my executors until such time as my daughter attains her age of twenty-one years and upon her attaining that age I do nominate and appoint her sole executrix   In witness whereof I have hereunto set my hand and seal this third day of December one thousand seven hundred and eighty three.

Hen. Tracy   (l.s.)

> Signed sealed published and declared by the above named Henry Tracy as and for his last will and testament in the presence of us
>
> John Crossman   W. Evans.

Upon my decease I give and bequeath the following sums to the persons undermentioned if living at that time   To miss Mary Harrison one thousand pounds to miss Constant Harrison one thousand pounds and to the following servants if living with me or my daughter at that time the following sums   To Mary Kindall four hundred pounds to Elizabeth Podmore four hundred pounds to Robert Cook two hundred pounds to every servant that has lived with me above three years fifty pounds each to those that have lived under that time one year's wages.

Portman street, May yᵉ 2ᵈ 1796.   Tracy.

N.B. I desire to be buryed at Toddington in as private a manner as possible.

> Proved at London with a codicil 3ʳᵈ June 1797 before the worshipful John Sewell doctor of laws and surrogate by the oath of the right honble Henrietta Susanna Tracy spinster the daughter and sole executrix named in the will she having attained her age of twenty-one years to whom admŏn was granted having been first sworn duly to administer.

Then Mr. Clarke was further asked :—

(*Mr. Hedley.*)   Do you produce an examined Copy of that Will ? I do.

The same was delivered in.

Mr. Hedley stated, That he next proposed to prove that Charles Tracy, the Second Son of John the Third Viscount by Elizabeth his Wife, died without Issue, by producing an Epitaph from a Monument in Toddington Church.

Then

Then Mr. Clarke was further asked :—

(*Mr. Hedley.*)   What do you produce?
A Copy of the Inscription on a Monument in Toddington Church, which I have examined with the Inscription.

It is a true Copy?
It is.

The same was delivered in, and read as follows :

M. S. nobiliss¹ juvenis Caroli Tracy filii tertii honoratiss¹ ɗni Joħ vicecomitis Tracy juvenis non natalibus solum sed et egregiâ indole et summis ingenii dotibus illustriss¹ qui post pueriles annos fœliciter studiis liberalibus impensos migravit Oxonium   Ibi sesquiano vix dum elapso non sine suspiriis omnium quibus innotuit immature (proh dolor) obiit 3° die Maii 1676.

No. 38.

Sed heus lector oculis cave si enim vivum nosses cujus jam mortui epitaphium legis verendum esset ne instar Niobes indulgens lacrymis rigeres in statuam.

ʼΟν φιλει Θεος θνησκει νεος.

The Counsel were informed, That it appeared on the Face of the Pedigree that he was the Second Son, whereas the Inscription just read stated him to be the Third, and they were directed to explain that.

Mr. Hedley stated, That he was not at the present Moment in a Situation to explain that, but that Inquiry should be made into the Facts : That he proposed next to prove that Ferdinando, described in the Pedigree as the Third Son, married Catherine Keck, and that they had a Son named Ferdinando, who died young.

Then Mr. Mussett was further asked :—

(*Mr. Hedley.*)   What do you produce?
A Book of Administrations for the Year 1783.   There is an Entry, headed Ferdinando Tracy, that on the 7th of June 1683 a Commission issued to the Honourable Catherine Tracy, the natural and lawful Mother of Ferdinando Tracy an Infant, late of Saint Dunstan in the East, London.

The same was read as follows :

Junii 1683.
Ferdinando Tracy   Septimo die emᵗ comᵒ honorabili Catherini Tracy matri ñrali et ĩtimæ Ferdinando Tracy infantis nup põæ Sc̃i Dunstani in Occideñ London def ħentis &c. ad aɗstranɗ bona jura et creɗ dc̃i def de bene &c. jurat̃.

No. 39.

Then Mr. Clarke was further asked :—

(*Mr. Hedley.*)   Do you produce an examined Copy of that Document ?
I do.

The same was delivered in.

Mr. Hedley stated, That Ferdinando and Catherine had a Second Son, John ; that he referred to the Will of John the Third Viscount to prove that Ferdinando the eldest Son died an Infant ; and that he next

(46.2.)   K   proposed

Mr. G. J. Mussett. proposed to prove that John, the Second Son of the Honourable Ferdinando Tracy by Catherine his Wife, married Ann daughter of Sir Robert Atkins.

(*To Mr. Mussett.*) Do you produce the Will of Mrs. Tracy?
Yes; it is the Will of Anne Tracy of Coscombe in the County of Gloucester, Widow.

How does she describe herself?
Of Coscombe in the County of Gloucester, Widow.

Widow of whom?
Nothing more is stated in the Description.

What is the Date?
It is dated the 12th of June 1746.

When was it proved?
The 29th of March 1762, with a Codicil.

The same was read as follows :

No. 40.   In the name of God Amen I Anne Tracy of Coscombe in the county of Gloucester widow being in good health and of sound and disposing mind and memory praised be God do make and ordain this my last will and testament in manner following (that is to say) first I commend my soul to God who gave it in hopes of a joyful resurrection thro' the merits of my blessed and merciful Redeemer And for my body it is my desire that it may be buried in the vault belonging to my family in the parish church of Stanway with no more expence than what decency requires attended only by my own servants & some of my tenants to be bearers & that six pounds may be given to the poor of that parish and that neither rings or money to buy mourning may be given to any one on that occasion it being my principal care and design as to my worldy affairs that after my just debts are duly paid and satisfied the residue of my estate may be left to those of my family who have not had so plentiful a provision as the rest of them have had therefore as for such worldly goods and estate wherewith it hath pleased God to bless me I give and dispose thereof as followeth And first I give and bequeath unto my beloved children Thomas Tracy Catherine Tracy Martha Tracy Elizabeth Tracy and Frances Tracy all the distributive part share & proportion of the personal estate of my late dear husband John Tracy esqʳᵉ who died intestate and also all other my goods chattels personal estate arrears of rent and whatever I shall die possessed of to be equally divided between them share and share alike except the plate jewells and other things herein-after mentioned that is to say To my son Thomas Tracy I give the picture of my son Keck & the diamond ring which he gave me and my table clock to my daughter Travell I give ten guineas to pay for a copy of her dear father's picture if I do not give it in my life time with my new silver coffee pot To my daughter Catherine Tracy I give all the jewells she is in possession of (except the largest diamond which I desire may be given to my daughter Frances Tracy (or the value of it which they shall choose) and to my said daughter Catherine Tracy I give a pair of my largest silver candlesticks & my snuffers belonging to them & the stitch'd quilt us'd in her chamber & the service of china which I bought for my table To my daughter Martha Tracy I give all the jewells she is now in possession of with the other pair of my large silver candlesticks

1

& my

& my mahogany chest & the card table given me by my brother Chute
& my tea table and all belonging to it To my daughter Elizabeth Tracy
I give all the jewells she is now in possession of with my silver hand
candlestick & what belongs to it my silver milk pot & the painted
bureau given me by my uncle Keck To my daughter Frances Tracy I
give all my rings not yet disposed of with my gold watch & chain &
seal belonging to it & all my lockets & a pair of silver candlesticks fit
for wax candles with the snuffers belonging to them and the tent-stich-
screen given me by the lady Tracy & the wrought bed not yet made
up I desire that all the rest of my plate household linen china pictures
& books may be equally divided between my son Thomas Tracy & my
four youngest daughters To my grandsons m^r Francis Travell & m^r Ferdinando Favell I give ten guineas to each of them to buy them a piece
of plate To m^{rs} Mary Dodwell I give the picture of herself (drawn by
m^r Worsdale) and make it my request to her (if she thinks I have
discharged the trust faithfully which s^r William Dodwell repos'd in me
in the care of her education) that she will in gratitude to my memory
be a friend to those of my family who shall most stand in need of her
favour and assistance To my servants Anne Newman & Hannah Chesley
(if they are with me at the time of my death) I give to each of them
five pounds And to all my other servants who shall then belong to my
family I give to each two guineas And I do make appoint & ordain my
daughters Catherine Martha & Elizabeth Tracy joint executrixes of
this my last will I desire the silver boiler which was given me by my
uncle Keck may be continu'd in my family if any of my sons or
daughters will pay the summ of seventy pounds (at which price it was
valued to me) towards the discharge of my debts but if they refuse it
I desire it may be offer'd to m^{rs} Mary Dodwell on the aforesaid terms
And I do declare these two sheets to each of which I have subscribed
my name (the whole being written with my own hand) to be my last
will & testament In witness whereof I have hereunto set my hand
& seal the 12th day of June in the year of our Lord 1740 & in the
14th year of the reign of our sovereign lord George the 2^d by the grace
of God of Great Brittain France & Ireland king defender of the
faith &^{c}.

ANNE TRACY. (L.S.)

Sign'd seal'd publish'd & declar'd by the said
  Anne Tracy to be her last will and testament
  in the presence of us who have hereunto set
  our hands as witnesses at the request of the
said Anne Tracy

JOHN CAPEN.
JN^o APPLEGATH.
ANNE ARNOLD.

    A codicil or supplement to the last will and testament of Ann Tracy
of Coscomb in the county of Gloucester widow I the said Ann Tracy
do give and bequeath unto my four daughters Catharine Tracy Martha
Tracy Elizabeth Tracy and Frances Tracy all that my leasehold mes-
suaage or tenement with the appurtenances in Wood Stanway in the
said county of Gloucester late in the tenure of Robert Gibbs and which
were granted to me by my son Robert Tracy esq^{re} for ninety-nine
years if my son Thomas Tracy esq^r the said Elizabeth and Frances
Tracy

Tracy or either of them should so long live as by the indenture of lease bearing date the fifteenth day of December last past will appear to hold the said leasehold premises unto my said four daughters their executors administrators and assigns from and immediately after my decease for and during all the then residue and remainder of the said term of ninety-nine years determinable as aforesaid they my said daughters from time to time paying the rent and discharging and performing the covenants reserved and contained in the said lease and on the lessees part to be paid done and performed and I order and direct this present codicil to be a part of my last will and testament hereunto annexed In witness whereof I the said Ann Tracy have hereunto sett my hand and seal the fourth day of February in the year of our Lord one thousand seven hundred and forty-six.

ANNE TRACY. (L.S.)

> This codicil was read unto the said Ann Tracy
> the testatrix and by her signed sealed and
> delivered in the presence of us
> > JN° APPLEGATH.
> > MARTHA NASH.

> Proved at London with a codicil the 29th of March 1762 before the worshipful George Harris doctor of laws and surrogate by the oaths of Catherine Tracy and Elizabeth Tracy spinster the daughters and two of the executrixes to whom admon was granted having been first sworn duly to administer power reserved of making the like grant to Martha Tracy spinster the daughter and other executrix when she shall apply for the same.

(*To Mr. Clarke.*)   Do you produce an examined Copy of this Will ?
I do.

The same was delivered in :

Mr. Hedley stated, That he should put in the Will of Francis Keck, to show that John Tracy had Six Sons by Anne his Wife.

(*To Mr. Mussett.*)   What do you produce?
The Will of Francis Keck of Great Lew in the County of Oxford, Esquire, dated the 29th Day of June 1728, and proved the 27th of January 1728.

The same was read as follows :

No. 41.

In the name of God Amen I Francis Keck of Great Tew in the county of Oxon esquire doe make my last will and testament in manner following I most humbly commend my soul into the hands of my most gracious God and my body to be buried in the earth in hope of an happy resurrection to eternall life through the infinite mercies and goodness of God in and by our blessed Lord and Saviour Jesus Christ As concerning the disposition of my worldly estate I haveing lately married my dear daughter to s[r] John Dutton of Sherborne and paid him sixteen thousand pounds as a marriage portion and obliged my heirs and executors to pay him four thousand pounds more within six months after my decease and my said dear daughter having in
consideration

consideration thereof assigned to mee the sume of two thousand pounds charged or chargeable on my Oxonshire estate for or towards her marriage portion soe that the said two thousand pounds is now part of my personall estate and for the better and more sure payment of the said four thousand pounds which it is my will and desire should bee most punctually paid I doe hereby charge and subject my two messuages or houses in Bell Yard London and all my estate as well of inheritance as leasehold in the county of Middlesex to for and with the payment and security thereof and if there be occasion would. have them sold for that purpose   And my will is and I desire my dear daughter Dutton should have the things herein-after mentioned (in case I shall not in my lifetime have delivered them all to her as I have already delivered some of them) viz. her dear mothers best pearle necklace and her dear mothers silver dressing plate and the blew satin mantle laced with a broad rich gold lace which her dear mother was christened in and the quilt of her dear mothers work not yet made up or ever used and the pillar cases of her owne dear mothers worke   And I do hereby give to my dear son m' John Keck his heires and executors for ever all my lands and estate in and about Sandford near the city of Oxon   And as concerning the revertion and inheritance in fee simple of my dear wifes estate in Hampshire and the Isle of Wight and in Berkshire which by the settlements thereof I have power to dispose off subject to the uses limitted to my dear son and his issue male and the joynture now charged thereon for his wife and to the estate limitted to my said dear daughter and the heires of her body all which uses and limitaçons I would have stand and continue in full force and virtue and doe hereby allow ratifye and confirm the same   I do give all my said dear wifes estates (subject to the debt owing thereon to my dear fathers executors) unto my said dear son and the heires of his body and for want of such issue I give all my said estate in Berkshire unto my cosin Anthony Keck and his heires and all my said estate in Hampshire and the Isle of Wight I give to my nephew m' John Nicoll for the terme of his life without impeachment of wast and after his decease to the first son of the said John Nicoll and the heires male of the body of such first son with the like remainder to the second third and all and every other son and sons of the said John Nicoll severally and successively one after another according to their seniority of age and priority of birth and the heires male of their respective bodyes issuing the elder and his heires male to take before the younger and his heires male and for default of such issue to my nephew Anthony Chute esq. of the Vine in Hampshire and to his heires   And as concerning the the revertion and inheritance of all my estate in the county of Oxon (except the lands and hereditaments in Sandford near Oxford by mee devised to my dear son as aforesaid) And as concerning the revertion and inheritance of all my estates in the countys of Wilts and Warwick all which by the settlement made on my sons marriage I have power to dispose off subject to the uses thereby limited to my son and his wife for joynture and to the issue male of my son   I doe hereby give and devise all the same estates to my dear son and the heires of his body and for want of such issue to my said daughter Dutton and the heires of her body and for want of such issue I doe hereby give all my said estate in the county of Warwick unto my said cosin Anthony Keck and to his heires for ever   And I doe give all my said estates in the county of Oxon (except as aforesaid) and in the county of Wilts unto Ferdinando Tracy (third son of my nephew John Tracy esq.) for the life of the said Ferdinando and after his

 decease

Mr. G. J. Mussett.

decease to the first son of the said Ferdinando and the heires male of the body of such first son with the like remainder to the second third and all and every other the son and sons of the said Ferdinando severally and successively one after another according to their seniority of age and priority of birth and to the heires male of their respective bodyes issueing the elder and the heires male of his body to take before the younger and the heires male of his body and for default of such issue to Anthony Tracy fourth son of my said nephew for the life of the same Anthony and after his decease to the first second third and all and every other the son and sons of the said Anthony Tracy severally and successively one after another according to their seniority of age and priority of birth and to the heires male of their respective bodyes issuing the elder and the heires male of his body to take before the younger and the heires male of his body and for default of such issue to Thomas Tracy fifth son of my said nephew for the life of the said Thomas and after his decease to the first second and all and every other the son and sons of the said Thomas severally and successively one after another according to their seniority of age and priority of birth and to the heires male of their respective bodyes issuing the elder and the heires male of his body to take before the younger and the heirs male of his body and for default of such issue to William Tracy sixth son of my said nephew Tracy for the life of the said William and after his decease to the first second and all and every other the sons of the said William severally and successively one after another according to their seniority of age and priority of birth and to the heires male of their respective bodyes issueing the elder and the heires male of his body to take before the younger and the heires male of his body and for default of such issue to John Tracy second son of my said nephew for the life of the said John Tracy the son and after his decease to the first second and all and every other the son and sons of the said John Tracy the son severally and successively one after another according to their seniority of age and priority of birth and to the heires male of their respective bodyes issueing the elder and the heires male of his body to take before the younger and the heires male of his body and for default of such issue unto Robert Tracy eldest son of my said nephew for the life of the said Robert and after his decease to the first and all and every other the son and sons of the said Robert severally and successively one after another according to their seniority of age and priority of birth and to the heires male of their respective bodyes the elder and the heires male of his body to take before the younger and the heires male of his body and for default of such issue to my owne right heires And my mind and will is that my said cosin Ferdinando Tracy and all and every his brothers when he and they respectively be in the actual possession of the lands and premises hereby devised to him and them shall have power to make and lymitt thereout a joynture not exceeding five hundred pounds per annum to any wife he or they shall respectively marry for the life of such wife or woman before or after her marriage soe as nevertheless the premisses shall not at any one time stand charged in possession or revertion with more than one such joynture made by any of my said cosins And all the devises to my said cosin Ferdinando and to his brothers and to his and their sons in tayle male as aforesaid I doe hereby will and declare to be with and under this limittacon and provisoe that hee and they shall and do immediately after and as soon as hee and they shall bee by virtue of this my will in the present and actuall possession of all or any the premisses hereby devised use and

take

take on him and them and stile name and write himselfe and themselves and his and their issue male by the surname of Keck and by noe other surname whatsoever And in case of refusall or neglecting soe to doe by my said cosins or any of their sons or issue male the estate hereby given to him or them soe refusing or neglecting to doe for life or in tayle male shall cease determine and be utterly void as if the person or persons soe refusing or neglecting were naturally dead And in such case the person or persons next in remainder who shall then use and take the surname of Keck as aforesaid shall enter into and hold and enjoy the premisses hereby to him and them devised according to the purport and true intent of this my will provided also and I doe hereby declare that the severall devises hereby by me made to my said cosin Anthony Keck and his heires of my estates in Warwickshire and Berkshire are soe made and intended upon this trust and confidence in him and them reposed And my mind desire and will is that if and soe soon as any of his grandsons by discent from him or their mother or by deed grant or devise by or under him or her shall happen to come into the actuall possession of all or any the said devised premisses or of any part or parts of them that then every one of the said grandsons doe and shall immediately from such time of his or their soe being in the actuall possession of any of the premisses leave and change his and their surname of James and use and take on him and them and still name and write himselfe and themselves and his and their children by the surname of Keck only and noe other surname whatsoever and in case of any of their neglect or refusall so to doe my will and desire is that my heires at law should enter upon him or them soe neglecting or refuseing and out them and have and retaine the said estates in their own right and to their own use if such entry or eviction can by law or equity bee made and effected I doe give unto s^r John Dutton and to my dear daughter his wife the sume of one hundred pounds a peece and to my dear daughter my sons wife one hundred pounds to buy her a peece of plate in remembrance of mee And I give to my dear sister Vernon one hundred pounds and to my brother m^r Nicoll and to my dear sister his wife one hundred pounds a peece and to m^{rs} Seyliard my dear wifes half sister one hundred pounds and to my said cosin Anthony Keck and to my cosin his wife one hundred pounds a peece And I give to m^r Chetle one hundred pounds and to my servant Richard Cole fifty pounds and to Thomas Aske my servant at Pusey fifty pounds and to every one of my other servants that shall be living with me at my house at the time of my decease one yeares wages over and above what shall be then due to them And I give to the poor of Great Tew Pusey Blunsden Baddesley and Hampstead ten pounds a peece to be given and distributed in such manner as my executor shall think fitt and order my will and desire is to be buried by my dear wife at Blunsden And I leave to my dear son and executor the ordering of my funerall the expence whereof I would not have to be great And all the residue and overpluss of my reall and personall estate whatsoever after and subject to the payment of my debts legacyes and funerall expences I give to my said dear son his heires executors and administrators respectively for ever and I hereby make my said dear son sole executor of this my last will and testament not doubting of his care and kindness in the due and punctuall performance of the same And I do hereby revoke all former wills by me made In witness whereof I have to this my last will conteyned in this and the four foregoing sheets of paper subscribed my name at the bottome of each of the same sheets and to this last have sett

(46.2.)   my

Mr. G. J. Mussett.
Mr. A. Clarke.

my hand and seale and my seale at the top of the first sheete where they are tyed together this nine and twentieth day of June anno Dñi 1728 and in the second yeare of the reigne of our soveraigne lord king George the second &c.

FRAN. KECK. (L.S.)

> Signed sealed and published by Francis Keck esq. as and for his last will and testament in the presence of us who in the presence of the said Francis Keck have subscribed our names as witnesses thereunto
> RICHARD HATTON.
> EDW. PORTER.
> GILES JAMES.

> Probatum Londini &c. coram domino &c. vicesimo septimo die mensis Januarij anno Domini 1728 juramento Johannis Keck armigeri filii et executoris &c. cui &c. de bene &c. vigore commiś juraẗ.

(*To Mr. Clarke.*)   Do you put in a Copy of that Will?
I do; it is correct.

The same was delivered in.

Mr. Hedley stated, That he proposed next to prove the Death of all those Sons without Male Issue.

(*To Mr. Mussett.*)   Do you produce the Will of Robert Tracy?
I do; it is the Will of Robert Tracy of Stanway in the County of Gloucester, dated the 16th of October 1766, proved the 4th of February 1768 by the Oath of John Tracy, Esquire, called in the Will John Tracy Atkyns, the Brother and one of the surviving Executors.

Is there any Mention made of Thomas Tracy?
With a "Power reserved of making the like Grant to Thomas Tracy Esquire, the Brother also, and Vansittart Hudson, Esquire, the other Executors, when they or either of them shall apply for the same."

The same was read as follows:

No. 42.

In the name of God Amen   I Robert Tracy of Stanway in the county of Gloucester esquire being of sound and disposing mind memory and understanding thanks be to God do this sixteenth day of October one thousand seven hundred and sixty-six make and ordaine this my last will and testament in manner and form following that is to say   First and principally I recommend my soul to the mercy and protection of Almighty God being fully persuaded by his Holy Spirit that through the death and passion of my dear Lord and Saviour Jesus Christ I shall obtain full pardon and remission of all my sins and inherit everlasting life to which Holy Trinity to one eternal and undivided Deity be all honour and glory for ever and ever Amen   And as to such worldly estate wherewith it hath pleased God to intrust me I dispose of the same as followeth   Whereas I entered into one bond or obligation bearing date on or about the eighteenth day of December one thousand
seven

seven hundred and forty seven in the penal sum of eight hundred pounds or some such sum with condition to pay to my brother Thomas Tracy his heirs executors and administrators the sum of four hundred pounds within six months after my decease pursuant to an agreement in writing between me and the said Thomas Tracy of the same date with the said bond   Now if the said Thomas Tracy or his heirs executors or administrators shall and will at the time of my death relinquish all right title claim and interest whatsoever in and to the said sum of four hundred pounds and also deliver up to my executors the said bond and agreement to be cancelled then I do hereby give and devise the said sum of four hundred pounds in equal shares and proportions to my three sisters Martha Tracy Elizabeth Tracy and Frances Guidickens late Frances Tracy   And I do also give to my said three sisters the further sum of six hundred pounds in like shares and proportions and also interest for the said two respective sums of four hundred pounds and six hundred pounds herein and hereby respectively given and appointed to them after the rate of four pounds for every one hundred pounds by the year from the time of my decease until the respective principal sums are paid and satisfied to them respectively   And if either or any of my said sisters Martha Tracy Elizabeth Tracy and Frances Guidickens should die in my lifetime then my will and intention is that the share or shares of her or them so dying either in the said sum of four hundred pounds or six hundred pounds shall go to the survivors or survivor of them her or their executors administrators or assigns   Item after all my just debts funeral expences and legacys given or that may be given by this my will are fully paid and satisfied I give and bequeath all my goods chattels and personal estate whatsoever and wheresoever and all and every sum and sums of money that shall or may be due and in arrear for rent from all and every part of my estate at the time of my decease unto my loving wife Anna Maria Tracy her executors administrators and assigns for her sole use and benefit   Item I give bequeath and devise all and every my manors messuages farms lands tenements hereditaments and premises with their and every of their rights members and appurtenances in the countys of Gloucester and Worcester or elsewhere in the kingdom of England and all my estate use benefit trust in reversion remainder or expectancy therein or thereto subject to the several charges limitations estates remainders and uses limited and declared to all my brothers severally and their respective first and every other sons in tail male in and by my marriage settlement bearing date the fifth day of August one thousand seven hundred and thirty five expressed limited and declared and likewise subject to a term of two hundred years created by a deed bearing date the twenty sixth day of September one thousand seven hundred and sixty for the raising three thousand pounds for my sisters immediately after my decease to Vansittart Hudson of Sunbury in the county of Middlesex esquire John Frederick of Burwood in the county of Surry esquire and Edmund Bœhm of Size Lane in the parish of St Antholins in the city of London esquire and the survivor of them and the heirs of such survivor for ever upon the special trusts and confidences and to and for the intents and purposes hereinafter limitted and declared that is to say   That in case I the said Robert Tracy and my brothers John Tracy Atkyns Thomas Tracy and Anthony Keck should all of us die without issue male or the issue male of my body or of either or any of my said brothers should die before he or they attain the age of twenty one years then and in such case I

Mr. G. J. Mussett. will direct and appoint that my said trustees and the survivor of them and the heirs of such survivor shall stand and be seized and possessed of all and every the said manors messuages lands tenements and hereditaments in the countys of Gloucester and Worcester or elsewhere and the reversion or reversions of such estate and all my estate use benefit and trust in reversion and expectancy therein and thereto to the several uses intents and purposes following (that is to say) To the use and behoof of Henrietta Charlotte Keck eldest daughter of my said brother Anthony Keck for and during the term of her natural life And from and after her decease to the use and behoof of the first and every other son of the said Henrietta Charlotte Keck and the respective heirs males of their bodys respectively to take according to their seniority of age and priority of birth every elder of such sons and the heirs male of his body being always preferred and to take before the younger of them and the heirs male of his body and in default of such issue to the use and behoof of Susan Keck second daughter of my said brother Anthony Keck for and during the term of her natural life and from and after her decease to the use and behoof of the first and every other son of the said Susan Keck and the respective heirs males of their bodys respectively to take according to their seniority of age and priority of birth every elder of such sons and the heirs male of his body being always preferred and to take before the younger of them and the heirs male of his body And in default of such issue to the use and behoof of my nephew Francis Travell eldest son of John Travell late of Severford in the county of Oxford esquire deceased for and during the term of his natural life and from and after his decease to the use and behoof of the first and every other son of the said Francis Travell and the respective heirs male of their bodys respectively to take according to their seniority of age and priority of birth every elder of such sons and the heirs male of his body being always preferred and to take before the younger of them and the heirs male of his body And in default of such issue to the use and behoof of Ferdinando Tracy Travell the second son of the said John Travell for and during the term of his natural life and from and after his decease to the use and behoof of the first and every other son of the said Ferdinando Tracy Travell and the respective heirs males of their bodys respectively to take according to their seniority of age and priority of birth every elder of such sons and the heirs male of his body being always preferred and to take before the younger of them and the heirs male of his body And in default of such issue to the use and behoof of my sister Frances Guidickens late Frances Tracy the wife of Gustavus Guidickens of Heston in the county of Middlesex esquire for and during the term of her natural life and from and after her decease to the use and behoof of the first and every other son of the said Frances Guidickens by the said Gustavus Guidickens or by any after taken husband and the respective heirs male of their bodys respectively to take according to their seniority of age and priority of birth every elder of such sons and the heirs male of his body being always preferred and to take before a younger of them and the heirs of his body And in default of such issue to the use and behoof of the eldest daughter of my said sister Frances Guidickins by the said Gustavus Guidickens or by any other after taken husband and the heirs of her body issuing And in default of such issue then to the second third fourth fifth and every other daughter of my said sister Frances Guidickens by the said Gustavus Guidickens or any after taken husband severally and successively according to their seniority of age and priority of birth and the several and respective

heirs

heirs of the bodys of such daughters issuing every elder of such daughters and the heirs of her body being always preferred and to take before a younger of them and the heirs of her body   And if my said sister Frances Guidickens should have no issue living at her decease or any issue she may leave at the time of her death should all happen to die before she or they attain the age of twenty one years and my said nieces Henrietta Charlotte Keck and Susan Keck and my said nephews Francis Travell and Ferdinando Tracy Travell should all and every of them die without issue male or the issue male of the bodys of all and every my said nieces and nephews should all die before he or they attain the age of twenty one years then my will and intention is that the said trustees Vansittart Hudson esquire John Frederick esquire and Edmund Bœhm esquire and the survivor of them and the heirs of such survivor do and shall in such case stand and be seized and possessed of all my said estate to the use and behoof of the eldest daughter of my said niece Henrietta Charlotte Keck by any husband or husbands lawfully begotten and the heirs of her body issuing   And in default of such issue to the second third fourth fifth and every other daughter of my said niece Henrietta Charlotte Keck by any husband or husbands lawfully begotten severally and successively according to their seniority of age and priority of birth and the several and respective heirs of the bodys of such daughters issuing every elder of such daughters and the heirs of her body being always preferred and to take before a younger of them and the heirs of her body   And in default of such issue to the use and behoof of the eldest daughter of my said niece Susan Keck by any husband or husbands lawfully begotten and the heirs of her body issuing   And in default of such issue to the second third fourth fifth and every other daughter of my said niece Susan Keck by any husband or husbands lawfully begotten severally and successively according to their seniority of age and priority of birth and the several and respective heirs of the bodys of such daughters issuing the elder of such daughters and the heirs of her body being always preferred and to take before the younger of them and the heirs of her body   And in default of such issue to the use and behoof of the eldest daughter of my said nephew Francis Travell on the body of any wife or wives lawfully begotten and the heirs of her body issuing   And in default of such issue to the second third fifth and every other daughter of my said nephew Francis Travell on the body of any wife or wives lawfully begotten severally and successively according to their seniority of age and priority of birth and the several and respective heirs of the body of such daughters issuing every elder of such daughters and the heirs of her body being always preferred and to take before a younger of them and the heirs of her body   And in default of such issue to the use and behoof of the eldest daughter of my said nephew Ferdinando Tracy Travell on the body of any wife or wives lawfully begotten and the heirs of her body issuing   And in default of such issue to the second third fourth fifth and every other daughter of my said nephew Ferdinando Tracy Travell on the body of any wife or wives lawfully begotten severally and successively according to their seniority of age and priority of birth and the several and respective heirs of the body of such daughters issuing the elder of such daughters and the heirs of her body being always preferred and to take before a younger of them and the heirs of her body And in default of such issue to my heirs and assigns for ever   Provided always that it shall and may be lawful to and for every person and

persons

Mr. G. J. Mussett. persons to whom any estate use and trust is herein devised limitted and declared from and after such time as they and each of them shall be in the actual possession of the premises or any part thereof by virtue of any devise or limitation herein contained to limit a jointure to any wife or wives which he or they may marry out of all or any of the manors lands and tenements devised provided such lands and tenements so limited in jointure do not exceed in value one hundred pounds by the year for every thousand pounds which he or they shall receive for the fortune of such wife or wives And further that every such person and persons being in the actual possession of the said premises by virtue of any devise herein contained may make or execute one or more lease or leases of all or any part of the said premises (save only the capital messuage commonly called Stanway Hall with the appurtenances and all such lands as have been usually occupied and enjoyed therewith) for any term of years not exceeding one and twenty years Provided there be reserved on every such lease or leases the best and most improved rent that can be got for the respective lands therein comprized Provided also that at the time of making such lease or leases the person to whom such lease or leases are made do make and execute one or more counterpart or counterparts thereof Provided also and I do hereby declare that all and every the devises limitations and uses to all and every the person and persons above mentioned to whom any devise limitation or use of and in and to my real estate in and by this my will is limited or declared is and are hereby declared to be upon this condition that all and every the person and persons mentioned shall within twelve calendar months from and after they shall respectively come into possession of the premises or any part thereof by virtue of any limitation devise use or title claimed or devised under this my will or any clause or part thereof respectively take upon himself herself and themselves the sirname of Tracy only and shall in all deeds and writings stile and write him her or themselves by the surname of Tracy only and shall bear the arms of the Tracy family and no other sirname or arms whatsoever and that all and every the person and persons aforesaid shall within twelve months next after such possession accrued respectively procure one or more act or acts of parliament to be passed for changing and altering his her and their and every of their respective names to and for the sirname of Tracy only And further if all any or either of the persons to whom any estate use devise limitation or remainder is herein limited made or declared shall refuse for the space of twelve months ~~(except as before excepted)~~ next after he she or they shall be in possession of all or any part of the premises by force of any devise limitation or use to take upon him her or themselves the sirname of Tracy and to procure one or more act or acts of parliament as aforesaid then and in such case I do revoke and make void all and every the limitations uses trust and benefit for or in respect of such person or persons in and by this my will limited declared or contained and moreover that from and after such refusal it shall and may be lawful to and for every such person and persons as shall be entitled by virtue of the next and immediate remainder to the premises or any part thereof to enter hold and enjoy the same or any part thereof in as full and ample manner as if such person or persons so refusing was or were actually dead And if I the said Robert Tracy and my said brothers John Tracy Atkyns Thomas Tracy and Anthony Keck should all of us happen to die without any son living at our or either of our deaths or the sons of either or any of us should die before he or they attain the

age

age of twenty one years and the aforesaid sum of three thousand pounds and the interest thereof shall then be actually raised and paid and all and singular the premises shall be actually discharged therefrom or so soon after as the same shall be raised and paid and the premises be discharged therefrom then I charge all my manors messuages farms lands tenements and hereditaments in the several countys of Gloucester and Worcester with the sum of two thousand pounds to be paid and payable in the manner and proportions following that is to say the sum of five hundred pounds part of the said sum of two thousand pounds to my neice Frances Travell eldest daughter of my late sister Ann Travell deceased who was the wife of John Travell late of Swerford in the county of Oxford esquire also deceased and the like sum of five hundred pounds part of the said sum of two thousand pounds to my neice Ann Travell second daughter of my said sister Ann Travell and the like sum of five hundred pounds part of the said sum of two thousand pounds to my neice Catharine Travell third daughter of my said sister Ann Travell and the like sum of five hundred pounds being the remainder of the said sum of two thousand pounds to my neice Agnes Travell fourth daughter of my said sister Ann Travell at her age of twenty-one years with interest after the rate of four pounds for every one hundred pounds by the year to be computed from and after the aforesaid contingencys on which the said sum of two thousand pounds is to be raised shall happen And if either or any of my said neices Frances Travell Ann Travell Catharine Travell and Agnes Travell shall happen to die before her or their share or shares of the said sum of two thousand pounds shall become due and payable then my will is that the share or shares of her or them so dying of and in the said sum of two thousand pounds shall go and be paid to the survivors or survivor of my said neices as an addition to their said legacys the same to be likewise equally divided amongst them (if more than one) share and share alike at such time and with such interest as their original shares are hereby directed to be paid and if but one then the same to be paid to such only neice at the time and with such interest as her original share is hereby directed to be paid And if my said four neices Frances Travell Ann Travell Catharine Travell and Agnes Travell shall all die before all the said contingencys have happened then I revoke the said legacy of two thousand pounds so given to them as aforesaid and hereby direct my said estate shall not be charged with the same or any part thereof Item I give twenty pounds to the poor people of the parish of Stanway aforesaid to be disposed of in such manner as my executors shall see fit Item I give five pounds apiece to all my servants who shall be in my service at the time of my decease over and besides what shall be due to any of my aforesaid servants for wages And I do hereby nominate constitute and appoint the said John Tracy Atkyns Anthony Keck Thomas Tracy and Vansittart Hudson executors of this my last will and testament to whose great care and fidelity I commend all things relating to my family desiring that my body may be buried in the parish church of Stanway in a decent but not costly manner Item I give the sum of fifty pounds apiece to such of my said executors John Tracy Atkyns Anthony Keck Thomas Tracy and Vansittart Hudson as shall act in the said executorship for their care and trouble therein And I do hereby revoke and make void all former and other wills and testaments by me at any time or times heretofore made and do publish and declare this only to be my last will and testament In witness whereof I the said Robert Tracy have to this my last will and testament contained in eight sheets of

Mr. G. J. Mussett.
Mr. A. Clarke.

paper fixed together at the top and sealed with my own coat of arms set my hand only to the seven first sheets and to the last sheet have set my hand and seal the day and year first above written.

ROBERT TRACY. (L. S.)

Signed sealed published and declared by the above named Robert Tracy as and for his last will and testament in the presence of us who at his request and in his presence and in the presence of each other have subscribed our names as witnesses thereunto as we have likewise done to a duplicate of the above written will at the same time CYPRIAN TAYLOR Stanway Gloucestershire — THOMAS TAYLOR of the same — JAMES BAUGHAM of the same

Proved at London the 4th February 1768 before the worshipful William Wynne doctor of laws surrogate by the oath of John Tracy esq. called in the will John Tracy Atkyns the brother and one of the surviving eхtors to whom admon was granted having been first sworn duly to administer power reserved of making the like grant to Thomas Tracy esq. the brother also and Vansittart Hudson esq. the other eхtors when they or either of them shall apply for the same

(*To Mr. Clarke.*) Do you produce a correct Copy of the Will of Robert Tracy of Stanway ?
I do.

The same was delivered in.

Mr. Hedley stated, That when he attempted to prove the Pedigree from the Heralds College it was with the Intention of introducing Two Wills ; that he proposed to prove those Two Wills now de bene esse, the Will of Sir Richard Tracy of Stanway and Sir John Tracy of Stanway, referred to in the last Page but one of the printed Case, on the right-hand Side of the Leaf.

(*To Mr. Mussett.*) What do you produce ?
I produce the Will of Sir Richard Tracy of Stanway in the County of Gloucester, Knight and Baronet, dated the 17th of July 1637, and proved the 6th of December 1637.

The same was read as follows :

No. 43.

In the name of God Amen The 17th day of Julye anº Dñº 1637 I sʳ Richard Tracy of Stanway in yᵉ countye of Gloucʳ knᵗ & baronett being weake in body but of good and perfect memory (thankes be to God therefore) doe here make & declare my last will & testamᵗ in manner following imprimis I commend my spirit into the handes of Allmightie God who gave it relying only uppon the all sufficient merits of Jesus Christ my Redeemer for the remission of my sinnes & the salvation of my sinfull soule and for my body I commit it to the earth whereof it was made to be buried within the church of Stanway at the discretion of my executor hereafter named wᵗʰout funerall pompe Item I give and bequeath unto my 2 sonnes Richard and John Tracy

8

seᵛally

se͡ally the some of one hundred marks a pece to be paid unto them by my executor during their minorities & after they attayne the severall ages of xxi yeeres then the some of two hundred poundes a pece during the terme of their naturall lives the s^d se͡all legacies *annuityes* to be paid unto them at the usual feasts of St Michaell the Archangell & the Annunciation of St Mary the Virgin by even & equall portions the first paym^t to beginne at such of the said feasts as shall first happen next after my decease the s^d se͡all & respective annuities to bee issuing & going forth of all or any of my mannors messuages landes or tene͡mts and if it shall happen the said annuities to bee behinde & unpaid in p^rte or in all over & above the space of 20 dayes next after either of the s^d feast dayes then my will is & accordingly I doe devise & appointe that it shall & may bee lawfull to & for my s^d 2 sonnes respectivelie into all or any of my said mannors messuages landes or tenem^ts (my wives jointure excepted) to enter & distreyne & the distresse or distresses then & there had & founde to take leade & carry away & the same to keepe & deteyne untill the said annuities & the arrearages of them (if any bee) shallbee fully satisfied and paid unto my s^d 2 sonnes & either of them respectivelie and when it shall please God that my said two sonnes or either of them shall dye then my will & meaning is that the s^d annuities shall not be paid to the ͡svivor of them or to the executor or ad͡mistrator of them or either of them but that in such case the same shall become extinguished as if the same had never bene given nor, bequeathed and that the benefit thereof shall res͡ply accrue unto my executor but my will & desire is that my wellbeloved wyfe (in case she live sole & unmarried shall have the disposing of the s^d annuities of one hundred markes a yere for the maintenance & education of my s^d 2 sonnes during their minorities in such manner as she in her discretion shall thinke most fit for their good (whome I especially trust in this behalfe well knowing her tender care over them & thereon much relyinge) Provided neverthelesse that it shall not be lawfull to or for my s^d sonnes Ri͡c and John Tracy or either of them to graunt lease assigne or set over or by any wayes or meanes whatsoever directlie or indirectlie to conveye or passe awaye the s^d s͡vrall & respective annuities or any p͡rte thereof for any time or terme whatsoever wch if in case they or either of them shall doe contrary to this my meaninge that then the same soe graunted or passed away shall cease and determine & shall not be due payable or leviable out of any my said mannors messuages landes or tenements and to avoide all doubte & ambiguitie my meaning is that my said 2 sonnes shall have noe benefit by the death of each other nor no augmentation of annuitie thereby nor that both the s^d annuities shall ever bee united but the s^d one hundrede marks annuitye to bee paid during their se͡vall minorities & as they attayne severallie to the age of xxi yeares then the same to cease & the s^d annuitie of 200^l. then & not before to beginne as afores^d Item I give & devise unto my daughter Phillip & her children the some of fifteene hundred poundes of lawfull money of England wch my will is shall remayne in the hands of my executor untill my brotherlaw FitzW^m Connisbye & my s^d executor shall agree to dispose of it in lands or otherwise to bee set^ld uppon my s^d daughter for her maintenance during her life & after her decease then to the benefit of her children but my will & meaning is & accordinglie I do declare & appointe that untill the s^d fifteene hundred pounds shall bee disposed of (as afores^d) my s^d executor & his heires shall pay unto my s^d daughter yeerelie during her life the some

ot

Mr. G. J. Mussett.
Mr. A. Clarke.

of six skore poundes for the consideration of the said money and after her death the same some to be likewise paid to the use & benefit of her s^d children at the 2 usuall feasts before named by equall portions & the first paym^t to beginne at such of the s^d feast dayes as shall first happen next after my decease Item I give and bequeath unto my beloved wyfe the some of five hundred pounds of current English money to bee disposed of at her will & pleasure & to bee paid unto her wthin 2 yeeres next after my decease and I further give unto her my s^d wiffe her plate & jewells the furniture of her chamber her coach & horses & my little bay nagge called Hibbetts Item I give to the poor people of the sev̊all p̃rishes of Stanway Haffielde Tewkesbury & Winchcombe the some of five poundes a yere to bee delivered by my executor whⁿ one month after my decease unto the churchwardens of the sev̊all parishes by them to be distributed yet soe as the common beggars may have least parte thereof Lastly I doe hereby make nominate & appoint my wellbeloved sonne Humphrey Tracey sole executor of this my last will & testam^t to whome I give & devise all the rest of my estate both reall and psonall beseeching Allmightie God to blesse him therewth and I doe hereby revoke & annihilate all former and other wills by me made or published In witnesse whereof I the s^d s^r Richard Tracy have to both these sheets of paper subscribed my name the day and yeare first above written.

RICHARD TRACY.

Published & declared & the worde annuities in the first leafe being first interlined in the presence of

Wm HILL.
JOHN GYNES.

Probatum apud Londoñ coram veněli viro dño Henrico Marten milite commissario &c. sexto die mensis Decembris anno Dñi 1637 juramento Humfredi Tracy ař filii dči defuncti et executoris &c. cui &c. de bene &c. coram Ambrosio Jenkes c̃lico viğe commissionis jurat̃.

(*To Mr. Clarke.*) Do you produce an examined Copy of that Will ? I do.

The same was delivered in.

(*To Mr. Mussett.*) Do you produce the Will of Sir John Tracy ? Yes ; this is the Will of Sir John Tracy of Stanway in the County of Gloucester, Baronet, dated the 12th of June 1673, and proved the 10th of May 1678.

The same was read as follows :

No. 44.

In the name of God Amen I s^r John Tracy of Stanway in the county of Gloucester baronett being in good health and of sound and perfect mind and memory praised be God for the same and calling to mind the certainty of death and the uncertainty of the time when doe make and ordayne this my last will and testament in writing in manner and forme following First I most humbly surrender upp my soule into the hands of Almighty God my Maker hopeing by his infinite goodnes and mercy through Jesus Christ my Lord and only Saviour and by his meritts to receive free pardon for all my sinnes and eternal life and salvation and for my body I will it be buried in decent manner by my executers hereafter named in the church of Stanway And as touching my reall and personal estate wherewithall it hath pleased God to blesse me in this world I doe hereby make this my last will and testament disposing of the same in manner and forme following Whereas upon or shortly before my marriage with my now wife dame Juliana one of the daughters of s[r] Erasmus de la Fontaine late of Kirby Bellars in the county of Leicester knight deceased I the said s[r] John Tracy have setled and conveyed diverse of my manno[rs] messuages farms lands tenements and hereditaments in the countye of Worcester and Gloucester to the use of myself for one hundred yeares if I shall soe long live and afterwards to the use of my said wife for the terme of her life for her joynture with the remainder to the first sonne of my body to be begotten on the body of the said dame Juliana and the heirs males of the body of such first sonne issuing and for default of such issue to the use of the second third and other the sonne and sonnes of my body on the body of the said dame Juliana to be begotten severally and successively one after another as they and every of them shall be in seniority and priority of age and birth and of the severall and respective heirs males of the bodyes of all and every such sonne and sonnes issuing th'elder of such sonnes and the heires males of his body issueing being alwayes preferred before the younger of such sonnes and the heires male of their bodyes issueing and for default of such issue to the use of such afterborne sonne of me the said s[r] John Tracey and the said Juliana as should happen to be borne after my death and to the heires males of his body issueing and for default of such issue to the use and behoofe of the right heires of mee the said s[r] John Tracy for ever And as to some other of my manno[rs] messuages farmes lands tenements and hereditam[ts] I have by the same conveyance setled and conveyed them to the same uses (omitting onely the use to my said wife for her life) soe as that the inheritance remainder or reversion in fee for want of issue male by me begotten on the body of my said wife remaineth in mee and my right heires and is at my dispose And whereas I am also siezed in fee to mee and my heires of the said manno[r] of Stanway and the capitall messuage or mannor house thereunto belonging with the appurtennĉs and of all other my manno[rs] farmes messuages lands tenements and hereditam[ts] with th'appurtenances in Church Stanway and in diverse other places in the said county of Gloucester not comprized in the aforesaid settlement or conveyance expectant upon a terme of two hundred years which was devised by my late brother s[r] Humphry Tracy baronett (who was heretofore owner of all and singular the said manners messuages lands tenements and premises) by his last will and testament in writing unto John Barton late of the Middle Temple London esquire now serjeant att law and my cozen William Stratford esquire for the severall ends and purposes in the said will mentioned who have made and granted severall termes for yeares thereout to severall persons and afterwards assigned the said terme of two hundred yeares to my loveing friend Hopton Shuter of the Inner Temple London esquire (in pursuance of a decree in chancery) in trust for me my heires executo[rs] and assignes who alsoe upon my desire did upon or before my marriage assigne the same terme to s[r] Thomas Meres knight and Erasmus De Ligne esquire or some other persons or trustees nominated by the said s[r] Erasmus de la Fontaine as a collaterall security for my said wives joynture and for a provision for raising portions for such daughters as it should please God I should

Mr. G. J. Mussett. begett on the body of my said wife in case I happen to dye without
issue male and afterwards to be in trust for me my heires and assignes
or such person or persons as I should by my last will and testament in
writing direct or appoint as by the severall conveyances and assigne-
ment whereunto relačon being had more at large appeareth And
whereas I have noe issue neither male nor female as yet borne of the
body of my said wife now I the said s⃰ John Tracy for a full and plaine
declarațon of my will and meaning how all and every my said manno⁗
messuages farmes lands tenements and hereditaments and how the said
terme of two hundred yeares or so much thereof as shall bee to remaine
and come att the time of my decease and the benefitt and profitt of all
my said manno⁗ lands tenements and hereditaments shall goe and be
disposed off after my death in case I shall dye without issue begotten
on the body of my said wife borne in my lifetime or after my death doe
hereby ratifie allow and confirme the said joynture made by mee unto
or uppon or to the use of my said wife for her life as fully and amply
as the same is thereby limitted and granted and all the uses and trusts
contayned in the said deeds or indentures made by mee upon or before
my said marriage as aforesaid And I doe hereby further declare my
mind and will to bee that the said s⃰ Thomas Meers and Erasmus De
Lygne or the survivo⁝ or survivo⁗ of them and all and every other person or persons that hath or have or shall come to have any estate or
interest by or under the said lease of two hundred yeares shall assigne
and convey the same and all their estate and interest therein and the
residue of the said terme of two hundred yeares that shall bee to come
at my death without issue as aforesaid to the said Hopton Shuter his
executors administrators and assignes yet subject to and lyable to make
good the said joynture made by mee to my said wife before her marriage
as aforesaid and for the raising of porčons for such daughters as I shall
have by my said wife in case I dye without issue male by her as aforesaid as is lymitted appointed and expressed in the said assignment of the
said terme of two hundred yeares made by the said Hopton Shuter to
the said s⃰ Thomas Meres and Erasmus De Ligne as aforesaid and not
otherwise and upon further trust that the said Hopton Shuter his
executors and assignes shall permitt and suffer my said wife during her
widdowhood for soe long a tyme or soe much of the said terme of two
hundred yeares as shall be then to come and as she shall continue my
widdow and unmarried and no longer to inhabite and enjoy the capital
messuage or manno⁝ house of Stanway wherein I now reside with the
gardens orchards barnes stables outhouses and edifices thereunto belonging with the appurten⁗nčs and all the profits thereof to her owne
use without rendring any accompt for the same or other matter or thing
whatsoever and likewise the rents issues and proffits of all and singular
other the manno⁗ messuages farmes lands tenements and hereditaments
in the said lease comprized soe long and for such time as she shall continue my widdow and unmarried in case I have no issue by her and not
otherwise and soe as she doe pay and sattisfie thereout the yearly annuities or rent charges which were charged or are issuing and payable
out of the same to any person or persons by the graunt of the said John
Barton and William Stratford or by the will devise or other disposičon
or graunt of the s⃰ Humphrey Tracy and if my said wife shall faile to
doe the same or shall happen to marry againe that then it is my will
and meaning in case I dye without issue by my said wife as aforesaid
that the said Hopton Shuter his executors and assignes shall and may
receive and take the rents issues and profitts of all and singular the
manno⁗

mannoᵗˢ messuages farmes lands tenements hereditaments and premisses
in and by the said lease of two hundred yeares comprized other than
such part thereof as is conteyned within my said wives joynture and
all those lands alsoe after her death and shall thereout pay and satisfie
all and singular the aforesaid annuities and rent charges and other rents
whatsoever the premises are charged or incumbred with and my owne
debts if any shall happen to be unpaid and also all such other legacies
hereafter mencͨoned as my personall estate shall not extend to pay and
shall deduct all such costs and charges as he the said Hopton Shuter
his executors administratoʳˢ or assignes shall be put unto or susteine by
the receiueing of the rents issues and profitts of the premisses and
paying the same over as aforesaid or otherwise by reason of the premisses and trust hereby reposed in him as aforesaid and afterwards shall
pay whatsoever shall then remaine of the cleere yearly rents and profitts
of the premisses to the proper hands of my said wife or to suche
person or persons as she shall appoint to receiue the same during her
widdowhood and noe longer   And I doe further will declare devise
lymitt and appoint that after the marriage or death of my said wife
the overplus of the yearly rents and proffitts more then what will pay
and satisfie the said annuity rent charges legacies and other incumbrances shall be paid by the said Hopton Shuter his executoʳˢ administratoʳˢ or assignes unto such person or persons to whom the freehold
or inheritance of the premisses shall belong or apperteine by vertue
of any the lymittacͨons appointmᵗˢ or devises hereinafter mencͨoned
and that the said lease or residue of the said terme of two hundred years shall wayte and attend upon the freehold and inheritance of
the premisses   And as touching the said freehold and inheritance of
all and singular the said mannoʳˢ messuages farms lands tenements
hereditaments advowsons rectories tithes and premisses whatsoever in
the said counties of Gloucester and Worcester or either of them which
were heretofore the lands of the said sʳ Humphrey Tracy and which by
the death of sʳ Richard Tracy baronett his sonne came or descended to
mee the said sʳ John Tracy other than what are in joynture to my said
wife as aforesaid and the revercͨon of those lands soe in joynture as
aforesaid as alsoe of all other my mannoʳˢ lands tenements and hereditaments with the appurteñnces I doe hereby give devise lymitt and
bequeath the same and every part and parcell thereof with their appurteñnces from and imediatly after my dyeing without issue male as aforesaid by my said wife or of some afterborne sonne by me begotten on
the body of my said wife as aforesaid to Charles Tracy esquire second
sonne of the right honorable John lord viscount Tracy for and during
his naturall life and from and after the determinacͨon of that estate to
the use and behoofe of sʳ William Juxon of Little Compton in the
county of Gloucester knight and baronett and William Dutton of Sherborne in the said county of Gloucester esquire and their heirs for and
during the naturall life of the said Charles Tracy to the intent onely to
preserve the contingent uses hereafter mencͨoned and for that purpose
to make entryes to and upon the premisses and any part thereof as
there shall be occasion but not to take any benefit or profitt thereby
unto themselves   And after the decease of the said Charles Tracy I
give devise bequeath lymitt and appoint the same premisses to the use
and behoofe of the first sonne of the body of the said Charles Tracy
lawfully to be begotten and to the heires males of the body of such
first lawfully to be begotten and for default of such issue to the use
and behoofe of the second sonne of the body of the said Charles Tracy

(46.2.)   lawfully

Mr. G. J. Mussett.

lawfully to be begotten and to the heires males of the body of such second sonne lawfully to be begotten and for default of such issue to the use and behoof of the third sonne of the body of the said Charles Tracy lawfully to be begotten and to the heires males of the body of such third sonne lawfully to be begotten and soe in like manner to every other sonne and sonnes of the body of the said Charles Tracy lawfully to be begotten successively one after another as they shall be in priority of birth and seniority of age and to the heirs male of the body of such other sonne and sonnes the elder and the heires males of his body being always preferred before the younger and the heires males of his body And for default of such issue male of the body of the said Charles Tracy I doe devise lymitt and appoint the said manno[rs] lord-shipps messuages farms lands tenements hereditaments and all other the premisses with th'appurteninces and the reverĉon and the reverĉons thereof to Ferdinando Tracy third sonne of the said John lord viscount Tracy for and during his naturall life and from and after the determin-aĉon of that estate to the use and behoof of the said s[r] William Juxon and William Dutten for and during the naturall life of the said Ferdi-nando Taacy to the intent only to preserve the contingent uses herein-after menĉoned and for that purpose to make entries to and upon the premises as there shall be occasion but not to take any benefitt or proffitt thereby unto themselves. And after the decease of the said Ferdinando Tracy I give and bequeath the same premises to the use and behoofe of the first sonne of the said Ferdinando Tracy lawfully to be begotten and to the heires males of the body of such first son lawfully to be begotten and for default of such issue to the use and behoofe of the second sonne of the body of the said Ferdinando Tracy lawfully to be begotten and to the heires males of the body of such second sonne lawfully to be begotten and for default of such issue to the use and behoofe of the third sonne of the body of the said Ferdinando Tracy lawfully to be begotten and to the heires males of the body of such third sonne lawfully to be begotten and soe in like manner to every other sonne and sonnes of the body of the said Ferdinando Tracy lawfully to be begotten successively one after another and to the heires males of the body of such other sonne and sonnes the elder and the heires males of his body being always preferred before the younger and the heires males of his body and for default of such issue I doe hereby devise lymitt and appoint the said manno[rs] lordshipps messuages farmes lands tenements hereditaments and all other the premisses with their appurteninces and the reverĉon and reverĉons thereof to Robert Tracy the first sonne of the right honorable Robert lord viscount Tracy father of the said John lord viscount Tracy by his the said Robert lord viscount Tracyes last wife for and during the naturall life of the said Robert Tracy and from and after the determinaĉon of that estate to the use and behoofe of the said s[r] William Juxon and William Dutten and their heires for and during the naturall life of the said Robert Tracy to the intent only to preserve the contingent uses hereafter mentioned, and for that purpose to make entryes to and upon the premisses as there shall be occasion but not to make any profitt or benefitt thereby unto themselves. And after the decease of the said Robert Tracy I give and bequeath the same premisses to the use and behoofe of the first sonne of the body of the said Robert Tracy lawfully to be begotten and the heirs males of the body of such first sonne lawfully to be begotten and the heires male of the body of such first sonne lawfully to be begotten and for default of such issue

4

to

of mercy in heaven.
She was married in
1798 to Charles Hanbury
3.d Son of John Hanbury
Esq.r of Pon ty Pool in the
County of Monmouth.
He afterwards took the
Name of Tracy and is
now M.P. for Tewksbury.

to the use and behoofe of the second sonne of the body of the said Robert Tracy lawfully to be begotten and to the heires males of the body of such second sonne lawfully to be begotten and for default of such issue to the use and behoofe of the third sonne of the body of the said Robert Tracy lawfully to be begotten and to the heires males of the body of such third sonne lawfully to be begotten and soe in like manner to every other sonne and sonnes of the body of the said Robert Tracy lawfully to be begotten successively one after another and to the heires males of the body of such other sonne and sonnes the elder and the heires males of his body being always preferred before the younger and the heires males of his body and for default of such issue male of the body of the said Robert Tracy to the use and behoofe of Benjamin Tracy second sonne of the said Robert lord viscount Tracy by his said last wife for and during the naturall life of the said Benjamin Tracy and from and after the determinacon of that estate to the use and behoofe of the said sᵣ William Juxon and William Dutton and their heires for and during the naturall life of the said Benjamin Tracy to the intent onely to preserve the contingent uses hereafter menconed and for that purpose to make entries to and upon the premisses as there shall be occasion but not to make any proffitt or benefitt thereby unto themselves and after the decease of the said Benjamin Tracy to the use and behoofe of the first sonne of the body of the said Benjamin Tracy lawfully to be begotten and to the heires males of the body of such first sonne lawfully to be begotten and for default of such issue to the use and behoofe of the second sonne of the body of the said Benjamin Tracy lawfully to be begotten and to the heires males of the body of such second sonne lawfully to be begotten and for default of such issue to the use and behoofe of the third sonne of the body of the said Benjamin Tracy lawfully to be begotten and soe in like manner to every other sonne and sonnes of the body of the said Benjamin Tracy lawfully to be begotten successively one after another and to the heires male of his body being always preferred before the younger and the heires males of his body and for default of such issue to the use and behoofe of William Tracy esquire eldest sonne of the said John lord viscount Tracy for and during the terme of his naturall life and from and after the determinacon of that estate to the use and behoofe of the said sᵣ William Juxon and William Dutten and their heires for and during the naturall life of the said William Tracy to the intent onely to preserve the contingent uses hereafter menconed and for that purpose to make entryes to and upon the premisses as there shall be occasion but not to take any benefitt or profitt thereby unto themselves and after the decease of the said William Tracy to the use and behoofe of the first son of the body of the said William Tracy lawfully to be begotten and to the heires males of the body of such first sonne lawfully to be begotten and for default of such issue to the use and behoofe of the second sonne of the body of the said William Tracy lawfully to be begotten and to the heires males of the body of such second sonne lawfully to be begotten and for default of such issue to the use and behoofe of the third sonne of the body of the said William Tracy lawfully to be begotten and to the heires males of the body of such third sonne lawfully to be begotten and soe in like manner toe evᵧ other sonne and sonnes of the body of the said William Tracy lawfully to be begotten successively one after another and to the heires males of the body of such other sonne and sonnes th'elder and the heires males of his body being always preferred before the younger and the heires males of his body

P body

Mr. G. J. Mussett.

body and for default of such issue to the use and behoofe of every other sonne and sonnes of the body of the said John lord viscount Tracy lawfully begotten or to be begotten and to the heires males of the body of every such other sonne lawfully begotten or to be begotten the eldest of such sonnes and the heires males of his body being always preferred before the younger of such sonnes and the heires males of his body and for default of such issue to the use and behoofe of the said John lord viscount Tracy and his heires for ever   Item I give five pounds to the churchwardens of the parish of Stanway to be distributed to and amongst the poore there   Item I give five pounds to the churchwardens of the parish of Winchcombe in the said county of Gloucester to be distributed amongst the poore there   Item I give to my well beloved wife dame Juliana Tracy all my plate of what sort soever and such coaches and horses with harnesse and furniture thereunto which I shall have att my death and all the furniture and goods belonging to her lodging chamber in my house att Stanway where she usually lodgeth and wherewith the same are now furnished or shall be furnished att the time of my death or the furniture and goods of any other chamber within my said house att Stanway which she shall choose or elect to bee att her owne free dispose   And I further give unto her the use of all other my goods household stuffe chattels cattle stocke and personall estate whatsoever in and about my dwelling house att Stanway aforesaid for and during her widdowhood and noe longer she paying my legacies herein menconed and such of my debts which are not secured or charged upon my said lande in case there shall be any such but if shee shall happen to marry againe after my death then it is my mind and meaning that all my goods househould stuffe chattels cattle stock and personall estate whatsoever remaineing in and about my dwelling house att Stanway aforesaid (other then such part thereof as I have before absolutely devised to my saidde are wife) shall be and remaine unto such person who by this my will is to have and enjoy my said house of Stanway from and after the marriage or death of my said wife to be enjoyed or disposed of by him as he shall thinke fitt   Item I give and bequeath to every of my servants male and female that shall be liveing with mee att the time of my death the sume of five pounds   Item I give and bequeath to my neece m⁰⁰ Mary Barcroft the sume of one hundred pounds to be paid unto her within twelve months next after my decease   Item I give and bequeath to my said loveing friend Hopton Shuter the sume of one hundred pounds to be paid to him within twelve moneths next after my decease   Item to my said worthy and loveing friends sr William Juxon and William Dutten the sume of tenn pounds a peece to be paid unto each of them within twelve moneths after my decease to buy each of them a ring or a peece of plate in remembrance of mee   Item to my loveing friend mrs Mary Clarke the sume of tenn pounds to be paid unto her within twelve moneths next after my decease   And of this my last will and testament I doe make appoint and ordaine my said deare and loveing wife during her widdowhood and my said good and loveing friend the said Hopton Shuter my executors and I doe alsoe desire my said wife in all things relateing to my estate and the future management thereof that she take the advice and assistance of the said Hopton Shuter whom I desire to be carefull and faithfull to her therein as he hath beene to me but in case my said wife shall happen to marry after my death her executorshipp to cease and then I doe appoint that the said Hopton Shuter from thenceforth shall be my full absolute and sole executor to

4

all

(*To face Page* 59.)

NATHANIELL, obiit sine prole.	JOHANNES, obiit sine prole.	VICESSIMUS TRACY, modo superstes.	**3** BARBARA vᵡ Riõdi Smith, de Medio Templo, Lonđ, juris consulti.	*(sic.)* Uᵫin m SUSANNA, mortua.	SUSANNA, superstes.	HESTER vᵡ Fran- cisca Kerle, de cofñ Heref.	MARGAR'.

all intents and purposes whatsoever and as for blacks or mournings to
be given att my funerall or otherwise and the whole ordering thereof I
leave it to the discretion of my said executo^{rs} And I do hereby revoke
annull and make void all former wills and testaments whatsoever by
mee att any time heretofore made and doe declare these fifteene sheets
of paper to every one whereof is subscribed my name att the bottome
of each sheet with my owne hand writing and to the labell that affixeth
them altogether att the topp I have sett my seale to be my very last
will and testament and in witness thereof I have hereunto sett my hand
and seale the twelveth day of June in the yeare of our Lord God
1673 and in the five and twentieth yeare of the reigne of our soveraigne
lord Charles the second by the grace of God of England Scotland
France and Ireland king defender of the faith &c.

JOHN TRACY.

Signed sealed published and declared by the said s^r
John Tracy to be his last will and testament in the
presence of

ROB. GILLMORE.   RICH. STAYLE.
FR. CORBETT.   BEN. TURBUTT.

Probatum apud Londoñ fuit huj^omõi testamentum decimo die mensis
Maij a° Dñi millimo sextentesimo septuagesimo octavo coram
ven^{bli} viro dno Richardo Lloyd milite legum dĉore surrogato
venblis et egregii viri dni Leolini Jenkins militis etiam ac legum
dĉoris curiæ prerogativæ Cant mağri custodii sive commissarii
litime constitut juramento dominæ Julianæ Tracy relictæ dicti
defuncti et superstitis ex^{tricis} in hujusmodi testamento nõiat cui
comissa fuit administraĉo omium et singulorum bonorum jurium
et creditoᵹ dict defunct de bene et fideliter administrand ead^m
ad Sancta Dei Evangelia jurat.

(*To Mr. Clarke.*) Do you produce a correct Copy of the Will just
read ?
I do.

The same was delivered in.

Mr. Attorney General stated, That having ascertained that the Facts
contained in the Pedigree, entered in the Book produced in a former
Part of the Day, were perfectly consistent with the Facts appearing in
other Evidence, he had no Objection to the same being put in, if it
appeared to their Lordships that the Book was sufficiently identified as
being one of a Series of Returns to Visitations.

The Counsel was informed, That he might put in the Pedigree.

Then THOMAS WILLIAM KING Esquire was again called in,
and further examined as follows :

(*Mr. Hedley.*) Do you produce an examined Copy of the Pedigree
you have referred to, contained in the Book you have produced ?
I do.

The same was delivered in, and read as follows. (*Vide* No. 45.)

The Witnesses were directed to withdraw.

(46.2.)   Mr.

Mr. Hedley stated, That he was not at present prepared with further Evidence, and that the Claimant was about to apply to the House for Permission to lodge an additional Case previous to the next Hearing.

The Counsel were directed to withdraw.

Proposed to adjourn this Committee *sine Die;*

Accordingly,

Adjourned *sine Die.*

Die Martis, 21° *Martii* 1843.

The Earl of SHAFTESBURY in the Chair.

Evidence on the
Tracy Claim of
Peerage.

THE Order of Adjournment was read.

The Minutes of the last Committee were read.

The Counsel and Parties were ordered to be called in.

And Mr. Solicitor General and Sir Harris Nicolas appeared as Counsel for the Petitioner ;

And the Attorney General appeared on behalf of the Crown.

Sir Harris Nicolas stated, That he would proceed to prove the Baptism and Burial of Horace Tracy, No. 7. in the Pedigree, a younger Son of Robert the Second Viscount.

Then the Reverend HENRY GLOSSOP was called in ; and having been sworn, was examined as follows :

Rev. H. Glossop.

(*Sir Harris Nicolas.*) Are you the Incumbent of the Church of Isleworth?
I am.

Do you produce the Register of that Parish ?
I do.

Do you find in it an Entry of the Baptism of Horace Tracy in the Year 1618?
I do.

Have the goodness to read the Entry ?

The same was read as follows :

" 1618.

No. 46.

" June 28. Horace yᵉ Sone of Sʳ Robert Trace ᴷⁿⁱᵍʰᵗ & Bridget his Lady — baptized."

Do you find an Entry of the Burial of the same Horace ?
I do.

Have the goodness to read it ?

The same was read as follows :

" 1619.

No. 47.

" Maii 20. Sʳ Robert Trace, Knight, Bridget his Lady, had Horace there Son — buryed."

The Witness.—I find other Entries in the same Form. I have found the Name of Trace in another Place, in 1616 ; there was Henry Trace,

March

(59.) Q

[*from* 46.³. *of* 1841.]

Rev. H. Glossop. March 21st ; Henry Trace, the Lord Deare's Kinsman. I have looked before and after. The Register appears to have been kept with great Care.

The Witness was directed to withdraw.

Sir Harris Nicolas stated, That he would next produce the Will of Dorothy the Second Wife of Robert the Second Viscount.

Mr. James Ford. Then Mr. JAMES FORD was called in ; and having been sworn, was examined as follows :

(*Sir Harris Nicolas.*) What Office do you hold?
I am a Clerk in the Prerogative Office, Doctors Commons, and Assistant to the Record Keepers.

What do you produce?
The Registration of the Will of Dorothy Tracy. I have not examined it; I know nothing of the Circumstances until I look at it. The Gentleman is here who examined it.

(*By a Lord.*) Have you the Will ?
We have a Copy when we have not the Original.

What is the Explanation of that?
We presume that the Original has been delivered out to the Executors.

That is the usual Course ?
It was at that Time.

Before they were delivered out they were copied into the Register ?
They were copied in Books of this Kind, which constituted the Registration.

(*Sir Harris Nicolas.*) Have you a Copy of that?
I have.

Mr. T. P. Mitchell. Then Mr. THOMAS PIKE MITCHELL was called in ; and having been sworn, was examined as follows :

(*Sir Harris Nicolas.*) You have been sworn to give Evidence ?
Yes.

Will you read the Original from the Book ?

The Witness read the same, as follows :

No. 48. In the name of God Amen The eleaventh day of September in the six and thirtyeth yeare of the reign of our most gracious soveraigne lord Charles the second by the grace of God of England Scotland France and Ireland king defender of the faith annoq Dñi one thousand six hundred eighty foure I the right honorable Dorothy viscountesse Tracy being in health and of sound mind and perfect memory praised be God for the same doe make this my last will and testament in manner and forme following First I commend my soule into the hands of Almighty God my Creator trusting through the merits and mediation of Jesus Christ my Redeemer to obtaine ever lasting life my body I desire may be decently interred at the discretion of my executors hereafter named And as for my worldly estate wherewith it hath pleased God to blesse me I give and dispose of the same as followeth Whereas I have two hundred pounds secured by a mortgage of certaine lands and tenements from sir Henry Purefoy taken in the name of m' Anthony
Best

Best in trust for me I doe here devise the same two hundred pounds and alsoe fifty pounds more out of my personall estate to the children of my sonne in law William Higford gent upon the body of Mary his wife my daughter now begotten or to be begotten to be equally divided amongst them upon this condicon nevertheless that my sonne in law William Higford his executors administrators or assignes doe well and truely pay unto my sonne Benjamin Tracey the sume fifteene pounds p annu^m duely out of the said two hundred and fifty pounds during my said sonne Benjamin's naturall life at two dayes in the yeare vizt Michaelmas and Lady day by equall porcons the first payment to begin the first of the said feast days next after my decease which shall soe happen to be And doe alsoe within six months next after my decease give such sufficient security to be taken in the names of my executors hereafter named for the due performance and payment of the said fifteene pounds p annu^m to my said sonne Benjamin Tracy during his naturall life as aforesaid as my executors shall approve of But if my said sonne in law William Higford his executors or administrators shall neglect or refuse to give such security to my executors within the time herein before limitted for the payment of the said fifteene pounds to my said sonne Benjamin during his life in manner as aforesaid then I doe hereby devise and giue the said two hundred and fifty pounds to my sonne Robert Tracy esq. upon the like condicon that if the said Robert Tracy his executors or administrators doe within twelve moneths next after my decease give such security to my executors or the surviv of them as they shall think fitt for the due payment of the said fifteene pounds p annū to my said sonne Benjamin Tracy during his naturall life at the severall dayes and times and in sort manner and forme hereinbefore mencõned and doe alsoe duely pay the same accordingly to my said sonne Benjamin Tracy but if my said sonne Robert Tracy shall neglect or refuse to give such security to my said executors or the survivor of them within .the time hereinbefore limitted for the payment of the said fifteene pounds p annū to my said sonne Benjamin Tracy during his naturall life as aforesaid then I doe hereby devise and give the said two hundred and fifty pounds to my said sonne Benjamin Tracey absolutely at his owne desposeall Item my will is that the sume of two hundred pounds be placed out upon a security at the discretion of my executors and that the interest thereof yearly accrewing and growing due I give unto my daughter Mary wife of the said William Higford for her sole benefit and advantage during her naturall life and after her decease I give the said last mencõned two hundred pounds to my grandchild Dorothy Higford if shee shall be then living but if shee shall happen to dye before her mother then I will the said two hundred pounds shall goe and be to such child or children as my said daughter Mary shall happen to have living at the time of her decease to be equally divided betwixt such children if there shall happen to be more than one Item I give and bequeath unto my sister Judith Try wife of Anthony Try gent one broad peice of gold to buy her a mourning ring Item I give and bequeath unto my said sonne Robert Tracey my best doüle bedd a bolster a rugg and two pillowes Item I give unto my said sonne Benjamin Tracy twenty guinneys of gold to buy him a ring alsoe the bedd I have in London in the possession of my s^d sonne Robert Tracy with all the furnature and what thereto belongs together with three silver spoones and two silver cups Item I give and bequeath unto my said sonne in law William Higford tenne pounds Item I give all my wearing apparel to my daughter Higford and such as shee shall not think fitt to use I give unto the

servant

servant that shall be living with me at the time of my decease Likewise to the servant that shall be living with me at my decease I give a yeares wages over and aboue what shall be then due Item I give unto my niece m^ra Penelope Harrison tenne pounds Item I give unto my brother Thomas Cocks esq' and my brother Charles Cocks gent five pounds a piece And doe hereby nõiate and appoint them sole execut^n of this my last will and testament and doe desire them to see this my will performed and that the sume of fourty pounds my will is be disburst and layed out on my funerall And I doe hereby revoke and make void all former wills at any time by me heretofore made and published declaring this to be my last will and testament And all the rest of my household goods and personall estate of what sort and kind soever not herein given and bequeathed after my debts legacies and funerall expences are paid my will is shall be equally divided betweene my said sonne Benjamin and daughter Higford share and share alike to hold a moyety thereof to my said sonne Benjamin for and during his natural life and after my will is the same shall remaine and be to the child or children of my said sonne and daughter Higford and that my said sonne Benjamin doe within twelve months next after my decease give his bond to my said executors for the due performance thereof of such penalty as they shall approve of In witnesse whereof I have hereunto sett my hand and seale to this my last will and testament containing one sheet of paper the day and yeare first above written vizt xj° die Septembris anno Dñi one thousand six hundred eighty four.

Doro. Tracy.

Signed sealed published and declared to be the last will and testament of the said Dorothy vice countesse Tracey in our presence and subscribed by us hereto as witnesses in her presence

John Kinman.
William Davis.
Frances Parker.

Tertio die mensis Octobris anno Dñi millimo sexceñmo octogẽmo quinto em^t com° honorabili Mariæ Higford (uxori Willīmi Higford gen^r) filiæ fīrali et Itimæ et uni legatariarum residuariarum nominat̃ in testamento prænobilis et honorandæ fœminæ Dorotheæ dñæ vice comitissæ dotissæ Tracy nuper defunctæ ñentis &c̃. ad admĩstrand̃ bona jura et credita dictæ deftæ juxta tenorem et effc̃um testi ipsius deftæ (eo quod Thomas Cocks ar̃ Carolus Cocks gen' executores in eodem testamento nominat̃ oneri ex̃cuc̃onis dicti testamenti expresse renunciarunt) de bene et fideliter admĩstrand̃ ead̃ ad Sancta Dei Evangelia jurat̃.

Tricesimo die mensis Decembris anno Dñi millimo sexceñmo octogẽmo quinto em^t com° Guilielmo Higford marito Itimo et admĩstratori bonorum honorabilis feminæ Mariæ Higford defunctæ dum vixit filiæ et unius residuar̃ legatar̃ nominat̃ in testamento sive ultima voluntate prænobilis et honorandæ fœminæ dñæ Dorothæ vice comitissæ Tracæ defunctæ habeñ &c̃. ad admĩstrand̃ bona jura et credita dictæ dñæ Dorothæ Tracey deftæ juxta tenorem et effc̃um testamenti ipsius defunctæ per pr̃fatam honorabilem fœminam Mariam Higford filiam et unam residuar̃ legatar̃ in eodem testo nominat̃ jam etiam demortuam non plene admĩstrata de bene et fideliter admĩstr̃ ead̃ ad Sancta Dei Evangelia jurat̃.

Then

Then Mr. JAMES WOODS was called in; and having been sworn, *Mr. James Woods.*
was examined as follows:

(Sir Harris Nicolas.) Did you examine that Paper in your Hand with the Original in the Book before you?
I did.

Is it correct?
It is; I examined it with the Original.

(By a Lord.) Have you examined every Page?
I have.

The same was delivered in.

(Mr. Attorney General.) You 'say you examined this with the Original?
Yes; with the Book.

Did you read the Book?
I did not read it.

Did you read a Word of it?
No; it was read to me.

Who read it to you?
One of the Clerks of Mr. Bourdillon.

All you know is that somebody read something, and that that is what he read?
Yes.

The Counsel being asked to what Point they read this Will, stated, That it was to prove that Dorothy Viscountess Tracy had Sons, Robert and Benjamin, Nos. 32. and 33. in the Pedigree.

Sir Harris Nicolas stated, That he would next prove the Burial of Robert the Second Viscount Tracy.

Then the Reverend JOHN RICHARD FREDERICK BILLINGSBY *Rev.*
was called in; and having been sworn, was examined as follows: *J. R. F. Billingsby.*

(Sir Harris Nicolas.) Are you the Officiating Minister of the Parish of Toddington?
I am.

Do you produce the Register of that Parish?
I do.

Have you searched for the Burial of Robert the Second Viscount Tracy, in the Year 1662?
I have not been asked so to do.

When does that Register commence?
In 1666.

Have you any earlier Register than that?
No earlier.

The Witness was directed to withdraw.

Then Mr. THOMAS HOLT was called in; and having been sworn, *Mr. Thomas Holt.*
was examined as follows:

(Sir Harris Nicolas.) What Office do you hold?
Registrar of the Diocese of Gloucester.

Mr. Thomas Holt.

Do you produce the Transcripts of the Diocese of that Register?
I produce one.
Is that an Original?
It is.
Do you find an Entry of the Burial of Viscount Tracy?
I do.

The same was read as follows :

No. 49.

" Robert Lord Viscount Tracy was buried the 11th of May 1662."

(*By a Lord.*)   Where is Toddington?
In Gloucestershire.

The Witness was directed to withdraw.

Sir Harris Nicolas stated, That he would next produce the Will of
Elizabeth Viscountess Tracy, the Widow of John Tracy the Third
Viscount.

Mr. James Ford.

Then Mr. JAMES FORD was further examined as follows :

(*Sir Harris Nicolas.*)   Have you the original Will of Elizabeth Vis-
countess Tracy?
It is a Copy taken from the File placed on the File when the Original
was taken away.
(*By a Lord.*)   Was there no Copy on the File of the last one?
There was not.
Was it usual to keep Copies on the File at the Date of the earliest?
It was usual, but occasionally we do not find them.
Were there other Copies filed at the same Period that ought to have
been on the File?
I should say not; but I cannot say.   I have not searched the
Register with that view.
Did you compare it?
I did not.

The Counsel being asked what they purposed proving by this Will,
stated, That it was the Existence of Children of Elizabeth.

The same was read as follows :

No. 50.

In the name of God Amen   I Elizabeth Vicountess Tracy being
under ye apprehention of an approaching death which shews my understanding perfect (praised be God for it) doe make and ordeign this my
last will & testament in manner and forme following   First I thankfully
surrender my soule to my Creator Redeemer & Sanctifier who together
make up the blessed & glorious Trinity   After this I leave my body to
be decently buryed by my deare lord at Todington in Glocestershire
without pompe and with as little ceremonie as may be   Then I give &
bequeath to my owne surviving sister ye lady Isham my little gold cup
& ten pounds to buy her mourning as likewise ten pounds a peece to
each of my sisters in law that shall be liveing att my decease   I also
give to my foure god children & my nephew Thomas Leigh gent.
twenty pounds a peece   To my daughter Mrs Every I give all my
trunks chests & boxes wth all therein contained except my books which
I give unto my grandson John Tracy with fifty broad peeces (there
being

being one hundred of them together in a drawer) but y⁰ other fifty I bequeath to my grand daughter Elizabeth Tracy Further I give vnto

Sic orig.

my daughter Every my necklace of pearle to her & her daughter for ever (if she has any) otherwise after her decease my grand daughter Elizabeth Tracy before mentioned is by my will to have it More over I give vnto my said daughter the third part of my plate or the worth of it in money y⁰ other two parts I would have devided equally betweene my son y⁰ p'sent Lord Tracy & my grandson John Tracy before nam'd And now my desire is y' y⁰ goods I have left in Hayles house should not be remov'd from thence but kept there for the vse & furniture of y⁰ said house Onely there is a suit of tapistry hangings (not yett hung up) which I leave to my son Tracy to dispose of as he pleaseth I give unto my kind friend m'ⁱˢ Pemberton five pounds in money & my two asses now at Leighton To my woman More I give five pounds beside her wages together with my cloths and to her brother (my page) I give five pounds also towards setting him apprentice Likewise I appoynt my executo'ˢ hereafter named to bestow on y⁰ minister of Leighton Todington & Hayles each a mourning gown And when my debts & legacies & funerail expencies are discharged the remainder of my money I give & bequeath to such charitable uses as my son the Lord Tracy

and my brother Charles Leigh ^esq' shall think best whom I joyntly make executors to this my last will and testament (and in token of my thankfullness to my brother I leave him twenty guineas there being forty together in one bag) In witness whereof I have hereunto sett my hand and seale this 30ᵗʰ day of January in y⁰ 3ᵈ yeare of our soveraigne lord king James y⁰ 2ᵈ annoq̄ Domini 168⁷⁄₈ I likewise give unto my neice

Sic orig.

Jane ^Leigh my lord my father's picture in ^* shagreene case Also I give to my son in law Henry Every esq' and to my two daughters in law ten pounds a peece for mourning Moreover I give my daughter Every all y⁰ pictures of my relations w⁰ʰ are ^in Hayles parlour.   E. TRACY (L.S.)

Sic orig.

Sic orig.

Published & declared
as my act & deed
in y⁰ p'sence of us
   JOSHUA PULFORD.
   ROBERT DEWNES.
   VNTON MOORE.

Now whereas I have given to my granson John Tracy as is within or above expressed (my books the third part of my plate and fifty broad peices of gold) my will is not that any of them shall be delivered to him till he arives to y⁰ age of eight-teen years compleat from his nativity.

The foure god children w'ᵗʰin named are y⁰ lord Leighs daughter. Mary s' W. Egertons daughter Elizabeth my nephew John Bromley and my my neice Anne Maine.

Sic orig.

Probatum Londini &ᶜ decimo quarto die Januarii anno Dn̄i (stilo Angliæ) 1688 coram dn̄o &ᶜ juram̄ hon̄di viri Caroli Leigh arm̄ vnius execut̄ &ᶜ cui &ᶜ de bene &ᶜ (vigore comm̄s) jurat̄ reservatâ tamen potestate similem comc̄ōem facienc̄ p'nobili et hon̄do viro Gulielmo dn̄o vicecomiti de Tracy filio et alteri execut̄ in dicto testō nōiat̄ cum venerit eandem petitur⁹.

Then

Then Mr. JAMES WOODS was further examined as follows :

(*Sir Harris Nicolas.*) Have you examined that with the Paper produced ?
Yes.

(*By a Lord.*) How was it examined?
It was examined in the same Way as the other,—read to me by a Clerk of Mr. Bourdillon's.

The same was delivered in.

Sir Harris Nicolas stated, That he would next prove the Matriculation of Three Sons of John the Third Viscount Tracy, William, Charles, and Ferdinando (Nos. 10, 11, and 12. in the Pedigree) at the University of Oxford.

Then the Reverend PHILIP BLISS, D.C.L., was called in; and having been sworn, was examined as follows :

(*Sir Harris Nicolas.*) What Office do you hold?
Keeper of the Archives in the University of Oxford.

What do you produce ?
The Book of Matriculations in the University of Oxford.

Do you find an Entry of the Matriculation of any Members of the Family of Tracy ?
I do.

Of what Date?
1674.

Have the goodness to read the same ?

The same was read as follows :

No. 51.

" 1674.   Coll. Reg.
" Vice-Canc. D^{re} Bathurst.

" Term. S. Mich.
Dec. 4.   D. Guilh. Tracy a. n. 17 Hon^{mi} Viri D^{ni} Joh Tracy
Vicecomitis Rhagul. de Toddington in agro Gloc.
filius   3. 6. 8.
D. Carolus Tracy a. n. 16 ejusdem Dñi filius   3. 6. 8.
D. Ferdinandus Tracy a. n. 15 ejusdem Dñi filius 3. 6. 8.'

What else do you produce ?
This is the Subscription Book. The first was written by the Officer of the University at the Time they entered. At the Time they entered they subscribed the Thirty-nine Articles, and here is the Subscription of the Parties themselves.

The Entry was read as follows :

No. 52.

" 1674.
" Dec. 4.   Guliel. Tracy e Coll. Reg. filius natu maximus Johannis
Vicecomitis Rhagulensis.
Carolus Tracy e Coll. Reg. filius natu secundus Johannis
Vicecom. Rahagules.
Ferdinandus Tracy e Coll. Reg. filius natu minimus Johannis Vicecom. Rhagulensis."

(*By*

(*By a Lord.*) The Ages are stated?

Yes; that Age is their last Birth-day; the Eldest, for instance, must have been Seventeen complete.

Rev. P. Bliss, D. C. L.

Sir Harris Nicolas stated, That he would next prove the Burial of Thomas Tracy (No. 6.), Third Son of Robert Second Viscount Tracy, without Issue Male.

Then the Reverend FRANCIS EDWARD WITTS was called in; and having been sworn, was examined as follows :

Rev. F. E. Witts.

(*Sir Harris Nicolas.*) Are you Vicar of Stanway in the County of Gloucester?

I am.

Do you produce the original Parish Register?

I do.

Do you find an Entry of the Burial of Thomas Tracy in 1669?

I do.

The same was read as follows :

" 1669.— 3. Mʳ Thomas Tracy buried Septembʳ 6ᵗʰ."

No. 53.

(*Mr. Attorney General.*) Have you looked at the other Entries about the same Time?

No.

This Person is entered " Mʳ Thomas Tracy." Is there any thing to connect him with any particular Family of that Name?

No otherwise than that the Entry is in the Stanway Register, in which there are a great many Entries of the Tracys.

What Tracys?

Of the Families of Stanway and Toddington, as I apprehend, being closely adjoining Parishes.

He is called " Mʳ"?

He is called " Mʳ Thomas Tracy."

Do you find the Use of that Title given in other Places?

As far as I have examined the Book there is great Irregularity in the Mode of Entry in that Register.

He was the Son of a Viscount Tracy?

In many Instances they are entered in Latin, and in others in English.

Do you find any of the Members of the Family entered with the Title which belongs to them as Honourable?

Sometimes Esquire, " Armiger "; sometimes the Ladies of the Family, " Generosa "; and at other Times I noticed that it was " Mʳ Thomas Tracy."

(*By a Lord.*) That appears to be in very pale Ink; is there much of that pale Ink in the Book?

It occasionally occurs.

Sir Harris Nicolas stated, That he would next prove the Admission of William Tracy (No. 8.) as a Member of the Society of the Middle Temple.

(59.)　　　　　　　　S　　　　　　　　Then

Mr. E. Eldred.

Then Mr. EDWARD ELDRED was called in; and having been sworn, was examined as follows:

(*Sir Harris Nicolas.*) What Office do you hold?
Sub-Treasurer to the Honourable Society of the Middle Temple.
What Book do you produce?
I produce the Admission Book of that Society.
Do you find an Entry of the Admission of William Tracy in 1649?
I do.

The same was read as follows:

No. 54.

" 8° Decembr 1649.
" Die et āno p̄dict
" Mr Willelm⁹ Tracy Fil' 3ᵘˢ Roḃti Vičcomitis Tracy admisŝs est in Societatē Meď Templ specialitr et obligatr una suᵃ.
Et dat p fine 4 ¹¹."

Sir Harris Nicolas stated, That he would next prove the Burial of the same Individual at Toddington.

Rev.
J. R. F. Billingsby.

Then the Rev. JOHN RICHARD FREDERICK BILLINGSBY was further examined as follows:

(*Sir Harris Nicolas.*) Do you find an Entry of the Burial of William Tracy in the Year 1706?
I do.

The same was read as follows:

No. 55.

" Anno Dom̄ 1706.
" The Honourable William Tracy Esqr of yᵉ Parish of St Andrews Holborn London was buried June 21. Certified in due time."

Sir Harris Nicolas stated, That he would next produce a Copy of a Monumental Inscription in the Parish Church of Trellick, showing the Death of Henry Tracy (No. 9.)

Rev. C. A. F. Kuper.

Then the Reverend CHARLES AUGUSTUS FREDERICK KUPER was called in; and having been sworn, was examined as follows:

(*Sir Harris Nicolas.*) What are you?
Vicar of the Parish of Trellick in Monmouthshire.
Is there a Monumental Inscription in that Church to the Memory of Henry Tracy?
There is.
In what Part of the Church is it?
In the Chancel of my Church.
Is it on a Slab or on a Monument?
On a Slab under the Communion Table.
On the Ground?
Yes.
(*By a Lord.*) Are you the Vicar of that Parish?
Yes.

How

How long have you been Vicar?
Since October 1841.

Did you know the Parish before?
I did not.

What Appearance has the Slab?
It has all the Appearance of an ancient Slab, to the best of my Knowledge.

It is nothing but a Slab?
No.

Are there any others of this Family?
Not to my Knowledge; I have seen none.

Have you searched the Register of Burials in that Parish?
Yes. We have no Register so far back; 1763 is the earliest Date of the Register.

There are no other Monuments of the Tracys in the Parish, to your Knowledge?
Certainly not, to my Knowledge.

(*Mr. Attorney General.*) You have only known the Parish Two Years?
Hardly Two Years.

I suppose there are Persons in the Parish who have been longer in the Parish?
Certainly; our Church contains many ancient Monuments similar to this; and I have not the slightest Doubt that this is genuine.

The Counsel were informed, That they must produce more satisfactory Evidence of the Antiquity of the Monument in question before the Inscription was adduced.

(*Mr. Attorney General.*) How far is your Parish from Toddington?
I do not know Toddington. I am not able to answer that Question.

The Witness was directed to withdraw.

Sir Harris Nicolas stated, That he would next prove the Death of Ferdinand (No. 12.) in 1682.

Then the Reverend JOHN RICHARD FREDERICK BILLINGSBY was further examined as follows :

(*Sir Harris Nicolas.*) Do you find an Entry of the Burial of Ferdinando Tracy in 1682?
I do.

The same was read as follows :

" Anno Dom̃i 1682.

No. 56.

Esq̃r
" Ferdinando Tracy ˄ was buried Feb. yᵉ 10ᵗʰ anno p̃dicto."

Sir Harris Nicolas stated, That he would next prove the Burial of John Tracy (No. 21.)

(59.)

Then

Rev. F. E. Witts.

Then the Reverend FRANCIS EDWARD WITTS was further examined as follows :

(*Sir Harris Nicolas.*) Do you find an Entry of the Burial of John Tracy at Stanway in 1735.
I do.

The same was read as follows :

No. 57.
" 1735.
" April' — Johannes Tracy de Stanway Armiger sepultus xxiiij°."

Sir Harris Nicolas stated, That he would next prove the Burial of John Tracy (No. 22.) in 1704.

Rev. F. E. Witts.

Then the Reverend FRANCIS EDWARD WITTS was further examined as follows :

Do you find an Entry of the Burial of John Tracy in 1704 ?
I do.

The same was read as follows :

No. 58.
" 1704.
" Octob' — Johannes Tracy Filius Johannis Tracy Armigeri sepultus iiij°."

Do you find an Entry of the Baptism of Anthony Tracy in 1712 ?
I do.

The same was read as follows :

No. 59.
" 1712.
" Maij — Antonius Filius Johannis Tracy Armigeri baptizatus 9°."

Do you find an Entry of the Baptism of Thomas Tracy in 1716 ?
I do.

The same was read as follows :

No. 60.
" 1716.
" Mar. — Thomas Filius Johannis Tracy Armigeri baptizatus xij°."

Sir Harris Nicolas stated, That he would next produce the Will of John Tracy (No. 24.), who took the Name of Atkyns.

Mr. James Ford.

Then Mr. JAMES FORD was further examined as follows :

(*Sir Harris Nicolas.*) Do you produce the original Will of John Tracy, proved in 1774 ?
I do ; and also the Codicil.

The same was read as follows :

No. 61.
In the name of God Amen I John Tracy of Parliament Street in the city of Westminster esquire cursitor baron of the Court of Exchequer being of good health of body and of sound and disposing mind and memory praised be God for the same and being desirous to settle my worldly affairs whilst I have strength and capacity so to do do make and publish this my last will and testament hereby revoking and making void all former wills by me at any time heretofore made and first and
principally

principally I commit my soul into the hands of my Creator who gave it hoping for free pardon and remission of all my sins and through the mediation and intercession of my blessed Saviour and Redeemer Jesus Christ to be admitted to those heavenly mansions where true joys are only to be found to whom with the Father and the Holy Ghost ever blessed and glorious Trinity be ascribed as is most due all honour power might majesty and dominion now and for ever and my body I resign to the earth to be interred at the discretion of my executrix herein after named and desire it may be done decently but not expensively and as to such worldly estate wherewith it hath pleased God to intrust me I dispose of the same as followeth   Imprimis I direct all my just debts to be paid and funeral charges and all the rest residue and remainder of my estate real and personal of what nature or kind soever I give and devise to my dearest wife Catherine Tracy and to her heirs executors administrators and assigns being a small proof only of my most un-feigned love and regard for her who for a long series of years and in the midst of all the changes and chances of this mortal life has ever approved herself my faithful adviser most amiable companion and steady friend and I do also hereby nominate and appoint her the whole and sole executrix of this my will   In witness whereof I have hereunto set my hand and seal this nineteenth day of October one thousand seven hundred and sixty-seven.

JOHN TRACY (L.S.)

Signed sealed published and declared by John
Tracy the above named testator as and for
his last will and testament in the presence of
us who at his request and in his presence and
in the presence of each other have subscribed
our names as witnesses thereto

JAMES PARKINSON of Castle yard Holborn gentleman.
WILLIAM SOAME servant to Jnᵒ Tracy esquire.
ELIZABETH EDWARDS servant to Jnᵒ Tracy esquire.

This is a codicil to the last will and testament of me the honourable John Tracy lately called John Tracy Atkyns cursitor baron of his majesty's court of exchequer at Westminster dated the nineteenth day of October one thousand seven hundred and sixty seven   Whereas under the will of Francis Keck late of Great Tew in the county of Oxford esquire deceased bearing date the twenty ninth day of June one thousand seven hundred and twenty eighth I am as one of the heirs at law of the said Francis Keck and of his sisters who survived him and died without issue or otherwise intitled to certain shares or proportions of the reversion in fee and inheritance of and in certain estates in the several counties of Oxford and Wilts and which said reversion in fee is expectant upon the determination of certain estates tail created in and by the will of the said Francis Keck in favour of myself and my brothers who were living at the time of the testator's death now I the said John Tracy do hereby give and devise all and singular my right title interest shares and proportions whatsoever of in to or out of all and singular the said estates or any or either of them or the reversion or reversions thereof unto the right honourable Thomas lord viscount Tracy the honourable and reverend doctor John Tracy warden of All Souls Oxon James Dagge and Henry Dagge of Lincoln's Inn in the county of Middlesex esquires and their heirs and to the survivors and survivor of them and their and his heirs in trust that they my said trustees or the survivors or survivor of them and his heirs do and shall

T   as

as soon as conveniently may be after the said reversion shall come into possession sell and dispose of my share or proportion thereof either together or in parcels for the best price or prices that can be got for the same and lay out the money that shall arise by such sale in the purchase of government stocks or annuities or on real securities and do and shall pay the dividends and interest thereof unto my dearly beloved wife Catherine Tracy for and during the term of her natural life and from and immediately after her death I do direct that my said trustees or the survivors or survivor of them his executors or administrators do and shall pay assign transfer or deliver over the said purchase money or the stocks annuities or other securities in which the same shall be then invested in manner following (that is to say) one third part thereof unto my nieces the honourable Henrietta Charlotte Keck and Susanna Keck equally to be divided between them share and share alike and in case of the death of either of them without issue and before the same shall become payable then the share of her so dying to go to the survivor of them but in case of issue then the share to go to such issue one other third part thereof unto my nephews and nieces Francis Ferdinando Tracy Ann Catherine and Agnes Travell sons and daughters of my late sister Ann Travell equally to be divided between them share and share alike and in case of the deaths of any or either of them without issue and before the same shall become payable then the share or shares of him her or them so dying to go to and be equally divided amongst the survivors of them and if they shall all die but one then the whole to such survivor except in case of issue when the share is to go to such issue and the other third part thereof unto my sisters Martha and Elizabeth Tracy and Frances Guydickens wife of Gustavus Guydickens esquire equally to be divided between them share and share alike and in case of the death of either of them then the share of her or them so dying to go to the survivors equally to be divided between them and if they shall all die but one then the whole to such survivor save only with respect to my sister Frances Guydickens and in case of her death then I do direct that her share thereof with what she may take by survivorship shall go to such child as she may leave behind her or if more than one to such children equally to be divided amongst them share and share alike and in case she shall leave no children then her said share to go to my said sisters Martha and Elizabeth Tracy or the survivors of them and I do direct that the rents issues and profits of the said premises until sale thereof shall go to belong and be divided amongst such person and persons and in such manner and proportions as the produce thereof when sold is hereby directed to go to belong and be divided amongst   In witness whereof I have to this my codicil to the first and second pages set my hand and to this third and last page my hand and seal this first day of August in the year of our Lord one thousand seven hundred and sixty-eight.

JOHN TRACY. (L.S.)

Signed sealed published and declared by the said John Tracy as and for a codicil to his last will and testament in the presence of us who in his presence and at his request and in the presence of each other have subscribed our names as witnesses hereto

JAMES PARKINSON of Castle yard gentleman.
WILLIAM SOAME servant to John Tracy esq^r.
ELIZABETH EDWARDS servant to the said John Tracy esq^r.

Proved

Proved at London with a codicil 4ᵗʰ August 1774 before the worshipful Andrew Coltee Ducarel doctor of laws and surrogate by the oath of Catherine Tracy widow the relict of the deceased and sole extrix named in the said will to whom admͨon was granted having been first sworn duly to admͪster.

Then Mr. JAMES WOODS was further examined as follows :

(*Sir Harris Nicolas.*)   Is that in your Hand a Copy of the Will now produced ?
It is ; I have compared it.

The same was delivered in.

The Counsel being asked for what Purpose this Will was produced, Sir Harris Nicolas stated, That it was intended to show that the Testator left no Issue, having mentioned no Issue, and having disposed of his Property elsewhere.

Then Mr. JAMES FORD was further examined as follows :

(*Sir Harris Nicolas.*)   .Do you produce the Will of Anthony Keck ?
I do.

The same was read as follows :

In the Name of God Amen   I Anthony Keck of Great Tew in the county of Oxford esqʳ being in good health of body and of sound and disposing mind & memory (praised be God for the same) and being desirous to settle my worldly affairs do make & publish this my last will & testament hereby revoking and making void all former wills by me at any time heretofore made   And first and principally I commit my soul into the hands of my Creator who gave it and my body to the earth to be interred at the discretion of my executrixes hereinafter named   And as to such worldly estate wherewith it hath pleased God to entrust me I dispose of the same as followeth   Imprimis I will & direct that all my just debts as shall be by me owing at my death together with my funeral expences and all charges touching the proving of or otherwise concerning this my will shall out of my personal estate and effects be fully paid & satisfied   And from and after payment thereof I give & bequeath unto my dear sisters Martha Tracy Elizabeth Tracy and Frances Guydickens the sum of two hundred pounds equally to be divided amongst them share and share alike   And as to all the rest & residue of my personal estate of what nature & kind soever I give & bequeath the same unto my two dear daughters Henrietta Charlotte Keck and Susan Keck equally to be divided between them share & share alike   And do hereby constitute & appoint them the said Henrietta Charlotte Keck & Susan Keck executrixes of this my last will   In witness whereof I the said Anthony Keck have to this my will set my hand & seal this seventh day of December in the year of our Lord one thousand seven hundred and sixty-three.

ANTHONY KECK.   (L.S.)

Witness J. TRACY ATKYNS.
CATH. TRACY ATKYNS.

(59.)

Proved

Mr. James Ford.

Proved at London the 9ᵗʰ of July 1767 before the worshipful James Marriott doctor of laws surrogate by the oath of Henrietta Charlotte Keck spinster the daughter and one of the extrixes to whom admicon was granted having been first sworn duly to admister Power reserved of making the like grant to Susan Keck spinster the daughter also of the deced and the other extor when she shall apply for the same.

Mr. James Woods.

Then Mr. JAMES WOODS was further examined as follows :

(*Sir Harris Nicolas.*)   Have you examined the Copy you produce of that Will ?
Yes.

The same was delivered in.

The Counsel being asked the Object of the Production of this Will, stated, That it was to show that the Testator left only Two Daughters and Co-heirs, and no Male Issue.

Rev. F. E. Witts.

Then the Reverend FRANCIS EDWARD WITTS was further examined as follows :

(*Sir Harris Nicolas.*)   Do you find an Entry of the Burial of Edward Tracy in 1723 ?
I do.

The same was read as follows :

No. 63.

" 1723.
" Junij — Edwardus Filius Johannis Tracy de Stanway Armigeri sepultus iiij°."

Do you find an Entry of the Baptism of Charles Richard Tracy in 1724 ?
I do.

The same was read as follows :

No. 64.

" 1724.
" Dec. — Carolus Richardus Filius Johannis Tracy Armigeri baptizatus xiiij°."

Do you find an Entry of the Burial of Charles Richard Tracy in 1725 ?
I do.

The same was read as follows :

No. 65.

" 1725.
" Martij — Carolus Richardus Filius Johannis Tracy Armigeri sepultus xxij°."

Do you find an Entry of the Burial of Robert Tracy in 1767 ?
I do.

The same was read as follows :

No. 66.

" 1767.
" Robert Tracy Esqʳ was buried September 5ᵗʰ."

Do

Do you find an Entry of the Burial of the Honourable John Tracy in 1773 ?   *Rev. F. E. Witts.*
I do.

The same was read as follows :

" 1773.   No. 67.

" Hon^bl John Tracy Esqr dy'd 24th July & buried August 4th."

Do you find an Entry of the Burial of Thomas Tracy of Sandywell in 1770 ?
I do.

The same was read as follows :

" 1770.   No. 68.

" Thomas Tracy of Sandywell Esqr was buried July 2nd."

Do you find an Entry of the Burial of Dodwel Tracy in 1768 ?
I do.

The same was read as follows :

" 1768.   No. 69.

" Dodwel only son & heir of Thomas Tracy Esqr & Mary his wife of Sandywell was buried Feb. 18th in ye 21st year of his age."

Sir Harris Nicolas stated, That he would next produce a Monumental Inscription in Whittington Church to Thomas and Dodwel Tracy.

Then Mr. GEORGE RUSK was called in ; and having been sworn, was examined as follows :   *Mr. George Rusk.*

Have you been to Whittington Church ?
I have.
Did you see a Monument in that Church ?
I did ; it was against the Wall.
(*By a Lord.*)   What are you ?
Clerk to the Claimant's Solicitor.
Did you see it for the first Time when you went to look at it ?
I did.

The Counsel were informed, That more satisfactory Proof of the Antiquity of the Monument must be produced before it could be received in Evidence.

Sir Harris Nicolas stated, That he would next prove the Admission of Robert Tracy the Judge (No. 32.) as a Member of the Middle Temple.

Then Mr. EDWARD ELDRED was further examined as follows :   *Mr. E. Eldred.*

(*Sir Harris Nicolas.*)   Do you find an Entry of the Admission of Robert Tracy ?
I do, in the Admission Book of 1673.

The same was read as follows :

(59.)   U   " Aprilis

No. 70.
" Aprilis 15to 1673°

" Robtus Tracy Aī filius quintus Robti vicecomitis Tracy de Tod‌dingtoñ in coī Gloucestr̃ admissus est in Societatem Medij Templi spēaliter et obligatur una sum.   Et dat p fine £4."

Sir Harris Nicolas stated, That he would next prove the Marriage of Robert Tracy the Judge (No. 32.) with Ann Dowdeswell at Bushley.

Rev. W. Prosser.

Then The Reverend WILLIAM PROSSER was called in ; and having been sworn, was examined as follows :

(*Sir Harris Nicolas.*)   Are you the Incumbent of the Parish of Bushley ?
I am.

(*By a Lord.*)   Where is that Parish ?
In the County of Worcester.

(*Sir Harris Nicolas.*)   Do you produce the Register of that Parish ?
Here is the Register.

Do you find an Entry of the Marriage of Robert Tracy ?
I do.
The same was read as follows :

No. 71.
" 1683.

" Mar.—Robert Tracey Esqr & Anne Dowdeswell Gent. Aug. 29th 1683.   Tracy."
The Witness was directed to withdraw.

Sir Harris Nicolas stated, That he would next prove the Death of Robert Tracy (No. 32.)

Rev. John Eddy.

Then the Reverend JOHN EDDY was called in ; and having been sworn, was examined as follows :

(*Sir Harris Nicolas.*)   Are you the officiating Minister of the Church of Didbrook ?
I am.

Do you produce the Register of that Parish ?
I do.

Do you find an Entry of the Burial of The Honourable Robert Tracy in 1735 ?
I do.
The same was read as follows :

No. 72.
" The Hon^{orable} Robert Tracy Esq. was buried September 19th 1735."

Do you find an Entry of the Burial of Robert Tracy of Coscomb in 1756 ?
I do.
The same was read as follows :

No. 73.
" 1756.

" Robert Tracy Esqre of Coscomb was buried May 30th."

(By

(*By a Lord.*)   Where is Coscomb ; how far is it from where the
Judge was resident ?
About a Mile.

Sir Harris Nicolas stated, That he would next prove the Burial of
Ann the Widow of the Judge.

Then the Reverend CHARLES KINGSLEY was called in ; and   *Rev. C. Kingsley.*
having been sworn, was examined as follows :

Are you Rector of Chelsea ?
I am.

Do you produce the Register of that Parish ?
I do.

Do you find an Entry of the Burial of Ann Tracy in 1697 ?
I do.

The same was read as follows :

"1697 buried   No. 74.
" Feb^r 23 Mrs Ann Tracy wife of the Hon^bl Robt Tracy Esqre."

The Witness was directed to withdraw.

Sir Harris Nicolas stated, That he would next prove the Admission
of Robert Tracy, (No. 34. in the Pedigree,) as a Member of the
Temple, and his Death ; and also the Admission of Richard Tracy
(No. 35.)

Then the Reverend WILLIAM HENRY ROWLATT was called in ;   *Rev. W. H. Rowlatt.*
and having been sworn, was examined as follows :

(*Sir Harris Nicolas.*)   You are the Reader of the Temple ?
I am.

Do you produce the Register of that Church ?
I do.

Do you find an Entry of the Burial of Robert Tracy in 1732 ?
I do.

The same was read as follows :

" Tracey { Robert Tracey Esqr a member of the Middle Temple   No. 75.
was buried in the Middle Temple vault on Thursday the
seven'th day of September 1732."

The Witness was directed to withdraw.

Then Mr. EDWARD ELDRED was further examined as follows :   *Mr. E. Eldred.*

(*Sir Harris Nicolas.*)   Do you find an Entry of the Admission of
Robert Tracy in 1700 ?
I do.

The same was read as follows :

Mr. E. Eldred.

No. 76.

" Novembris 9ᵇᵒ 1700.

" Mʳ Robtus Tracy filius et heres apparens Robti Tracy Ar servient ad legem admissus est in Societatem Medij Templi spĕaliter et obligatur una sum.

Et dat p fine nil."

Do you find an Entry of the Admission of Richard Tracy in 1708.
I do.

The same was read as follows :

No. 77.

" Januarij 24° 1708°.

" Mʳ Ricus Tracy filius sĕdus honorabilis Robti Tracy unius Justiciariorum de Cõi Banco admissus est in Societatem Medij Templi spĕaliter et obligatur una sum.

Et dat p fine nil."

Sir Harris Nicolas stated, That he would next prove a Monument in Didbrooke Church to the Memory of Robert Tracy (No. 32.), by the officiating Minister.

Rev. John Eddy.

Then the Reverend JOHN EDDY was further examined as follows :

(*Sir Harris Nicolas.*)   You are Curate of Didbrooke Church ?
I am.

How long have you been Curate ?
Eighteen Years.

How long have you known the Parish ?
Thirty Years.

Have you known the Church Thirty Years ?
Yes.

There is a Monument in that Church to the Memory of Robert Tracy ?
There is.

How long have you known that Monument ?
Thirty Years.

All the Time you have known the Church ?
Yes.

(*By a Lord.*)   There has been no Alteration in it ?
No.

No additional Inscriptions ?
No.

(*Sir Harris Nicolas.*)   It is in the same State as you have always known it, with the Exception of Age ?
Yes.

(*By a Lord.*)   Is it on the Wall or the Ground ?
On the Wall.

Is it in Marble ?
Yes.

The same was read as follows :

" Near

" Near this Place
Lies interred the Body of
The Honourable Robert Tracy Esq.
Son of the Right Honourable Robert
Late Lord Viscount Tracy
Of Todington
He was a Judge Twenty-six Years
In the Courts of Westminster
But being struck with the Palsy
In the Year 1726 resign'd a Commission
Which he had so long executed
With the greatest Knowledge
Moderation and Integrity
To the Honour of his Prince
And the universal Satisfaction
Of his Fellow Subjects.
Obiit 11° Sept.   Anno 1735.
Ætat. 80.
Bene facere magis quam conspici."

The Witnesses were directed to withdraw.

The Counsel were directed to withdraw.

Proposed to adjourn this Committee to the First Tuesday after the
Recess at Easter;

Accordingly,

Adjourned to the First Tuesday after the Recess at Easter.

Die Martis, 2° Maii 1843.

The Earl of SHAFTESBURY in the Chair.

Evidence on the
Tracy Claim of
Peerage.

THE Order of Adjournment was read.

The Minutes of the last Committee were read.

The Counsel and Parties were ordered to be called in.

And Mr. Solicitor General and Sir Harris Nicolas appeared as Counsel for the Petitioner ;

And Mr. Attorney General and the Attorney General for Ireland appeared on behalf of the Crown ;

Sir Harris Nicolas stated, That he was about to give further Evidence of the Antiquity of the Monument referred to on a former Day.

Then the Reverend STEPHEN PARRY was called in ; and having been sworn, was examined as follows :

Rev. S. Parry.

(*Sir Harris Nicolas.*)   Are you the Curate of the Parish of Trellick in Monmouthshire ?
I have been from 1821 until Midsummer of last Year. I am now Curate of Penalt, the next Parish.

During the whole of that Period you served that Church ?
I did.

Do you know of a Monument in that Church to the Memory of Harry Tracy ?
I do.

Was it there when you first took the Charge of that Church ?
Yes.

What is the Shape of that Monument ?
A flat Grey Tombstone, even with the Pavement, of a different Colour from any other Stone of the Church, and a shining Surface, something like Marble.

Have you made a Copy of the Inscription on that Tomb ?
I have.

Did you make it yourself ?
I did.

(59.)   Y   Have

Rev. S. Parry.

Have the goodness to read it?

No. 79.

The same was read as follows:

" HERE LYETH THE HON:ᴮˡᵉ

HARRY TRACY

OF TODINGTON, ESQ^ʳ

Anno Dñi 1699

OBIIT 30 Aug.

Ætatis Suæ 73

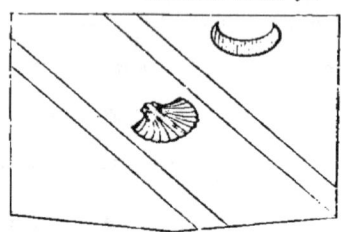

RESURGET "

(*By a Lord.*) From its general Appearance should you suppose that it was there at the Time that it purports to bear Date?
It has every Appearance of it.

Cross-examined by Mr. Attorney General.

You say you were Curate formerly of Trellick?
I was Curate of Trellick with Penalt from March 1821 until Midsummer of last Year. Since then I have been Curate of Penalt, the annexed Parish, only.

When did you take this Copy of the Inscription on the Tombstone?
In August 1842, when Mr. Tracy wrote to me first, while I was in Possession of the Parish Registers.

Can you state at what Time you first took any Notice of this Tombstone?
The first Time that I entered on the Curacy, in 1821.

Whereabouts is it; is it in the Church or the Yard?
In the Chancel, within the Communion Rails, on the South-east Corner.

Was it there when you left the Church?
Yes.

Can you speak to its having been there during the Time you mentioned,—above Twenty Years?
To the best of my Knowledge and Belief it has not been disturbed the whole of that Term.

Is there any Account of any of the Monuments of that Church in any Book you are aware of?
Not the Monuments.

Is

Is there any Account of the Church any where to be met with ?
Nothing in the Parish Chest of old Date.

Is there any printed Book, you are aware of, giving any Account of the Church ?
Not any thing within the Parish or the Parish Chest.

Are you aware of there being any published Account of the County or the Place, or the Country around, which gives any Account of the Church of Trellick ?
There are many Books descriptive of Places in the County, but I have never met with one with an Account of the Monuments in Trellick.

You had the Custody of the Parish Books?
I had from March 1821 until August 1842.

How far back do the Parish Books go ?
1763 is the earliest Date of Burials and Baptisms.

Do you know what is the Date of the earliest Monument in the Church ; are there any Monuments older than this ?
The earliest Date I have noticed is 1622.

What is that ? Whom is it to ?
The Name I do not recollect, but the Date is fixed on my Memory from its being the earliest ; the Situation I know ; it is in the North Aisle of the Church.

Have you any Account in the Parish, or have you any Means of stating, at what Time the Chancel was built ?
I do not know ; I never heard.

Is this you produce the Form of the Inscription ?
That is a rough Fac-simile.

In what County is Trellick ?
In Monmouth.

What is the Market Town that it is nearest to ?
Monmouth, the County Town ; Five Miles distant.

The Witness was directed to withdraw.

Sir Harris Nicolas stated, That he proposed next to put in Two Acts of Parliament, to enable Charlotte and Susan to take the Name and Arms of Tracy under the Will by which they inherited Property, in order to prove that their Father died without Issue Male, as a Son, if he had had one, would have taken the Property.

Then EDWARD PARRATT Esquire was called in ; and having been sworn, was examined as follows :

(*Sir Harris Nicolas.*) Do you produce a Private Act of Parliament of the 14th of George the Third ?
I do.

Have the goodness to read the Title ?
" An Act to enable the Honourable Henrietta Charlotte Keck, Spinster, and her Issue, to take, use, and bear the Surname and Arms of Tracy, pursuant to the Will of Robert Tracy, Esq', deceased."

The same was read as follows :

(59.)

Anno

Anno, 14° Georgii 3.—No. 67.

An act to enable the honourable Henrietta Charlotte Keck spinster, and her issue, to take, use, and bear the surname and arms of Tracy, pursuant to the Will of Robert Tracy esquire, deceased.

Whereas Robert Tracy of Stanway in the county of Gloucester, esquire, deceased, made and duly executed his last will and testament in writing, bearing date the sixteenth day of October one thousand seven hundred and sixty-six, and did thereby give and devise all and every his manors, messuages, lands, farms, tenements, hereditaments, and premises, with their and every of their rights, members, and appurtenances, in the counties of Gloucester and Worcester, and elsewhere in the kingdom of England, and all his estate, use, benefit, trust, in reversion, remainder, or expectancy, therein, and subject to certain estates therein which have since determined, to trustees therein named, and their heirs, to the use and behoof of the honourable Henrietta Charlotte Keck, therein described as the eldest daughter of his the testator's brother Anthony Keck, for and during the term of her natural life ; and from and after her decease to the use and behoof of the first and every other son of the body of the said Henrietta Charlotte Keck, and the respective heirs male of their bodies respectively, according to seniority of age and priority of birth, every elder of such sons and the heirs male of his body being always preferred and to take before the younger of them and the heirs male of his body ; and in default of such issue to the use and behoof of Susan Keck, second daughter of his said brother Anthony Keck ; with divers remainders over ; in which said will is contained a clause whereby the said testator declared, that all and every the person and persons therein before named, within twelve calendar months from and after they should respectively come into possession of the premises or any part thereof, by virtue of any limitation or devise therein contained, should respectively take upon himself, herself, and themselves the surname of Tracy only, and should in all deeds and writings write him or themselves by the surname of Tracy only, and should bear the arms of the Tracy family, and no other surname or arms whatsoever, and that all and every the person and persons aforesaid should, within twelve calendar months next after such possession accrued, respectively procure one or more act or acts of parliament to be passed for changing and altering his, her, and their and every of their respective names, to and for the surname of Tracy only ; and further, if all or any or either of the persons to whom any estate, use, devise, limitation, or remainder is therein limited, made, or declared, should refuse, for the space of twelve months next after he, she, or they should be in possession of all or any part of the premises by force of any such devise, limitation, or use, to take upon him, her, or themselves the surname of Tracy, and to procure one or more act or acts of parliament, then and in such case the said testator revoked and made void all and every the limitations, uses, trusts, and benefit for or in respect of such person or persons in and by his said will limited or contained ; and the said testator by his said will declared, that from and after such refusal it should be lawful to and for every such person and persons as should be entitled by virtue of the next and immediate remainder to the premises or any part thereof to enter, hold, and enjoy the same or any part thereof in as full and ample

ample manner as if such person or persons so refusing was or were actually dead : And whereas the said testator died in the month of September one thousand seven hundred and sixty-seven, without revoking or altering his said will : And whereas the said Henrietta Charlotte Keck did, within twelve calendar months last past, become entitled, under the limitations of the said will, to the manors, lands, hereditaments, and premises thereby devised as aforesaid, subject, as to part thereof, to certain estates limited to the respective widows of the said testator and John Tracy Atkins his brother, deceased, for their respective lives, by way of jointure : And whereas the said Henrietta Charlotte Keck is now in the actual possession and receipt of the rents and profits of the said hereditaments and premises, except as to such parts thereof as are limited to the respective widows of the said testator Robert Tracy and John Tracy Atkins for their respective lives, as aforesaid : And whereas the said Henrietta Charlotte Keck is desirous to comply with the condition contained in the said will : Wherefore your majesty's most dutiful and loyal subject, the said Henrietta Charlotte Keck doth most humbly beseech your majesty that it may be enacted ; and be it enacted by the king's most excellent majesty, by and with the advice and consent of the lords spiritual and temporal, and commons, in this present parliament assembled, and by the authority of the same, that the said Henrietta Charlotte Keck and her issue shall and may from henceforth and at all times hereafter have, use, assume, and take upon her or them and every of them the surname of Tracy instead of the surname of Keck, and bear and use the coat of arms of the name and family of the said testator Robert Tracy deceased, and shall and may write herself and themselves and be styled and called by the surname of Tracy in all deeds, writings, or letters, instruments of writings, and evidences whatsoever, and set and subscribe and write their respective surnames of Tracy to all and every such deeds, writings, letters, and instruments, and that the said surname Tracy shall be and is hereby confirmed to the said Henrietta Charlotte Keck, and that the said Henrietta Charlotte Keck and her issue taking and using the surname of Tracy, and bearing the coat of arms of the said testator's name and family, by virtue of this act shall at all times hereafter be deemed and taken to be a performance of the direction in the will of the said Robert Tracy. Provided always, and it is hereby enacted, that the alteration or change of the surname of any of the persons authorized or required by this act to take and use the surname of Tracy shall not in anywise interrupt, defeat, or prevent the descent of lands, tenements, or hereditaments which she, they, or any of them is, are, or may be entitled unto, or prejudice, interrupt, defeat, or prevent any right or title to her, them, or any of them accrued or to accrue in or to any real or personal estate, by any purchase, limitation, devise, gift, or bequest, in or by any other name, title, or designation whatsoever, but that she, they, and every of them shall and may have and take all such estates, right, interest, benefit, and advantage by such descent, purchase, limitation, devise, gift, or bequest, or otherwise, as she, they, or any of them respectively could or might have done in case this act had not been made, any thing herein contained to the contrary thereof in anywise notwithstanding.

(*Sir Harris Nicolas.*) Do you produce an Act of the 58th George the Third ?
I do.

(59.)   Z   Have

E. Parratt, Esq.

Have the goodness to read the Title?
" An Act to enable the Right Honourable Susan Charteris commonly called Dowager Lady Elcho to take and use the Surname of Tracy, and to bear the Coat of Arms of the Name and Family of Tracy, pursuant to the Will of Robert Tracy, Esquire, deceased."

The same was read as follows :

No. 81.

Anno 58° Georgii 3.—No. 180.

An act to enable the right honourable Susan Charteris commonly called dowager lady Elcho to take and use the surname of Tracy, and to bear the coat of arms of the name and family of Tracy, pursuant to the will of Robert Tracy esquire, deceased. (28th May 1818.)

Whereas Robert Tracy of Stanway in the county of Gloucester, esquire, deceased, made and duly executed his last will and testament in writing as by law is required for passing real estates by devise, bearing date the sixteenth day of October one thousand seven hundred and sixty-six, and thereby gave and devised all and every his manors, messuages, lands, farms, tenements, hereditaments, and premises, with their and every of their rights, members, and appurtenances, in the counties of Gloucester and Worcester, and elsewhere in the kingdom of England, and all his estate, use, benefit, trust, in reversion, remainder, or expectancy, therein, subject to certain estates therein which have since determined, to trustees therein named, and their heirs, to the use and behoof of Henrietta Charlotte Keck, eldest daughter of his the testator's brother Anthony Keck, for and during the term of her natural life, and from and after her decease to the use and behoof of the first and every other son of the said Henrietta Charlotte Keck, and the respective heirs males of their bodies respectively, to take according to their seniority of age and priority of birth, every elder of such sons and the heirs male of his body being always preferred and to take before the younger of them and the heirs male of his body, and in default of such issue to the use and behoof of Susan Charteris dowager lady Elcho, then Susan Keck spinster, and therein described as the second daughter of his the testator's brother Anthony Keck, for and during the term of her natural life ; and from and after her decease to the use and behoof of the first and every other son of the said Susan Charteris dowager lady Elcho, and the respective heirs males of their bodies respectively, according to their seniority of age and priority of birth, every elder of such sons and the heirs male of his body being always preferred and to take before the younger of them and the heirs male of his body ; with divers remainders over ; in which said will is contained a proviso whereby it is declared that all and every the devises, limitations, and uses to all and every the person and persons therein-before mentioned, to whom any devise, limitation, or use of, in, and to the said testator's real estate in and by his said will was limited or declared, were to be upon this condition, that all and every the person and persons therein-before named should, within twelve calendar months from and after they should respectively come into possession of the premises or any part thereof, by virtue of any limitation, devise, use, or title claimed or devised under his said will, or any clause or part thereof respectively, take upon himself, herself, and themselves

6

the

E. *Parratt*, *Esq*.

the surname of Tracy only, and should in all deeds and writings style or write him, her, or themselves by the surname of Tracy only, and should bear the arms of the Tracy family, and no other surname or arms whatsoever; and that all and every the person and persons afore-said should, within twelve months next after such possession accrued, respectively procure one or more act or acts of parliament to be passed for changing and altering his, her, and their and every of their respec-tive names to and for the surname of Tracy only; and further, if all, any, or either of the persons to whom any estate, use, devise, limita-tion, or remainder was therein limited, made, or declared, should refuse for the space of twelve months next after he, she, or they should be in possession of all or any part of the premises, by force of any devise, limitation, or use, to take upon him, her, or themselves the surname of Tracy, and to procure one or more act or acts of parliament as afore-said, then and in such case the said testator revoked and made void all and every the limitations, uses, trust, and benefit for or in respect of such person or persons in and by his said will limited, declared, or con-tained, and, moreover, declared, that from and after such refusal it should and might be lawful to and for every such person and persons as should be entitled by virtue of the next and immediate remainder to the premises, or any part thereof, to enter, hold, and enjoy the same, or any part thereof, in as full and ample manner as if such person or persons so refusing was or were actually dead : And whereas the said testator died in the month of September one thousand seven hundred and sixty-seven, without having revoked or altered his said will : And whereas, some time after the death of the said testator, the said Hen-rietta Charlotte Keck, afterwards dowager viscountess of Hereford, under the limitations in the said will contained, became entitled for her life to the manors, lands, and hereditaments thereby devised, and entered into the actual possession thereof : And whereas the said Henrietta Charlotte dowager viscountess of Hereford departed this life on or about the twenty-fourth day of June one thousand eight hundred and seventeen, without issue, leaving the said Susan Charteris dowager lady Elcho her surviving, who thereupon became entitled, as tenant for life in remainder under the limitation of the said testator's will, to the manors, lands, hereditaments, and premises thereby devised as afore-said, and she is now in the actual possession and receipt of the rents, and profits of the said hereditaments and premises : And whereas the said Susan Charteris dowager lady Elcho is desirous of complying with the condition contained in the said will of the said testator : Where-fore your majesty's most dutiful and loyal subject, the said Susan Charteris dowager lady Elcho, doth most humbly beseech your majesty that it may be enacted ; and be it enacted by the king's most excel-lent majesty, by and with the advice and consent of the lords spiritual and temporal, and commons, in this present parliament assembled, and by the authority of the same, that the said Susan Charteris dowager lady Elcho shall and may from henceforth and at all times hereafter have, use, assume, and take the surname of Tracy instead of the surname of Charteris, and bear and use the coat of arms of the name and family of the said testator Robert Tracy, deceased, and shall and may write herself and be styled and called by the surname of Tracy in all deeds, writings, or letters, instruments of writing, and evidences whatsoever, and set and subscribe and write her surname of Tracy to all and every such deeds, writings, letters, and instruments, such arms being first duly exemplified according to the

law

E. Parratt, Esq.

law of arms : Provided nevertheless, and .it is hereby declared and enacted, that the said Susan Charteris dowager lady Elcho shall and may retain and use the style or title of Elcho, and sign or subscribe any deeds, writings, letters, or instruments by such style or title, together with and in addition to the surname of Tracy, without being chargeable with or accountable for any breach or contravention of the condition herein-before set forth or referred to, and without committing, incurring, or suffering any forfeiture of or prejudice to her estate, right, title, interest, or claim of, in, or to the premises or any part thereof, by virtue of or under the said will, any thing herein contained to the contrary thereof in anywise notwithstanding ; and that the said Susan Charteris dowager lady Elcho taking and using the surname of Tracy in addition to the title of Elcho, and bearing the coat of arms of the said testator's name and family, by virtue of this act shall at all times hereafter be deemed and taken to be a performance of the direction in the will of the said Robert Tracy : Provided also, and it is hereby enacted, that the alteration or change of the surname of the said Susan Charteris dowager lady Elcho shall not in any way intercept, defeat, or prevent the descent of any lands, tenements, or hereditaments which she and her heirs is, are, or may be entitled unto, or prejudice, interrupt, defeat, or prevent any right or title to her, her heirs, executors, or administrators, accrued or to accrue in or to any real or personal estate, by· any purchase, limitation, devise, gift, or bequest in or by any other name, title, or designation whatsoever, but that she, they, and every of them shall and may have and take all such estates, right, interest, benefit, and advantage by such descent, purchase, limitation, devise, gift, or bequest, or otherwise, as she, they, or any of them respectively could or might have done in case this act had not been made, any thing herein contained to the contrary thereof in anywise notwithstanding.

The Witness was directed to withdraw.

Mr. James Woods.

Then Mr. JAMES WOODS was called in ; and having been sworn, was examined as follows :

(*Sir Harris Nicolas.*) Do you produce Copies of the Acts of Parliament just produced ?
I do.

Have you examined them yourself?
I have ; they are correct.

The same were delivered in.

Sir Harris Nicolas stated, That he should next give further Evidence of the Character of the Monument in Whittington Church referred to in the former Minutes.

Rev. W. Hicks.

Then the Reverend WILLIAM HICKS was called in ; and having been sworn, was examined as follows :

(*Sir Harris Nicolas.*) Are you Rector of the Parish of Whittington in the County of Gloucester ?
I am.

Is

Is there a Monument in that Church to the Memory of Thomas Tracy?   *Rev. W. Hicks.*
Yes.

And his Son Dodwel Tracy?
Yes.

How long have you been Rector of that Church?
Since 1811.

Was the Monument there when you became Rector of that Church?
It was.

Does it appear to be in the same State as when you first saw it?
Quite the same, notwithstanding it is Thirty Years since.

Have you a Copy of the Inscription on that Monument?
I have.

Have the goodness to read it?

The same was read as follows :

" To the beloved Memory   No. 82.
of Thomas Tracy, Esqr, of Landywell in Gloucestershire,
youngest Son of John Tracy, Esqr, of Stanway
in the said County,
who deceas'd June 24th 1770, Aged 53.
This excellent Man was distinguished in
Private Life
By an uncommon sweetness of Temper
And benevolence of Heart ;
And possessed in an eminent degree those social
And amiable Virtues,
Which not only procured him the Love of his
Relations and intimate Friends,
But the universal Esteem of all
His Acquaintance.
He was unanimously chosen by his Country
in two succeeding Parliaments to represent the
County of Gloucester,
Which important trust he discharged
with the strictest integrity
and
Disinterested Zeal.
He married Mary, only Daughter and Heiress of
Sir William Dodwell, Kn^t,
And had by her one only Son, Dodwell Tracy,
A Youth, from his amiable Disposition and
distinguished Parts, of the most
promising hopes ;
But these, alas, were blasted, when, in the
flower of his Age, he was snatched
From the Arms of his Afflicted Parents and Friends,
Jan. 11, 1768, at Paris, on his return
from his Travels,
in the 21st Year of his Age.

(59.)   A a   Mary,

Rev. W. Hicks.

Mary, their lamenting Wife and Mother,
placed this Mournful Testimony of
Her tenderest Affection
to her Dear Husband
and her beloved Son.
Their Remains are deposited in the Tracy Vault at Stanway."

The Witness was directed to withdraw.

Sir Harris Nicolas stated, That he proposed to put in the Will of Richard Dowdeswell, to show that his Sister married Robert Tracy, the Judge (No. 32.), who is the immediate Ancestor of the Claimant.

Mr. James Ford.   Then Mr. JAMES FORD was called in ; and having been sworn, was examined as follows :

(*Sir Harris Nicolas.*)   What Office do you hold ?
A Clerk in the Prerogative Office, Doctors Commons.

Do you produce the original Will of Richard Dowdeswell of Poole Court in the County of Worcester?
I do.

Will you read the Beginning of it ?

The Witness read the same as follows :

No. 33.

In ye the name of God Amen I Richard Dowdeswell of Poole Court in ye county of Worcester esq^r doe make constitute & ordain y^s my last will & testament revokeing all former wills by me made Impr̃is it is my will y^t all my just debts y^t I shall owe at ye time of my decease be punctually p̃d in the first place Item I doe give unto my deare wife one hundred pounds Item I doe give unto my daughter Judith the summ of four thousand pounds for her portion wth full interest for the same from the time of my decease Item I doe give unto my sonn Francis the summ of three thousand pounds for his portion to be p̃d as soon as he shall arrive at ye full age of twenty-one yeares wth full interest for ye same from ye time of my decease Item I doe give unto my daughter Margarett the summ of three thousand pounds for her portion to be p̃d her as soon as shee shall arrive at ye full age of twenty-one yeares or be married wch shall first happen wth full interest for ye same from ye time of my decease But in case my s̃d sonn Francis shall dye before he attains his age of twenty-one yeares or my daughter Margarett shall dye before shee attaine her age of twenty-one yeares & before shee be married then my will is y^t the portion or summ of money hereinbefore given to him or her soe dying shall not be p̃d And whereas my daughter Elizabeth hath lately married Mr. Roger Tuckfeild against my consent & their

Original so.

has been ~~as yett~~ noe settlement as yett made upon her I doe hereby give & bequeath vnto my executers herein-after named the summ of three thousand pound vpon ye trusts & to ye intents & purposes following (that is to say) upon trust that they shall pay ye summ of three thousand pounds vnto ye s̃d Roger Tuchfeild wⁿ such a settlement shall be made by him or her father vpon my s̃d daughter Elizabeth & her issue as my s̃d executors shall think reasonable & approve of & vntill such a settlement shall be made my will is y^t my s^d executors doe pay ye interest of ye s̃d summ of three thousand pounds vnto ye proper hands of my s^d daughter

daughter Elizabeth where wth her husband shall noe wayes ~~intermeddle~~ Original so.
intermeddle & her owne receipts wth out her husband shall be sufficient
discharges for the same   And if the s^d Roger Tuchfeild ˏbefore my s̃d Original so.
daughter & before any settlement shall be made upon her as affores̃d
then my will is y^t the s̃d summ of three thousand pounds shall be p̃d
unto my s̃d daughter to be absolutely at her owne disposall butt if my s̃d
daughter shall happen to dye before her husband & before such a settlement shall be made upon her as affores̃d y^n my will is y^t the s̃d summ of
three thousand pounds shall be p̃d unto my daughter Judith my sonn
Francis & my daughter Margaret equally   And my will & meaning is y^t
my personall estate shall in ye first place be applyed towards ye payment of
my debts & ye legacyes portions & summs of money herein-before given
And for ye further secureing ye payment of all my just debts wch I shall
owe at ye time of my decease & allsoe of ye s^d legacyes & portions I have
herein-before given I doe give & devise unto my deare b^r Robert

Tracy esq^r of Serjents Inn in Fleet Street one of her maj^ties ᵗⁱᵉˢ of ye court Original so.
of Common Pleas at Westminster Francis Winnington of Broadway in
ye county of Worcester esq^r & Thomas Wylde of Sidbury in ye county
of Worcester esq^r & theyr heires my mannors of Rushley Boredon &
Mitton in ye s̃d county of Worcester and all other my mannors lands
tenements & hereditaments of wch I have a power to dispose as well
those I hold by any lease or leases for lives or otherwise from
or under ye dean & chapter of Westminster or ye dean & chapter
of Glocester as those of wch I am seized or any person in trust
for me of any estate of freehold or inheritance upon ye trusts & to
& for ye intents & purposes herein-after mentioned (that is to say)
upon trust y^t they the s̃d Robert Tracy Francis Winnington & Thomas
Wylde & ye survivor of y^m & ye heires of such survivor shall by y^e
perception of ye rents & proffitts & by leaseing mortgageing (or if
necessity require) by selling all or any p^t of ye s̃d mannors lands tenements or hereditaments to y^m devised raise pay & satisfie all my just
debts wch I shall owe at ye time of my decease & all ye legacys & portions & summs of money wch I have herein-before given or such part
thereof as shall not be p̃d out of my personall estate in such manner as
I have herein-before directed ye same to be p^d   And my will & meaning
is y^t after my s̃d debts & all ye s̃d legacys portions or summs of money
wch I have herein-before given shall be p̃d & satisfied then ye s̃d Robert
Tracy Francis Winning^ton & Thomas Wylde & theyr heires shall stand
& be seized & possessed of such & such part of ye s̃d mannors lands
tenements & hereditaments to y^m devised as shall not be sold subject
never ye less to such leases & mortgages as shall be by y^m made for y^e
purposes afores̃d in trust for my sonn William & his heires And my will
& meaning is & I doe hereby declare y^t the severall portions & summs
of money wch I have here given to my sonn Francis & to my s̃d daughters are intended by me to be in full satisfaction of all such portions or
summs of money wch they or either of y^m might claime by virtue of my
marriage settlement   And I doe hereby constitute & appoint the s̃d
Robert Tracy Francis Winnington & Thomas Wylde to be the sole
executors of ye my will   And my will is y^t they shall pay & satisfie y^m
selves out of my reall & personall estate all such charges & expences as
they shall be put unto in ye execution of ye my will   Item I doe give &
devise unto ye s̃d Robert Tracy Francis Winnington & Thomas Wylde
twenty pounds each   In witness of ye my last will & testament I
(59.) have

Mr. James Ford.

have hereunto put my hand & seale y° sixth day of Aprill in y° yeare of our Lord one thousand seven hundred & eight.

R. DOWDESWELL.   (L. S.)

Signed sealed & published by y° above named Richard Dowdeswell as his last will & testament in y° presence of us who subscribed our names as witnesses there unto in his presence

FRA BROMPTON.
ROB^t DICKESON.
JN° SOUTHALL.

Vicesimo tertio die mensis Jan^ii anno Dñi 1711 em^t com° Willielmo Dowdeswell arm filio ñrali et ltimo et legatario priñli nominat̃ in testament° Richardi Dowdeswell nuper de Poole Court in com̃ Wigornie defti habeñ &c. ad adstrand̃ bona jura et credita dicti defti juxta tenorem et effectum testañti ipsius defti de bene &c. jurat̃ hoñli viro Roberto Tracy arm̃ uno justiciaror̃ dñe ñræ regine de com̃uni banco Francisco Winnington arm̃ et Thoma Wylde arm̃ ex̃ribus prius renunciañ.

Did you examine the Copy you produce of that Will ?
I did.
Is it correct ?
It is.

The same was delivered in.

Sir Harris Nicolas stated, That he would next put in the Will of Robert Tracy, the Judge (No. 32.)

(*To the Witness.*). Do you produce the Will of Robert Tracy ?
I do.
Have the goodness to read it ?

The Witness read the same as follows :

No. 84.

Original so.

In the name of God Amen I Robert Tracy of Coscomb in the parish of Didbrooke in the county of Glouc^r esq^r late one of the justices of the court of Common Pleas at Westminster being I praise God of sound mind and memory doe make this my last will and testament in writing ~~and~~ hereby revoaking all former wills and codicells by me heretofore made And first I resigne my soul into the hands of Almighty God hopeing through his infinite mercyes and the mediation and meritts of my blessed Saviour Jesus Christ to receive remission of my sins and a joyfull resurrecc̃on to life immortall I desire to be buried in as private a manner as is consistant with decency in the chancell of the parish church of Didbrook aforesaid neare the communion table And my will is that my executors erect a monument for me on the side of the wall near my grave the charge whereof shall not exceed fifty pounds haveing leave of the right hoñble the lord viscount Tracy impropriator of the said church for the purposes aforesaid And as for my worldly estate wherewith it hath pleased Almighty God to bless me I give and dispose thereof as followeth I give and devise unto my grandson Robert Tracy and to the heires of his body lawfully begotten all that my new built house at Coscomb aforesaid wherein I now
dwell

dwell with all the gardens stables and outhouses therewith used and enjoyed and all that farme called Coscomb farm in the parish of Didbrook aforesaid now in the posšion of Richd Bryan and all lands tenements and hereditaments therewith used and enjoyed and all my farms and lands in Norton aĩs Bishops Norton in the said county of Glouc^r and all other my freehold messuages lands tenements and hereditaments whatsoever in Coscomb and Norton aĩs Bishops Norton aforesaid or elsewhere in that part of Great Britain called England but so as my said grandson shall ^{not} be lett into the percepčon receipt or enjoym^t of the rents and proffitts thereof untill he shall attaine the age of one and twenty years unless such part as is herein-after directed and left to ye dissrečon of the trustees of this my will to be applyed for and towards his educačon and maintenance and in default of heires of the body of my said grandson Robert Tracy I give and devise all the aforesaid premĩes unto my daughter Anne wife of Thomas Wylde esq^r during the term of her naturall life and immediately after her decease I give and devise all ye aforesaid premisses unto my grandson Robert Pratt sonn of my daughter Dorothy dečed by John Pratt esq^r and the heires male of his body lawfully begotten & in default of such issue I give and devise all the aforesaid premisses to the heires of the body of my said daughter Wylde and in default of such issue I give and devise all the aforesaid premisses unto my owne right heires for ever Provided always and my will meaning and direcčon is that when the aforesaid premisses shall come in possession to my said grandson Robert ~~Pratt~~ by vertue of the devise and limmittačon thereof by this my will that then he and his issue male shall take upon him and them the sirname of Tracy only and use the same in all letters instruments and writings whatsoever and in case he or the heires male of his body shall refuse or neglect to take upon him and them the sirname of Tracy only and so use the same as aforesaid that then the devise to him or them so refuseing or neglecting shall be void I give and devise all the rents issues and proffitts of all the aforesaid premisses untill my said grandson Robert Tracy shall attain the age of one and twenty years or untill his death in case the same shall happen before that time unto my said two sons in law Thomas Wylde and John Pratt and Henry Barnes gent. formerly my clerk and now secondary to mr. Borrett one of the prothonotaries of the court of Common Pleas and to the survivors and survivor of them and to the exŏrs and adm̃ors of such survivor upon trust and to the intent and purpose that they and the survivors and survivor of them and the exŏrs and adm̃ors of such survivor shall lay out and dispose of the same in the purchase or purchases of lands and tenements of inheritance in that part of Great Britain called England in their owne names and shall forthwith convey and settle the same in such manner as councell shall advise and direct to or to the same use and uses of such person and persons and for such estate and estates and in such manner as my said new built house at Coscombe and Coscomb farm are herein-before limĩtted and devised or as neare the same as may be upon the death of partyes or other alteračons of circumstances which may happen before such settlement canbe made and I should chose to have such purchases made in the county of Glouc^r and near to Coscombe if ye same may be made in convenient time and at reasonable prizes otherwise not And my will is that untill such rents and proffitts so received shall be laid out in the purchase or purchases ~~as~~ aforesaid the same shall be put out at interest by my said trustees in their

their names or in the names of the survivors or survivor of them or the exōrs or admōrs of such survivor upon government or such other security or securityes as they shall think fitt and the interest or produce thereof shall from time to time be received by such person & persons who would have been entituled to the proffitts of the lands to be purchased and settled according to this my will Item my will is and I doe hereby direct that my sudy of books and all my goods and furniture which shall be in my new built house at Coscomb at the time of my death shall continue therein and goe along with the same and be used and enjoyed from time to time by such person and persons who shall be entitled to the said house by vertue of the devises and limittačons aforesaid as far as the rules of law or equity will permitt Item I give to my said sons in law Thomas Wylde and John Pratt and the said Henry Barnes tenn pounds apiece to buy them mourning and to each of them a ring of twenty shillings value Item I give to the twelve judges liveing at my decease and to each of them a ring of twenty shillings value as a small token of my respect to them Item I give to my daughter Wylde to my daughter in law mrs Margarett Tracy to the right honōble the lord viscount Tracy to my nephew John Tracy of Stanway esqr to my brother William Higford esqr and his daughter my cousin Elianor Higford to Robert Wylde esqr and his wife and to my friend mr Thomas Mander of Toddenham and to each of them a ring of twenty shillings value Item I give to my said daughter Wylde one hundred pounds for her great kindness and tender care of me during my late illness in London Item I give to my servant George Daken twenty pounds Item I give to all the rest of my servants that shall live with me at my death halfe a year's wages apiece besides what shall be then due to them Item I give to ye said Henry Barnes the further sume of fifty pounds besides what is hereinbefore given to him Item as to all the rest and residue of my personall estate after my debts legacyes funerall charges and the expence of the said monumt shall be paid I give devise and bequeath the same unto the said Thomas Wylde John Pratt and Henry Barnes to the intent and purpose that they or the survivors or survivor of them and the exōrs and admōrs of such survivor shall turn the same into money and shall with all convenient speed lay out and dispose the same in the purchase or purchases of lands and tenements of inheritance in that part of Great Britain called England in their own names and shall forthwith convey and settle the same in such manner as councell shall advise and direct to or to the use and uses of such person and persons and for such estate and estates and in such manner as my said new built house at Coscomb and Coscomb farm are hereinbefore limitted and devised or as neare the same as may be upon the death of partyes or other alteračons of circumstances which may happen before such settlement can be made and I should chose to have such purchases made in the county of Gloucr and neare to Coscomb if ye same may be made in convenient time and at reasonable prices otherwise not And my will is that untill the residue of my personall estate shall be laid out in the purchase or purchases aforesaid the interest and produce thereof shall from time to time be received by such person and persons who would have been entitled to the proffitts of the lands to be purchased and settled according to this my will Provided always and my will and meaning is that it shall and may be lawfull to and for the said Thomas Wylde John Pratt and Henry Barnes and the survivors and survivor of them and the exōrs and admōrs of such survivor if they shall in their discrečon think

fitt

fitt and find it necessary as the circumstances of the case may happen and require during the life time of my said daughter in law m^rs Margarett Tracy mother of my grandson Robert Tracy either by and out of the rents issues and proffitts of my said new house & farm at Coscomb

and farms lands and premisses in Norton ~~and~~ *or* by and out of the interest or produce of my money & personall estate to allow pay and apply to and for the maintenance and educačon of my said grandson Robert Tracy any sume of money not exceeding fifty pounds per ann̄ till he shall attain ye age of twelve years and after he shall ~~arise~~ *arise* to that age any sume of money not exceeding the sume of one hundred pounds per ann̄ untill he shall attain ye age of one and twenty years or untill the death of his said mother which shall first happen any thing herein contained to the contrary thereof in anywise notwithstanding Item it is my will direcčon and meaning that ye said trustees of this my will shall not be answerable or lyable for ye receits or disbursem^ts the one of the other nor for ye act or deed the one of the other but for his owne respective act and deed only nor for any more of the trust money than

he and they shall respectively actually receive nor for the failing *or* ~~and~~ insufficiency or any security or securityes to be taken for any sume of money to be placed out at interest pursuant to ye dicčon of this my will unless the same shall happen by any willfull neglect or default and that the said trustees and the survivors and survivor of them and the exors and adm̄ors of such survivor shall be reimbursed and satesfyed out of the said trust money and estate all such lawfull and reasonable costs charges and expences as they or any or either of them shall expend lay out or be put unto in or about ye execučon of ye aforesaid trusts And I doe hereby nominate and appoint the said Thomas Wylde John Pratt and Henry Barnes executors of this my last will In witness whereof I the said Robert Tracy have to this my last will and testament consisting of three sheets of paper ~~I have~~ putt my hand to the bottom of the two first sheetes and to the last sheet putt my hand and seale this p^rsent fifteenth day of December in the sixth yeare of the reign of our soveraigne lord *George* the second king over Great Britain, &c. annoq̄ Dn̄i 1732.

R. TRACY. (L. S.)

Signed sealed published and declared by the testator Robert Tracy for and as his last will and testament in the p^rsence of us who att his request and in his p^rsence have hereunto subscribed our names as witnesses

ELE. HIGFORD.
THO. MANDER.
EDM^d WHITLEY,
Cl. to m^r Mander.

June 15th 1733.

I give and bequeath to my servant Martin Clark ten pounds for his great kindness to me in my illness and I desire this may be taken as a codicel ~~to~~ to my will.

R. TRACY.

Witness GEORGE DAKEN.

(59.)

Proved

Proved at London the fourth day of October (with a codicil annexed) before the worshipfull Thomas Walker doctor of laws surrogate by Thomas Wylde esqʳ John Pratt esqʳ and Henry Barnes gent. to whom ad̃con was granted being first sworn duly to administer.

Did you examine the Copy you produce with the Original?
I did.

Is it correct?
It is correct.

(*By a Lord.*)   Did you examine that yourself with the Original?
I did.

In what Way did you examine it?
I examined it with a Fellow Clerk, who held one while I read the other.

Did you do it crosswise?
We did.

The same was delivered in.

Sir Harris Nicolas stated, That he would next put in the Will of Robert Tracy (No. 37.); the Grandson of the Judge (No. 32.)

Do you produce the Will of Robert Tracy the Grandson?
I do.

Have the goodness to read it?

The Witness read the same as follows:

No. 85.

I Robert Tracy of Coscombe in the county of Gloucester esquire do hereby make my last will & testament as follows that is to say I give devise & bequeath my capital messuage at Coscombe aforesaid & all other my messuages lands tenements & hereditaments whatsoever in the counties of Gloucester Worcester Warwick or elsewhere in England to my cousin Robert Pratt son of my aunt Dorothy daughter of my late grand father the honorable mʳ Justice Tracy deceased & to his heirs and assigns for ever subject to the incumbrances thereupon by me made I further give and devise all my reversionary interest in an estate in Wales wherein my mother has an estate for life under my father's marriage settlement to the said Robert Pratt his heirs & assigns for ever and I do hereby charge all my real estate in possession & reversion with payment of my just debts and legacies I hereby give & devise to my servant William Morgan all the goods furniture books wearing apparell watches rings trinketts & other things in my chambers in the Temple to detain & keep the same till he is paid what I owe him which is above one hundred pounds but upon payment of his full demand he is to deliver up all the said goods furniture books watches rings and other things (wearing apparell excepted) to my executor herein-after named I acknowledge to owe to Henry Barnes of the Middle Temple London gentleman one hundred pounds   I leave to my said servant William Morgan six pounds for mourning and to my old nurse Legg and to my laundress Charlotte Ward five pounds each for mourning
I hereby

I hereby appoint the said Henry Barnes executor of this my last will &   *Mr. James Ford.*
testament   Dated the fourteenth day of May 1756.

Robt Tracy.   (L. s.)

Signed sealed published & declared by the testator as and for his last will and testament in
the presence of us who have subscribed our
names as witnesses thereto in his presence
and at his request

        J. Bell.
        Arthur Murphy.
        Sam¹ Coppock.

Proved at London the 25th day of May 1756 before the worshipful
Andrew Coltree Ducarel doctor of laws and surrogate by the
oath of Henry Barnes the sole executor to whom admͦon was
granted having been first sworn duly to ad^{ster}.

Do you produce a Copy of that Will, compared by yourself?
I do; it is correct.

The same was delivered in.

Do you produce the Will of Richard Tracy, dated the 16th of
January 1731-32?
   I do.

Be good enough to read it?

The Witness read the same as follows :

In the name of God Amen   I Richard Tracy of Coscomb in y^e   No. 86.
county of Glöster esq^r being weak in body but of a good disposing
mind and memory praised be God for ye same do make this my last
will & testament in writing in manner following   First I resign my
soul into ye hands of Almighty God hoping thro' his infinite mercies
and the merits & mediation of Jesus Christ my Savior for a joyful
resurrection to life immortal And I desire to be bury'd in as private
a manner as is consistent wth decency wch I leave to ye discretion of
my executrix hereafter namd   And as to my wordly concerns one prin-
cipal part whereof is the care & education of my only son (who is now
very young) & ye management of his estate during his minority I give
& devise unto Margaret my dearly beloved wife the custody &
tuition of Robert my son untill he shall attain his age of twenty one
years   Provided nevertheless and my will is that as the same will
cease on the death of my said wife so if she shall marry again the
said custody & tuition hereby devised to her shall also cease & be
void & in either of these cases I give & devise ye custody and tuition
of my said son untill he shall attain his age of twenty one years unto
s^r William Wynn of London knight standard bearer of his majesties band
of gentlemen pensioners & to Robert Meyrick of Ucheldre in ye county
of Merioneth esq^r & ye survivor of them being persons well acquainted
with & therefore best able to manage the estate in Wales wch will come
to my said son after the decease of his mother wch is much more likely
to happen than her marriage But I desire my said wife & ye said s^r
William Wynn & Robert Meyrick to advise with my honor'd father

as long as he lives & after his death with my worthy freinds & kinsmen Thomas Cha. l^d viscount _{Tracy} & John Tracy of Stanway in ye county of Glŏster esq^r in all things relating to ye education of my said son And I do hereby constitute & appoint my dearly belov'd wife to be executrix of this my will & I give & devise to her all my real estate & all my goods & chattels & personal estate whatsoever And lastly I doe hereby revoke all former wills by me made And in witness of this my last will and testament (all of my own handwriting) I have hereunto sett my hand & seal this sixteenth day of January anno Doṁ 1731-2.

R^d TRACY. (L. s.)

> Signd seald and publishd by the said testator
> as his last will and testament in the presence
> of us who set our names as witnesses here-
> unto in his presence
>
> JOYCE WINDE.
> ELIZABETH LEGG.
> ROBERT COLLINSON.

Proved at London before the judge the eleventh day of May 1734 by Margaret Tracy widow the relict and extrix to whom admĉon was granted she being first sworn by coṁ duely to administer.

Is that in your Hand a Copy of that Will, examined by yourself? It is.

The same was delivered in.

Is there any Indorsement, showing the Date of the Death of the Testator, on the Back of that?
There is not.

(*By a Lord.*) When was the Will proved?
It was proved the 11th of May 1734, by Margaret Tracy, Widow, the Relict.

The Counsel being asked, whether they could prove the Date of the Death, Sir Harris Nicolas stated, That the most careful Searches had been made, but that he was not in a Situation to prove it.

(*By a Lord.*) Is not it the Practice in Doctors Commons to make an Oath of the Time of the Death, at the Time of the Proof of the Will?
It is now; it was not at that Time.

Sir Harris Nicolas stated, That he proposed to put in Letters of Administration, granted on the 19th of October 1732, of Robert Tracy (No. 34.), the eldest Son of the Judge, to his Father.

Do you produce Letters of Administration on the Death of Robert Tracy?
I produce the Bond.
What is the Date of it?
The 19th of October 1732.
Have the goodness to read it.

The Witness read the same as follows:

Noverint

Noverint universi per præsentes nos Robertum Tracy de Coscomb in com̃ Glouĩ aȓ Georgium Daken de Coscomb p̃d geñ & Thomam Mander de Toddenham in com̃ Glouĩ prã geñ teneri & firmiter obligari reverendissimo in Christo patri ac domino domino Gulielmo providentia divina Cantuariensi archiepiscopo totius Angliæ primati & metropolitano in quatuor cenĩ libris bonæ & legalis monetæ Magnæ Britanniæ solvendis eidem reverendissimo in Christo patri aut suo certo attornato executoribus administratoribus vel assignatis suis ad quam quidem solutionem bene & fideliter faciendam obligamus nos & quemlibet nostrum per se pro toto & in solido heredes executores & administratores nostros firmiter per presentes Sigillis nostris sigillatis Datis decimo nono die mensis Octobris anno Domini millesimo septingentesimo tricesimo secundo.

R. TRACY.   (L.S.)
GEO. DAKEN.   (L.S.)
THO. MANDER.   (L.S.)

Signaĩ sigillaĩ & deliberaĩ in præsentia
        JOSEPH CALLOU.
        WILLIAM SMART.

The condition of this obligation is such that if the honourable Robert Tracy esqʳᵉ within bounden the natural and lawful father and administrator of all and singular the goods chattels and credits of Robert Tracy esqʳ late of the Middle Temple London batchelor deceased do make or cause to be made a true and perfect inventory of all and singular the goods chattels and credits of the said deceased which have or shall come to the hands possession or knowledge of him the said Robert Tracy esqʳ or into the hands & possession of any other person or persons for him and the same so made do exhibit or cause to be exhibited into the registry of the prerogative court of Canterbury at or before the last day of April next ensuing and the same goods chattels and credits and all other the goods chattels and credits of the said deceased at the time of his death which at any time after shall come to the hand or possession of the said Robert Tracy esqʳ or into the hands and possession of any other person or persons for him do well and truly administer according to law and further do make or cause to be made a true and just accompt of his said administration at or before the last day of October which shall be in the year of our Lord God one thousand seven hundred and thirty-three and all the rest and residue of the said goods chattels and credits which shall be found remaining upon the said administrator's accompt (the same being first examined and allowed of by the judge or judges for the time being of the said court) shall deliver and pay unto such person or persons respectively as the said judge or judges by his or their decree or sentence pursuant to the true intent and meaning of an act of parliament (intituled an act for the better settling of intestates estates) shall limit and appoint and if it shall hereafter appear that any last will and testament was made by the said deceased and the executor or executors therein named do exhibit the same into the said court making request to have it allowed and approved accordingly if the said Robert Tracy esqʳ within bounden being thereunto required do render and deliver the said letters of administration (approbation of such testament being first had and made) in the said court then this obligation to be void and of none effect or else to remain in ~in~ full force and virtue.

(59.)

Is

Mr. James Ford.

Is the Copy you produce of that a true Copy ?
It is.
Have you examined it yourself ?
I have.

The same was delivered in.

Sir Harris Nicolas stated, That he would next prove the Baptism of William Tracy (No. 36.), the Third Son of the Judge, the Ancestor of the Claimant.

Rev. J. T. Robinson. Then the Reverend JOHN TRAVERS ROBINSON was called in; and having been sworn, was examined as follows :

(*Sir Harris Nicolas.*) Are you the Rector of the Parish Church of St. Andrew's, Holborn ?
I am.
Do you produce the Register of that Parish ?
I do.
Do you find a Register of the Baptism of William Tracy in 1692 ?
I do.

The same was read as follows :

No. 88.

" 1692, February.
" William son of Robert Tracey esq' & Ann, in Turks Co', was bap' 22."

Do you know of any Court called Turk's Court in the Parish ?
No; there is no Court now known by that Name.

Mr. Solicitor General stated, That he proposed to offer Evidence touching the Prayer Book which had been referred to in the Course of the Inquiry; that it was received from the Claimant by the late Solicitor, who was not now present, and was handed to him by Mr. Bourdillon, the present Solicitor; that, not being prepared to prove the Delivery of it by the Claimant, he would proceed, with the Permission of their Lordships, to prove it to have been in the Possession of a Member of the Family many Years ago.

Mary Atkin. Then MARY ATKIN was called in; and having been sworn, was examined as follows :

(*Mr. Solicitor General.*) How old are you ?
Seventy-six.
Are you the Widow of Mr. Richard Atkin ?
Yes.
What was he by Trade ?
He was an Engineer and Machine Maker of all Sorts.
In London ?
Yes, in London and at Manchester.
I believe he has been dead some Years ?
Yes; he died in 1831, I think.
Where were you yourself born ? Are you an Irishwoman ?
I am; I was born in the County of Kildare, at a Place called Kilrush, Twenty-five Miles from Dublin.

What

What was your Maiden Name ?
Mary Corcoran.

I believe your Father was a Farmer there ?
He was a very extensive one.

Were you at any Time in Dublin at all acquainted with a Family of the Name of Tracy ?
Yes.

Whom did you know of that Name ?
I knew Mrs. Tracy ; I worked for her several Years.

In what Way did you work for her ?
Dress-making, plain Work, or any thing.

Were you in the habit of being much at her House ?
Yes ; I frequently stopped to work for her ; all the Day, sometimes.

Where did she live ?
In Exchequer Street, Dublin.

At the Time you knew her, was she a Widow, or a Married Woman, or what ?
She was a Widow, and had been for several Years.

Did you know a Family of the Name of O'Brien ?
Yes.

Where did they live ?
They lived in Francis Street, Dublin ; they were Woollen Drapers.

Were they any Connexion of Mrs. Tracy ?
Yes ; Mr. O'Brien was a Brother of Mrs. Tracy. I dealt at his House, and made several Purchases at his House, which I required in my Business ; having been brought up a Dress-maker, I had it in my Power to deal with him.

Have you had any Conversation at any Time with Mrs. Tracy respecting her Family ?
I have very often heard her speak of her Family.

What have you heard her say about her Family, or her Husband's Family ? You say Mr. O'Brien was a Brother of this Mrs. Tracy ?
Yes.

You say you have heard Mrs. Tracy speak of her Family ? have you heard her speak of her Husband's Family ?
Yes.

Will you state what it was that she stated about her Family, or her Husband's Family ?
I have heard her speak of her Husband's Family ; she said they were very much aggrieved at the Neglect of the Family in England.

Will you tell us whether she told you at any Time who her Husband was, or who his Connexions were ?
At one Time when I was working there my Father came to Mrs. Tracy to Tea with her ; I was there at work, and she told my Father whose Son her Husband was.

(*By a Lord.*) In your Presence ?
Yes. She told my Father that her Husband was the Son of the Honourable Robert Tracy, a Judge in England.

D d   In

In what Year was this?

It was about a Year before she died; it was in 1786, I think, to the best of my Knowledge.

How old was Mrs. Tracy at this Period?

She was very old indeed; I believe she was nearly Eighty Years of Age.

(*Mr. Solicitor General.*) You say she mentioned at that Time who her Husband's Father was; have you heard her at other Times speak respecting her Husband's Family?

I have at different Times heard her speak; she said that she thought, on account of her being a Tradesman's Daughter, they were not satisfied that her Husband married into a Tradesman's Family, and that that was the Cause of the Neglect of her and her Children.

(*By a Lord.*) When was this?

The same Day that my Father was there,—that she told him about who her Husband's Father was.

How old were you at that Time?

I was about Twenty or One-and-twenty; I was in Business for myself at the Time.

(*Mr. Solicitor General.*) You say that she said that her being a Tradesman's Daughter was the Reason they had neglected her and her Children?

Yes.

Do you recollect at any Time seeing any Prayer Book, or any Book whatever, produced to you with any Entries in it?

Yes; it was at the same Time that my Father came there to Tea, and she told him who her Husband's Father was. Mrs. Tracy produced a Prayer Book with Entries of her Marriage and her Children's Births. My Father looked at the Entries, and so did I.

You saw in that Book Entries of her Marriage, did you?

Yes.

You say this was about a Year before she died?

Yes.

Have you any Recollection, as you say that she produced a Prayer Book, of the Size of the Prayer Book; whether it was a large or a small Book?

It was not a large Book,—a middle-sized Book; it might be a Book about that Length (*about Five Inches*).

(*By a Lord.*) Have you seen it lately?

No; I have never seen it since.

Do you mean to swear you have never seen it since, that it has never been shown you?

I have never seen it but once.

(*Mr. Solicitor General.*) Have you not been shown any Book by the Parties when they examined you? Did they ask you whether that was the Book, or any thing like that?

I do not recollect.

You do not recollect having seen the Book, except at the Time you were speaking of?

No, I do not.

(*By a Lord.*) How old are you?

Seventy-six, last February.

(*Mr.*

(*Mr. Solicitor General.*) You say you saw a Book upon that Occasion ; were you in the habit of seeing Mrs. Tracy afterwards, before her Death ?

Yes, I have seen her afterwards.

Do you recollect having any Talk with her at any other Time about her Family ?

She often mentioned about her Family in England ; very often.

Cross-examined by Mr. Attorney General.

How old were you at the Time that Mrs. Tracy died ?
I was about Two-and-twenty, I think.

How long had you known her at that Time ?
I had known her for Two or Three Years before.

What was the Age of her Husband at that Time ?
I do not know.

Did you know him ?
I did not.

You did not know him ?
I did not.

Did you never see him ?
Not as I know of. I never saw him. I understood he was dead long before that.

You understood he had been dead some Time ?
Yes.

How long had you been working for Mrs. Tracy before that Conversation ?
About Two Years, I think.

Did you never hear from her, as she spoke of her Husband, how long her Husband had been dead ?
No ; I do not recollect having asked the Question.

(*By a Lord.*) How long had he been dead before you worked for Mrs. Tracy ?
I do not know ; I understood he had been dead some Years.

She was out of Mourning ?
She was not in Mourning at the Time.

(*Mr. Attorney General.*) In the course of your Conversation with her, did you never learn whether she had been a Widow Two or Three Years, or Forty or Fifty ?
I do not recollect how long ; I never asked the Question, but I understood she was several Years a Widow.

Did you see any of the Family besides Mrs. Tracy ?
Yes ; I have seen Mr. Tracy's eldest Son James, and his Wife Mary, and their eldest Son Joseph.

When did you first become acquainted with James Tracy ?
That was some Time before Mr. Tracy's Death, but I do not know how long ; I did not take any Account. I became acquainted with Mrs. Tracy on account of my purchasing Goods at her Brother's Shop in Francis Street.

Where did you first see James Tracy ?
At Mr. O'Brien's, in Francis Street.

(59.)

Did

Mary Atkin.

Did you ever see him at his Mother's?
Yes, I think I have; but I am not certain that I have.

How old was he at that Time?
I really do not know what his Age might be; he was upwards of Twenty, I suppose, but I do not know; I cannot answer the Question.

Of course you cannot know precisely; but how old do you think he was at that Time?
He was between Twenty and Thirty; but I cannot say precisely.

You did not know Mrs. Tracy at all, except Three or Four Years before her Death, I understand?
Yes, thereabouts.

Therefore you must have seen the Son, James Tracy, during that Time?
Yes.

You say he was between Twenty and Thirty?
I think so; he was married, and had a Son.

How old was the Son?
He was a young Man grown; I do not know exactly his Age.

The Son was a young Man grown; is that so?
Yes.

Where did you see him?
I have seen him at Mr. O'Brien's.

How old should you take him to be at that Time — Joseph Tracy?
I really do not know.

About how old?
Upon my Word I cannot say.

You say the Father was between Twenty and Thirty; how old was the Son?
I really cannot tell.

You say he was a young Man grown?
Yes.

Was he above Twenty?
No, I do not think he was.

Was he a Youth?
Yes, he was a Youth.

Under Twenty?
It may be; I cannot exactly say his Age; it is impossible, for I took no Notice about his Age at that Time.

Did you ever hear Mrs. Tracy speak of her Husband's Father, except at that Time when your Father was present?
I did once or twice, when I have been sitting at work with her, hear her talk of him.

About her Husband's Father?
Yes.

What did she say of him?
That the Honourable Robert Tracy was the Father of her Husband William; a Judge of the Common Pleas in England; that was what she always said of him.

She

She always called him the Honourable Robert Tracy, a Judge of the Court of Common Pleas in England ?
Yes.

On this particular Occasion, you say, your Father was there ?
Yes, he was.

And the Prayer Book was produced ?
Yes.

Have you a very distinct Recollection of that Prayer Book ?
I have remembered it; if I was to see it I think I should know whether it was the Book.

What Colour was it ?
It was a reddish,—a dark reddish Colour, if I recollect right.

About what Size ? Can you point out something about the Size of it ?
It might be about the Size of Half this Book ; not quite so long ; about this Size. (*About Five Inches.*)

> The Witnesses on this Part of the Case were directed to withdraw from the House.

Do you mean to say that you have never seen that Prayer Book again since that Time ?
I do not recollect ever having seen it but once.

That is about Fifty Years ago, is it not ?
Yes.

Have you been examined by any body before you came here To-day to give this Evidence ?
No, I have not been examined.

Has nobody asked you what you knew about it ? Has not some Gentleman come to you to ask you what you knew about the Matter ?
I do not recollect having seen any body but Mr. Tracy since I answered his Advertisement, and he called upon me after.

When was that ?
That was in February.

In what Year ?
In this Year.

February in this Year ?
Yes.

That is about Two Months ago ; do you mean that ?
Yes.

(*By a Lord.*) You had said nothing about it before to any body ?
No.

(*Mr. Attorney General.*) You saw an Advertisement ?
Yes ; addressed to elderly Persons well acquainted with Dublin Fifty-seven Years ago.

Was that the Sort of Advertisement ?
Yes.

What more did it say ; was there any Reward offered ?
No, none at all ; not the least.

E e

What

Mary Atkin.

What else did it say?

It said, to elderly Persons well acquainted with the City of Dublin Fifty-seven Years ago, and that knew a Family of the Name of Tracy, —a Mr. Tracy who resided in Exchequer Street, Dublin; and I knowing it, answered it.

Is that all there was in the Advertisement; what were the elderly People well acquainted with Dublin to do?

If they knew Mr. Tracy they were to give Account of him.

To whom?

To the Advertiser.

Who was the Advertiser?

Mr. Tracy.

You read that Advertisement last February?

Yes.

Where did you go to, or what did you do, on reading that Advertisement?

I did not go anywhere; I answered it by Letter.

To whom did you write the Letter?

To no Name; but X.X., at the Exeter Coffee House, Strand.

In London?

Yes.

Where have you been living; in London, or in Dublin?

I was living in London. I have been in London a good many Years.

When you wrote that Letter what was the next Thing that happened?

Mr. Tracy called upon me, being the Writer of the Answer to the Advertisement.

What Mr. Tracy is that who called upon you?

The Mr. Tracy that this Business is about, I suppose.

Who is he?

He is a Relation of Mrs. Tracy's; I do not know how near of Kindred he is.

You understood him to be the Claimant?

Yes.

Did you tell your Story to him, or to the Attorney?

I told him I was acquainted with Mrs. Tracy, and that I worked for her, and that I knew her Brother and his Family.

Did you see any one else except Mr. Tracy?

Nobody else called upon me.

Did you go to any Place of Business,—any Office?

Yes.

Where did you go?

It was in the City; I do not exactly know the Name of the Place.

Did you see any Gentleman whom you have seen here To-day?

I think I did see a Gentleman.—Oh yes, that is the Gentleman *pointing out Mr. Bourdillon, the Solicitor for the Claimant*).

Did not you tell him your Story?

I did.

Did

Did he put any Questions to you?

He asked me whether I was acquainted, and how long.

And you told him what you had to say about it?

Yes.

Did not he show you the Prayer Book?

I do not recollect seeing it; we talked about it.

You are quite sure he did not show you the Prayer Book; are you quite sure he did not show it you?

No.

Have you any Recollection about it?

No, I have not.

When did you see this Gentleman; upon what Day was it?

It was in February or March.

Of this Year?

Yes.

You have no Recollection of having seen the Prayer Book since you saw it Fifty-seven Years ago?

No; I do not recollect having seen it but once.

Re-examined by Mr. Solicitor General.

You say your Husband was an Engineer or Machine Maker in London and Manchester?

Yes.

He died in 1831?

Yes.

Where have you been living since 1831?

I have been living in Castle Street and in Queen Street; and I have been living in Regent's Park for the last Seven Years.

Were you left well off by your Husband, or in what Way have you supported yourself?

I supported myself by Needlework, and since my Husband's Death I supported myself by monthly nursing, which I do now, and Needle-work.

You say this was about a Year before the Death of Mrs. Mary Tracy; do you recollect that Time?

Yes; I recollect when she died, by the House being shut up.

Were you at her Funeral?

I was not at her Funeral; but I lived very near to Exchequer Street, and I saw the House shut up, and knew she was dead.

Do you know where she was buried?

Yes; she was buried at the round Church called St. Andrew's Church, near College Green, nearly opposite the Commercial Buildings.

(*By a Lord.*) Who directed your Attention to the Advertisement in the Newspaper?

Myself; I saw it in the Newspaper. I called upon my Brother; my Brother saw it first, and pointed it out to me: I said I had a great Mind to answer it; it might be somebody I knew, and I should like to see them.

Who is your Brother?

He lives in Soho, and is a Manufacturer of Machines and Mangles.

(59.)   Is

Is he your Husband's Brother, or your own?
My own Brother, of the Name of Corcoran.

What Age is he?
He is about Sixty-one.

Where did you become acquainted with your Husband?
In England; in London.

When did you leave Dublin?
I left Dublin in 1806, to the best of my Recollection; it was after the Second Rebellion there.

How old were you then?
I do not exactly know how old I was when I came to London.

What brought you to London?
My Parents were here, and my Brother and Sister. My Father came over; he went from Dublin to Manchester, and came back to Dublin again before I was out of my Time; and it was after I was out of my Time that those Interviews took place with my Father and Mrs. Tracy, when I was there.

What did you do in Dublin from 1786 to 1806?
At Dress-making.

On your own Account?
Yes.

You left Dublin and came over to London in 1806?
Yes.

You forget how old you were then?
I do not exactly recollect how old I was then.

Have you seen Mr. James Tracy, the Claimant?
I have seen him To-day here in this Court.

Is this the first Time of your seeing him?
I saw him Yesterday.

Have you not seen him before Yesterday?
Yes.

When did you first see him?
It was in February, when I went to the City.

It was him whom you saw?
Yes.

How often have you seen him since?
I have not seen him except twice.

When was that?
He called upon me the Day after I answered the Advertisement, at my own Place in Regent's Park, and I saw him once in the City.

Where was that?
Where I saw this Gentleman.

At the Solicitor's Office?
Yes.

When first you saw Mr. Tracy did he remind you of the Prayer Book?
No; he did not speak to me about any thing particular the first Time.

You mentioned it to him first?
No; I never thought about it.

From

From the Time of the Death of old Mrs. Tracy had you had any Communication at all with the Family?
No.

Did Mr. Tracy introduce himself to you as a Grandson of your old Friend?
No, he did not; but he said he was a Relative, and it was to identify Mrs. Mary Tracy that he wrote for anybody that knew her personally.

Whom have you seen upon the Business besides Mr. Tracy?
Nobody else.

When was the Subject of the Prayer Book first mentioned to you?
The Day I went into the City it was mentioned, but I do not know what passed about it.

Did you mention it the first Time you saw Mr. Tracy at your House?
No; I never mentioned about the Book, or any thing particular.

Was it first mentioned at the Solicitor's Office?
Yes; the Solicitor asked me Questions.

Did he ever ask you whether you ever saw the Prayer Book?
I believe he did.

And if you had ever seen any Entry in the Prayer Book?
Yes.

Did he tell you what the Entry was?
No, he did not; but I saw the Entries when I was at Mrs. Tracy's House.

Do you recollect the Question he put to you respecting the Entry?
When?

When he saw you at his Office?
No, I do not.

Did not he describe the Prayer Book to you?
He asked me if I saw the Book, and what Description of Book it was; and I described it as I have done here,—that it was a small-sized Book.

What Sort of Book did he ask you whether you had seen? Did he merely ask you, " Have you ever seen Mrs. Tracy with a Prayer Book?"
He asked me whether I had seen this.

Did he ask you whether you had seen a Prayer Book in Mrs. Tracy's Possession with some Entries respecting Marriages and Baptisms?
He did not.

Did you tell him you had?
I told him I thought I could well recollect the Prayer Book, and what passed respecting it.

Did not he ask whether the Prayer Book in his Possession was the one?
No.

Where did she keep it?
I think it was in a Drawer or Bureau in the same Room where we were sitting at Tea.

(59.)　　　　　F f　　　　　Will

Will you swear you have never been shown any Prayer Book as being the Prayer Book which belonged to Mrs. Tracy?

No; I never saw one, except the one Mrs. Tracy had in her Possession.

Since you answered the Advertisement, will you swear you have never been shown any Prayer Book as being the Prayer Book of Mrs. Tracy?

No; I do not recollect having seen it.

Has no Prayer Book been shown to you for the Purpose of asking you any Question about it?

No, only the Size; I described the Size of it.

Has no Prayer Book been shown to you?

I say I described the Size of the Book, and the Colour of it, as nearly as I can recollect.

The Question is, whether you will swear that no Prayer Book has been shown to you since you first saw Mr. Tracy?

I do not recollect it.

Do you recollect what the Entry was which you read in the Prayer Book in 1786?

It was the Entry of her Marriage with Mr. William Tracy, Son of the Honourable Robert Tracy, Judge in the Common Pleas of England.

Did it state the Date of that Marriage?

I do not recollect any thing about the Date of it;—and the Birth of her Two Sons, James and Timothy.

Are you quite confident that they did not show you a Book, and ask you whether it was that Kind of Book?

No, I did not see the Book; I showed the Size of the Book, as near as I could recollect.

Did the Prayer Book which Mrs. Tracy showed you state that her Husband's Father was a Judge of the Court of Common Pleas?

Yes; I think the Honourable Robert Tracy.

Did it describe him as a Judge of the Court of Common Pleas?

I do not recollect; but I saw the Entry of the Marriage, and the Entry of the Two Sons.

Do you recollect how it described the Honourable Robert Tracy, —who his Father was?

No; I think it stated that he was the Third Son of the Honourable Robert Tracy.

Did it state whether the Father was a Judge of the Court of Common Pleas?

I always understood so from Mrs. Tracy.

Was that stated in the Prayer Book?

I cannot say whether it was in the Book or not.

According to the best of your Recollection, what was in the Book?

There was an Entry of the Marriage, and an Entry of the Births of the Two Sons; that is all I can recollect was in it.

Was it signed by any body?

I do not know. Mrs. Tracy said it was in the Handwriting of her Husband William Tracy.

In what Year were you married?

I was married in 1827.

Did

Did you know Timothy Tracy?
I have seen him.

Had he any thing to do with that Prayer Book?
Not as I know of.

What Age were you when you married; do you recollect?
I am sure I cannot recollect.

Have you any Family?
No; I have none living.

You have had some Children?
No; I have had none.

Have you had a Family?
I have not.

What did you mean by saying you had none living?
I have had no Family.

You forget what Age you were when you married?
I do; it was in 1827.

What Age were you at that Time?
I was about Sixty, I think.

Who was it that said anything to you first about the Prayer Book; who asked you about it?
I think they first asked me whether I ever saw or heard Mr. Tracy speak about a Prayer Book.

You had not mentioned that previously to any body?
No.

Was that at this Office?
Yes.

Then you told him you had?
Yes, I recollected it.

Did you know at that Time that Mr. Tracy was claiming to be a Viscount?
I did not understand what his Claim was, nor did I ever make such Inquiry. I understood he was claiming something of a Title or Property. I never asked Mr. Tracy half a Question on any Business.

Where were you born?
In the County of Kildare, at a Place called Kilrush, which is Twenty-five Miles from Dublin.

Your Father was a Farmer?
Yes.

Was he a Roman Catholic or a Protestant?
He was a Roman Catholic, and my Mother was a Protestant.

You were bred a Protestant?
Yes.

You said that Mr. O'Brien was a Linen Draper?
A Woollen Draper.

In a very large Business?
Yes.

Was he a Roman Catholic or a Protestant?
I do not know, indeed.

(59.)

Was

Was Mrs. Tracy a Roman Catholic?
I do not think she was.

In what Condition was Mrs. Tracy living in Dublin?
She was in Business in a Pastrycook's Shop in Exchequer Street.

Did she state that her Family had any Property?
I cannot say that she did; all she ever said about it was, that she felt very much neglected by Mr. Tracy's Family.

Did she say that she ever had any Communication with the Family?
No.

That she had ever made any Application to them for Assistance?
No; I never heard her say any such Thing.

What is your present Direction?
No. 51, Cumberland Market, Regent's Park.

You say you were acquainted with James Tracy the Son of Mrs. Tracy?
I have seen him frequently at Mr. O'Brien's.

Did you ever hear of his having any Communication with the English Tracys?
No; I never did hear any thing about it; he might, for any thing I know.

Did you ever hear him say any thing about his Family?
No, I have not.

In what Condition of Life was he?
I do not know, I am sure, in what Condition of Life he was; he was frequently at his Uncle O'Brien's; he was a young Man.

Was he ever present at any of the Conversations you had with his Mother?
No. When I went there I sat at work in a Room where they did not come in or out to Mrs. Tracy; I always sat where she did, when she was disengaged.

You never heard James say any thing about his being descended from the Judge?
No.

Should you know the Prayer Book again if you saw it?
I think I should recollect it; I do not know that I could exactly, for it is a great many Years ago, and I took very little Notice of it.

In what Part of the Book was the Entry?
It was in a blank Leaf at the Beginning of the Book.

Did you see any other Entry besides that?
No; I did not notice any other Entry but those Three Entries.

(*Mr. Solicitor General.*) Is that the Description of Book you recollect? (*A small Prayer Book bound in Red being produced.*)
That is very like the Size and the Colour to my Eye; may I look at it?

Yes.
I cannot see it without my Spectacles. (*The Witness put on her Spectacles, and added*) I think that is very like the Book, and very like the Writing.

(*By a Lord.*) You never saw it but once?
No.

Have

Have you any Register of your Baptism?
I have not.

Was there any Entry of that Nature in any Book?
The same as in that Book; our Births were all entered in a Prayer
Book or Bible. When my Father was in Manchester, and coming up
to London, the Box which contained the Books was lost or stolen on
the Way between Manchester and London, and we have often regretted
the Loss of our Ages in the Bible.

You were baptized a Protestant?
Yes.

Was not your Baptism registered in a Church?
No; I never knew any registered there; nothing but entered in a
Prayer Book or Bible; it was not customary in those Days.

Are you quite sure that you are as much as Seventy-six?
I am indeed, the 22d of last February. Mrs. Tracy was Eighty
Years of Age when she died. I was born the same Year that the Duke
of Kent was born.

You are sure she said those Entries were made by her Husband?
In the Handwriting of her Husband William.

That is what she told you?
Yes; she told my Father.

Do you recollect whether you saw any Entry of the Name of O'Brien
in that Book?
No. I did not look at any but in the One Page where the Entries of
the Marriage and the Births was; I took no more Notice of it, but just
looked at them; it was in my Father's Hand at the Time.

(*Mr. Attorney General.*) Just turn to the Entry which was said
to be in the Handwriting of William Tracy? (*The Book being handed to
the Witness.*)
That is it.

Just read it?
" Married in Dublin, April 17th, 1728, William, Son of the Honourable Robert Tracy, late One of the English Judges, to Mary, Daughter
of Mr. James O'Brien, Merchant. James Tracy the eldest Son, born
January 27th, 1729; Timothy Tracy, the Second eldest, born January
20th, 1730."

You read that at that Time, Fifty-seven Years ago?
Yes, I did; I just glanced it over; I never had it in my Hand at
the Time, for it was in my Father's Hand at the Time.

(*By a Lord.*) Did Mrs. Tracy ever tell you what Condition her
Husband had been in in Dublin?
No.

Had he been a Pastrycook?
I do not know what he was, I am sure; but Mrs. Tracy kept on the
Business at the Time I knew her. I never heard nor inquired whether
her Husband was a Confectioner or not.

Should you have called Mr. O'Brien a Merchant or a Linen
Draper?
They are called Merchants or Woollen Drapers. It is the same as in
Oxford Street or Regent Street. It is not confined to One Article alone,
but they deal in every thing suitable for Ladies or Gentlemen.

G g (*By*

Mary Atkin.

(*By a Lord.*) You knew this Family of Tracy; you knew the Mother, the Son, and the Grandson; can you state of what Religious Persuasion they were? Were they Roman Catholics or Protestants?
I do not think they were Roman Catholics, but I cannot positively say, for I never inquired any thing about their Religion.

You might know whether they went to Mass or to Church?
I do not.

Do you know whether they kept Meagre Days—Fast Days?
No, I do not; I have been there almost every Day in the Week besides.

Did you never know, from what you saw of the Son or the Grandson, whether they were Protestants?
Yes, they were Protestants.

Where was she buried?
At Saint Andrew's Church.

Is that a Protestant Church?
Yes.

You believe the O'Briens were Protestants?
I do not know one Way or another; I never was there much, except going into the Shop to purchase any thing I wanted.

The Witness was directed to withdraw.

Sir F. Madden.

Then Sir FREDERICK MADDEN was called in; and having been sworn, was examined as follows:

(*Mr. Solicitor General.*) You are the Assistant Keeper of the Manuscripts at the British Museum?
I am at present the Keeper of the Department of Manuscripts in the British Museum.

How long have you been in that Office, or the Office of Assistant Keeper?
I have been Keeper from July 1837, and previously Assistant Keeper from the Year 1828.

Have you acquired the Knowledge of the Handwriting of different Periods from your Acquaintance with the Manuscripts there?
A large Mass of the Papers of different Periods must necessarily pass through my Hands from the Nature of my Office, and I think myself sufficiently conversant to give my Opinion of the Age of any Writing which may come before me.

Will you have the goodness to look at this Writing in this Book. I believe you have seen it before? (*The Book being shown to the Witness.*)
I have seen this before.

Are you able to tell me about what Age you should suppose that Handwriting to be?
I should say that I see no Reason why this should not have been written at or near the Period of the last Date on the Page.

You say at or near the Period of the last Date, which is the Year 1780?
Yes.

Does

Does the Handwriting appear to you to be the Handwriting of that Time?

It does.

From your Acquaintance with the Handwriting of that Time?

It does.

From your Acquaintance with the Handwriting of different Periods, are you able to give an Opinion whether the Handwriting in that Page is the Handwriting of about the Year 1730?

In my Opinion; I see no Reason to the contrary.

From your Knowledge of the Handwriting of different Times are you able to state an Opinion as to that being the Writing of the Date of 1730; is that your Opinion?

It is my Opinion.

(*By a Lord.*) That is the Character of the Handwriting that was then common and usual?

I believe it to be so.

Was not it equally common and usual Fifty Years afterwards?

I should say, no.

Is it the Handwriting of Men of Education of that Period?

I should say, the Person who wrote this must have acquired a sufficient Education from the Style of the Writing. I call it a fair Hand,—not a good Hand,—but a fair Hand for the Period, from the Way in which the Capital Letters are formed.

Is that the Character of the Handwriting of Men of Education of that Period, according to the best of your Judgment and Skill in Handwriting?

Yes; I should say it was a Man of some Education.

Do you know any thing of the Handwriting of Persons of Education at that Time in Ireland?

I have been accustomed to see a great many Letters written both in Ireland as well as in England. It is from the general Character of the Handwriting I judge.

Is there any Difference in the Character of the Handwriting of that Period in England and in Ireland?

I think there is a considerable Difference between the Writing in Ireland and the Writing in England at that Time.

Look at the Corner of the Page over Leaf; you will see a Name; read it?

"James O'Brien, September 1st, 1730."

Does that appear to you to be the same Writing; look at the last Date?

I should doubt whether it was written by the same Hand that wrote this Page.

Do you mean that you doubt it from the Inspection?

I doubt it from a Comparison of the Form of the Letters; the C's and P's are made differently.

Is there any Resemblance between them?

There is some Resemblance, certainly.

Is there any Resemblance in the Character of the Handwriting?

I cannot answer the Question, except by saying there is a certain Resemblance; but I consider that it is by a different Hand; the Letters are

Sir F. Madden.

are so differently formed that I think it is not the same ; the O's and P's and the B's are formed differently.

Is it not the same Style of Handwriting ?
It is the same Style of Handwriting, certainly ; it is rather a better Hand, I should say.

Do you say that that is the Character of the Handwriting of the Beginning of the Eighteenth Century ?
If I were asked, without any Date whatever, I should say it would be written in the first Half of the last Century.

Is that the Character of the Handwriting of Queen Anne's Reign ?
It is impossible for me to fix any particular Period to a particular Writing ; particularly after the Year 1700.

Have you seen Writing of the Date of Queen Anne's Reign ?
Yes, plenty.

In that Style of Writing ?
Yes, in this Style of Writing. I should say it would depend on the Grade of the Individual.

Did many Persons of Education in the Reign of Queen Anne write in that Style ?
I cannot recollect any particular Instance.

Have you seen any Autographs of Pope or Swift ?
Yes ; I know them perfectly well.

Is there the slightest Resemblance between those Autographs and that Character of Handwriting ?
No, certainly not the slightest.

Is there any Handwriting of that Period you have seen at all resembling that ?
I should say this Entry is of the Character of the Handwriting of a Person far inferior in Grade to Pope or Swift.

Should you say it was the Handwriting of a Gentleman, the Son of a Judge, educated in England ?
I cannot answer that Question.

Why cannot you answer that Question ?
It depends so much on Circumstances. We know so many Noble Lords at present who write very bad Hands.

It does not depend upon whether it is a good or bad Hand, but whether it is the formed Hand of a Man accustomed much to write ?
I should say it is not the Hand of a Man accustomed to write very much, for it is not a current Hand ; it is a set Hand.

Did you ever see the Writing of Craig, the Secretary of State ?
I do not recollect that I ever did.

Have you seen Addison's Handwriting ?
Yes ; I know that as well as I know my own.

It does not bear much Resemblance to that ?
Not the least.

Does not it appear to be the Writing of an uneducated or half educated Man ?
I should say, not a highly educated Man like Pope or Addison, for a Moment ; but I should say a Man who had received a fair Education.

Such

Such as the Son of a Judge might be expected to receive ?
I cannot say what Education the Son of a Judge of that Period would receive.

Would you suppose that a Judge himself would have written such a Hand?
I should say that a Judge would write a far more current Hand, from the Quantity of Writing he would probably have to execute.

Did you ever see the Handwriting of a Noble Lord—Lord Wynford?
No; I do not recollect at this Moment that I have.

Supposing you had been asked whether that might be the Hand-writing of the latter Part of the Eighteenth Century, should you say that it was not?
I should say, decidedly not.

Were not Contractions almost universal in the early Part of the Eighteenth Century?
No; very few indeed, scarcely any.

For "the" was not "yᵉ" generally put?
Yes; or "y" with "ʳ" or "y" with "ᵐ."

Almost universally?
No; very commonly.

Did Swift, and Pope, and Addison use those Contractions?
They used them very frequently.

Cross-examined by Mr. Attorney General.

Your first Answer to my Learned Friend, I think in Substance was, that you saw nothing inconsistent with this having been written at the Time that it purports to be written; was that so?
Yes.

Is there any thing inconsistent with its having been written Yesterday or last Year?
I think so, indeed.

What is the Inconsistency?
I judge from the Character of the Writing.

Will you point out the Shape of a single Letter, a Contraction, or any one Particular in the Writing, which indicates that it might not have written by a School Boy within the last Ten Years?
As far as my Opinion goes, I should judge not.

I must beg you to point out the Shape of any Letter whatever which appears there to be of one particular Date rather than another; take the Book into your Hand, and point out any single Letter the Shape of which, the Character of which, the Contraction, or any other Circumstance about which, is inconsistent with its having been written within the last Ten Years by a School Boy or an uneducated Person?
I should say the Numerals, the Character of the Numerals, would be against that Supposition.

Which of them?
The Figure 2, for instance.

(59.)   H h   I beg

Sir F. Madden.

I beg to ask whether upon your Oath you mean to say there is any Particularity in that 2 that is connected with the Period of 1728 rather than 1832 ?

It is, to my Belief. All the Figures are made large. It is only from general Appearances. I cannot deny that it may not have been written at the Period, but it is only to the best of my Belief.

That is not the Evidence you are entitled to give to their Lordships, without connecting it with the Age in which it is supposed to be written ?

It would appear to me that the Figure 2 more resembles what would be written in the first Half of the last Century than since.

In what respect ?

I cannot say, except that it is in a round Form, and rises above the next Figure which follows.

Is there any other Shape of either Letter or Figure which you can point out that indicates that it was not written within the last Ten Years ?

I confess that I am not able to point out any particular Letter which would show positively that it might not have been written within the last Ten Years.

With respect to the Autographs of the Time of Queen Elizabeth and King Charles, and the latter Part of the Year 1600, I believe there are certain Forms of Letters which distinctly mark out about the Period when they were made ?

Previous to the 1700 there is no Difficulty, but there is considerable Difficulty after that Period.

Previous to 1700 there is no Difficulty whatever in fixing the Period of Writing, if it is genuine ?

Yes, if it is genuine.

With reference to the Forms of the Letters and the Contractions used ?

I should say there was little or no Difficulty.

For instance, I mean there were certain Capital Letters written, and certain Contractions and Joinings of the Letters ?

Yes ; the general Character of the Writing ; I cannot particularize any Letter ; it is merely from the general Character I judge. I have never made Alphabets of each Period ?

Have you any Doubt that an Alphabet could be made of each Period ?

Certainly ; I have no Doubt but that an Alphabet could be made of the Age of Queen Elizabeth ; but in the Seventeenth Century, after they began to vary so much, there might be Difficulty.

Can you point out any single Shape of any one Letter that is there used which varies from the Shape that a School Boy might make now ?

Certainly it might be ; I cannot deny that.

Are you able to point out the Shape of a single Letter that has any Tendency to fix it of the Date of 1728 ?

I cannot point out any single Letter ; it is from the whole general Appearance that I judge.

Have you been frequently a Witness in Cases of this Sort ?

No.

Have

Have you ever given Evidence before?
I have not; I was subpœnaed, but my Evidence was not admitted.
Where was that?
That was in a Case at Westminster.

Have you ever given Evidence before?
No, never.

(*By a Lord.*) When were you first shown this Prayer Book?
In 1837.

By whom?
By Mr. Tracy, I think.

The present Claimant?
Yes.

Will you have the goodness to look at that Page, and tell their Lordships at what Period you suppose that to be? (*Page 86.*) Have you seen that before?
I have seen it before, but I have not examined it. I should say this Writing was written by a Person not so well educated as the former.

Of the same Period?
No; I should say not the same Period. I should say also that this Page is so exceedingly dirty as well as the other it is very difficult to give an Opinion, on account of the State of the Page.

That applies to both?
Yes.

Re-examined by Mr. Solicitor General.

You have been asked about the Character of different Letters; independently of the Shape of different Letters, is there a Difference in the Character of Handwriting of different Times?
The general Character. I think there is a sufficient general Difference of Characters certainly before the Year 1700 to be able to decide to which Period it belongs.

Is not the Character of the Handwriting of a Gentleman or Person of ordinary Education of the present Day entirely different from the Writing of a Person of the same Rank in the last Century?
The ordinary Hand is different.

A Person looking at the Handwriting, without a Comparison of the Shapes of the Letters, would be able to tell whether it was of one Century or the other?
Yes.

Since the Year 1700 has there not been a Difference in the Character of the Writing?
I think there is a general Difference in the Character of the Writing of educated Persons, showing whether it was written in the last Fifty Years of the Century, or previously.

Is the Difference very apparent between the Handwriting of the present Day and the Handwriting of the earlier Part of the last Century?
I should say, generally speaking, it is; but it depends upon the Grade of Life and the Mode of Writing.

(59.)   (*By*

Sir F. Madden.

(*By a Lord.*) Do you mean to say that there is a striking Difference between that Writing and the Writing of the present Day?
From the whole Appearance of it, I should judge it to be of the First Part of the last Century.

Is there a striking Difference between that Handwriting and the Handwriting of the present Day; aye or no?
We must take a Man of the same Grade in Life.

Just answer the Question in the Form in which it is put?
I cannot answer it precisely in this Form. A well educated Man would write, no doubt, better now.

Suppose a Person skilled in Writing were to see that for the first Time, would he at once say that could not have been written within Fifty Years?
I should say so.

(*Mr. Solicitor General.*) Do you give that Opinion from the Appearance of the Writing, that this was not written within the last Fifty Years?
Yes; that is my Opinion.

(*By a Lord.*) Have you made an Affidavit on this Subject?
Yes; I think I made an Affidavit in 1837, shortly after I saw the Book.

At whose Request?
I believe at the Request of the Claimant, as far as I can recollect.

Did you know at that Time that Mr. Tracy claimed to be a Viscount?
No; I cannot say that I recollect much. I recollect there was some Claim to a Peerage, but what the Question was I had no Knowledge of, nor have I any Knowledge now; so little have I felt interested about it. I never saw the Claimant's Pedigree till this Day.

The Witness was directed to withdraw.

Sir T. Phillips.

Then Sir THOMAS PHILLIPS was called in; and having been sworn, was examined as follows:

(*Mr. Solicitor General.*) I believe you have had a great Acquaintance with the Handwriting of different Times?
I have, for some Years.

Have you been engaged in Researches in ancient Documents so as to ascertain the Difference of Handwriting in various Periods?
I have.

I believe you have in your own Possession a very valuable Collection of Manuscripts of different Times?
I have a great many of all Times.

Are you well acquainted with the Character of the Writing of the earlier Part of the last Century?
I am.

Will you look at this, and tell me whether, in your Judgment, that is the Handwriting of the earlier Part of the last Century? (*The Entry being shown to the Witness.*)
Not of the earlier Part; I think about the Middle.

Does

Does it appear to you to be the Handwriting of a Person of Education, or of what Class in Society?

Not of a Person who has had a Classical Education; there is great Care taken with the Letters, apparently.

Speaking generally, from the Character of the Handwriting, should you come to the Opinion that it was written about the Middle of the last Century?

Yes, I should.

Looking at that Page, and judging from the Character of the Handwriting only, at what Period should you say, from that Comparison, that it was written?

I should think about 1750; 1740 or 1750; between 1740 and 1750.

Cross-examined by Mr. Attorney General.

Are we to understand that a particular Age has a Character of Handwriting independent of the Forms of the Letters? When you speak of the Character of the Writing of the earlier Part of the last Century, and the Character of the Writing of the Middle of the last Century, you fix on this as probably being written some Time between 1740 and 1750?

Yes.

Can you point out any Shape of the Letters, or Contraction, or any Circumstance that is inconsistent with that having been written within the last Ten Years?

The general Character of the Letters altogether is totally different from any thing lately written.

In what respect? What do you mean by " Character"?

The Darkness of the Page in the first place is sufficient to show an Age of many Years.

By that do you mean the Colour of the Paper?

Yes.

Is that the first Reason you would assign for giving so old a Date to this Writing?

I do not call it a very old Date; that is not considered an old Date.

Is that the only Answer you mean to give to my Question?

Perhaps I do not understand the Question.

You assign to this Writing a Period from 1740 to 1750?

About the Middle of the last Century.

Is the Colour of the Paper one of the Reasons you fix on for that Opinion?

It is because of the great Use generally made of Paper such as has been frequently met with that there is in this Paper a great Degree of Antiquity.

Will you mention any other Reason, if there be any other, why you assign a Date so far back as 1740 to 1750?

I do not know that I can say more than the general Appearance of the Writing and the Book.

What do you mean by the general Appearance of the Writing?

The Darkness in the first place. I think the Writing is of that Date. a Change took place about that Time.

Sir T. Phillips.
———

What Change?

I have observed I thought there was a Change in the Letter " e " which belonged to the last Century, but the Form given to it depended entirely on Education.

Is not the Letter " e " of the most recent Fashion of Handwriting?

It certainly is not of the Period of the Beginning of the last Century.

Is not the Shape of the Letter " e " in a Handwriting inconsistent, if you look at it?

Yes, it does look so.

Is there any Letter you can point out that has from its Shape or any thing about it the least Character of Antiquity?

Not older than the Date I speak of.

Is there any Shape of any Letter there that might not have been written within the last Ten Years?

I think the Letters were similar at the Date I speak of.

That may be; but the Question I am putting is this :—Although it may be consistent with your Knowledge of Writing that that might be written in the Middle of the last Century, I ask whether there is any thing inconsistent with its having been written Ten Years ago?

As far as the Writing itself is concerned the Imitation may be exact.

Is there a single Letter there which from its Shape and the Mode of writing it, or any other Circumstance connected with it, you can say is distinctively of the Character of the Middle of last Century, and not the Beginning of this Century?

I do not know that I can decidedly.

We will take the Letter "m". Is there any thing in that " m " which is inconsistent with its having been written within the last Ten Years. Is not that an " m " that is now in use?

It depends a great deal upon the Person who writes ; that is a round Style of " m " ; but I do not think there is any thing to distinguish any Letter here from what was written during the last Half of the last Century.

Is there any thing to distinguish it from the Writing of the Beginning of this Century?

I do not know that there is ; I think a Person might write like this in the Beginning of the present Century.

No doubt he might ; but is there any thing inconsistent, from the Shape of any One of the Letters there, with that having been written within the last Ten Years? Is there a single Form of Letter in that Manuscript before you that has fallen out of Use so as to enable you to fix upon it as being about a Hundred Years old?

No, certainly not.

Is there a single Shape of any Letter that is not consistent with its having been written according to the Handwriting of the Party writing within the last Ten Years?

Certainly the Forms of the Letters have a modern Appearance. I know that I have seen Writing very like this of the Middle of the last Century.

Whose Writing was that?

Some Relation of my own.

Is

Is there any thing in the Shape,—take " Daughter"—is there any one Letter there that is not shaped exactly as a Schoolboy, or a Person not accustomed to write a running Hand, might shape it now ?

A Schoolboy not well educated now writes a similar Style of Writing. I have seen Writing like that.

Lately ?

Yes ; with Schoolboys.

Is there any thing inconsistent in the Appearance of that with the Supposition that it may have been written within the last Ten Years ?

The Appearance of the Paper and the Book.

When I ask you one Thing do not fly off to another. I am not asking you whether that is a genuine Entry, or this is a good Piece of Evidence about the Tracy Peerage. With your Knowledge of Manuscripts, is there any thing in the Face or Appearance of the Letters that is at all inconsistent with this having been written within the last Ten Years. Do answer that Question plainly ; yes, or no. If there is, point it out ?

I do not think there has so great a Change taken place as to prevent this being of the Period of the Middle of the last Century.

Do you mean their Lordships to understand that as an Answer to my Question. My Question is this :—Has any such Change taken place since the Middle of the last Century as to make it inconsistent with that having been written within the last Ten Years ?

I do not think there has, because, as I said before, Schoolboys would write now very much like that.

Illiterate People would write like that now ?

Yes ; a Boy who had learned about Eight or Nine Years.

Or a Man who had written about Eight or Nine Years ; is there any Difference ?

A Man has not so flexible a Hand.

The Result is, then, that a Boy who had written about Eight or Nine Years might, you say, write very much like that ?

I think he might.

Re-examined by Mr. Solicitor General.

You say you have looked at the Manuscripts of different Times, and when you looked at that Book you said you thought it appeared to be the Writing of the Middle of the last Century. Have you seen much of the Writing of the Middle of the last Century ?

Yes ; my Pursuits have led me to much more ancient Documents.

You have seen the Handwriting, or become acquainted with the Handwriting, of the Middle of the last Century ?

Yes, I have.

Do you consider yourself acquainted with the Character and Style of the Handwriting of that Period ?

Yes ; not so perfectly as the former ones.

Without reference to the Possibility of Schoolboys writing, as they now do, the ordinary Character of that Period ?

Not the ordinary Character. It depends very much upon the Man

who

Sir T. Phillips.

who writes. A Person who had had a good Education would not have made that " D " to " Daughter " in that Way.

Will you inform their Lordships what you have considered to be the Character of the Writing of the Middle of the last Century? On what did you form your Judgment? What made you say this was of that Date?

The general Appearance of it; that whoever has had any Acquaintance with Manuscripts must know there is a general Appearance at first View; that a Thing strikes them at once to be of such an Age, independently of the Shape and Character of the Letters.

From their general Appearance you formed your Opinion?
Yes.

(*By a Lord.*) Will not the Character of Handwriting depend much more upon the Circumstance where the Person who wrote was born and educated than the Year when the particular Writing was executed by him?

Hands of course will change as a Man advances in Life.

The Hand will change, but will the Character change, and adapt itself to the varying Change of Character which may be introduced among younger Men?
No, I do not think it would.

Do you think that that could be the Handwriting of a Gentleman of Education who was born in the Year 1692?
No, I do not think it could.

The Witness was directed to withdraw.

T. Davis, Esq.

Then THOMAS DAVIS Esquire was called in; and having been sworn, was examined as follows:

(*Sir Harris Nicolas.*) What Office do you hold?
I am a Clerk in the Prerogative Office, Doctors Commons.

What is the Nature of your Duties?
I have passed through the various Situations in the Office. I have been there upwards of Thirty-one Years, and since that Time I have held various Situations in the Office.

What are the Duties of those Situations?
The Duty of which I should more especially speak is, having been the Librarian or Book-shower in the Office.

Do you mean Books or Manuscripts?
The Manuscripts.

Have you had Occasion to look at the Character of the Writing of different Periods?
I have had Occasion to examine them, all the Books of various Dates having passed through my Hands.

Your Attention has been drawn to the Subject?
Yes.

Have the goodness to look at that Book? Look at that Writing, and state at what Period you believe it to have been written? (*The Entry being shown to the Witness.*)
I have before examined this, and my Impression was then ————.

What is your Impression now?
That it is the Handwriting of the Date which it purports to bear?
What

What Date ?
1729 and 1730.

Judging from your Knowledge of Manuscripts in general, and having seen many Manuscripts of that Period, it is your Opinion that that was written about the Period of 1730 ?
That is my Opinion.

Cross-examined by Mr. Attorney General.

That being your Opinion, I suppose it is a Matter of perfect Indifference how old the Person was who wrote it ?
No; it would not be so.

Can you tell whether it was written by a very young Person with an unformed Hand, or a very old Person with a well-formed Hand ?
I should say, that consistently with its being in the Character of the Day at which it bears Date, it might have been written by a young Person, but I do not follow that up by saying that it was so.

What is your Opinion ?
The Handwriting of these Periods was of the same old-fashioned Order as the Writing of this is.

What is there old-fashioned there ?
It is the round Schoolboy-like Hand.

Can you give an Opinion of the Age of the Person who wrote that ?
No; I should think it very difficult, and almost impossible, as to the Age of the Party, for I know many old Men of the present Day who write modern Hands.

And many young Men who write ancient Hands ?
Plain round Schoolboy Hands.

(*By a Lord.*) Is not that a round Schoolboy Hand ?
It is that Sort of Hand.

(*Mr. Attorney General.*) Does that differ in any respect whatever from the Handwriting which a Schoolboy might write in the present Day, or Twenty Years ago, or Thirty, or at any Time since the Beginning of the present Century ?
When I use the Term Schoolboy Hand, I mean in a round Character of Handwriting, but I should be inclined to say this would be the Handwriting of an older Person.

(*By a Lord.*) What Person would this, in your Opinion, be applied to?
An old Man.

(*Mr. Attorney General.*) How old ?
If this were put into my Hand as being the Writing of a Man who had written it recently, I should say it was written by a Man of Eighty or Ninety.

(*By a Lord.*) There appears nothing here of Tremulousness in it ?
No.

(*Mr. Attorney General.*) Do you mean to say you believe that it was written by a Man of Eighty or Ninety ?
I cannot say.

(59.)   K k   (*By*

T. *Davis, Esq.*

(*By a Lord.*)   Do not you think the Subject is of so obscure a Kind it is difficult to form an Opinion upon it ?

It is very difficult.   When I was first asked to look at it I expressed my Opinion that it was the Handwriting of a particular Era.

(*Mr. Attorney General.*)   There is nothing inconsistent in its Appearance with its being so ?

No.

By that Time they had got rid of the old-fashioned Mode of writing very much like German Text ?

No, I do not say that, for that is like the old Writing.

Is that like German Text ?

The Law-hand was of that Character, but not generally.

When did that Character of Handwriting come in ?

I cannot say ; I believe it to be the Writing of that Period.

(*By a Lord.*)   Is that what they call Round-hand ?

Yes.

(*Mr. Attorney General.*)   When did that Species of Hand come in ?

I do not profess to have a Knowledge of that.

About what Time did it come in ?

I do not profess to have a Knowledge of that.

Is it consistent with the Fact that that might be the Writing of Fifty Years before that Time ?

No, certainly not.

Thirty ?

No, certainly not.

Twenty ?

No ; I should say it is precisely the Handwriting of that Date.

(*By a Lord.*)   It would not have done for 1731 then ?

I am speaking of the Period generally.

(*Mr. Attorney General.*)   How many Years do you include in that Period ?

The particular Era ; some Twenty or Thirty Years.

How far back would you go ?

I would not go further back than the Year 1729 or 1730 ; I do not believe it was written prior to that Period.

It is not very usual for People to use Dates before the Time, is it ?

No.

Did you ever see an Instance of that Sort ?

No, I never did.

You believe it was written so late as 1728 ?

That is my Impression.

Will you point out the general Character or Shape of any Letter there which is not in use at the present Hour by Schoolboys and Persons who have not acquired a running Hand ?

Yes, I can ; the Figures more especially.

Which Figures ?

The " 17," for instance ; the " 7 " is brought straight down.

Which " 17 ?"

Both of them.

What

What is the Character of the "7"; point it out?
The "7" is broad, thick, and straight down; there would be a thin Stroke a Part of the Way down; there is the same Thickness which would not be the Character of the Sevens of the present Day.

Can you point out any Letter the Shape of which is not in use at the present Moment?
I will examine it again, if you please.

(*By a Lord.*) Will you look at that "7," and point out any marked Difference from that which is in use in the present Day?
There is that Difference in the modern Writing, the top Part is thinner than the lower Part.

A little Pressure more or less on the Pen,— a Glass of Wine more or less the Day before?
That is the Difference.

Was there any Handwriting such as that in the Reign of Queen Anne?
I should say not.

Should you think that a Person born in the Reign of William the 3rd, would write in that Hand?
I should say not.

When must a Man have been born to have written that Hand?
I have before said, that it is possible it may have been written by a young Man in the Reign of Queen Anne.

Could it be the natural Writing of a Gentleman of Education born in the Year 1692?
I do not see any thing in the Diction to interfere with the Education of the Gentleman at all.

You are not asked as to the Diction; but will you read the last Entry of that Page, and state whether you think a Gentleman of Education wrote that?
"Timothy Tracy, second eldest," presuming I suppose, Son "born June."

Is that the usual Diction of Gentlemen, "the second eldest?
Possibly there may have been an Error; that he may have left the "Son" out, or it might have been read the other Way, the eldest Son having been mentioned.

You would call them the Second, the Third, the Fourth, and the Fifth eldest?
Yes, that may be done; the First is the eldest Son, and the Second is the Second eldest.

The Witness was directed to withdraw.

Sir Harris Nicolas stated, That he would next proceed to prove the Burial of Mary Tracy.

Then the Reverend WILLIAM BOURNE was called in; and having been sworn, was examined as follows:

(*Sir Harris Nicolas.*) Are you the Vicar of the Church of Saint Andrew's, Dublin?
I am.

Do

Rev. W. Bourne.

Do you produce the Register of that Church?
I have it here. (*Producing the same.*)
Do you find an Entry of the Burial of Mary Tracy, in the Year 1787?
I do.
Have the goodness to read it?

The same was read as follows:
" On 13th Sep. 1787—Widow Tracy."

The Witness was directed to withdraw.

Rev. W. H. Dickenson.

Then the Reverend WILLIAM HENRY DICKENSON was called in; and having been sworn, was examined as follows:

(*Sir Harris Nicolas.*) Are you Curate of St. George's Hanover Square?
I am.
Do you find an Entry in the Register of that Parish of the Burial of Joseph Tracy in 1836?
I do.
Have the goodness to read it?

No. 88.

The same was read as follows:

Name.	Abode.	When buried.	Age.	By whom the Ceremony was performed.
Joseph Tracy -	Chapel Court	March 20 1836	75 y.	Revd R. H. Millington.

The Witness was directed to withdraw.

Mr. Solicitor General stated, That he would next proceed to prove the very imperfect State of the Parochial Registries in Dublin.

Mr. W. Courtenay.

Then Mr. WILLIAM COURTENAY was called in; and having been sworn, was examined as follows:

(*Mr. Solicitor General.*) Did you go to Ireland to make any Searches of Registries relating to this Case?
Yes. I live in Ireland.
Have you made any Searches in the Churches in Dublin?
I have. I searched all the Parish Churches in Dublin.

Are you able to state whether the Registers generally of the Parish Churches in Dublin were kept regularly during the early Part of the last Century?
No, indeed they were not. In some Parishes they have been; in other Parishes they were very irregular. I searched all the Parishes where there were any Registers kept.

Were there many Parishes where they had been without Registry at all?
No, none where there were none at all.

When

When did they begin ?
Some in 1750 and 1729, and 1619, 1698, 1636, 1729; some in 1704 and 1782.

You found them varying; some beginning about the Period of 1700, and some so late as 1750?
Yes.

I believe you searched every Parish Church in Dublin?
I did.

Were you able to find in Dublin any Entry of the Marriage of William Tracy with a Person of the Name of O'Brien?
No.

(*By a Lord.*) Did you find many Persons of the Name of Tracy?
In some Parishes I did; in the Parish of St. Michan's.

There are several Tracys in Dublin; it is not an uncommon Name?
Not so many as I expected to find. There are some in the Parish of St. Michan's.

Did you look in the Parish of St. Peter's?
I did.

Did you find none there?
Not during the Period I searched.

You did find some Tracys in St. Peter's?
No, I did not, during the Years I searched.

Do you recollect when the Register of St. Peter's begins?
In the Year 1669 for Baptisms, and for Marriages in 1670.

Where is Gurteen?
That is in the King's County.

How far from Dublin?
I suppose about, perhaps, Fifty Miles.

The Witness was directed to withdraw.

Sir Harris Nicolas stated, That he would next give Evidence of the Existence, many Years ago, of an Inscription on a Tombstone to the Memory of William Tracy, the Son of the Judge.

Then PATRICK CULLETON was called in; and having been sworn, was examined as follows :

(*Sir Harris Nicolas.*) What is your Name?
Patrick Culleton.

What are you?
I am a Farmer now.

Who is your Landlord?
Sir Charles Coote.

In what Parish?
The Parish of Rurie in the Queen's County.

How old are you?
I am about Seventy.

Where were you born?
I was born in the Place where I live.

Patrick Culleton.

Do you know a Place called Castlebrack?
I do, very well. I live within Two Miles of it.

Is there a Churchyard at Castlebrack?
There is.

Have you ever been in it?
I have, several Times.

How long ago?
It might be within these Four Years.

How long ago, at first?
Fifty Years ago; and if I say Sixty, I should not be saying too much.

Did you take any Notice of any particular Tombstone in that Church?
I did.

What did you see on it?
That was the Tombstone of the Son of an English Judge.

Do you recollect any thing else about it?
Erected by Mary Tracy, in Memory of her Husband William Tracy, the Son of an English Judge. There was more upon it that I do not recollect at this Moment.

Where was your Mother buried?
In Castlebrack.

How long ago is it since you saw this Tombstone to the Memory of the Son of the Judge?
I think it is about Fifty Years ago, the first Time.

Have you seen it repeatedly since that Time?
Repeatedly till about the Twenty last Years; I have not seen it since.

Do you know of any Circumstances which would account for this Stone not being there now?
It was broken when I saw it first into Three or Four Pieces.

What is the Sort of Churchyard; is there a Wall round it?
No; it is an open Place by the Roadside. It was a Place for Cock-fighting and throwing Stones,—what we call shoving Stones, to see which is the best Man. The far End of the Churchyard there was a Fair for Horses and Cows.

Where do you throw those Stones; into the Churchyard?
Yes, into the Churchyard.

Was not there Care taken in throwing those Stones that they did not hurt any Tombstones, or did not fall upon the Tombstones?
They could not help falling upon them.

(*By a Lord.*) That is the Way they got broken, I suppose?
I cannot say; I have seen them broken, but I never saw any one breaking any one.

Was this Tombstone standing upright, or laying down?
It was on the Ground; the Two Ends were rather higher than the Middle, and the other Part was broken.

Was there any Inscription upon it?
There was.

What was it?
I cannot remember; there was more than I can recollect; there was Part of it where the Crack went in the Centre.

(*Sir*

(*Sir Harris Nicolas.*) Is there a Church in this Churchyard, or
near it?

No ; no Church in the Parish.

Is it a mere Burying Place detached from a Church ?
Yes.

Did you know James Tracy ?
I did.

What did you know of him ?
I know that he lived in Gurteen.

Where is Gurteen ?
It is in the King's County, about, I think, Four Miles from Castle-brack.

You knew him ?
I did.

Did you know when he died ?
I did.

How did you know when he died ?
Because I attended his Funeral.

Do you know when it was ?
I do.

When was it ?
It is in or about Forty-eight Years, to the best of my Recollection, ago.

Where was he buried ?
He was buried in Castlebrack.

Was he buried near or at a Distance from the Tombstone you speak of?
He was buried by the Side of it.

Do you know whom he married ?
No.

Do you know whether he had any Children ?
He had.

How did you know him ?
Because I was working near his Place, and he was an old Man, and I was only a young Boy at that Time, and that was the Way I became acquainted with him ; I just came in to the next House.

And you attended his Funeral ?
Yes. He was telling me about his Son ; he had a Son, Joseph, and he was about getting above being in any Business, and leaving it to his Son.

Was this a general Burying Place ; were there many buried there ?
There were Numbers of them close.

Did you take any Notice of the other Tombs ?
Oh, many. I have seen more Tombs, but that was one.

(*By a Lord.*) Is Philip Tracy's Tomb there ?
It is.

A good many Tracys are there?
There were Three Tracys ; Philip Tracy, his Brother Hugh Tracy, and his Brother Bryan Tracy, buried there.

(*Sir*

Patrick Culleton.
_____

(*Sir Harris Nicolas.*) Do you recollect any other Particulars of this Tombstone? When first you saw it was there any one attracted your Attention to it?

I was with a Friend; he and I went up to a Cock-fight one Sunday Night, and we were walking about waiting for the Cocks, and he said, " Come over here, and I will show you the Son of an English Judge who was buried here ;" and he brought me here.

Who was that Friend?
He was named Tracy.

His Attention was attracted by its being the Son of an English Judge?
Yes.

Do you mean that you were surprised at this Son of an English Judge being buried there?
Yes; there were many very much surprised what brought the Son of an English Judge there.

This Tombstone became well known in the Neighbourhood from the extraordinary Circumstance of the Son of an English Judge being buried there?
There were many there surprised at it.

Cross-examined by Mr. Attorney General for Ireland.

In what Parish do you live?
The Parish of Rarie.

Is that in King's County?
No; in Queen's County.

How far from Castlebrack Church is that?
In or about Two Miles.

What Quantity of Land do you hold under Sir Charles Coote?
About Twenty-four Acres.

Do you hold under Lease?
Yes, I do.

For how long a Period?
Two Lives, or Twenty-one Years.

Have you paid all your Rent to Sir Charles?
I have paid it pretty well. I do my best.

How much do you now owe of your Rent?
Indeed I do not think it is requisite to tell these Things.

I should wish to know how many Years you owe to Sir Charles Coote?
I think it is not requisite to tell you.

I am connected with that Part of the Country, and I have a Curiosity to know?
Then I owe for Three Half Years Rent.

To last March?
No; to Yesterday; but he always lets a little hanging upon the Land.

He always lets a Year and a Half's Rent lie?
Oh no.

I will

I will not ask you when you mean to pay Sir Charles; that would not be a fair Question?

As soon as I can.

I have a Curiosity, which may be very inquisitive, to know where you bought that Coat; I never saw a Person in Queen's County wear that Sort of Coat before?

Indeed I bought this Coat in Queen's County.

Where?

In Mount Melick.

When did you buy it?

I suppose it is near Two Years ago.

You have been in the habit of wearing that Coat every Sunday when you have been going to Chapel since?

Yes.

Are you in any way connected with the Tracy Family?

Yes.

How is that; is it through your Wife?

No; by my own Family.

What Connexion are you of the Tracys?

This present Claimant's Mother was a Friend of mine; she was a Cousin of mine.

What Cousin was she; was she First Cousin or Twentieth Cousin?

Not my First; I cannot exactly tell.

Was she pretty near?

Yes, she was.

When did she die?

She died, I think, well on about Two Years ago.

You are a Descendant of Judge Tracy's, are not you?

No, no.

Who was your Father?

My Father's Name was Culleton.

What was your Mother's Name?

Tracy.

Whose Daughter was your Mother?

Bryan Tracy's.

Do you happen to know whose Son Bryan Tracy was?

I forget now.

When did you first hear of any thing being said about this Tombstone?

The first Time I heard of its being looked for is Five Years ago.

You spoke of it, you say, in Castlebrack Churchyard, with a Man of the Name of Tracy; how long ago was that?

About Fifty Years ago.

What Relation was that Tracy in whose Company you were to the present Claimant? What was his Name?

Thomas Tracy.

Which Thomas Tracy was it?

He lived just by Castlebrack.

Patrick Culleton.

What Relation was he of yours ?

He was a Second Cousin, I believe, of mine.

Did you know James Tracy, the Grandfather of the present Claimant ?

Yes.

What Relation was he to James ?

None at all.

What Relation was he to you ?

Second Cousin.

Are you connected with the present Claimant ?

I am, on account of his Mother.

Did you ever see that Tombstone from the Time of Fifty Years up to the present Time ?

No ; I did not see it up to the present Time.

You were there Twenty Years ago ?

I think thereabouts.

Have you been in the Church of Castlebrack within these Twenty Years ?

I have ; Ten or Fifteen or Twenty Times.

Has that Tombstone been in that Churchyard for the last Twenty Years ?

No, I think not, for it has been moved from where it was.

Is there any Ruin of the Church in the Churchyard ?

There is Part of the Ruin up still.

Was that Tombstone within or without the Wall you saw there ?

It was at the South, on the Outside.

How far from the South Wall was it ?

Three or Four Graves.

Do you know a Man of the Name of Moran ?

Yes, I do.

Is he in London now.

He is.

What is his Christian Name ?

Philip.

Do you know of a Man of the Name of Martin Higany ?

Yes.

Are they from that Part of the Country too ?

No.

From what Part of the Country are they ?

From Queen's County.

The Parish of Castlebrack ?

I think it is.

Are you only Two Miles from Castlebrack ?

That is all.

How far do they live from you ?

I think they live Four Miles from me, or beyond Four Miles.

Is there any other Man from Ireland that is here ?

Yes ; there is Paddy Quarter, and another Man, I forget what his Name is.

Is

Is it Behan?
Yes.

Is there any other Man from Ireland except you and the Persons I have mentioned?
I do not know.

Are you living in the same House together?
We are in One House, but not together.

Do you dine together, or live together?
We often dine together.

Have you been talking this over since you came to London?
No.

You never mentioned the Subject of the Tombstone to those Persons since that Time?
I did not.

In what Part of the Town are you living?
In Leadenhall Street.

When did you first mention the Circumstance of your having seen this Tombstone?
At the Time I heard Mr. Tracy's Brother inquiring for a Tombstone of that Description in Castlebrack; it was talked about, and I was in the Fair of Maryborough, and as I was coming home I called at his House; he was not at home.

Who was not at home?
Mr. Tracy. I desired his Wife to let him know that if he came to my House I thought I could give him some Account of that Stone; I knew some of it, but I did not know it all.

When was this?
About Four Years ago.

What did you mean by saying you did not know it all?
Because there was more upon it that I did not recollect.

How often have you seen Mr. Tracy, the Claimant, since that?
Egad, I never saw him till I saw him here.

You saw him here last Night?
No; I mean when I saw him in England.

In what Part of England?
In London.

Have you seen him, since those Four Years when you first saw him, until you saw him in London?
No.

Have you been in communication with any other Persons besides Mr. Tracy about this Tombstone?
A good many.

Who were they?
The Neighbours; they talked about it.

Do you know a Person of the Name of Rice Meredith?
I do.

Did you ever tell him you were going to London?
I did, I believe.

Are you not certain you did?
I am not certain upon that.

(59.)   Had

Patrick Culleton.

Had you not some Conversation with Mr. Rice Meredith about it ?
I think I had.

Are you not sure?
I am pretty sure.

Are not you very sure ?
I cannot say I am very sure, but I think I had.

If Mr. Meredith was to walk in, and say that he did have a Conversation with you, what would you say ?
I would say I think I had.

Would not you say you were sure of it ?
Indeed I do not know but I should.

Did you tell him you were coming to London about this ?
I did.

Did he ever tell you you would never come back ; that you would be transported ?
Egad, I do not know.

Do you think, if your Relation Tracy was made Viscount Tracy, you would be able to pay your Year and a Half's Rent to Sir Charles Coote ?
I do not expect he would do it ; I think he would be able to do it, but I do not know whether he would.

Do you not think he would be most ungrateful, if he were to be Viscount Tracy, if he were to forget you, his Cousin ?
Faith, I cannot account him ungrateful.

Is there any other Tracy buried in any other Place in the Queen's County ?
I cannot say.

Do you know Killee ?
I do.

Are there not several of the Family buried in Killee ?
No, I never heard of any but One ; there is One Stone there.

How far is that from Castlebrack ?
About Two Miles.

Were there any buried in Gasheel Churchyard ?
I do not think there were.

What brought you to Castlebrack Churchyard ? How often have you been there for the last Fifty Years ? Have you been in the habit of going there ?
A hundred Times.

You have been in the habit of attending Funerals ?
Yes.

Of Persons buried in Castlebrack Churchyard ?
Yes.

How many Times have you been attending Funerals for the last Twenty Years ?
It was in my Youth when I went there.

How many Cock-fightings have you been at at Castlebrack Churchyard in the last Twenty Years ?
Not One.

You

You have given up Cock-fighting? *Patrick Culleton.*
Yes.

Do you know what has become of the Tombstone?
I do not know any thing of it.

Did you ever say you believed or had heard that it had been put as a Hearthstone of any Kind?
I cannot say that I believed, but I heard Talk of Tombstones being put in Hearthstones.

Did you say any thing about that Tombstone in particular?
No; but I have heard of Tombstones being put in Hearthstones.

Did you ever say to Mr. Rice Meredith that you had seen it, and it was now in Mile Mackavoy's, the Grange, near Castlebrack, with the Face down, but no Writing on it?
No, I never did.

Nor any thing of the same Kind?
No, never.

How long ago is it since this Tombstone was first spoken of; about Four Years ago, was not it?
It was often spoken of.

About the present Claimant?
Four or Five Years.

When you first heard they were looking for the Peerage?
We were looking for the Tombstone in the Churchyard.

You heard that his Brother was looking for the Tombstone to show that some Relation of his was the Son of an English Judge?
Yes.

Did not you think it was a very wrong Thing for the Son of an English Judge to be buried in an Irish Churchyard?
The Church being so old and so wild a Place, I thought it a very strange Thing.

(*By a Lord.*) There were a good many Tracys there?
There were.

There is no Trace of this Stone remaining?
No.

Have you looked for it lately?
There is not a Bit of it left.

Have you looked for it since?
I have often looked at the Spot, but I never went to try for it on purpose; I only looked when I have been in the Churchyard.

There are very few Protestants in that Part of the Country, are there?
There are a good many.

Were the Tracys of the Roman Catholic Religion or the Protestant?
There are Tracys Protestants, and Tracys Roman Catholics.

In that Part of the Country?
Yes.

Was it a large Stone? What was the Size of it?
I think it was well on about Six or Seven Feet long and Four Feet wide.

Patrick Culleton.

Was it a white or a grey Stone?
A very thin flat Stone.

White or grey?
It was rather a grey; it was Mountain Gritstone; a soft Stone.

(*Mr. Attorney General for Ireland.*) You recollect James, the Father of the Claimant?
Yes.

Did he go to Church or to Mass?
I cannot tell whether he went to Mass or to Church.

Did you know Joseph Tracy, the Brother?
I did.

Did he go to Church or to Mass?
I suppose he went to Mass.

Did not you meet him in the Chapel?
No.

What makes you think he went to Mass if you have never seen him?
I knew his Wife to go to Mass, and that makes me think so.

Have you any other Reason for knowing that Joseph Tracy was a Roman Catholic?
No.

(*By a Lord.*) Is there any Protestant Clergyman belonging to that Parish?
There is Mr. Kemmis.

He is the Minister of that Parish?
Yes.

Wher does he live?
At a Place called Kemia.

How far is that from Castlebrack?
Five Miles.

How long has he been there?
Not over Six or Seven Years.

Who was there before him?
Mr. Pickett.

Is he living?
No.

(*Mr. Attorney General for Ireland.*) Mr. Joseph Tracy was in the Parish of Gasheel?
Yes.

Who was the Clergyman of the Parish of Gasheel?
Mr. Wingfield.

(*By a Lord.*) How long has he been there?
I cannot say.

(*Mr. Attorney General for Ireland.*) Upon your Oath has he not been there Twenty Years and upwards?
I do not know.

Did you know Dean Digby, who was Vicar there?
I did.

Dean

Dean Digby had been in that Parish a great many Years before Mr. Wingfield?
I suppose so.
Do not you know it?
I do not.
Mr. Wingfield has been there for Twenty or Thirty Years?
No, I do not think he has.]

Has not he been there upwards of Thirty Years?
No; I think not so long as that.

At all events he was there before 1836, when Joseph Tracy died?
He was.

Is he alive now?
He was when I left.

Could not he tell whether Joseph Tracy went to Church or to Chapel?
He could.

(*By a Lord.*) You say you were at James Tracy's Funeral?
Yes.

Who buried him?
I suppose his Son Joseph.

What Minister?
I only met the Funeral; there was no Minister in the Churchyard.

Did any one ever tell you that James Tracy was the Son of the Tracy whose Tombstone you saw?
I heard them say he was buried near the Side of his Father.

Who said so?
His Neighbours.

You knew him, you say?
Yes.

Did he ever tell you he was the Son of that Man?
There was some Conversation of that Kind passed. He was an old Man, and I was a young Boy.

Was there any Tombstone upon his Grave?
Not one.

What was he?
He was a Farmer.

Was that Tombstone you speak of remaining when James was buried?
It was there.

How many other Tombstones do you suppose there were in Castlebrack Churchyard?
Forty, Fifty, or Sixty.

Were there Inscriptions on the others?
There was.

Can you tell us the Inscriptions there were on any others?
Here lies the Body, we will say, of such a Man, who departed this Life on such a Day. There was an Inscription on that of Brian Tracy. Here lies the Body of Brian Tracy, who departed this Life,—I forget the Date,—in such a Year, and his Age was put on it after that.

You

Patrick Culleton.

Re-examined by Mr. Solicitor General.

You have been asked about the Tombstones of the Tracys in Castlebrack; do you recollect any other Tombstone of any other Person of the Name of Tracy in Castlebrack?

I do.

What Tracys do you recollect?

I recollect Philip Tracy, Hugh Tracy, and Brian Tracy.

Were those the only Tombstones belonging to the Tracys in the Churchyard?

I did not see any others, except that which had the Son of the Judge upon it, in the Churchyard.

Brian Tracy was a Connexion of yours, was not he?

He was my Grandfather.

What Relation was Philip Tracy to him; his Brother?

I believe so.

Who was Hugh Tracy?

He was another Brother.

There being these Three Brothers, there was no Tombstone of the Tracys besides that of the Son of a Judge?

Not one that I saw.

You say you have seen a Stone of a Person of the Name of Tracy in the Yard at Killee?

I heard of it; I never saw it; I only heard of it.

Do you know of any Tombstone besides that you have mentioned?

No; only this I have mentioned.

(*By a Lord.*) Were Brian and Hugh and Philip of the same Family as the Judge's Son?

Oh no.

They were Tracys who had been settled there before he came?

Yes.

Are there a good many Tracys in that Part of Ireland?

There are.

It happened that he came to a Part of the Country where there were a good many of his Name before?

I suppose so. I do not know. There were a good many of his Name.

You did not go up to the Churchyard with the Funeral of James Tracy?

I did, and into it.

And saw him put into the Ground by this old Tombstone?

Yes.

And there was no Clergyman by?

There was not.

Would any Protestant have been so buried?

I have often seen it.

With no Service said over him?

Not a Word; I have seen Protestants buried, and not a Word said over them.

You do not know that he had not any Mass or Service said over him before he was taken to the Churchyard?

I cannot tell.

You

You say he was buried about Forty Years ago?
I think I said about Forty-eight.

What do you date it by?
By the Year of the Rebellion in Ireland.

In what Year was that; was it the Year of the Rebellion?
No; it was about Four Years before the Rebellion he died.

There were a good many others who saw this Tombstone besides yourself?
I suppose there were.

Are they all dead besides you?
I suppose not.

Some of them are here, are not they?
Yes, they are.

Did the Inscription cover the whole of the Stone, or nearly so?
No; it did not cover the whole of the Stone; it went a good Way on it; it covered a good deal of it.

There was no other Member of the Family mentioned besides William and his Father?
No, not a Word; only that he was Son to an English Judge.

Was there any Latin upon it?
No Latin upon it.

No Text of Scripture?
Not that I recollect.

Can you repeat what was on it?
That it was erected by Mary Tracy in Memory of her Husband, William Tracy, Son to an English Judge.

Was not it said that he had been a faithful and affectionate Husband?
Egad, I believe it did, but I do not recollect any more.

(*By a Lord.*) The Gentleman has brushed up your Memory?
I know there was more upon it that I do not remember.

Did it say any thing about an affectionate Wife?
I do not remember that.

A disconsolate Wife?
I do not remember that at all.

Was there any Coat of Arms upon it?
No; there was no Coat of Arms upon it.

The Witness was directed to withdraw.

Then MARTIN HIGANY was called in; and having been sworn, was examined as follows:

(*Mr. Solicitor General.*) You are an Irishman?
Yes.

From what Part of Ireland do you come?
Queen's County; the Parish of Castlebrack.

Do you hold any Lands there?
Yes.

Who is your Landlord?
Captain Sandys.

Do you know the old Churchyard at Castlebrack ?
I do.

Were you born at Castlebrack ?
At Kilcaven.

Is that near it ?
Yes ; within Two Miles.

Have you known this Churchyard all your Life ?
Yes.

About how old are you now ?
About Forty-five or Forty-six.

When you first recollect that Churchyard do you remember there being a Tombstone to any one of the Name of Tracy in it ?
I do.

Have you any Recollection at all what was upon the Tombstone ?
Yes.

What was it ?
" Erected by Mary Tracy to the Memory of her Husband William Tracy, late of Ross in the King's County, Son to Judge Tracy of England."

When you recollect that Tombstone first, was it lying on the Ground, or erect, or in what Way ?
Lying on the Ground ; flat on the Ground.

Was it broken at that Time ?
Yes, it was.

What Sort of Churchyard was this at that Time ? Was it open to the Road, or were the People in the habit of playing any Games in it.?
It was always open ; it was broken always at Fair Time.

Was there a Fair held near it ?
Yes, there was.

How long back is it since you saw this Tombstone, to your Recollection ?
It is Twenty-four or Twenty-five Years since I saw it.

Do you know what was done with it ?
I do not.

Before that Time had you seen this Tombstone often ; had you seen the Inscription upon it often ?
Yes ; I often saw it Ten Years before that.

Was there any other Tombstone there to any other Person of the Name of Tracy ?
I do not know ; I do not remember any other Tracy but that.

You say he was of Ross ; do you know where Ross is ?
I do not.

Cross-examined by Mr. Attorney General.

When did you come to London ?
I believe it is Three Weeks or Four Weeks since I came.

Surely you can remember the Date nearer than that ? Do not you know the Date ?
I never recollect the Date. I think to the best of my Recollection it is Four Weeks ago.

Do

Do not you remember what Day of the Week you came?
It was Monday, I think; last Monday Three Weeks, to the best of my Knowledge.

Yesterday Three Weeks?
Yes; it may be a Week more. I do not recollect at this Time whether it was or not.

Where did you come from?
From Kilcaven.

How far is that from Castlebrack?
Two Miles, to the best of my Knowledge.

How long have you lived there?
I was born there.

And you have lived there at all Times?
Yes.

When did any body first ask you about this Tombstone?
About Twenty-five or Twenty-six Years ago.

I do not ask you when you saw it, but when did any body first ask you any thing about it?
I cannot recollect that.

You must remember something about it; who asked you about it, and brought you here?
It is about Two Months ago since I received a Letter from Mr. Joe Tracy, requesting me to meet him.

Who is Joe Tracy?
He is the Brother of the Claimant.

Where does he live?
Near Maryborough.

He wrote to you about Two Months ago?
Yes.

Is that the first Time that there were Inquiries made about your recollecting it?
Yes, it is.

Did you see him?
No. I wrote a Letter to him that I could not go up; but I told him what I knew about it, and that I would come here if he wished.

Till the Time you got that Letter had you not talked about it, or any body spoken to you about it, in any way whatever?
Yes; the Neighbours; but no Person about coming here.

No Person came to you about coming to this House to give Evidence?
No.

Did you know Joe Tracy?
I never knew him till then.

Did you know James Tracy?
No.

Did you know any of the Tracys?
No.

How came he to write to you?
By Report, I suppose; he heard of my speaking about it.

Did

Did you ever see any of the Tracys there ; Joe, or his Brother ?
No, not till lately.

(*By a Lord.*) How far is Ross from Dublin ?
I do not know.

(*Mr. Attorney General.*) You say it is Twenty-five or Twenty-six Years ago since you saw this ?
Yes.

Whereabouts was it ?
It was nearly in the Middle of the Burying Ground, by the old Wall, the Church Wall.

Was that one of the Church Walls ?
Yes, so I understood.

On which Side was it ; the West, North, East, or South ?
The South Wall.

(*By a Lord.*) Was it outside the South Wall ?
Yes, it was.

How far from the Wall ?
About the Breadth of Three Graves.

Did you observe any other Tombstones with Inscriptions upon them in that Churchyard ?
Oh yes.

But none of the Tracys, that you remember ?
No, I do not remember any other Tracy Tombstone but that.

When did you first miss this Tombstone about the English Judge ?
I could not exactly say, but a good many Years.

Were not you rather struck by remarking that it had disappeared ?
I was.

Did you make any Observation to any body that the Gravestone had disappeared ?
Yes ; I remarked that that Stone we used to be speaking of was not there.

Did you make any Remark what had become of it ?
I did not.

Was there any other Tombstone in that Churchyard which disappeared ?
Yes, a good many.

Had they taken Flight ?
I suppose they were taken out of it.

To make Hearthstones ?
I could not tell for what Purpose ; I used to hear of many.

Was there any other Tombstone that bore an Inscription upon it that disappeared ?
Yes.

Can you tell us the Inscription on any other Stone that disappeared ?
There was One erected to a Man of the Name of Hoyland.

In what Part of the Churchyard was that Stone ?
It was on the Side of the old Wall ; the other Side of the Wall.

That

That had been taken away?
Yes.

Was this taken away in One whole Piece?
No; it was broken when I saw it.

Much?
It was broken in Two or Three Pieces; I cannot say exactly how much.

Was it a large Stone?
It was the common Size.

Was there a Fracture that interrupted the reading of the Inscription?
It did, a Line,—One Line across the Stone,—but a good deal of it could be read.

Was there only One Line across the Stone that was broken?
There was another Break, but that was on a Part of the Stone where there were no Letters.

What Kind of Stone was it; White, or what?
It was partly White.

Did the Inscription cover the whole Stone, or how?
No; it covered a good deal of it; not the whole.

Was there any Space left for adding the Name of the Widow when she should be interred in the same Grave?
To the best of my Knowledge there was.

Did you know Joseph Tracy, the Father of James?
No.

You did not know him at all?
No.

Re-examined by Mr. Solicitor General.

You say that " late of Ross " was on the Tomb, but you do not know where Ross was?
No.

Have you been asked to read this to other Persons?
Yes.

It was talked about?
Yes; it was wondered at by Persons there.

(*By a Lord.*) What was wondered at?
At a Judge's Son being buried there.

Although his Name was Tracy?
Yes.

The Witness was directed to withdraw.

Then PATRICK QUARTER was called in; and having been sworn, was examined as follows :

(*Sir Harris Nicolas.*) What Age are you?
Seventy.

What are you?
A labouring Man.

(59.)   P p   Where

Patrick Quarter.

Where do you live?
I live in Kinnyhinch.

How far is that from Castlebrack?
About Four Miles.

Do you know Castlebrack?
Yes.

How long have you known it?
I have been Twenty-five Years out of it, and I was Fifty Years in it; between Forty and Fifty in it.

You knew it well Fifty Years ago?
Yes.

When did you know it?
I was in it between Forty and Fifty Years ago.

Were you ever in the Churchyard in Castlebrack?
Yes, oftentimes; I lived very near.

What sort of a Place is it?
A Country Place.

Is there any Church in it?
Yes; the Walls of a Church.

Did you ever notice any Tombstones in it?
I did.

What Tombstones have you noticed in it?
I have seen this Tombstone belonging to Mr. Tracy.

Do you recollect what was upon it?
Yes, I do.

What was it?
It was erected by Mary Tracy in Memory of her Husband, William Tracy, Son of an English Judge.

What made you recollect this Tombstone?
On account of a great Man's Son being buried there.

Did you notice it yourself first, or was your Attention called to it?
A Man lived on the Churchyard, one James Dunn, who is dead now, who was the first Person I ever heard notice the Stone in the Churchyard.

Do you recollect what he said?
He said there is a Stone to an English Judge, and he was surprised such a Man's Son should be buried there.

What Sort of Stone was it?
It was a Grit Stone; what we call Mountain Stone.

Is there a Fair held in the Churchyard?
Yes, once a Year.

Is the Churchyard used for any other Purpose besides the burying Persons there?
Yes.

(*By a Lord.*) Did you read the Inscription yourself?
Yes.

You are a good Scholar?
Yes, I can read.

(*Sir*

(*Sir Harris Nicolas.*) For what other Purpose is the Churchyard used than Funerals ?
Cock-fighting.
Did you ever attend Cock-fighting there ?
Yes, I did.
Were any other Games played in it ?
Yes ; Hurling, when I was a Boy.
What Sort of hurling ?
A Ball from one to another.
Of what is the Ball made ?
Yarn, and covered with Leather.
Where was your Father buried ?
In Castlebrack.
How long ago ?
Forty Years ago.
Can you tell what was the last Time you recollect having seen this Tombstone ?
I have not seen it these Twenty Years ; I was out of it since that ; but a short Time before I left I saw it.
Did you see it more than once ?
Yes.
A great many Times more than once ?
Yes, I have ; but I cannot say how many I may have seen it.

Cross-examined by Mr. Attorney General for Ireland.

I understood you to say you were in Castlebrack Fifty Years, and out of it Twenty-five Years ?
Yes.
How long were you in it altogether ?
Between Forty and Fifty Years 1 was living in it.
And have been out of it Twenty-five Years ?
Yes.
How old are you ?
Seventy.
Under whom do you live ?
Mr. Dunn.
How old is Mr. Dunn ?
He is Seventy-six.
Does he live at Castlebrack ?
No ; he lives in the Parish of Killochy, about Seven Miles from Castlebrack.
Are his Family buried in Castlebrack Churchyard ?
No.
What is the nearest Chapel to Castlebrack ?
Cloncunden.
How far is that from Castlebrack ?
About a Mile and a Half or Two Miles.
How many Priests are there at Cloncunden Chapel ?
They are at Mount Melick.
How many Priests are there belonging to the Chapel of Cloncunden ?
Three.

(59.). How

Patrick Quarter.

How old is the oldest of them ?

I cannot say.

How old about, do you believe ?

I cannot say.

Are there any of the Three Priests that may have been there above Twenty-five Years ?

No, I think not.

Do you remember the Name of the Priests who were in Cloncunden Chapel when you left it ?

Father Dewan ; he was the only Priest I remember.

Who were the other Priests ?

Himself and his Nephew, Father Anthony.

Who was the other ?

Father Haley.

He was there when you left, Twenty-five Years ago ?

No, he was not.

Do you know the Names of the Priests who were there Twenty-five Years ago ?

Father Dewan was there Twenty-five Years ago.

Is Father Dewan alive ?

No.

Is Father Anthony alive ?

No ; they are both dead.

Do you know any other Gentleman living in the Neighbourhood who was living there Twenty-five Years ago ?

Mr. Meredith.

Is he a Gentleman ?

A Gentleman Farmer.

Was he resident there Twenty or Twenty-five Years ago ?

Near where I live now.

When you left Castlebrack, Twenty-five Years ago, when you saw the Tombstone, were there any Gentlemen resident there who are now living ?

The Son of Mr. Mackavoy was there.

Was he alive when you left Castlebrack ?

Yes.

Is he alive still ?

Yes.

(*By a Lord.*) How old is he ?

I cannot say.

Is he of your own Age ?

Very near it.

(*Mr. Attorney General.*) He knew the Churchyard of late Years ?

Yes.

Is there any other Gentleman of that Neighbourhood besides Mr. Mackavoy who was there Twenty-five Years ago ?

There is One.

Who is he ?

Mr. Delaney.

Is

Is he as old as you?
Yes.

How near to the Churchyard does he live?
Two Miles, or a Mile and a Half.

Did he ever go to the Churchyard?
Yes.

Were his Family buried there?
Yes, I suppose they were.

He is still alive?
Yes.

About your Age?
Yes, I believe so.

Is there any Protestant Clergyman living now who was living then?
No; they are dead now.

Who was the Protestant Clergyman?
One Mr. Mash.

Do you remember any other Gentlemen besides Mr. Mackavoy and Mr. Delaney who were living at that Time, and are now alive?
There is Peter Malone.

Is that one of Peter's Family?
No.

How old is he?
Nearly as old as I.

What is he?
A Gentleman Farmer.

Were his Family buried there?
Yes.

And he of course attended the Funerals?
Yes.

Do you remember any other?
Yes; Mr. Gibb's People.

They are nearly as old as you?
Yes.

Are his Family buried in Castlebrack?
They are not.

How near does he live to Castlebrack?
Within Half a Mile.

Do you think he attended the Funerals of other Persons there?
Yes; I have no Doubt he did.

(*By a Lord.*) Has your Landlord much Land about Castlebrack?
No; none at all.

(*Mr. Attorney General.*) When did you first hear any Conversation about this Tombstone?
Not these Twenty-five Years.

About how lately is it that you heard of it?
About Six Weeks ago.

Patrick Quarter.

Who informed you then?

Being the oldest Man, and living near the Churchyard, Mr. Tracy thought I knew more of it than any other Man, and I voluntarily came with him.

He said, " Do not you recollect the Tombstone about Judge Tracy's Son?"

Yes.

Do you recollect the Tombstone of Mr. William Tracy, the Son of an English Judge, who had a Fancy to be buried in an Irish Churchyard?

Yes ; it was a Wonder.

You earn your Bread as a Labourer?

Yes.

What are you earning now ; what are your Wages?

We have Ten-pence and Eight-pence a Day.

You are now living in a House with Culleton and Patrick Quarter?

I am Patrick Quarter myself.

You do not live in the House with Paddy Quarter?

Yes, I do.

Are not you very anxious to get back to Ireland?

Yes ; I should be very glad to get back, but this is the best Place I ever had to do with.

For eating and drinking?

Yes.

They do not give you Whiskey?

Oh dear no.

What do you get to drink?

They make up a Cordial called sweet Water.

(*By a Lord.*) Do not they treat you well?

Yes.

(*Mr. Attorney General.*) Do you and Higany and Culleton live together?

Yes.

(*By a Lord.*) Do not you drink Success to the Tracys?

I wish well to the Family.

(*Mr. Attorney General.*) How long have you known the Tracys?

I have known the Tracys as long as I have known any one.

You have no Illwill towards the Tracys?

No ; that would be bad.

(*By a Lord.*) Did the Tracys go to Mass, or to Church?

Some of them went to Mass, and a good many of them to Church ; not of this Family, but of the Tracys.

(*Mr. Attorney General.*) Did you know James Tracy, the Father of the Claimant?

No.

Did you know Joe Tracy?

No.

The Witness was directed to withdraw.

Then

Then JOHN BEHAN was called in ; and having been sworn,
was examined as follows :

(*Mr. Solicitor General.*)   Do you know the Churchyard of Castlebrack ?
Yes.

Do you live in the Neighbourhood ?
I do ; within Forty Perches of it.

What are you ?
A Labourer.

Do you recollect any Tombstones taken away from the Churchyard
there ?
I do.

When was that ?
Some of them have been out these Twenty Years or very tight
upon it—these Fifteen or Sixteen Years ; there was not so much Harm
done since Mr. Kemmis came in as there was Twenty Years ago.
There used to be Cock-fights upon it, and People drunk, and it used
to be used as a Fair.   The Two People that held the House upon the
Graveyard were stupid, and did not take care of the Place.

Do you know of Tombstones being taken away ?
Yes, I saw them broken, and there may be some not larger than that
Piece of Paper, and some of them better.   I had some Pieces to
sharpen a Hatchet on, or any thing of that Kind.

Since Mr. Kemmis has been there they have taken more Care of
them ?
Yes, and his Son is living there ; old Jem Dunn and his Son.

Before that Time, did you see any of those Stones broken up and
carried away in the Way you have spoken of ?
Yes.

What did you say about sharpening your Hatchet ?
We used to go and sharpen our Hatchets on a Mountain Flag ; but
there is a better Quality come in since that.   We call them Lime-
stones.

(*By a Lord.*)   Do you say that this was broken to Pieces ?
I know nothing of any particular Tombstone, or whose they were ;
only I saw Stones lying on the flat Ground broken.

What was upon them you do not know ?
No.

Can you read or write ?
No ; but I have been living within Forty Perches of it for Forty-six
Years.

How old are you ?
Forty-six my last Birthday.   I was a Year old at the Time of the
Irish Rebellion, and that is the Way I know it ; and that is all I know
about it.

The Witness was directed to withdraw.

Then

Then DENNIS MORAN was called in; and having been sworn, was examined as follows:

(*Sir Harris Nicolas.*)   What are you?
A Farmer.

Were do you live?
In Ireland.

How old are you?
I am about Sixty-six.

Do you hold Land under any one?
Yes.

Who is your Landlord?
Captain Sandes, Son to the Lord Bishop of Killaloe, who is dead now.

Do you know Castlebrack?
Yes.

What do you know of it?
I know Castlebrack Churchyard.

Is any body belonging to your Family buried there?
Yes.

Who?
My Father, and my Mother, and my Grandfather.

How long have you known the Churchyard?
I have known it since I came to be grown up; the Practice was to go to the Churchyard, and to Cock-fights and Fairs.

Do you know any of the Tombstones in that Churchyard?
I do.

What Tombstones have you known?
I was in Castlebrack with a Funeral; there was a Man standing at a Distance from me; I standing over the Remains of my own poor Father, he called me to him to show me where the Son of an Honourable Judge lay from England, and he explained the Letters on the Stone, and explained to me first " Erected ———.

(*Mr. Attorney General.*)   Can you read yourself?
Yes, I can; but he first explained it, I say.

What did you see?
I saw, "Erected by Mary Tracy to the Memory of her Husband William Tracy, Son of Judge Tracy of England."

(*Sir Harris Nicolas.*)   You saw that on that Occasion?
I did.

Have you ever seen it since?
I have.

When?
I saw it at different Times; I cannot tell how often.

Did you ever see it in company with any body else?
I showed it to People myself.

Why did you take notice of that Tomb?
That Tomb I would not distinguish from any other, except from what appeared upon it; it appeared more remarkable than any other Stone.

About

About how long ago is it since you saw it ?
I suppose Twenty Years.

In what State was it when you last saw it ?
Broken.

Much broken, or a little ?
Broken across it, and Pieces broken off of it.

Cross-examined by Mr. Attorney General.

What, do you know, was written upon it ?
" Erected by Mary Tracy to the Memory of her Husband, William Tracy of England."

" William Tracy of England ?"
Yes. There was more that I do not recollect.

Do not you recollect any thing else ?
That comes into my Mind more than any thing else.

You said something about a Judge ?
" William Tracy, Son to Judge Tracy of England."

(*By a Lord.*) Was it " the Honourable Judge Tracy of England ?"
It was.

(*Mr. Attorney General.*) You can read, 1 suppose ?
Yes.

Just read that ?
I cannot read without Spectacles. (*The Witness put on his Spectacles.*)

Was that the same that was on the Tombstone ?
(*By a Lord.*) Read it aloud ; we want to hear your Scholarship.
" The Will of Robert Tracy of Coscomb in the County of Gloucester, Esquire ; dated May the 14th 1756, and proved 25th May."

(*Mr. Attorney General.*) Did you say he was an English Judge ?
I did.

Was that there ?
It was there ; that I do not call to Mind now.

Did you come here to give Evidence ?
I did.

When were you first spoken to by any body about this ?
I cannot exactly say how long back it is.

About how long ?
More than a Year since I heard it spoken of.

Who spoke to you about it ?
Mr. Joe Tracy.

Where did you see him ?
He came to my House.

Where to ?
To Haley Moor in the Parish of Castlebrack.

About what Time was that ?
I believe it was somewhere in the Spring of last Year.

Last Year ?
No ; I think the Year before.

R r   Recollect ;

Dennis Moran.

Recollect ; was it last Year, or the Year before ?
It was the Year before last, to the best of my Knowledge.
The Year 1841 ?
Yes, I think it was.

Will you swear it was ; are you sure it was Two Years ago ?
It is Two Years ago.

Joe Tracy spoke to you about it ?
He did.

Had he ever spoken to you about it before ?
No, never.

How long before that had you seen the Tombstone ?
I had seen it many Times before that.

How long before ?
Upwards of Forty Years.

Re-examined by Mr. Solicitor General.

Do you mean that it is upwards of Forty Years since you first saw
the Tombstone, or since you last saw it ?
This Gentleman asked me how long it was before Mr. Tracy spoke
of it to me ; I say it was upwards of Forty Years ?

Had you seen the Tombstone Forty Years before he spoke to you ?
Yes.

(*By a Lord.*)   Did you know Joe Tracey, James's Father ?
I did ; I just came to know him.

Was he ever at Castlebrack ?
It was in Gasheel I knew him.

Do you know whether Joseph claimed to be Viscount Tracy ?
I am not able to enter into the Case of the Claimant ; I do not know
that Case at all. I only certify what I know, and any thing else I do
not want to go into.

Did not you know Joseph Tracy ?
I hope you will be satisfied with the Truth.

I want to know the Truth ?
It is the Truth I want to tell you.

You say you knew Joseph ?
Yes.

How shortly before his Death had you seen him ?
I do not know that I had seen him for Three or Four Years before
his Death.

Did not you know that he was making the same Claim as James is
now prosecuting ?
I had heard of it.

Did you tell him of this Tombstone you had seen ?
No.

It would have been very welcome Intelligence to him, but you did
not mention it ?
No.

How far did he live from Castlebrack ?
About Three or Four Miles.

The Witness was directed to withdraw.

Sir

Sir Harris Nicolas stated, That he would prove Conversations of the last Viscount Tracy, tending to recognize this Branch of the Family in Ireland. Being asked whether there had been Evidence of that Nature laid before the late Attorney General, he stated that he believed there was not.

Then JOSEPH ARKELL was called in ; and having been sworn, was examined as follows :

(*Sir Harris Nicolas.*) Where do you live ?
At Cow Honeyborne.

Where is that ?
Near Evesham in Gloucestershire.

What are you ; a Farmer ?
Yes.

Who is your Landlord ?
Sir Thomas Phillips. I rent Part, and Part I have of my own.

When did your Father die ?
In 1815.

Who was your Grandmother ?
Her Name was Susan Writ ; I believe it was.

Was she related to the Tracy Family in any way ?
Yes, I believe she was.

In what Way ?
I do not know in what Way.

Was your Father a Tenant of the Lords Tracy ?
Mr. Tracy of Sandywell, and my Grandfather before him.

Did you ever hear your Father speak of the Tracys ?
Yes.

Had you ever any Conversation with the late Lord Tracy ?
No.

The Witness was directed to withdraw.

The Counsel were directed to withdraw.

Proposed to adjourn this Committee to Tuesday the 16th instant ;

Accordingly,

Adjourned to Tuesday the 16th instant.

Die Martis, 30° Maii 1843.

The Earl of SHAFTESBURY in the Chair.

Evidence on the
Tracy Claim of
Peerage.

THE Order of Adjournment was read.

The Minutes of the last Committee were read.

The Counsel and Parties were ordered to be called in :

And Mr. Solicitor General and Sir Harris Nicolas appeared as Cousel for the Petitioner ;

And Mr. Attorney General and the Attorney General for Ireland appeared on behalf of the Crown.

Then BARRAKIA LOWE TARLTON was called in ; and having been sworn, was examined as follows :

B. L. Tarlton.

(*Sir Harris Nicolas.*)   Where do you live ?
In Killee in the King's County, in Ireland.

Have you resided long at Killee ?
Yes, I have ; since I have been born.

Were your Family long resident in that Place ?
Yes ; upwards of Two hundred Years.

That is the Tradition of your Family ?
Yes.

What are you ?
I am a Farmer ; I hold Land and have Property.

Who is your Landlord ?
Earl Digby.

Are you a Juryman ?
Yes ; a Nisi Prius Juryman these Thirty Years, and a Grand Juryman at the Sessions.

Did you ever serve in the Yeomanry ?
I did.

What Rank have you held in it ?
I was Lieutenant in the dismounted Infantry of Gazehill,—the disbanded Cavalry I mean.

(*By a Lord.*)   How many Acres do you occupy ?
In One Farm I have about Fifteen in my own Possession along with my House ; in another I have One hundred and odd.

What Rent do you pay ?
75*l.* a Year Irish.

In the whole?
Yes, in the whole ; a very old Take.

(*Sir Harris Nicolas.*) Had you an Uncle called Warren Tarlton?
I had.

Did he come on a Visit to you some Years ago?
He did.

In what Year did he come on a Visit to you?
In the Year 1812.

Where?
At Killee.

Do you know the Churchyard of Castlebrack?
Very well.

For how many Years have you known it?
I have known it for Forty Years or more.

(*By a Lord.*) How near is that to your Residence?
Two Miles, to go round the Road ; but it is a shorter Distance to come from my Property to it.

(*Sir Harris Nicolas.*) Were any Part of your Family buried in Castlebrack?
No, not of mine.

Were any of your Uncle's Family?
Yes.

Who?
His Father-in-Law and Mother-in-Law.

Did you go to the Churchyard of Castlebrack in company with your Uncle at any Time?
I did.

When?
The latter End of July or the First Week in August 1812.

For what Purpose did you go?
He came to my House on Business, and he asked me to go to Castlebrack with him to see the Burying Ground of his Wife's Father and Family, who were a very ancient Family, as they intended to erect a new Tombstone.

To some of his Family?
Yes ; he and his Brother-in-Law, I suppose.

Did you notice any other Tombstones on that Occasion?
Oh yes, many.

State what Tombstones you recollect to have seen?
I have seen the Conroy Tombstones, and I have seen the Tracy Tombstones, and many others ; and the Dunns.

Do you recollect any Inscriptions on any Tombstones you saw?
Yes, I do, Part.

State what you recollect?
As to the Dunn Tombstone?

As to the Tracy Tombstone?
It was my Uncle first discovered this Stone, and he had been reading it, and he called me over to him : he said " Barry, is this any of our Family?" " I am sure I cannot say," said I. " I wish you would try and clean it for me," said he ; so I got some Grass, or Dock Leaves, as they

call

call it in Ireland, and rubbed the corner Part of it for him; and it mentioned the Stone being erected by Mary the beloved Wife of William Tracy, a Son of a Judge in England, the Honourable—I cannot swear nor say whether Robert or Richard,—an English Judge, or one of the English Judges; I could not swear whether it was Robert or Richard.

Do you recollect its being said he was an English Judge?
Yes.

You cannot recollect whether it was Robert or Richard?
No, I cannot.

In what State was the Stone at that Time?
One Corner was broken off; it was cracked in the Centre, and it was on a Centre and Half-through,—Half in the Ground and Half over.

Did you see the Tombstone on any other Occasion?
I have seen it since; a Part of it.

How long since?
From Ten to Twelve Months afterwards.

Was there any Difference in the Appearance of the Stone?
There was Part of it gone.

(*By a Lord.*) What Part?
The upper Part was broken off,—the Top Half.

That was gone?
Yes.

On what Part was the Inscription?
That Part went nearly through the Centre of it.

Was the Part which had the Inscription on it gone?
The greater Part of it.

(*Sir Harris Nicolas.*) Some Part remained with the Inscription?
Yes.

(*By a Lord.*) What Part of the Inscription remained?
An English Judge, or a Judge of England; I cannot be certain which.

That remained?
Yes; the Name of Tracy was off it.

Have you ever seen it since?
No; I cannot swear that I have.

No Part of it?
I could not swear that I have.

(*Sir Harris Nicolas.*) Was the Churchyard used for any other Purpose than burying?
Oh yes.

For what other Purpose?
I have frequently seen Cattle grazing in it, and Cows; it belonged to a poor Person, and they used to make use of it for Grass.

Mr. Attorney General submitted, That if this Evidence was offered for the Purpose of proving the supposed Ancestor of the Claimant an English Judge, it was not Evidence admissible for that Purpose.

The

B. L. Tarlton.

The Counsel were informed, That this, connected with the Evidence which had been given, appeared to their Lordships to be admissible as Evidence.

Cross-examined by Mr. Attorney General.

When were you first applied to, to come here and give Evidence?
About the 9th of this Month; the 8th or 9th?

The 9th of May?
Yes.

Before that had you ever heard that any Person was claiming the Title?
Two or Three. I have heard of Two or Three.

How many different Claimants have you known or heard of?
I have heard of Three.

Who are the Three you have heard of?
The present Claimant of course one, and a Man of the Name of Tracy, who lived in Tullamore, another.

What was his Christian Name?
Patrick.

Who was the other?
William Welden Tracy of Ard was another; I did not know that Claimant; they told me he had made a Claim.

When did you first hear of any one making this Claim?
A good many Years ago.

Was it before you saw this Tombstone in 1812?
No, I cannot say it was.

Since?
Yes.

When did you first hear of the present Claimant making his Claim?
I suppose Two or Three Years ago; I might have read of it in the Papers; I did not know the Gentleman at that Time.

(*By a Lord.*) How far off does he live from you?
His Father lived about Five Miles.

Has he got a Residence there?
They had.

Does he live there?
No; he lived in Dublin; I understood he was a Wine Merchant in Dublin; I had the Honour of the Acquaintance of the Gentleman very lately, and knew who he was.

(*Mr. Attorney General.*) You say you were first applied to on the 9th of May?
Yes; by the present Claimant.

Who applied to you?
My Son came over from London: after Breakfast I asked him, and says, " How is this Case of Mr. Tracy's going on?" " I do not know," he says, " much about it." But then we got into a Conversation: I told him what I had seen Years ago, and there had been an Application to me some Years ago by a Man of the Name of Patrick Tracy about the Family.

That was the first Time you had heard of it for some Years?
I had heard they had been looking about it, but I did not know but that the Stone might belong to some Relatives of my own.

Fo

For any thing you know, now, it might have done?
Indeed it may.   I do not know to whom it belonged.

Are there many Families of the Name of Tracy round about there?
There are Two or Three that I am acquainted with.

You say you saw this first in 1812?
Yes.

And then the Year after?
Yes, then the Year after; about Ten Months or Twelve; I could not be positive.

Have you ever seen it since?
No, I never did.

At the Time you first saw it, when you wiped it and cleaned it with Grass or Dock, was it perfect at that Time?
The Stone perfect!   Oh no; it was broken at that Time.

At first?
Yes; a Corner of it.

Was the Inscription of it perfect?
Part was and Part not; where the Crack was it was not very perfect.

It was imperfect when you first saw it?
Yes; the Corner was off it, and there was a Crack across it.

What Part of the Inscription was wanting?
I do not say any Part of it was wanting.

Could you make out the whole of the Inscription?
Yes, the whole of it.   I made out what I have repeated, and probably more.

What was the Name of the Person who was stated to be buried there?
William Tracy.

When did he die?
I could not exactly say that.

Can you say at all?
No; I would not take upon me to say the Year.

What was the Age of the Man?
It was an elderly Age, rather an oldish Age; but I would not take upon me to say exactly the Age.

Have you any Recollection, or any Idea in your Mind, of how long he had been buried, or when he was buried?
No, I have not.

Was there any thing said about his leaving any Children?
Oh yes.   All I can recollect on it was, that the Stone was erected by Mary his beloved Wife.

Was there any thing on the Stone about his leaving Children?
Do you mean William?   Yes, there was.

What was there on the Stone about his leaving Children?
I could not exactly say.

Give us the best Impression you have on your Mind.   What did the Stone record about his Family?   How many Children did he leave?
All it mentioned was One, I think; all I can recollect.

(*By a Lord.*)   What was the Name of that Child?
[No Answer.]

B. L. Tarlton.

(Mr. Attorney General.) In what Manner did it mention that one ; was it a Son or a Daughter ?

It was a Son, I think.

What was the Name ?

I could not take upon me to swear to the Name.

Have you any Recollection of it, or none ?

I wont swear I have none.

Do you mean to say distinctly that you have no Recollection what the Name was ?

[The Witness hesitated.]

(By a Lord.) Answer the Question. Why do not you answer the Question one Way or the other ?

My Lord ———

Why do you not answer the Question which has been put Two or Three Times ?

(Mr. Attorney General.) Do you mean to say you have no Recollection of the Name ?

Yes; either Robert or Richard.

The Name of the Son ?

I think the Name was William, if I recollect right ; but I will not be positive ; it is so many Years ago I cannot be positive.

(By a Lord.) Did it state how old the Son was ?

I could not say.

(Mr. Attorney General.) It recorded the Name of Mary the Wife of the Person buried ?

Yes.

It recorded the Name of Mary the beloved Wife ?

Yes ; I have the greater Part of it in Writing at the Time by my Uncle, but I could not find it ; I searched for the Paper, but could not find it.

(By a Lord.) Your Uncle took it down in Writing ?

Yes, he did.

And gave it to you ?

I had a Copy ; I never knew it would ever be wanted or inquired after.

Not knowing it would ever be wanted or inquired after, you took no Pains to take care of it ?

No ; my Aunt was married to William Tracy, and that was my Reason.

(Mr. Attorney General.) Did he take a Copy of any other Tombstone at that Time ?

He took a Copy of his own Relations, the Dunns.

Did he take a Copy of any other except those Two ?

I cannot say whether he did or not ; he might have done so.

There was the Name of " Mary the beloved Wife "?

Yes.

Of William, the Husband ?

Of William Tracy.

His Father was mentioned ; but whether Richard or Robert, you do not remember ?

Yes.

And

And a Son, whose Name was William ?   *B. L. Tarlton.*
I think so.

(*By a Lord.*)   Was it stated whether that Son William was alive or
dead ?
Of course he was dead.

William the Son ?
Yes.

What did it say about the Son ?
The Tombstone ?   It mentioned a Son.

As dead ?
Of course.

(*Mr. Attorney General.*)   Why do you say " of course" ?
Because if he was not dead his Name would not be on it.

Did, then, the Tombstone record the Death of a Son named William,
as well as of the Father ?
Yes.

(*By a Lord.*)   Was there any other of the Family ?
I cannot say, indeed.

Cannot you say whether there was or was not ?
There might have been ; there were Two Names upon it that I
recollect.

Was the Tombstone erected to the Memory of Two Persons ?
No ; only One.

(*Mr. Attorney General.*)   The Tombstone was erected to the Memory
of William the Son of the Judge ?
Yes ; by Mary his Wife.

But it recorded the Death of a Son of that William ?
Yes.

Did it mention whether that William, the Son of the Judge, left any
Children surviving him ?
I cannot say.

You had a Copy, but took no Notice of it ?
Yes, it is so long ago.

You were not certain whether the Tombstone belonged to one of
your own Relations ?
Yes.

You would surely take more Interest in your living Relations than
your dead ones ?
Certainly.

I want to know whether that Tombstone recorded, that William left
any Sons who were alive ?
I cannot say.

(*By a Lord.*) This Person that came to you from London was a Son
of yours ?
Yes.

What is that Son ?
He is in the Police here ; he is a Sergeant of a Division.

How long has he been in England, do you know ?
Six or Seven Years ; he has never been in Ireland since.

Was

Was he sent over for the Purpose of getting some Information?

He came over with the Solicitor from England. I do not know for what Purpose he came, I am sure.

What is your Son's Name?

Edward Tarlton.

He came to pay you a Visit?

Yes; he came to my House about Four o'Clock in the Morning, Saturday Morning.

How long did he stay with you?

Till the Tuesday; not any more; he was in Tullamore and different Places.

This Conversation took place by Accident?

Yes; he asked me to go with him to Castlebrack, to show him where I saw the Stone, and I did. I knew nothing of the Solicitors nor Mr. Tracy till Two Days after.

What brought him over with the Solicitor?

I cannot tell that. He is here; he will answer for himself.

How long did you keep that Copy of the Inscription?

Oh, it might have been, may be, Ten or Twenty Years in my Possession; I never went to look for it till my Father wanted to search for some old Papers that had been in my Father's Possession and my own for many Years, and it was not to be found.

When did you search for it?

On the 8th or 9th of this Month, when I was asked these Questions.

Did you ever show it to any body?

I showed it to a Man of the Name of Tracy, who came to me Years ago,—a Man of the Name of Tracy. He told me afterwards he had given up his Claim; that he was not the Person.

He was claiming the Title himself?

Yes, he was.

Where is he now?

He is dead.

Did you show it to any of the other Claimants?

No; they never asked me.

Did you mention it to any of the Claimants?

I do not know that I have; probably I may have.

Did you, or did you not?

I cannot say.

Do you believe you mentioned it to any one?

Indeed, I believe, I may have mentioned it to them.

Did you consider it material and important to this Claim?

No; I did not consider it material at all; the first Claimant that was looking for it or looking about it was a Relation of my own.

You cannot say whether you showed it to any of them?

No, I cannot say; it was known by many in that Country.

The Tombstone was known to many?

Yes.

Any Persons who went where the Tombstone was might see it?

Yes; it was a Place for People congregating on many Occasions.

Were

Were you connected with the Family?
With other Families; not this Family.

How happened you to have your Attention called to the Tomb-stone?
By my Uncle going to see about erecting a Tombstone to his Family. There are some more Tombstones to the Memory of the Tracy Family.

You did not know that the Paper was lost till you looked for it the other Day,—the Paper I refer to?
No, I did not.

You did not look for it till the other Day?
No.

Are you on good Terms with the Family of Tracy who live near you,—Five Miles off?
Oh yes, very good Terms.

Did you know they were claiming the Title?
Oh yes.

Where did you keep this Paper?
Among my Papers in my Desk.

What Sort of a Desk?
Mahogany; a good deal older than myself.

How old is that?
Fifty-six next Christmas.

What Desk was it?
A Mahogany Desk.

Had it been long in your Possession?
It belonged to my Grandfather.

What did you keep in it besides Papers?
Sometimes Money, when I had it.

Did you lock it?
Yes.

Where was the Key kept?
Sometimes in my Pocket, sometimes in my Wife's.

You generally went about with the Key in your Pocket?
Yes.

How came it out?
When I took it out, I suppose.

When did you take the Paper out?
I cannot say; I might have taken the Paper out, and it might have been lost; or others might have taken it out.

How could others take it out when you had the Key in your Pocket?
I would not have the Key in my Pocket always; they might take it out when they had the Key.

Where did you keep it generally?
In my Pocket.

When was it not in your Pocket?
When my Wife or any of my Family wanted it.

What would they want out of it?
Oftentimes Money.

Then your Family were used to go and take Money out?
Yes.

U u   That

B. L. Tarlton:

That was the Way you kept it ?
Yes ; we do not keep separate Purses in Ireland.

What do your Family consist of ? Answer the Question with common Respect to the House, and remember you are upon your Oath ?
I remember I am.

What do your Family consist of ?
Four Daughters and a Son.

What Age are your Daughters ?
The eldest is Thirty-three the youngest Fourteen.

And the Son ?
Sixteen.

At the Time the Paper was lost, how, to the best of your Knowledge, was that Paper lost ?
I cannot say ; we never had Occasion to look for it till I was asked this Question.

How many Years is it since you have seen it ?
I have not seen it these Fourteen or Fifteen Years.

What was the last Occasion of your seeing it ?
When old Tracy of Tullamore came to ask me about it I said "Pat" says I, "I have never known nothing of it but about the Stone in Castlebrack, and I dare say I have the Inscription of it."

Then your Daughter must have been under Age at that Time ?
Yes.

At that Time do you mean to swear, on the Oath you have taken, you allowed your Daughter, as well as your Wife, to take what Money out of your Desk they wanted ?
I have often given them the Key to go and take the Money out to pay for Work.

Did you not say just now that you kept a common Purse ?
Yes ; the Money I put into the Desk there, and they went to get the Money.

Whatever Money they wanted they might take ?
They came first to me.

You were understood to say you kept a common Purse, and that any who chose might go and take what Money they pleased out of it ?
No, not without my Consent.

All you mean is, that sometimes you went yourself, and sometimes sent them to get Money out of it ?
Yes ; and sometimes, if they wanted Money to get any thing, they would come to me.

Did you ever authorize them to go and get other Things than Money ?
Yes ; I have sent them to fetch me some Papers.

What became of this Paper when you took it out ?
I generally put it back again.

Did not you always put it back again ?
Yes ; I think I did, unless any of them went by Accident.

Then how could this Paper be lost ?
I had Papers belonging to many Persons : my Father was left Executor to Two or Three Families, and there were often Papers

8

remaining

·remaining with me, which Papers I have given up to the Claimants, that I would not have any thing to do with.

Then you gave those up, and did not lose them ?
Of course I do not wish to lose Papers.

How can you account for this being lost ?
I cannot account for its being lost, unless it went away with some of the other Papers. I did not consider it of any Vaue.

It was written in Ink ?
Yes.

And the Original from which it was copied was also in Ink ?
It was ; or I will not say, indeed, whether it was written on the Tablet in Pencil or Ink.

Who wrote the Copy your Uncle gave you ?
I wrote it myself.

Where ?
In my own Parlour.

On what ?
On the Paper.

On what ; a Table or a Desk ?
My Table.

Who was by ?
My Uncle.

Any other living Person ?
Perhaps my Wife was there ; I cannot say.

Did any other Person who is alive see it besides yourself?
I dare say they did. My Wife may have seen it.

Is your Wife alive ?
Yes, she is.

Is she here ?
She is not ; and she wouldnot wish to be here ; nor should I wish to be here, if I could help myself.

When did you make the Copy of that Inscription ?
Either that Evening or the next Day ; I cannot say which.

Was your Uncle living with you in the House at that Time ?
He was only on a Visit for a few Days.

You cannot say whether the Paper from which it was copied was written with Pencil or with Ink ?
I should rather say it was written with Pencil, what he took in Castlebrack.

Did you make yours in Pencil or in Ink ?
In Ink.

How many Years is it since you made that Copy ?
In August 1812.

Did he take any other Inscription in the Churchyard ?
Yes ; I think he did.

What ?
Some belonging to his own Relatives Tombstone.

(59.)

How

B. L. Tarlton.

How long after his copying this in Pencil was it that you made that Copy in Ink?

It might be that Evening, but I think it was the next Day; he stopped only Two or Three Days with me.

Will you swear it was not more than a Day after he took it down in Pencil?

No, I would not. It was during the Time he was with me.

You would not swear it was not Two Days after he had taken the Copy himself?

No, I would not.

Will you swear it was not Three Days?

No, indeed, I will not.

During the whole of that Time, between his copying it and your copying it, where did he keep it?

In his Pocket.

Which Pocket; his Waistcoat or his Breeches Pocket?

I cannot say indeed.

Do you swear that when you copied it it was distinctly readible?

Yes.

Though in Pencil?

Yes; it was in an Envelope, shut up.

Rubbing in his Pocket all the Time?

I suppose he carried it here (*his Waistcoat Pocket*); I cannot say.

Did not you say it was in his Breeches Pocket?

I cannot say.

It was not in his Coat Pocket?

I cannot say.

Which do you think it was in?

I think it was in his Breast Pocket.

What Trade was he? What did he do for his Living?

He was a Hearth Money Collector.

During the Time he was with you with this Inscription in his Pocket how was he employed?

He came to me on Business.

Did he remain with you the whole Time on Business?

Two or Three Days.

What was he doing during the Time he was there on Business?

He spent the Time walking about with me.

What Time of the Year was it?

It was in July or August.

Fine Weather?

Indeed it was; we were beginning to mow at the Time.

Did he go out and help them to mow?

No; he went to see his Friends.

He went about the whole Day?

Yes, and sat in the House; he went to see one old Acquaintance and another.

Was the Copy your Uncle made in a running Hand, or was it in Imitation of the Inscription?

It was in a running Hand,—in the Manner he wrote himself.

It

It did not profess to be what we call a Fac-simile of the Inscription ? B. L. Tarlt
No, it did not.

The Conversation you have referred to with your Son commenced, you say, accidentally ?
Yes.

Who began it, you or he ?
When he came in the Morning, at Half past Four in the Morning, I did not know him.

Who commenced this Conversation respecting this Tomb ?
I think I commenced it. I asked him at Breakfast, " What are you doing in London about Mr. Tracy ?" He said, " I know very little about it, but being in Dublin I have come down here."

Did he say how he happened to know any thing about it ?
No, he did not.

He did not state that he came to Ireland for the Purpose of making Inquiries with the Attorney ?
No, he did not ; if he had I should not have told him any thing I knew about it.

Re-examined by Mr. Solicitor General.

Did I understand you that you are connected with a Family of the Name of Tracy ?
Yes.

By Marriage ?
Yes.

You say you went to this Churchyard with your Uncle, and you saw other Tombstones with the Name of Tracy upon them ?
Yes.

He called your Attention to this ?
Yes.

You say, if I understand you rightly, the Copy was made in Pencil by the Person with whom you were,—your Uncle ?
Yes.

And that you copied it afterwards at your House ?
Yes.

Will you have the goodness,—for I did not understand, from the Way in which the Question and Answer were put, what William — what Person you were speaking of ? What was upon the Tomb. What do you recollect yourself was the Inscription on the Tomb ?
What I recollect of it is, that the Tombstone was erected by Mary the beloved Wife of William in Memory of her Husband.

Was there any other William upon the Tombstone ? Were you, in the Answer you gave, speaking of William the Husband of Mary ?
Yes ; William the Husband of Mary, the Son of one of the Judges, —an English Judge, or a Judge of England.

Was there any other William mentioned, or were you speaking of William the Son of the Judge ?
Of course.

Will you state to their Lordships what was the Inscription upon the Tomb as near as you can recollect it,—the whole of it from the Beginning ?
" This Stone erected by Mary the beloved Wife of William Tracy,

(59.)   X x   Son

B. L. Tarlton.

Son to Robert;" I will not say whether one of the Judges of England, or an English Judge.

Was that the whole of the Inscription you recollect upon the Tomb? That is the whole that I can recollect, as near as I can go.

As nearly as you can recollect, is that the Inscription that was copied by you from the Paper of your Uncle? It is; it was that Word,—an English Judge or a Judge of England,— that attracted my Uncle's Notice, and he called to me to know was he any Relative of ours; and I said, "I am sure I do not know."

When do you first recollect having seen the Paper yourself? I think Fourteen or Fifteen Years ago; I cannot say the Year, it was at the Time that Patrick Tracy of Tullamore was speaking, I suppose, about his Claim.

Was that the first Occasion of your seeing him? Yes; I have had no Occasion to look any thing more about it.

From that Time you have not seen it? No.

(*By a Lord.*) Did you not say, that, in addition to William the Son of the Judge, the Tombstone mentioned a Son of that William? I must have misunderstood; if you will allow me,—I cannot recollect anything of the Name of William but One.

Did not you say that? I might have said that; but I have said it wrong, if I have.

Did you not likewise say, that you were not sure what the Name of the Son was, but that you believed his Name was William? Yes, I did.

You now say that you cannot say whether the Tombstone mentioned a Son of that William or not? It mentioned none but One William, that I saw.

Did not you say that the Tombstone was placed there also to the Memory of William, a Son? To the Memory of William.

Did not you say it was also to the Memory of a Son of that William? " By Mary the beloved Wife."

Did you not say that the Tombstone said, upon the Face of it, that it was placed there to the Memory of a Son of that William? Probably I did, but I did not understand.

If you did, it was false, was it? Certainly; I can recollect only One Name of William; but then through Ignorance I might have said it, probably.

Did you not say, whether through Ignorance or Knowledge, that the other William who was mentioned upon the Tombstone was dead, and that for that Reason his Name was upon the Tombstone? Of course that was the Reason why, I suppose, the Name was put on it.

You were asked whether it was a Son or a Daughter? If the Name was William, it was a Son of course.

Though you said Half an Hour ago that it was erected to the Son as well as to William the Husband, you now say that was false? I say that I cannot recollect any Name but One; I might have answered
the

the Question wrong, not intentionally, but all I can recollect is One
Name William.

Half an Hour ago you recollected another?
I took it wrong; it was through my Ignorance, if I did.

(*By a Lord.*) It was a Son, and not a Daughter?
Of course.

A Son of the beloved Wife, a Son of William?
I should not say that.

I thought you said it was a Son, and not a Daughter?
I said William was a Son.

You spoke to a Son of William?
That was a Mistake entirely.

The Witness was directed to withdraw.

Then PATRICK BOYNE was called in ; and having been sworn, was
examined as follows :

(*Sir Harris Nicolas.*) How old are you?
About Fifty-eight Years of Age.

What are you?
I am a Farmer living on my own Property.

Where?
At Dureen in the King's County, near Portarlington in Ireland.

Is that near Castlebrack?
Within about Four Miles.

Whom did you marry?
I married a Daughter of Mr. Wyer of the Place where I now reside.

Did you go on a Visit to your Father-in-Law in the Year 1813?
I did; in October 1813.

Did you on that Occasion go with your Father-in-Law to the Churchyard of Castlebrack?
No; I went on that Occasion with my Wife and my Sister-in-Law
to the Churchyard of Castlebrack.

What induced you to go to the Churchyard of Castlebrack?
The Family Tomb of my Wife is at Castlebrack.

Did you see any other Tomb upon that Occasion than the One to
your Wife's Father?
I did.

What did you see?
I saw a Tomb, quite near my Family Tomb, with the Name of Tracy
upon it.   I was then a Resident in Dublin.

Have you any Recollection of there being an Inscription on that
Tomb?
Yes; to the best of my Recollection I recollect an Inscription.

State what you recollect?
To the best of my Recollection it ran, " Erected by Mary Tracy to
the Memory of her Husband William Tracy, the Son of an Honourable
Tracy ;" I do not know what the first Name was,—" an Honourable
Tracy, an English Judge."

Did

Did you see that Tomb on any other Occasion ?
I did.

When ?
On the Burial of one of my Daughters ; early in 1816 I perceived it.

Did you see it on any other Occasion but those Two ?
No. I think it was in January 1816.

Have you never seen it since that ?
No, I have not.

In what State was the Tombstone at the Time you saw it ?
When first I saw it, it appeared to be cracked in the Centre or near it.

(*By a Lord.*) Was the Inscription quite legible?
I recollect some of the Letters. I got my Knife to take off some of the Moss and clean it ; and being Tracy, I was the more curious.

Could you read it ?
Yes ; I could read the whole of it distinctly.

Being Tracy you were the more curious?
Yes ; because my Father-in-Law's Mother was a Tracy, and connected with the Tracys.

What was the Inscription upon your Family Tombstone ?
My Family Tombstone runs, "Here lieth the virtuous and charitable," exceedingly flattering to the Party, "Catharine Wyer, Wife of Mr. Patrick Wyer," of such a Place in the "Queen's County, Esquire, who departed this Life" I think "July 1793." Then it went on with the Inscription on his Son ; then it went on further on my Tomb,—on the Family Tomb, with the Inscription of my Wife.

Was not it a few Months after you married that you went there ?
Yes ; I went there in October 1813 ; but I thought I was asked what was the Inscription on my Tomb.

You were asked what you saw on that Tomb in 1813 ?
I saw, in October 1813, the Inscription I allude to, with the Exception of my Wife's, for she was then living.

Was there any thing else upon it besides that you have mentioned ?
No.

Did you look at any other Tombstone except that ?
I believe there was a Tombstone, a small Distance to the Eastward of mine, of the Name of Gorman. I recollect looking at that.

What could lead you to go there so immediately after you were married to see the Tombstone ?
I was very desirous to see the Family Burying Place.

You seem to have been making very early Provision for such a lamentable Event. You went again, you say, to see this in 1816 ?
Yes.

You read this Inscription of the Tracys again ?
I saw it.

Was it in the same State as it was in 1813 ?
I think not ; I think it was a good deal broken.

Did you look at the Inscription ?
I did not.

Cross-

Cross-examined by Mr. Attorney General for Ireland.

You have stated that you are a Freeholder, and live on your own Property; are you registered?
I am.

As a 50*l.* or a 10*l.* Freeholder?
A 50*l.* Freeholder.

How far is it from Castlebrack?
Perhaps it might be more than Four Miles.

Are you able to state whether there was any other Inscription on the Tombstone except that you have stated?
No; I do not think there was.

Are you positive whether there was or not?
I cannot be positive, it is so long ago; but the Inscription was quite short; it appeared to be quite short.

Was there any thing about any Children of William?
No; I perceived nothing of the Kind.

When were you first applied to to give Evidence in this Case?
About the Beginning of April last.

Who applied to you?
I met the Claimant's Brother at the Hotel where I stopped in Dublin.

You had a Conversation with him?
The Conversation arose at the Hotel.

When did you come to London?
About Fourteen Days ago.

Did you tell his Brother you had seen this Tombstone?
I told him I had a Recollection of seeing the old Tracy Tomb.

When did you receive the Application to come over?
It was out of the Conversation arose the Application to come over.

When?
Some Time about the latter End of April, I think.

In Dublin?
No; in the Country where I live.

Who applied to you? Was it a Solicitor?
The Claimant's Brother wrote to me to know whether I had any Objection to meet a Solicitor.

In Dublin?
In the Country.

The Solicitor went over to Ireland to look for Witnesses immediately after the Proceedings in this House?
I cannot say.

You saw him in Ireland?
Yes.

It was in the early Part of April you communicated to the Brother of the Claimant your having seen this Tombstone?
Yes.

You were not summoned over to this Country until the latter End of April?
No.

Patrick Boyne.

(*By a Lord.*) Is that the Gentleman you saw, Mr. Bourdillon?
Yes, that is the Gentleman.

(*Mr. Attorney General for Ireland.*) Did you know the Father or Grandfather of the Claimant?
I knew the Father.

Not the Grandfather?
No.

Are you able to state of what Religion the Family was?
I saw him at our Chapel; he lived in the same Parish with me.

That is Roman Catholic?
Yes.

He went to Mass?
Yes, he did.

Who are the Roman Catholic Clergymen of that Chapel? What Chapel was it you saw him at?
My Parish Chapel, called Rahene.

Who were the Roman Catholic Clergymen in that Parish?
The Reverend Mr. Kinsella is the Rector, and he has Two Curates.

How many Years have they been at that Chapel?
I believe Mr. Kinsella, the present Parish Priest, has been there Twenty Years.

He probably knew the Grandfather of the present Claimant?
I cannot tell.

Do you know whether the Grandfather of the present Claimant died within Twenty Years?
I cannot tell.

Do you think there is any Person in that Parish who could tell whether the Grandfather of the present Claimant went to Church or to Chapel?
I cannot tell.

(*By a Lord.*) Are not the Tracys connected in some Way with you?
No.

You stated that they were connected with your Wife?
Not this Family; another Family of the Name of Tracy.

(*Mr. Attorney General for Ireland.*) Are there any elderly Gentlemen of Family and Fortune living in the Neighbourhood of Castlebrack?
No; I do not think there are any Gentlemen.

Are there no Gentlemen of high Respectability living in that Neighbourhood?
There is a Mr. Kemmis, a Clergyman, lives there.

I am speaking, not of young Men, but old Men of Sixty or Seventy, or more?
I should think there is; but I cannot tell distinctly.

Do you mean to say that you live within Five Miles of Castlebrack, and cannot tell whether there are any Gentlemen of Respectability and Family living in the Neighbourhood?
I cannot tell.

Do you know who your Neighbours are?
Yes, I do.

Are

Are any of them Persons having large Properties ?
There are, near me.

State the Names of any Gentlemen of Property near you ?
There is Mr. Warburton ; he is in Life.

What is his Age ?
Near Sixty.

(*By a Lord.*) How near to Castlebrack does his House stand ?
About Six Miles, perhaps.

Is he a Protestant or a Catholic ?
A Protestant.

Is his House in the Parish of Castlebrack ?
No.

(*Mr. Attorney General for Ireland.*) Is Mr. Warburton's Burying Place in the Parish of Castlebrack ?
No, I think not.

Is there any other Gentleman of Respectability and Property in that Neighbourhood, or within Five or Six Miles of it ?
There are.

Can you name any of them ?
Yes ; I will name Mr. Wingfield of Gashell near it.—Four or Five Miles.

Do you think he has been ever at Castlebrack ?
Oh, I cannot tell.

Do you know any other ?
Mr. Newcombe, a Man of Property near me.

What is his Age ?
About Fifty, or perhaps not quite so much.

(*By a Lord.*) How near to Castlebrack is he ?
About Four Miles.

Is he a Protestant ?
Yes, he is.

Are there any Persons of some Property living in the Parish of Castlebrack ?
No ; I do not think there are any of Rank ; there are perhaps a few.

Is there a Justice of the Peace, for instance ?
No ; there is One Justice of the Peace within about Two Miles or Two Miles and a Half of me.

What is his Name ?
Tarlton.

What is his Age ?
About Fifty.

He has lived all his Life there ?
As long as I have known the Country,—perhaps Two Miles and a Half.

He lives in the Parish ?
I rather think not. I think he lives in the Parish of Gashell.

Does he ever go to Castlebrack Church ?
There is no Church at Castlebrack.

To

Patrick Boyne.

To the Churchyard ?
I do not know that he does.

(*Mr. Attorney General for Ireland.*) Are there any Roman Catholics buried in the Churchyard of Castlebrack ?
There are.

Is it usual for the Priest of the Parish to attend ?
No ; he seldom or never attends.

(*By a Lord.*) What Age is the Clergyman of Castlebrack ?
He is near Fifty, I should think.

Is he living there ?
Yes, he is there. No ; I beg your Pardon ; Castlebrack is in another Parish, in the Queen's County, and my Parish Priest is in the King's County.

Who is the Clergyman of Castlebrack ?
Mr. Hayley.

What Age is he?
Between Forty and Fifty, I think.

How long has he been there ?
It is the neighbouring Parish, and I do not exactly know.

Cannot you state about what Time ?
Yes ; I dare say about Ten Years.

Where was he before that ?
He was in some Part of the County of Carlow before that ; I think in another Part of the Diocese.

It was in the Year 1813 you first went ?
Yes ; October 1813.

That you are sure of ?
Yes, perfectly. It was the Day Month after I was married.

Though there was a Crack across the Tombstone you could then read it perfectly ?
Oh yes, I could read it perfectly.

It was in 1813 you saw this Tombstone ?
It was.

How long after that was it that you were first spoken to about the Inscription ?
I was only spoken to about it last April.

Therefore for Thirty Years you had no Conversation upon the Subject with any one ?
None.

Had you taken any Copy of it ?
I am inclined to think I might have taken a Memorandum of it in Pencil, but I have no Recollection of it.

You might or you might not ; do you think you took it in Pencil ?
I am not clear upon that.

Do you think you took down the Inscription upon your Wife's Family Tombstone in Pencil ?
No ; but I recollect what was upon it.

The only one that you might have taken down was this Tracy one ?
I might have taken this, but I cannot be sure that I did. I could have

have no Occasion to take the Inscription of my own, because I knew the Parties entered upon it.

Did you take the Inscription of any other Tombstone except the Tracy one ?
No ; I have no Recollection of taking any Note.

If you did take a Note in Pencil of the Tracy Tombstone where did you keep it ?
I might have it with my Papers, but I have no Recollection of it.

Is it not a mere Fancy of the Moment that you took something of a Note ?
It is pure Fancy ; I have no Recollection of having taken it.

Have you any Recollection whatever of having taken it ?
No, I have not.

How came you to say you had taken a Note ?
I say I might have taken a Note ; I have not a distinct Recollection of having taken a Note.

You might have taken that and the other too, but you swear you did not take a Copy of the other ?
I did not take it of my own Family Tomb, for I had no Occasion.

You did not take it of any other ?
No, I did not.

Nobody ever spoke to you upon the Subject of the Tombstone for Thirty Years after you saw it ?
No.

When was it that this Conversation took place ?
The Beginning of last April.

Did you know any of the other Claimants ?
I have heard of the Claimant's Father,

When ?
A good many Years ago.

Did you know him ?
I did.

Had you any Conversation with him about this Tombstone ?
No.

You did not tell him you recollected having seen this Tombstone ?
Not the Father ; I have with the Son.

That was in April last ?
Yes.

Had you any Conversation with the Father before that ?
No ; never with the Father.

You knew he was a Claimant ?
I heard that.

You saw the Man ?
Yes.

But you never said a Word about the Tombstone to him ?
No ; I did not think I was called upon to do it.

Were you aware that this Tombstone would be a material Piece of Evidence for the Claimant, whoever he might be ?
I was not.

(59.)   Z z   When

Patrick Boyne.

When was it you saw the Solicitor who came over to Dublin?
It was the 20th of April, the latter End of April, I met him in the Country.

As late as the 20th?
I should imagine so; some Time in April, or the latter End of April.

Did he come to you, or did you go to him?
I met him.

Where?
At Tullamore.

At what Place in Tullamore?
At the Inn.

Did you go there by Accident?
The Brother of the Claimant called upon me, and we went direct from my House to Tullamore.

How far is it from your House to Tullamore?
About Eleven Miles; and what I stated he took down, I suppose.

He took it down in your Presence?
He did.

Then why do you suppose?
He took it down certainly.

The Witness was directed to withdraw.

Rev. John Dunn.

Then the Reverend JOHN DUNN was called in; and having been sworn, was examined as follows:

(*Sir Harris Nicolas.*) You are a Clergyman?
I am.

Are you Rector or Curate?
I am the Curate of Killochee.

Is that in the Neighbourhood of Castlebrack?
Yes; it is about Seven Miles or Eight Miles.

How long have you been in that Neighbourhood?
Twenty Years, about.

Do you know the Churchyard of Castlebrack?
I do.

How long have you known it?
My Ancestors have been buried there; it has been their Burial Place longer, a great deal, than any one I can recollect.

When did you first know the Churchyard of Castlebrack?
I went in the Year 1825 to inter my Mother; I think that was the first Time I ever recollect having been in Castlebrack Churchyard; after that I went to inter an Uncle of my Father, of the Name of John Dunn, in the Year 1830, and I went in last May to inter my Father.

Have the goodness to state in what State the Churchyard was when you first saw it as to its Preservation,—of the Walls and Monuments?
The Churchyard was very badly fenced, and at all Times that I have seen it it has been in that badly fenced State, and I believe it is in that State at this Moment; that there is free Ingress and Egress, very nearly.

Have

Have you any Knowledge of Tombstones being removed from that Churchyard, I do not mean any particular Tombstone?

In the Year 1825 my Tombstone of my Family was within the interior Walls of the Churchyard of the Church or Chapel, and the Walls were then standing about Six or Seven Feet high, and in the Year 1830, the Stones of the Walls were broken down, and very nearly levelled to the Ground.

(*By a Lord.*) Was that the Wall of the Chapel or the Yard?

The whole of the Chapel or the Church; I remonstrated with the Sexton.

Cross-examined by Mr. Attorney General.

In the Year 1825 was the first Time you saw Castlebrack Churchyard?

I think so; about 1825, the first Time I took particular Notice, my Mother being interred there.

You say that it was very badly fenced?

It was, very badly.

And had been so for many Years?

I cannot say prior to that, as that was the first Time I saw it.

Did it appear to have been for many Years in that badly fenced State?

Yes.

Any body had Access to it?

I should think any Person had Access to it.

To take Stones away?

Certainly.

Or to bring them there?

To erect any Tombstone of course. There seemed to be a small Gate, and at the Sides of that Gate Cattle or Pigs could go in.

It was under no Care or Superintendence?

There was a Sexton.

Did he take care of it?

I conceive he did not.

(*By a Lord.*) What Age was that Sexton?

I think it was a Sextoness; I think it was a Woman.

Do you know whether she is alive now?

I do not.

What Age was she apparently?

Indeed I think she could not be above Fifty or Sixty.

Have you seen any other Sexton since?

No.

Have you seen any Sexton at all except that Woman?

No.

The Appearance of the Churchyard the last Time you saw it was very much the Appearance when you first saw it?

It was.

Did you miss any Stones taken away from the Ruins after the first Time you were there?

I did.

From

Rev. John Dunn.

From the Ruins?
Yes, from the Ruins.
From the Ruin of the Chapel or Church?
Yes.
From what Part of it?
All surrounding it.
Were any of those which had been removed Gravestones?
I did not observe any.
From what you know of your Countrymen, the common People in Ireland, who would be likely to take Stones for building, would they not have a Preference of any Stones taken from some Building rather than a Tombstone?
The Impression on my Mind is that they would take all they could meet with.
You think that they would take any Stone, and equally a Tombstone with any other?
That they would take any Stone they could get.
Did you ever see any Tombstone taken?
I did not.
Do you mean to represent the Nature of your Countrymen to be such that they have no Reverence for a Place of Repose for the Dead?
Indeed I do not.
Have they not on the contrary, very great?
They have, very great.
Is not that their known Character?
Yes.
They have great Horror of any Sacrilege committed on the Persons of the Dead?
Yes.
Is not this an ancient consecrated Place of Burial?
It is.

The Witness was directed to withdraw.

Patrick Boyne.

Then PATRICK BOYNE was again called in, and further examined as follows :

(*By a Lord.*) In what Part of the Churchyard did that Stone stand on which you say you saw the Inscription about the Tracys?
It stood a few Graves to the Southward of the Church.
Was it near the outer Fence?
No; more in the Middle of the Churchyard.
Was it near the old Wall?
It was; but I should suppose about Seven Graves from the old Wall.
What Shape was it?
About Two Feet and a Half, I think; where the Inscription was on, it appeared to be pretty much square.
Less than a Yard square?
What the Inscription was on; but I am not alluding to the original Tomb.
What do you mean by the original Tomb?
It appeared to me to be that Country Stone.

What

What Size was the whole Stone upon which the Inscription was?
I do not think it was more than Two Feet and a Half in Length.

And Two Feet and a Half in Breadth?
No; it was lying flat.

Not standing up?
No.

Was it fixed in the Ground?
It appeared to be loose.

Two Feet and a Half square?
Yes; that was what the Inscription was on.

Was there another Part besides that on which the Inscription was?
I am not clear about that, for, as I have said, Half of the lower Part appeared to be loose.

How thick was it.
What we call our Mountain Flags, about Two to Three Inches thick.

The rest was buried in the Grass?
I am not clear about that.

In what Part was the Crack?
In the Middle.

About a Foot from the Top?
The Crack was Two Feet from the Top.

Then the Crack was at the Extremity?
No; the Crack appeared to be in the Middle of the Stone.

Of which Stone?
Of this Tombstone.

The Inscription?
Yes.

Did the Crack run through the Letters?
No; it did not.

Then how could it be in the Middle of the Inscription?
The Letters were quite distinct before you came to the Crack.

Then came the Crack, and then more Stone?
I will not say, for I am not sure.

Do you mean that it was Two Feet, independently of the Crack?
I think it was.

The Crack was Two Feet and a Half from the Top of the Stone?
I think it was.

What was upon the rest?
To the best of my Recollection it was Grass.

Was the Crack in a straight Line?
Yes, right across.

You cannot say whether that was the whole of the Stone or not?
No, I cannot.

You cannot tell whether the Stone was Two Feet and a Half long or not?
I cannot.

Patrick Boyne.

Under the Grass it might have been twice as long?
No; generally speaking the Stones are not more than Six Feet,—those old Flags.

Have you ever been in that Ground since 1818?
I was there in 1816.

Did it appear to be in the same State then?
I took very little Interest in it; it appeared to be very much abused.

Abused in what respect?
I think it appeared to be stamped.

Do you mean by People's Feet?
I think it appeared to be loosened in its original Position.

It was still there in 1816?
I think it was.

Have you seen it since?
No.

Did it appear to be of the same Size in 1816?
I do not remember; I think it was very much abused.

Was it of the same Size?
I am not clear; I am inclined to think it was quite broken.

It was not taken away?
No.

Did you read the Inscription again in 1816?
I did not.

You say there were Letters?
Yes, I saw the Letters; it was quite near my own Tomb.

Were the Letters as visible as they were before?
They were; if you went very near it you could see it.

(*Mr. Attorney General for Ireland.*) Was it to the North or the Southward in the Line of the Chapel?
It was Southward of it.

The Witness was directed to withdraw.

B. L. Tarlton.

Then BARRAKIA LOWE TARLTON was again called in, and further examined as follows:

(*By a Lord.*) Have you heard the Examination of the last Witness?
No.

Have you ever had any Conversation with him out of Court about this?
No.

Do you know him personally?
I do.

Did you come over with him in the same Boat?
I did.

And you did not converse at all on the Subject?
Not a Word.

But

But you talked on every other Subject?
I was not along with him on board long till we went to Bed, and then we went into the Steam Carriage Four or Five together and came up.

And never said a Word about that you were coming upon?
No.

You never mentioned the Word " Castlebrack "?
I do not think we did.

Nor mentioned the Name of Tracy?
No; I do not think we did.

How did you know what he was coming for?
He told me at Dublin he was summoned up on this.

Had you no Conversation with him on the Subject of this?
No; not about the Stone.

About the Cause?
Yes; certainly about the Cause, but nothing about the Stone. I knew what he was coming for, but we had no Conversation about it.

You told him you were coming about the Tombstone?
Yes.

And he told you he was coming about the Tombstone?
No; he did not. I told him I was coming about the Tracy Peerage.

And about the Tombstone?
No; I do not think I did.

In what Part of the Churchyard was it?
It was just back at a Portion of the old Wall now standing, a Part of which is down.

What Wall do you mean?
The Wall at the End of the Church I understand it to be.

Close by the Fence?
No; the Fence is at a Distance from it; it was pretty much in the Centre.

What Size was the Stone you saw?
The usual Size, I suppose; from Five to Six Feet long.

Was the great Crack going through the Inscription?
Yes; through a Part of One Line.

Was it lengthways or crossways?
First the Corner was broken off, and it went across.

The Length of the Stone, and not across the Stone?
No; across the Letters.

Suppose this to be the Length of the Stone, Six Feet; did the Crack go that Way or the other,—that Way?
Across the Stone.

When was it you first looked at this Stone?
In the Year 1812 I was directed to it by the Circumstances I have stated.

You read it, and a Copy was taken?
Yes.

About Ten Months afterwards you went and found it almost gone?
There was a Part of it broken off, and moved away from it.

3 B   A great

A great Part of the Inscription was gone?
Yes.

At what Time of the Year was this?
It was in the Winter Season of 1812, or the Beginning of 1813.

Were you ever there in 1816?
I have been there every Year of my Life.

It was quite gone in 1816?
It was then; I cannot say the Year; it was gone away totally at last.

In 1814 or 1815 it was gone?
I cannot say whether it was gone entirely then; I have not seen it some Years; a good many Years.

You say a great deal of it was gone in the Winter of 1812?
Yes; one part of it was broken off.

Very few Letters remained in that Year?
There were some Letters, but they were very much defaced.

Were you there again in 1814?
I might be.

Were you there in 1813?
Yes, I was.

Was it quite gone then?
There was a Part of it gone when I saw it then.

In the meantime there was more gone, probably?
That precise Time, I cannot say whether I saw it or no.

Was it gone altogether then?
I cannot say; the People were in the habit of taking Stones away.

In the July of 1812 you first saw it?
Yes.

It was the following Winter you saw it again, when it was so broken and defaced?
It was broken at first.

In the Year 1812 it was so defaced you could only read Part of it?
As in 1813; I cannot be positive as to the Month.

That was Ten or Twelve Months after you first saw it in July?
Yes.

(*Sir Harris Nicolas.*) You have stated that there was a Crack through the Stone, and that you think that Crack was through Part of the Letters; do you mean it to be understood that the Crack was through a particular Line of the Letters?
Through One Line.

And that there might be other Letters below it?
Yes.

(*By a Lord.*) Did you see any Letters below the Crack?
A Part of the Letters.

It ran through One Line?
Yes.

Did you look for this Stone in 1816?
No, I cannot say that I did; I was in the habit of attending Fairs, and going to Funerals of my Friends, and so on; I cannot say whether I looked for it.

The Witness was directed to withdraw.

Sir

Sir Harris Nicolas stated, That he would next call a Witness to prove that the Prayer Book referred to on the Minutes of the former Day had come out of the Possession of the Claimant.

Then Mr. GEORGE BOLTON was called in; and having been sworn, was examined as follows :

(*Sir Harris Nicolas.*) Are you a Solicitor ?
I am.

Were you employed for the present Mr. Tracy in the Claim to the Viscounty of Tracy ?
I was, in 1837.

Look at that Book ; was that Book ever in your Possession ? (*The Prayer Book being shown to the Witness.*)
It was.

From whom did you receive it ?
I received it from the present Claimant.

Of this Peerage ?
Yes.

When ?
When I presented it to the then Attorney General in June 1837, the Day it was produced before Sir John Campbell.

(*By a Lord.*) Had you ever seen it before the Claimant produced it to you ?
Not before the Claimant produced it that Evening.

Were you Agent for the Claimant ?
I was.

You had got up the Case for the Claimant, had not you ?
I had.

And yet you had never seen it before ?
No ; never before till that Evening.

(*Sir Harris Nicolas.*) You had had a Copy of the Inscription given you ?
Of course I had.

(*By a Lord.*) When did you first take up the Case ?
In March 1837.

You were employed by whom ?
By Mr. Tracy.

Not the present Claimant ?
Yes.

Did you know his Father ?
Oh dear no.

How long have you been his Solicitor ?
From 1837 to the Time of obtaining the Report.

Till the Attorney General's Report ?
Yes.

The Prayer Book referred to was delivered in, and the following Entry, referred to in Page 116 of the printed Minutes, was read from the Fly Leaf.

(59.)   " Married,

Mr. G. Bolton.

" Married, in Dublin, April 17ᵗʰ 1728, Willᵐ Son of the Honᵇⁱᵉ Robᵗ Tracy (late One of the English Judges) to Mary Daughter of Mᵣ James O'Brien, Merchant.

"James Tracy, their eldest Son, born January 27ᵗʰ 1729.

" Timothy Tracy, 2ⁿᵈ eldest, born June 26ᵗʰ 1730."

The Witness was directed to withdraw.

The Counsel being desired to state whether he had closed his Case, Sir Harris Nicolas stated, That he had been lately informed that the Claimant had received an Intimation of documentary Evidence, which would be of Importance to his Case.

The Counsel being asked the Nature of the documentary Evidence to which he referred, Sir Harris Nicolas stated, That he did not consider it prudent at the present Moment to state the Nature of it.

The Counsel were informed, That further Time could not be allowed, unless the Nature of the Evidence proposed to be adduced was stated, and it appeared to be material.

The Counsel were informed, That they must be prepared to sum up their Case for the Claimant on Friday Week.

The Counsel were directed to withdraw.

Proposed to adjourn this Committee to Friday the 9th of June next ;

Accordingly,

Adjourned to Friday the 9th of June next.

Die Veneris, 9° Junii 1843.

The Earl of SHAFTESBURY in the Chair.

THE Order of Adjournment was read.

The Minutes of the last Committee were read.

The Counsel and Parties were ordered to be called in :

And Mr. Solicitor General and Sir Harris Nicolas appeared as Counsel for the Petitioner ;

And Mr. Attorney General appeared on behalf of the Crown.

Mr. Attorney General requested that a Statement made in 1836 by Joseph Tracy, the Father of the present Claimant, who was then Claimant, and the Affidavit of William Carroll, both of which were laid before the then Attorney General in 1836, and annexed to his Reports on the Claim to Her Majesty, and now on the Table of the House, might be read, to show the Variance between the Facts at that Time deposed to with respect to the Prayer Book which had been given in and the Facts as now sworn by Mary Atkins.

The same were read, and are as follow :

I, Joseph Tracy formerly of Geashill in the King's County, Ireland, now of Chapel Place North, South Audley Street, London, whose Petition is before the House of Lords claiming to vote as Viscount Tracy for the Representative Peers of Ireland, and aged Seventy Years and upwards, do declare, that I was principally reared by my Uncle, the late Timothy Tracy of Coole in the County of Westmeath, Ireland; that on the 10th Day of August 1796 he gave me a Prayer Book, which he then told me, as well as on several other Occasions, that he received it from his Mother, Mary Tracy otherwise O'Brien, in or about the Year 1748, and that the Entry of her Marriage, and the Births of her eldest Son James and her Second Son Timothy Tracy, was written in the First Page of said Prayer Book by her Husband William Tracy, who was the youngest of the Three Sons of the Honorable Robert Tracy, an English Judge, and who resided at Coscomb in the County of Gloucester, by his Wife, formerly Miss Dowdswill, and that the Book formerly belonged to her Father James O'Brien ; and also that the Writing in Pages 86 and 89, dated 10th Day of August 1796, and signed Timothy Tracy, was written by my said Uncle in my Presence, at which Time he gave it to me ; and that my said

No. 89.

(59.)　　　　　　　　　3 C

said Uncle Timothy Tracy, on the Death of Henry the Eighth Viscount, in 1797, commenced Proceedings for the Recovery of the Title and Estates for me ; that he went about the same Period to Gloucestershire for the Purpose of obtaining Information relating to my Claim, and on his Return he told me that the Heirs Male of Robert the Judge's eldest Son became extinct, and that Richard the Judge's Second Son died young and unmarried, shortly after my Uncle Timothy died, and I was obliged to discontinue the Proceedings he commenced for Want of Means.

In 1798 I married the Daughter of Mr. Philip Tracy of Castlebrack in the Queen's County, by whom I have a Family of Four Sons and Two Daughters. In the Year 1815 I gave the aforesaid Prayer Book to my eldest Son James by my aforesaid Marriage on his going to reside in Dublin, and which Prayer Book he has this Day produced to me, which I solemnly declare, in the Presence of Martin Grady and Mrs. Harriet Brown, and on which Book they have put their Initials, to be the identical Prayer Book given to me by my Uncle, Timothy Tracy.

Dated the 16th Day of February 1836 six.

Witness,   JOSEPH TRACY.
MARTIN GRADY,
HARRIETT BROWN.

No. 90.

In the Matter of the Petition of James Tracy, Esquire, claiming the Dignity and Honor of Baron and Viscount Tracy of Rathcoole in the Kingdom of Ireland.

William Carroll of the Town of Tullamore in the King's County in Ireland, Tailor, but at present residing in 18, King Street, near Golden Square in the County of Middlesex in England, being weak of Body but of sound Mind and Memory, maketh Oath and saith, that he will be Seventy-two Years of Age the Eighth Day of August next ensuing ; that the longest Time back Deponent can recollect he was living in the Townland of Bonatern, Parish of Killoughy, Barony of Ballyboy, in the King's County in Ireland. Deponent saith, that his Father and Mother were living there ; that Ann Carroll's, Deponent's Mother's, Maiden Name was Ann Tracy ; that he, Deponent, was at that Time Six or Seven Years of Age, and had a Sister from Ten to Twelve Years of Age. Deponent further saith, that his Father held a Take of Land under Mr. Briscoe of Ross in the Barony of Ballycowen ; that the said Take of Land did not consist of more than Six or Seven Acres, with a House ; that Deponent's Father's People were living convenient, and had Takes of Land under Mr. Joseph Telford, who was their Landlord ; that Deponent's Mother, Ann Carroll formerly Ann Tracy, was born in the Parish of Lismally in the King's County ; that Deponent well recollects his Uncle James Tracy, and his Uncle Timothy Tracy, the Brothers of his Mother, Ann Carroll ; that Deponent's Grandfather, William Tracy, and Mary Tracy, Grandmother, on his Mother's Side, had been dead for several Years ; that Deponent's Grandfather, William Tracy, died first. Deponent saith, that at this Time he does not recollect to know his Uncle Timothy, who was at that Period abroad, engaged in the German War, but Deponent

ponent distinctly recollects, and says, that when he, Deponent, was about Twelve or Fourteen Years of Age his Uncle Timothy came home, accompanied by his Wife, an English Woman, and that Deponent's said Uncle Timothy gave his, Deponent's, Mother, Ann Carroll, Money to pay her Rent; and that Deponent's said Uncle Timothy afterwards gave Deponent's Mother Money twice a Year, namely, at Christmas and Easter, for the like Purpose; and this Deponent further saith, that his said Uncle Timothy was afterwards a Clerk in the General Post Office in the City of Dublin; that Deponent's Uncle Timothy after that Time became Agent to Lord Boyne, who had an Estate in the Parish of Lanelly. Deponent further saith, that his said Uncle Timothy was employed for many Years by Lord Portarlington, but Deponent's Uncle Timothy, not considering his Salary sufficient, entered into the Service of Mr. Smyth of the County of Westmeath; that the said Mr. Smyth was a Member of Parliament, and gave Deponent's Uncle Timothy a Freehold in the County of Westmeath, in a Townland called Coole, where Deponent's said Uncle settled and died. And this Deponent further saith, that his said Uncle Timothy was in the habit of writing to Deponent's Mother as often as Four Times a Year, in the Month of November, about the Months of March or May, and at Christmas and Easter; these Letters contained Money for the Purpose of paying Deponent's Mother's Rent, which was but trifling, about Fifty Shillings per Year, as Deponent's Mother held but about Two Acres and a Half; saith, his Mother used to give him, Deponent, his Uncle Timothy's Letters, and that he used to answer them; that said Letters came sometimes by Post and sometimes by Hand. Deponent saith, his Mother, Ann Carroll formerly Ann Tracy, died in the Year One thousand seven hundred and ninety-seven or One thousand seven hundred and ninety-eight, but in which Year Deponent does not recollect. Deponent was in Dublin at the Time, and did not attend his Mother's Funeral. Deponent further saith, that his Uncle Timothy died about the Year One thousand seven hundred and ninety-nine, or soon after the Death of Deponent's Mother. Deponent's said Uncle Timothy was buried at Coole, County Westmeath. Deponent saith, that when his said Uncle Timothy returned from the Wars, he came to the Country to see his Friends, and Deponent well recollects him on that Occasion; and again, when he, Timothy, was in Lord Portarlington's Service, he, Timothy, sent for Deponent and Deponent's Mother, and they went together to the House at the Spire Hill at Portarlington, and was also in Westmeath at his House there, but a good while before he died. Deponent saith, that when he was about Six or Seven Years of Age he recollects his Uncle James, the elder Brother of his Uncle Timothy, who was living in Gurteen in the Barony of Geashill in the King's County; that he had a small Take of Ground on Lord Digby's Estate, and that he used to come continually to see his Sister Ann, this Deponent's Mother. Deponent's Uncle James was at that Time married, and his Wife used to come with him to see Deponent's Mother; they had One Child about Deponent's own Age at that Time; this Child was called Joseph Tracy, and was the only Child at that Time of Deponent's Uncle James. James Wife's Maiden Name was Carrier; don't know what Part of the Country she came from, or any of her People. Deponent recollects his Uncle James and his Sister, Deponent's Mother, used to have frequent Communications about the Family; they used always, when

they

they met, to be talking about their Family; they used to say that Judge Tracy in England had Three Sons, Robert, Richard, and William, and that William was the youngest Son; that Mr. O'Brien, a Merchant in Dublin, came to London on mercantile Business, and that his Daughter was with him, and that William Tracy made his Acquaintance in London with her, and that some Time after they corresponded, and that William came over to Dublin, and was married to her; Mary O'Brien was her Maiden Name; they settled in Dublin; and they said Mr. O'Brien took him in Dublin as a Partner, they failed in Business, and that William Tracy and his Wife, with his Two Sons, went to the Country, to the Parish of Lanelly, in or about the Year One thousand seven hundred and thirty-one, and settled upon Lord Boyne's Estate, where Ann, Deponent's Mother, was born. Deponent does not know whether Mr. O'Brien was dead or alive at this Time; they did not talk any thing about him; saith, that he heard them also say that the said William Tracy (Father of Deponent's Mother) died there, and was buried at Castlebrack in the Queen's County, leaving his Widow, Mary, and Three Children. Deponent heard them also say that their Mother was buried at Castlebrack in the Queen's County with their Father; and heard them say, that at the Time William Tracy died his Sons James and Timothy were young, and that Mary Tracy otherwise O'Brien, their Mother, lived until in or about the Year One thousand seven hundred and fifty. Deponent heard them say, that old Ralph Briscoe, after Lord Boyne's Death at Summer Hill in Dublin, purchased his Estate and turned them out; (this was after the Death of William Tracy, but long before the Death of Mary his Wife;) that old Lord Boyne had told William Tracy to go to Dublin to get a Lease for ever of Eighty Acres of Land, but he neglected it. Deponent heard that Mary, William's Widow, and her Three Children went to a Townland called Ross, convenient to Lanelly; this was after they were turned out by Ralph Briscoe; she took some Ground there under one of the Briscoe Family, where she continued as long as she lived; that they had no Lease of the Ground in Ross, and after Mary Tracy's Death it was given up. Deponent recollects perfectly well that they said that their Father, Deponent's Grandfather, William Tracy, died in One thousand seven hundred and thirty-four. Deponent saith, that when he, Deponent, was about Fourteen Years of Age, he was bound Apprentice to one William Rooney, a Tailor, in Back Lane, Dublin; Deponent's Uncle John Carroll and his Mother bound him; during the Time Deponent was an Apprentice he went occasionally to the Country to see his Mother, and during the Time Deponent was in Dublin his Uncle Timothy had left the Post Office, and Deponent thinks he then went to do Business for Lord Boyne. When Deponent went to his Mother he saw his Uncle James there, and afterwards saw his Uncle Timothy at the Brazen Head, Bridge Street, Dublin, at one Mitchell's. The Way Deponent came to see his Uncle there was this: his Master worked for the Mitchells; Deponent called there one Day with some Work, and in Conversation heard from the Waiter that Mr. Tracy was there, and he thought he was his Uncle, and sent his Name up; his Uncle sent for him, Deponent, and gave him some Money. Deponent saith, that this was the only Time during his Apprenticeship he saw his Uncle in Dublin, at which Time he had been Three or Four Years an Apprentice at the Business. And this Deponent further saith, that

it

It is about Fifty Years since he got out of his Apprenticeship; he did Business afterwards for his Master, for several Years after. Deponent saith, that he recollects his Uncle James well, and his living in Gurteen; he recollects his Death about One thousand seven hundred and ninety-four, and that he was buried at Castlebrack in the Queen's County; he recollects his Children; that at his Death he left Joseph, his eldest Son, and Two other Sons, Andrew and Patrick, and One Daughter. Deponent further saith, that when he, Deponent, occasionally went down to see his Mother he often met his Cousin, the said Joseph Tracy, the Son of James Tracy, and renewed their Acquaintance, and became very intimate; after this Time said Joseph Tracy married, and went to live in Geashill, and Deponent was often at his House at Geashill. Deponent saw, some Years after, James Tracy there, and other Children; James Tracy was then a young Boy; saw Mrs. Tracy, the Wife of the said Joseph; they had some Land in Geashill, but what Quantity Deponent does not know. Deponent saith, that he, Deponent, went to see Timothy Tracy at his Place in Coole, near Castle Pollard, in the early Part of the Year One thousand seven hundred and ninety-six; he, Timothy Tracy, had been so kind to Deponent's Mother, Deponent went to see him; Deponent never sought any Compliment for himself, did not trouble him; he merely considered him as an Uncle; Deponent stayed a Couple of Days with him, Timothy Tracy; during the Two Days Deponent was with his Uncle, had Talk with him about the Family; he spoke to Deponent first; he said, as soon as he was able, he would come to London to look after the Property of the Judge Tracy for his Nephew, Joseph; he, Deponent's Uncle, was then very old and infirm; he told Deponent that Judge Tracy had Three Sons, Robert, Richard, and William, and that William, his Father, was the youngest Son; that Richard died on his Way to the East Indies, young and unmarried, that Judge Tracy was the Second Son of Lord Tracy, that the Judge's Father was married twice, and that the Third Lord was the Son by the First Marriage, and the Judge was by the Second. Deponent saw a Prayer Book at his Uncle Timothy's House; it was on a Desk; recollects looking at the Prayer Book, and that the old Man, Timothy Tracy, saw him looking at it, and said to him, Deponent, that it was his, Timothy Tracy's, Mother's Gift; that it was his Father's Prayer Book and hers, and that she told him to take care of it, and to keep it in Memory of his Father and her; that it contained the Entry of her Marriage to William Tracy, and the Births of her Two Sons, James and said Timothy. Deponent looked at the Prayer Book, and read distinctly the Entry of William Tracy's Marriage and the Births of his Two Sons in the First Page. Said Timothy also told Deponent that his Mother, Mary Tracy otherwise O'Brien, told him that the Entry that was written in the First Page of said Prayer Book was in the Handwriting of her said Husband, William Tracy. This was the first Time ever he, Deponent, saw the Prayer Book, but he, Deponent, saw it after with Joseph Tracy, the Son of James Tracy, and knew it when he saw it. He, Joseph Tracy, told him that he received it from his Uncle in August One thousand seven hundred and ninety-six. Deponent saw his Uncle's Writing in Pages Thirty-six and Thirty-nine of said Book, and signed Timothy Tracy, and dated August Tenth, which is in his Handwriting. Deponent saith, that in One thousand seven hundred and ninety-eight the Rebellion in Ireland broke out, and there were great Troubles, and Deponent thought it safe to leave Dublin; and in that Year he left Dublin, and went to his Uncle Timothy, to Coole, where he staid some Time, and from him went to Tullamore, where he settled, and set up in Business. Saith, that at his Time (in One thousand seven hundred and ninety-eight) his Uncle, who was an old and infirm Man, conversed with Deponent. He had given the Prayer Book to his Nephew, Joseph Tracy, which Book Deponent has seen with said Joseph on many Occasions in Geashill. Deponent recollects having heard of the Death of Timothy in One thousand seven hundred and ninety-nine, and that Joseph Tracy was left his Heir. Deponent settled in Tullamore in or about the Year One thousand seven hundred and ninety-nine, and remained there till he came over to London this present Year. Deponent further saith, that the Prayer Book now produced is the identical Book which he saw with his Uncle Timothy Tracy in One thousand seven hundred and ninety-six, and afterwards with the late Joseph Tracy in Geashill, and on last October with James Tracy, his eldest Son, at Tullamore, which he identified in the Presence of Mr. James Ferrall of London. Deponent saith, he knows that his Uncle Timothy was all his Life a Protestant, and heard that his Father was a Protestant also, but knew that James, his, Timothy's, Brother, who was a simple Man, was a Catholic,—he went with his Wife.

(Signed)   WILLIAM CARROLL.

Sworn by the above-named William Carroll, having been first duly read by him, this 4th Day of July 1836, at No. 18, King Street, Golden Square, Westminster.

W. WINGFIELD.

The Book marked A., produced and shown to him at the Time of his Examination, is the Book referred to in this Affidavit.

W. WINGFIELD.

The following Entries were read from the said Prayer Book :

(*On the Title.*)

" James O'Brien,
" Sept* 1**, 1730."

(*On the Backs of Two Copper Plates, at Page* 39.)

" This Book belonged to my Grandfather, James O'Brien, and afterwards to my Father, William Tracy, who was an Englishman. It contains the Entry of his Marriage, and the Births of my elder Brother, James, and my own. I now give it to my Nephew, Joseph Tracy of Geashill.

" Coole, Aug* 10, 1796,
" TIMOTHY TRACY."

Mr.

Mr. Solicitor General was heard to sum up the Evidence in support of the Claimant's Case.

Mr. Attorney General was heard on behalf of the Crown.

Proposed to resolve, That the Claimant hath not made out his Claim to the Title, Honor, and Dignity of Viscount Tracy of Rathcoole in the Kingdom of Ireland.

On the Question being put ;

It was resolved in the Affirmative.

Ordered, That the Chairman do report the said Resolution to the House.

Die Lunæ, 8° Maii 1843.

The Earl of SHAFTESBURY in the Chair.

THE Order of Adjournment was read.

The Minutes of the last Committee were read.

The Counsel and Parties were ordered to be called in.

Mr. Solicitor General and Deposition appeared as Counsel for the Claimant.

Mr. Kelly and Sir Harris Nicolas appeared as Counsel for Sir Hugh Hume Campbell of Marchmont, Baronet, in opposition to the Claim of Francis Home, Esquire.

Mr. Attorney General appeared on behalf of the Crown.

Mr. Pattison, having stated that he did not desire at present to adduce further Evidence in support of the Claim, was directed to sum up the same.

Mr. Pattison stated, That he had understood that the Committee was appointed for the Purpose of receiving the Evidence to be tendered on behalf of Sir Hugh Hume Campbell, and in consequence of this had not prepared himself to sum up.

The Counsel were informed, That their Lordships felt that they must adhere to the ordinary Practice of hearing the Case for the Claimant summed up before the Case of a counter Claimant, or a Party opposing the Claim, was heard; and that the Day having been appointed he must avail himself of the Privilege, or forego it.

Mr. Pattison was heard to sum up the early Part of the Evidence.

Mr. Kelly was directed to submit to the House any Observations he had to offer in opposition to the Claim.

Mr. Kelly, having commenced his Opening of the Case of Sir Hugh Hume Campbell opposing the Claim of Francis Home, Esquire, and having stated that a great Variety of Objections presented themselves on the Proof adduced by the Claimant, was directed to address himself to the Case in Sections, and was heard to observe upon the Pedigree of the Homes of Wedderburn, set out in Page 59. of the Case of Sir Hugh Hume Campbell, and to open the Evidence he proposed to adduce in relation to the same.

(103.)   5 E   Then

[*from* (33.) *of* 1842.]

Mr. W. Fraser.

Then Mr. WILLIAM FRASER was called in ; and having been sworn, was examined as follows :

(*Sir Harris Nicolas.*) What do you produce ?
I produce a Letter from Mr. Ninian Home of Billy to the Lady Wedderburn.

From whence do you produce it ?
From the Charter Chest of Billy.

What is the Date of it ?
The 9th of December 1720.

The same was read as follows :

No. 12.

Madam,   Edinb^r 9th Decemb^r 1720.
I am truly grieved for George unaccountable carriage for it seems he will have his humour wit zards however he shall not find his interest in behaving so er you are mistress of your contract of marriage and infeftmen better and I do not incline you should delay calling for ỹm and I presume you should insist upon his doing something immediately towards repairing the house if he intend reallie to do what he wryts for if it be delayed the next summer will go over also And y'for it will not be amiss you put him to declaré himself as you did with respect to the lads and if he refuses we must do the best we can The reason why I am for putting him to it is that should I proceed to do anything without him he will pretend his offer and friendship was slighted and I desire to shun giving him that pretext and you may wryt that if he be disposed in earnest to do you y^t kindness its fit he should do it immediately and if not beg of him to declare himself y^t you may think of some oy^r way and I do assure you the tyme is far gone already for if it be not set about presently it will not be got finishd this summer.
The state of my health is much as befor The cough continues still I give your lãps hearty thanks for your kindness and must own y^t I am not so easie in my own mind any wher from my own house as in yours Tell ffrankie I am glad to hear his ñïr is pleased with him for so David wryts and assure him I shall be mindful of his lances and anything els he needs Thess should have comed out with the carier if I had not been affraid of his loosing y^m because so small a thing your good frind and neighbour at a botle of wine last week in Steels as a gentleman in the company told me next day said it was a verry strange thing y^t the comñrs for ought he heard had given no directions about Wedderburn's estate for his part he did not envy any favour was shown to any person only he could not comprehend how y^r came not to appeal the lords sentence in the case of Whitfeild and not medle w^t Wedderburn tho' appeald qrby he pointed as if I had a way of manadging ỹm y^t none els had.

I am
Madam
Yo^r lãps most humble servant
NIN : HOME.

To
The Lady Wedderburn
att Wedderburn
This.

Is

Is that before you an examined Copy ?
It is.

The same was delivered in.

Cross-examined by Mr. Solicitor General.

Did you receive that at Billy ?
No ; I got it from Mr. David Milne, Advocate, who is the Judicial Factor on the Estate of Billy.

Where did he deliver it to you?
In his House, No. 10, York Place, Edinburgh.

The Counsel being asked for what Purpose this had been put in, Sir Harris Nicolas stated, That it was to prove that George Home went to America.

Mr. Solicitor General submitted, That this was not Evidence, not having been brought by the Witness from the Charter Chest, or delivered to him at the Place of Deposit.

(*Sir Harris Nicolas.*) When Mr. David Milne gave this to you, had he the Box before him ?
He had the Charter Chest before him at the Time. He is the Judicial Factor on the Estate, under the Authority of the Court of Session.

He gave it to you from the Charter Chest ?
Yes ; and marked his Initials upon it at the Time.

The Counsel being asked how this applied, Mr. Kelly stated, That it was in support of his Case ; that George Home had quarrelled with his Family, and that that, and not his Decease, was the Reason for his having been excluded from the Settlement made in 1733 ; and that he was instructed to prove, that George Home had gone to America, and that Children of his were living in America at a late Date.

(*Sir Harris Nicolas to the Witness.*) What do you next produce ?
I produce a Letter from George Home, dated Rappahannock River, in Virginia, the 20th of June 1723, addressed to Mr. Ninian Home of Billy, at his Lodgings forgainst the Magdalen Chapel in the Cowgate, Edinburgh.

(*By a Lord.*) Is there any thing that identifies this Letter ?
There is an Endorsement on the Back in the Handwriting of the late George Home of Paxton : " Letters from George Home, Second Son of George Home of Wedderburn, from Virginia, in June 1723 ; mentions his Uncle Francis's Death."

(*Mr. Solicitor General.*) You do not state that from your own Knowledge, that it is the Handwriting of George Home of Paxton ?
I am well acquainted with his Character of Handwriting from other Letters I have seen, and I have not a Doubt that this is in his Handwriting.

When did he die ?
He died in or about 1820.

You mean to say that he wrote this previous to his Death in 1820, indicating the Person by whom this was written in 1723 ?
Yes.

(103.)   Mr. Solicitor

Mr. Solicitor General submitted, That this was not Evidence, there being no Evidence of Handwriting, nor any thing to identify it with the George Home supposed to be the Author, and the Endorsement having been made by a Person who had died so late as 1820, and that the Contents of the Letter could not be referred to to make it Evidence.

The Counsel were informed, That, it appearing to have been written by a George Home at so very remote a Date, and being found in the Possession of a Member of the Family, the Contents of the Letter might be referred to to prove the Identity of the Writer.

The same was read as follows :

No. 13.

Sr,   Rappahannock River, June 20, 1723.

We had no sooner landed in this country but I was takne immediatly wth all ye most common distampers y^t attend it but ye most violent of all was a severe flux of wch my unkle died being the governour's factor att a place called Germawna in the upper parts of ye colony whom he berried their and put pails about his berrial place wch is not very common in y^s country I went & saw it as soon as I was able to ride Y^t distemper brought me so low in a very short time y^t I was scarse able to walk however I was oblidged to tend ye store for all my being so ill till we had done purchasing tobaco for ye ship's loadning w^h took me about six weeks when I was so much out of ordre y^t I was oblidged to go to Williamsburg by water where I met wth Dr Brown who I suppose gave you an account last year of my condition He declared to my selfe after he had almost cured me of ye flux y^t he did not expect I should have lived I waited on ye governour ye day after I went to town & delivred y^m Spotswood's letter He was seemingly very kind to me & talked to me very friendly but he told me it was out of his power to do any thing for me he being put out of his place and he had so many wth y^m that he was oblidged to put away some of y^m whom he could best spare then q^t to do I could not tell however I advised wth Dr Brown who was of ye oppinion I should return home as soon as I could What little money I had I was oblidged to spend it at W^{m}sBurg the time I was their sick wch was about five weeks indeed ye D^r took nothing for my druggs All that comes to this country have ordinerly sickness at first wch they call a seasoning of wch I shall assure you I had a most severe one when I went to town I got but very little for my store keeping for all y^t went to pay my passage for when ever my cosen John Watson at Port Glasgow told the merchants there q^t you had writtne to him was the occasion of my going away so hastely they would not allow me to go but to come home again and they sent to Whithaven (because we were driven in their by stress of wather) to desire our captain to send me home but he proved so much my friend when he saw me so fond of going (for he was always very kind to me) that he got me into an other ship and I was to keep ye store for my passage of wch I was very glad & accepted of it so y^t you may know by y^t I could be but very poor in purse & I did not know q^t hand to turn my selfe to for I could get no bussiness for unless one have very good recommendation there is no sort of bussiness to be got in y^s Indian country wherefore I would have traveled farer where I was informed I would have been better if I could have got any money but this is ye worst place for y^t I could have pitched upon for there is so little in ye country y^t I belive a great many of y^m does not

not know it if they saw it only   They make a parcill of tobaco wch they make to buy themselves cloaths and makes it to go from one to another innstied of money and that is all they seek after here so y^t if nothing fall out better for me next year if it be possable for me to get a little money & cloaths together I design for farrer abroad either to Jamaica or ye West Indies which ever of them I can get ye best accounts of   I thought to have gone to New York little after I came here when I found so little incouragement here wch is not far from y^s place but I could never be worth so much as to carry me it being very dear travling y^t way   I hear my brother Pattrick is there surgion of ye Grayhound man of warr lying on y^t station.

Mr Petter Chambers has been very kind to me in y^s place in assisting me wth severall necessaries which I could not want & which it had been very hard for me to get unless he had assisted me such as shoos & stokings for ever since I came into y^s country I have never gained any thing for my selfe unless it be sometimes a small parcill of tobaco wch I get for writting   Every thing of cloathing is most unreasonably dear here it being three times as dear as in Scotland so y^t y^t is ye greats^t strait I am att.

I have not my halth very well in y^s country as yet but however I have it much better then I had it last year only I am now and then trobled wth ye fever & ague wch is a very violent distemper here   This place is only good for doctors & ministers who have very good encouragem^t here.

, I must own I think it the hight of impudence for me to write to you wch was the occasion of my not writting last year but having incrotched so far on your good nature formerly and still have found you to be my very well wisher I hope you will excoose me for tho' at that time I did not adhere to your good advice yet now I see my folly and I wish to God I had given more ear to you and less to some others   It had been better for me and many a time now it makes me melencholy to think of my follies and despising my best of friends advice which you have always been wherefore dear s^r let this be my excuse.

I designed to have writtne to my mother but after I bethought with my selfe how much I had disoblidged and how far I had been out of the way to her who I may now say (if I had but considred it right at that time) was the best of mothers to me for which I pray God and she may both forgive me which as long as I am on this side of time I am oblidged to pray for and it makes me that I shall never forget the verse which I remember I learned long agoe which was

"O mihi præteritos referat si Jupiter annos."

Neither can I have the impudence to send my duty to her unless you will be pleased to give it and to interceed for me but you have interceeded there for me so oftne that I can scarse desire it and if I were to serve you on my knees while I lived it would scarce be a recompence for all such favoors which I have received from you   I have yet another favoor to ask of you which is that you will be pleased to let me hear from you how you and all friends are   I stay in the upper part of Essex county on Rappahannock river   If you please to write let it be directed to Mr. Chamberses care who will forward it to me He lives on the same river but farrer down   I desire you will be pleased

(103.)   5 F   to

Mr. W. Fraser.

to give my duty to all your family to my grandmother my aunt to
Mrs Home and all my brothers And I am and allways shall think
my selfe

* A Word torn
away after " to."

                                                    D^r sir
                                            your most humble and
Virginea June 20 1723.   obliged servant to *
                                                          G. HOME.

To Mr Ninian Home of Billie att his
  loodging forgainst the Magdalen
  chaple in the Cougate
                    Edinburgh.

  Is that you produce an examined Copy ?
  It is.

                The same was delivered in.

  (*Sir Harris Nicolas to the Witness.*)   Do you produce another Letter
of George Home ?
  I do.
  What is the Date of it ?
  The 20th of June 1723.
  To whom is it addressed ?
  To Mr. James Home.
  Did you receive this from the same Repository ?
  Yes ; it was put up with the other. This appears to have been
written to the Son of the Person to whom the other was addressed.

                The same was read as follows : `

No. 14.   Dear Jamie   Virginea Rappahannock River June 20, 1723.
  I would have writtne to you last year but I always delay'd it till
I saw if I could get in to any bussiness wch made me delay it so long
till all ye shiping were gone & besides y^t having so very highly disoblidged your father who I find now to have been my best of friends
I could not write to any unless to him which I could not have y^e
confidence to do tho I have takne it upon me ye year for I cannot let
my selfe think but he is still my very well wisher & if I had takne
more of his advice then I did it had been more to my advantage then
I can mention I find there is nothing to be got here without very
good recommendation Tho mine was good yet it did me no manner of
service because just as I came in to ye country ye go: lost his place &
another came in not long after but I thank God I make a shift to live
& y^t is all I cannot get a pint of good topany bere to drink your
halths for all our drink here is water & sometimes rum but y^t is very
dear & very little mony to buy it Cloaths and linnin are very dear
here in ye Indian country yea I truly think y^m three times as dear as
at home tobaco is all ye commodity here I have had but very ordinary
halth in ye country as yet especially last summer and fall but I begin
to take a little better with ye place wch I suppose you will hear from
your father for I have given him a full accompt of it I belive indeed
I should have died if Dr Brown had not stood my friend att Williamsburg from which place I am now at a great distance above an hundred
miles I hope I shall hear from you with the first shiping and direct
for me to ye care of Mr Petter Chambers on Rapahannock River
                                                          Virginea

Virginea I desire you will give my service to my friend Hendry Scrimsiour and Dickson Mrs Helen & May Rentons and all other friends and I am

Dr Jamie
Your most humble
and oblidged servant
G. HOME.

I desire you may not forget to give my service to Mr George Home and tell him I shall be very glad to hear from him.

To Mr James Home sone to
    Mr Ninian Home of Billy att
        Edinbrough.

Is that you produce an examined Copy ?
It is.

The same was delivered in.

The Counsel being asked who was the George Home referred to in this Letter, Mr. Kelly stated, That he was informed that Ninian Home had a Son named George; that he was not at present in a Situation to prove that Fact, but that Inquiry should be made against a future Day.

Mr. Kelly prayed, That he might have an Opportunity of cross-examining Mr. George Home, who had been examined in a former Stage of this Proceeding, but had not undergone Cross-examination.

Mr. Solicitor General stated, That Mr. George Home was in attendance, and ready to answer any Questions which might be proposed.

(*Sir Harris Nicolas to Mr. Fraser.*) Do you produce certain other Letters ?
I do; I produce a Letter from Mr. Francis Home, Advocate, to the Reverend Ninian Home, Minister of the Gospel at Sprouston, dated the 15th of April 1717.

From whence do you produce that ?
From the same Repository.

The Counsel were informed, That Mr. George Home being in attendance, it might be more convenient to suspend the Production of these Letters, and to proceed with the Cross-examination of Mr. Home.

Then GEORGE HOME Esquire was called in; and having been sworn, was cross-examined as follows:

(*Mr. Kelly.*) You have been examined as a Witness in this Case ?
I have.

You are the Brother of the Claimant ?
I am the only Brother now alive.

In the Event of your Brother dying without Issue, supposing this Claim established, would you be the next in Succession to the Earldom, Honours, and Dignities ?
Yes.

(103.)

Has

George Home, Esq. Has your Brother any Issue?
He never had any Issue; he was married, but his Wife is dead.
How old is he?
He is in his Fifty-seventh Year.

Is his Wife still alive?
She died Two Years ago.

You stated, in your Evidence, that you were acquainted with the late George Home of Paxton and Wedderburn, and you then stated a Conversation you had with him?
Yes.

What Relation was he to you?
Mr. George Home of Paxton and my Father were Second Cousins,— Cousins once removed, as near as I can trace it. Mr. George Home was the Son of Isabel Home, the Second Daughter of George Home of Wedderburn, I think the Tenth in the Pedigree; my Father was the Grandson of Francis Home, the Brother of George Home of Wedderburn, the Tenth in the Pedigree.

That Conversation you say took place in 1809?
Yes.

Where?
At Wedderburn House.

Where he lived?
Yes, one of his Residences.

How long did you stay at Wedderburn House upon that Occasion?
I cannot recollect whether it was Two Days, or Three, or One. I think it must have been either Two or Three Days. I was going to Sea, and was sent out on a Visit to my Relations from Edinburgh.

Had you become acquainted with this Gentleman before that?
I had seen him, I think. I cannot be positively sure whether I had seen him before or not. I had seen his Aunt, Miss Jane Home, with whom he lived.

I presume you had very little Acquaintance with him till that Time?
No Person of Thirteen can have a very extensive Acquaintance with a Man of Seventy-five; but I had seen Letters of my Father, exchanged with him.

You rather think that you had seen him before?
I may; but I cannot be sure.

You stayed there Two or Three Days?
Yes.

Did you ever see him again?
Oh yes. When I was paid off from the Navy, in 1815, I saw him at Paxton House, another of his Residences; and at that Time I had other Conversations with him upon the Subject.

Did you at that Time know that your Father had made a Claim to these Dignities?
Perfectly; from my Infancy I knew that.

Do you know how he began the Conversation in which he stated that Alexander had gone abroad?
The Conversation was not literally with me; it was with his Aunt Miss Jane Home, the Daughter of Ninian Home, I being present whilst
the

the Conversation about the Family of Home occurred. Mr. Home had had the Management of the Claim, being a Writer to the Signet, and latterly a Clerk of Session. *George Home, Esq.*

How old were you at that Time?
I was then Thirteen.

Your Relation, Mr. George Home of Paxton, was quite aware that this Claim had been made?
He was not only aware of it, but he had borne most of the Expenses of the Researches; many of them at least.

He knew, I presume, that it was necessary to show that this Alexander had died without Issue?
He knew, of course, that it was necessary to extinguish every one of them.

In answer to the Question "Are you aware whether that he had any Means of Information from the West Indies?" that is, whether you were aware that Mr. Home of Paxton had any Information from the West Indies, your Answer is, "His Brother, Mr. Ninian Home, was Governor of the Island of Grenada; there was a continual Correspondence between him and his Brother."
Yes.

Will you explain to their Lordships how it is that the Circumstance of Mr. Ninian Home being Governor of the Island of Grenada, and this continual Correspondence between him and his Brother, would give any Information to Mr. Home of Paxton about the Fate of Mr. George Home of Wedderburn?
I did not state that that gave him any Information; I merely stated the Fact which I knew, that Mr. George Home had a continual Correspondence with his Brother; that his Brother acquired large Property in Grenada; that Mr. George Home succeeded to his Brother's Property. He was murdered by the Africans in an Insurrection there.

Do you not know that this Brother, the Governor of the Island of Grenada, only became Governor in 1793?
I am not aware of the Time he became Governor at all.

Do you know whether he was Governor before that?
I only know it as it is put in Sir Hugh Campbell's Case. I know he went out, and was a little while in Grenada, and then came over and purchased Property, and built Paxton House, and then he returned. I believe the Family Interest got him the Governorship, so that he was many Years there.

Do you know of his having been Governor of Grenada at any Time before the Year 1793?
No, I do not; but I think he acquired Lands in the Island many Years before that; in fact the Family hold them yet.

(*By a Lord.*) In what Island?
His Lands lie all in St. Vincent and Grenada. The Representative of the Family came over only the other Day, who had been living on the Estate.

(*Mr. Kelly.*) When was it, according to the best of your Knowledge, that he first went to the West Indies at all?
I have a distinct Recollection of my Father's Statement of his being murdered; I also remember his further mentioning this: it was said

(103.)   5 G   that

George Home, Esq. that the late Mr. George Home never smiled after his Brother's Death, so deeply was he affected by it.

You say he must have been in the West Indies before he was Governor?

Certainly, as a Planter; and I believe he married a Creole Lady.

Can you state how many Years he had been out?

I cannot say; perhaps Twenty Years. I think he was about Forty when he came home; and that he purchased the Property, and built Paxton House.

When was that?

I cannot tell; I have spoken from my Father's Statements and the Statements of the Family.

Can you give me any Indication of his Age?

The late George Home was older than my Father; his Brother must have been born about the Year 1740; I should conceive, probably, Ninian Home was much about his Age.

Did he live in Scotland?

In Berwickshire, with his Father, Alexander Home of Jardinefield.

You say that this Statement was made to the Lady, his Aunt?

It was as much to her as to me; I think she made a Remark, (she was a very plain old Scotch Lady,) whether her Great Uncle Alexander was any Obstruction in the Way? And he said, Oh no, he was never married, and he died in the West Indies many many Years ago.

Re-examined by Mr. Solicitor General.

Do you know the Family of the Homes of Paddockmyre?

I do.

When you first recollect the Family, who was residing there?

My Grandmother, who was the Wife of my Grandfather.

What was the Name of your Grandfather?

John Home or Hume.

Do you recollect your Grandmother?

I have a sort of dreamy Recollection of once being in the House; but as she died in 1799, and I was born in 1796, its only like a Dream; I cannot speak to it; I have a faint Recollectio of her Face, but that is all.

You recollect your own Father and Mother?

Yes; I was Twenty-six when my Father died.

Did your Father and Mother live together as Man and Wife?

Always, from the Day of their Marriage, in 1783 or 1784, to the Day of my Father's Death.

(*By a Lord.*) Were there other Children besides you?

Yes; I had Four Brothers and Two Sisters.

(*Mr. Solicitor General.*) Who told you the Date of their Marriage?

It stands in the Parish Books of Coldinghame, and I have heard them refer to it.

They always lived together as Man and Wife?

Yes; at Buskin Burn in Berwickshire, a Property of their own.

(*By*

(*By a Lord.*) You never heard a Doubt expressed as to whether *George Home, Esq.* they were married?

Not a Shadow of a Doubt. My Mother enjoyed the Pension of a Captain's Widow, as my Father's Widow, Ten Years after his Death. They were twice married; first by the Church of England, and afterwards by the Church of Scotland.

(*By a Lord.*) Before any of the Children were born?

Before any of the Children were born, for any thing I know to the contrary; though I would not speak to the Family's Shame if it was after; they were all legitimate; but I have no Reason to believe that to have been the Case.

The Witness was directed to withdraw.

The Counsel and Parties were directed to withdraw.

Proposed to adjourn this Committee *sine Die;*

Accordingly,
Adjourned *sine Die.*

1.

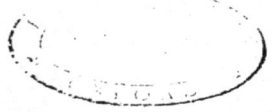

MINUTES OF EVIDENCE

GIVEN BEFORE

THE COMMITTEE OF PRIVILEGES

TO WHOM

THE PETITION OF JAMES TRACY, ESQUIRE,

CLAIMING, AS OF RIGHT,

To be VISCOUNT and BARON TRACY
OF RATHCOOLE,

TOGETHER WITH

HER MAJESTY'S REFERENCE THEREOF TO THIS HOUSE,

WAS REFERRED.

Ordered to be printed 23d March 1847.

(62.1.)

Die Martis, 23° Martii 1847.

The EARL OF SHAFTESBURY in the Chair.

THE Order of Reference was read.

The Petition of James Tracy, of No. 10, Albemarle Street, Piccadilly, Esquire, to Her Majesty, praying Her Majesty to direct and cause the Petitioner's Right and Title to the Viscounty and Barony of Tracy of Rathcoole, in the Peerage of Ireland, to be duly and sufficiently inquired into; and in case the Petitioner shall upon such Inquiry sufficiently prove and establish his Pedigree, as set forth in his former Petition to Her Majesty, that then and in that Case Her Majesty will be graciously pleased to declare and acknowledge the Petitioner to be Viscount and Baron Tracy, in the Peerage of Ireland, and to adjudge him to be entitled to the Honours and Dignities of Viscount and Baron Tracy; together with Her Majesty's Reference thereof to this House, and the Report of Her Majesty's Attorney General thereunto annexed, were read.

The Counsel and Parties were ordered to be called in;

And Sir Fitzroy Kelly, Mr. Fleming, Mr. Charles Bourdillon, and Mr. Hudson appearing as Counsel for the Petitioner, and Mr. Attorney General and Mr. Solicitor General and Mr. Solicitor General for Ireland appearing on behalf of the Crown;

Sir Fitzroy Kelly was heard to open the Allegations of the Petition of James Tracy, Esquire.

Mr. Fleming stated, That he proposed first to tender the Evidence given before the Committee of Privileges upon the former Petition of the Claimant.

Mr. Attorney General stated, That he did not object to that Course, it being understood that the whole of the Proceedings upon the former Occasion were to be taken as being now before the Committee.

Mr. Fleming stated, That he proposed to prove the Tombstone erected by Ann Wylde, the Daughter of Mr. Justice Tracy, to her First Husband, Mr. Dowdeswell.

Then Mr. JOHN WHITE was called in; and having been sworn, was examined as follows:

Mr. J. White.

(*Mr. Fleming.*)   Are you one of the Churchwardens of the Parish of Forthampton?
Yes.

Mr. J. White.

Are you acquainted with the Church of Forthampton?
Yes.

How long have you been acquainted with it?
I have been Churchwarden Twenty-one Years.

How long do you remember the Parish?
Nearly Seventy Years.

(*By a Lord.*) What Age are you now?
In my Seventieth Year.

(*Mr. Fleming.*) How long do you remember the Parish of Forthampton?
I have been in the Parish almost ever since I was born.

As long as you remember any thing do you remember the Parish of Forthampton?
Yes.

How long have you been acquainted with the Church of Forthampton?
These Fifty Years or more.

Do you remember a Tombstone erected in that Church to the Memory of Charles Dowdeswell?
Yes.

How long have you known that Tombstone?
Ever since I have been in the Parish.

Has it been ever since you have known it in the same State as it is now?
Yes, exactly.

(*By a Lord.*) When did you learn to read?
When I was a little Boy.

How old?
Between Seven and Eight Years old.

Cross-examined by Mr. Attorney General.

What are you?
A Farmer.

Whereabouts is this Tombstone which you speak of?
Up by the Communion Table.

On the Ground or in the Wall?
On the Ground.

Inside the Railing?
Yes.

Mr. B. Clubb.

Then Mr. BALTIMORE CLUBB was called in; and having been sworn, was examined as follows:

(*Mr. Fleming.*) Are you Clerk to Messrs. Bourdillon, the Solicitors of the Claimant in this Matter?
I am.

Have you got a Copy of the Tombstone erected in the Church of Forthampton to the Memory of Mr. Dowdeswell?
I have a Copy of the Inscription. (*Producing the same.*)

Is

Is that a true and correct Copy of the Inscription?
It is.

Did you compare it yourself with the original Tombstone?
I did.

Where does that Tombstone lie?
Within the Altar Rails of the Church.

The same was delivered in, and read as follows :

This marble stone was laid by the widow 1716.

In memory to her much hon^d husband Charles Dowdeswell esq^{re} late of Forthampton Court. He married Ann eldest daughter of ye hon^{ble} Mr Justice Tracy by whome he had two children. His son Charles is interr'd wth him his daughter Ann surviv'd him he dy'd very much lamented

The 30th of May 1713 in
The 26 year of his age.

Mr. Fleming stated, That as one of the Witnesses, a Clergyman, was desirous of leaving Town, he would, with the Permission of the Committee, examine him next.

Then the Reverend HAY M'DOWALL ERSKINE was called in ; and having been sworn, was examined as follows :

(*Mr. Fleming.*) Are you the Curate of the Parish of Forthampton?
I am.

Do you produce the Register of Baptisms of that Parish?
I do. (*Producing the same.*)

Do you find an Entry there, under the Date of 1612, of Ann, the Daughter of Charles Dowdeswell?
Yes, it is here.

Will you read it ?

The Witness read the same as follows :

Anno Dom. 1712.

Ann ye daughter of Charles Dowdeswell esq^r by Ann his wife was baptised July the 7th.

Cross-examined by Mr. Attorney General.

How long have you been Curate of the Parish ?
Between Six and Seven Years.

Was this Book delivered to you upon your becoming the Curate ?
It was.

By whom ?
By the Incumbent.

Where is it kept ?
In an Iron Chest in my House.

(*By a Lord.*) Have you ever looked at the Tombstones within the Altar ?
I have.

Rev. H. Erskine.
Mr. B. Clubb.

Did you ever see that of Charles Dowdeswell ?
Yes.

A Marble Tombstone ?
Yes.

With the Inscription which has been sworn to ?
The same.

(*Mr. Fleming to Mr. Clubb.*) Have you a Copy of the Entry which has just been read ?
I have. (*Producing the same.*)

Did you compare it yourself with the Original ?
Yes.

Is it a true and correct Copy ?
It is.

The same was delivered in.

Rev. W. H. Rowlatt.

Then the Reverend WILLIAM HENRY ROWLATT was called in ; and having been sworn, was examined as follows :

(*Mr. Fleming.*) Are you a Clergyman ?
I am.

Are you the Reader of the Temple Church ?
I am.

Do you produce the original Register of the Temple Church ?
I do. (*Producing the same.*)

Do you find, under the Date of 1719, an Entry of the Marriage of Thomas Wylde with Madam Dowdeswell ?
I do.

Will you read it ?

No. 3.

| Wylde and Dowdeswell. | Thomas Wylde esqʳ & Madᵐ Ann Dowdes- well were marry'd in the Temple church by the Revᵈ Dʳ Sherlock dean of Chichester & maʳ of the Temple on Saturday Febⁿ yᵉ 27ᵗʰ | 1719. |

(*To Mr. Clubb.*) Have you got a Copy of this Entry ?
I have.

Is it a true and correct Copy ?
It is.

Did you compare it yourself with the Original ?
I did.

The same was delivered in.

Mr. G. Hatchell.

Then Mr. GEORGE HATCHELL was called in ; and having been sworn, was examined as follows :

(*Mr. Fleming.*) Are you Clerk of Enrolments of the Court of Chancery in Ireland ?
I am.

Do you produce a Copy of Letters Patent, dated in the Second Year of George the First, appointing certain Persons Commissioners of Excise in Ireland ?
Yes, I do. (*Producing the same.*)

Is

Is that a true and correct Copy of the original Roll in Ireland?
Yes; I have compared it with the original Patent Roll of the Second
of George the First.

Will you read it?

The Witness read the same as follows :

George by the grace of God of Great Britain France and Ireland
king defender of the faith &c. To our trusty & welbeloved councellor
sir Thomas Southwell knt our trusty & welbeloved William Strickland
esq^r our trusty and welbeloved councellor William Conolly esq^r our
trusty and welbeloved Horatio Walpole esq^r our trusty and welbeloved
Thomas Medlicott esq^r our trusty and welbeloved Phillips Gibbon esq^r
and our trusty and welbeloved Thomas Wylde esq^r greeting. Whereas
by our letters patents under the great seal of that our kingdom of
Ireland bearing date the eleventh day of December in the first year of
our reign and in the year of our Lord God one thousand seven hundred and fourteen we lately constituted our right trusty and welbeloved
councellor sir Thomas Southwell knt our trusty and well beloved
William Strickland Wm Conolly esq^r sir Henry Bunbury and Thomas
Medlicott esq^r to be commissioners of our revenue of excise there and
the said sir Thomas Southwell William Strickland William Conolly
sir Henry Bunbury Thomas Medlicott and our trusty and welbeloved
Horatio Walpole and Phillips Gibbon esq^s to be our chief com^rs and
governours in and throughout our said kingdom of Ireland of and for
all and every other our revenues profits and incomes whatsoever due
or payable unto us in our said kingdome at a sallary of one thousand
pounds per annum to each of them as by the said letters patents relation
being thereunto had may more fully appear. And whereas we have
thought fitt to revoke determine and make void the said letters patents
whereby the said sir Thomas Southwell William Strickland William
Conolly sir Henry Bunbury and Thomas Medlicott were appointed our
commissioners of excise in our said kingdom of Ireland and also
whereby the said sir Thomas Southwell William Strickland William
Conolly sir Henry Bunbury Thomas Medlicott Horatio Walpole and
Phillips Gibbon were constituted and appointed our chief commissioners
and governours in and throughout our said kingdom of Ireland of and
for all and every other our revenues profits and incomes whatsoever
due or payable unto us in our said kingdom of Ireland. Now know ye
that we by and with the advice and consent of our right trusty & right
entirely beloved cousin and councellor Charles duke of Grafton & our
right trusty and right welbeloved cousin and councellor Henry earl of
Galway our justices and general governors of our kingdom of Ireland
and of the most rev^d fathers in God our right trusty and right entirely
beloved councellors William lord archbishop of Dublin and John lord
archbishop of Tuam & of our right trusty and right welbeloved cousin
and councellor Robert earl of Kildare our justices and general governors
of our said kingdom of Ireland and according to the tenor and effect
of our letters under our privy signett and royal sign manual bearing
date at our court at Saint James's the fourteenth day of Septr in the
year of our Lord God one thousand seven hundred & fifteen and in the
second year of our reign and now enrolled on the rolls of our high
court of Chancery in our said kingdom of Ireland have revoked determined and made void and by these presents we do revoke determine
and make void the said letters patents bearing date the said eleventh

day of December in the first year of our reign and in the year of our Lord God one thousand seven hundred and fourteen whereby the said sir Thomas Southwell William Strickland Willm Conolly sir Henry Bunbury and Thomas Medlicott were appointed commissioners of our revenue of excise in our said kingdom of Ireland and whereby the said sir Thomas Southwell William Conolly sir Henry Bunbury Thomas Medlicott Horatio Walpole and Phillips Gibbon were constituted our chief commiss^{rs} & governors in and throughout our said kingdom of Ireland of & for all and every other our revenues profits and incoms whatsoever due or payable unto us in our said kingdom of Ireland. Know yee further that we reposing special trust and confidence in the abilities integrities and fidelities of our right trusty & welbeloved councellor sir Thomas Southwell knt. our trusty and welbeloved William Strickland our right trusty and welbeloved councellor William Conolly Horatio Walpole Thomas Medlicott Phillips Gibbon and Thomas Wylde esq^s of our special grace certain knowlege & meer motion by and with the advice and consent aforesaid & according to the tenor and effect of our aforesaid letters have nominated constituted and appointed and by these presents do nominate constitute and appoint you the said sir Thomas Southwell knight William Strickland William Conolly Thomas Medlicott and Thomas Wylde esq^s to be our commiss^{rs} of our revenue of excise within our said kingdom of Ireland and you the said sir Thomas Southwell William Strickland William Conolly Thomas Medlicott and Thomas Wylde our governors and chief commiss^{rs} of and for the office of excise and new impost settled within our city of Dublin within our said kingdom of Ireland during our pleasure. And we do hereby give and grant unto you the said sir Thomas Southwell William Strickland William Conolly Thomas Medlicott and Thomas Wylde or any three or more of you or so many of you as by the laws & statutes of our said kingdom of Ireland are appointed to be a quorum full power and authority in and throughout our said kingdom of Ireland to exercise execute and put in due execution all and every the powers and authorities that by the act made in the parliament which was holden at Dublin in the fourteenth and fifteenth years of the reign of our late royal brother king Charles the second entitled an act for settling the excise or new impost upon his ma^{tie} his heirs and succ^{rs} according to the book of rates therein incerted are given granted and confirmed unto us or which are thereby directed or appointed to be done by us or by any person or persons who by virtue of or in pursuance of the said act are to be constituted and appointed commissioners governors officers and ministers for the execution thereof respectively in as full and ample manner as we they or any others thereunto authorized by the said act may might or ought to do by virtue of and according to the true intent & meaning of the said act. And we do hereby further give & grant unto you sir Thomas Southwell William Strickland William Conolly Thomas Medlicott & Thomas Wylde or any two or more of you full power and authority during our will & pleasure to exercise and execute all other the powers and privileges and authorities whatsoever of right to us belonging or appertaining for the due managing levying ordering and receiving our revenues arising by the said act of excise & new impost and the arrears thereof and all sums of money which are or shall be due and payable to us by virtue of the said act. And we do hereby further give and grant unto you the said sir Thomas Southwell William Strickland William Conolly Thomas Medlicott and Thomas Wylde and your deputies substitutes

collectors

collectors officers and agents full power and authority during our will and pleasure to demand sue for distrain prosecute and recover or cause to be demanded received levied collected sued for distrained prosecuted and recovered & by your deputies substitutes collectors officers and agents to receive levy & collect in the several and respective counties barronies places cities and townes corporate within our said kingdom of Ireland all such sum and sums of money due and in arreare or that shall grow due and payable to us by virtue of the aforesaid act of excise and new impost and to perform and execute all & sing^r the powers given unto us by force and virtue of the aforesaid act and to do all matters and things touching the well ordering governing and receiving levying & collecting the p̃misses as shall be agreeable to law. And we do hereby give unto you or any three or more of you in manner as afores^d full power & authority to nominate constitute and appoint in and throughout our said kingdom of Ireland subcom^{rs} deputies collectors accomptants clerks surveyors waiters searchers gaugers and other inferior officers resp̃ly at or in the several counties cities baronies burroughs towns parishes and places of this kingdom and the islands & territories thereunto belonging from time to time as fully as the late or any former com^{rs} of the excise or chief governour or chief governours and councill or the lord treasurer of Ireland or any others are by the said act of parliament or by the laws and statutes of this realme directed authorized or impowered or as may lawfully be done or granted by us and any commis^{rs} collectors receivers accomptants clerks surveyors searchers gaugers and other inferior officers already appointed or hereafter to be appointed in relation to the said revenue of excise and new impost to suspend remove and displace and to constitute and appoint others in their places resp̃ly according as you our said com^{rs} or any three or more of you shall think fit or requisite for our service to take receive or cause to be taken and received in our name & to our use such security from the respective collectors & other officers for the faithful discharge of their respective trusts as to you our said com^{rs} or any three or more of you resp̃ly shall be approved of and thought reasonable & to allow to the said com^{rs} collectors receivers accomptants clerks surveyors waiters searchers gaugers and other inferior officers such sallaries as are already or hereafter shall be allowed or settled by us or by our high treasurer or the commiss^{rs} of the treasury for the time being and where no sallarys are or shall be specially settled by us or by our high treas^r or the com^{rs} of the treasury for the time being in all such cases you our said com^{rs} or any three or more of you may allow to the said officers such sallaries as to you our said com^{rs} or any three or more of you upon due consideration of the services performed or to be performed shall be thought reasonable and fitting to be allowed and paid out of our revenue. And we do hereby give and grant unto you our said com^{rs} or any three or more of you full power & authority if you shall think fit with the approbation of our lord lieutenant or chief governors of our said kingdom of Ireland for the time being first had and obtained from time to time to farm our said revenue of excise upon beer & ale throughout our whole realme of Ireland or arising in any particular place thereof provided the said farm do not exceed the term of one year. And whereas the excise upon foreigne goods imported is not payable by the merchants till the goods are sold and yet in some cases it would be for our service to have the moneys advanced we do hereby give and grant unto you our said com^{rs} or any three of you full power and authority if you shall think

Mr. G. Hatchell.

think fit to agree with any such merchant for the excise of such goods imported and unsold and to allow him in the composition such reasonable satisfaction for the advance of his money as to you shall seem reasonable. And we hereby give & grant to you our said com" or any three or more of you resp̃ly or to so many of you as by law may have full power and authority where you shall find reasonable to compound dispence with remitt or mittigate any fine penalty or forfeitures whereunto we shall or may be intituled to by virtue of the said act so as no part of the duties thereby arising to us be lost or lessened & that the charges of recovery be reimbursed to us if any such charges shall be. And further of our special grace certain knowlege and meer motion by and with the advice and consent afores^d & of our privy councill of our said kingdom of Ireland & according to the purport & tenor of our afores^d letters we have nominated constituted and appointed and by these presents do nominate constitute & appoint you the said sir Thomas Southwell Wm Strickland William Conolly Horatio Walpole Thomas Medlicott Phillips Gibbon and Thomas Wylde our chief commiss^rs and governors in and throughout our said kingdom of Ireland of and for all and every other our revenues profits & incomes arising or which are or shall be answerable due owing in arrear or payable to us within our said kingdom of Ireland by virtue of all and every the several acts of parliament hereafter ment^d or any other ways or means whats^r that is to say one act entitled an act for settling the subsidy of poundage & granting a subsidy of tunnage & other sums of money unto his royal ma^tie his heirs and succ^rs the same to be paid upon the merchandizes imported & exported into or out of the kingdom of Ireland according to a book of rates hereunto annexed & an act entitled an act for the improvement of his ma^ties revenue upon the granting of licences for selling of ale & beer and also one other act entituled an act for the better ordering the selling of wines and aqua vite together with all sorts of strong waters by retaile and also one other act entitled an act for establishing an additional revenue upon his ma^tie his heirs and succ^rs for the support of his and their crown and dignity and also one other act entitled an addit^l act for the better ordering and collecting the revenue arising by hearth money and also out of and for all and every the quitt rents & other rents and payments arising or which are or shall be answerable or payable to us by virtue of one other act entitled an act for the better execution of his ma^ties gracious declaration for the settlement of his kingdom of Ireland and satisfacčon of the several interests of advent^rs soldiers and other his subjects there & also one other act intituled an act for the explaining some doubts arising upon an act intituled an act for the better execučon of his ma^ties gracious declaration for the settlement of his kingdom of Ireland and satisfacčon of the several interests of adventurers soldiers and other his subjects there & for making some alteračons of and additions unto the said act for the more speedy & effectual settlement of the said kingdom and also of & for all and all manner of chief rents rents services rents of inheritance rents of assize rents charge and rents seck or dry rents fee farms rents reserved upon leases made or to be made custodiam rents or composition money exchequer rents nomine decime et vicesime assart rents rents due for purprestures arrented coppyhold rents and all other certain antient rents and other crown rents or other rents payable to us our heirs or succ^rs within this our said realme of Ireland which now are or ought to be in charge or in being or existent or which at any time hereafter shall or may grow due or be answerable

or

or payable or of right ought to be paid to us our heirs or succ^{rs} by any person or persons bodies politick or corporate by reason of any term charter patent lease demise or grant made or to be made of any mannors messuages lands tenements or heredit^s or of any rights royalties offices liberties franchises or immunities whats^r within this our realm of Ireland and also of and for all & every other the revenues duties incomes profits benefits & advantages of what nature or kind soever which shall or may or ought to happen come arise grow due or be due answerable payable compounded accounted for reserved or appointed to be paid unto us our heirs and succ^{rs} for our use or uses from any person or persons bodies politick or corporate or for any cause matter or thing whats^r in our said kingdom of Ireland or whereunto we our heirs and succ^{rs} shall or may be any ways justly entitled by virtue or in purs^{ce} of all or any the statutes or acts last before mentioned or by any acts statutes laws or customs now in force in our said kingdom of Ireland or by any outlawry attainder or forfeiture or by any custome usuage p̃scripc̃on right p̃rogative covenant condition agreement tenure charters patents lease demise or grant made or to be made of any mannor messuages lands tenements or heredits or of any rights privileges liberties royalties franchises or immunities whats^r or which we our heirs or succ^{rs} by any lawful ways or means can or may receive within our said kingdom of Ireland whether the same be great or small branches of our revenue certain or casual ordinary or extraordinary or otherwise whatsoever or howsoever happening or arising within our said kingdom of Ireland. And we do give and grant by these p̃sents unto you the said sir Thomas Southwell Wm Strickland William Conolly Horatio Walpole Thomas Medlicott Phillips Gibbon & Thomas Wyle your deputies substitutes officers & agents full power and authority during our will and pleasure to demand sue for distrain prosecute and recover or cause to be demanded received levied collected sued for distrained prosecuted & recovered & by your deputies substitutes collectors officers & agents to receive levy and collect in the sev^l & respective counties baronies places cities and towns corporate & elsewhere within our said kingdom of Ireland all & every & other our revenues profits & incomes sume and sumes of money due and in arrear or that shall grow due and payable to us by virtue of the last before recited acts of parliament or any of them or otherwise howsoever and to do perform and execute all & sing^r the powers & authorities given unto us by force and virtue thereof & to do all matters & things touching the well ordering governing receiving levying & collecting the premes as shall be agreeable to law & we hereby require and command you our said chief commiss^{rs} and governors resp̃ly and every of you that you do from time to time observe perform fulfill and keep all & singuler the orders rules instructions and directions which now are or which shall from time to time hereafter be made or given you by us or by our lord high treasurer or from the lords comm^{rs} of the treasury for the time being when there is or shall be no lord treasurer touching or concerning the better ordering managing collecting & receiving the revenues herein before menc̃oned. And we do hereby give unto you our said respective com^{rs} or any three or more of you in manner afores^d full power & authority to nominate constitute and appoint such person & persons from time to time as you our said com^{rs} or any three or more of you shall think fit to be your secretary to be attendant upon you our said respective com^{rs} in the execution of your said respective commissions & from time to time to do execute and perform

Mr. G. Hatchell.

all & every the matter & things which to the said office and employment of secretary appertains as you or any three or more of you our said respective com^{rs} shall think fitt. And also we hereby likewise grant unto you our said com^{rs} or any three or more of you full power & authority from time to time to nominate and appoint such person and persons to be agent and solicitor to & for you our said respective commiss^{rs} in all such cases matters & things wherein you our said respective commiss^{rs} can or may stand in need of or have occasion to use the assistance or service of any agent or solicitor as you shall think fitt. And we do likewise give unto you or any three or more of you in manner afores^d full power and authority to nominate constitute & appoint in and throughout our said kingdom of Ireland subcom^{rs} deputies receivers collectors accomptants clerks surveyors waiters searchers gaugers or other inferior officers resp^{ly} at or in the several counties cities baronies burroughs towns parishes & places of this kingdom & the islands & territories thereunto belonging from time to time as fully as the late or any former com^{rs} chief governor or governors and councill of Ireland or the lord treasurer of Ireland or any others are by any act or acts of parliament or by the laws & statutes of this realm directed authorized or empowered as may be lawfully done or granted by us and such respective officers subcom^{rs} collectors receivers accomptants clerks surveyors waiters searchers gaugers & other inferior officers already appointed or hereafter to be appointed in relation to the said revenues last mentioned to suspend remove or displace & to constitute & appoint others in his & their place & places resp^{ly} according as you our said com^{rs} or any three or more of you resp^{ly} shall think fit & requisite for our services and to take and receive & to cause to be taken and rec^d in our names & to our use such securities from the respective collectors and other officers for the faithful discharge of their respective trusts as by you our said com^{rs} or any three or more of you resp^{ly} shall be approved of and thought reasonable and to allow the said secretary and agent or sol^{rs} or the sub-com^{rs} collectors receivers accomptants clerks surveyors waiters searchers gaugers & other inferior officers such sallarys as are already or shall be hereafter allowed or settled by us or by the high treasurer or com^{rs} of the treasury in Great Britain for the time being and where no sallaries are or shall be resp^{ly} settled by us or our high treasurer or our com^{rs} of our treasury for the time being in all such cases you our said com^{rs} or any three or more of you resp^{ly} may allow to such secretary or agent and sol^r & other officers such salary as to you our said com^{rs} or any three or more of you resp^{ly} upon due consideration of the service performed or to be performed shall be thought reasonable & fitting to be allowed and paid out of our said revenue. And wee doe likewise give and grant unto you our said com^{rs} or any three or more of you full power and authority if you shall think fit with the approbation of our lord lieuten^t or chief governor or governors there for the time being first had & obtained from time to time to farme out our hearth money & licences upon beer ale wine & strong waters throughout our whole realm of Ireland or arising in any particular place thereof provided the said farme do not exceed the term of one year. And we do hereby require you our said com^{rs} resp^{ly} from time to time to give an account to our lord lieu^t or other chief governor or governors and to our lord high treasurer or lord com^{rs} of our treasury of Great Britain for the time being of your actings and proceedings in purs^{ce} of this our commission as often as

it

it shall be demanded of you by our lord lieu^t or other chief governor or governors of Ireland or lords com^{rs} of our treasury or lord treasurer for the time being. And we do hereby give and grant unto you our said com^{rs} or any three or more of you resp̄ly or so many of you as by law may have full power and authority where you shall find it reasonable to compound and dispence with remit or mittigate any fine penalty or forfeiture whereunto we shall or may be entitled by virtue of the said acts or any of them so as the same extend not to any forfeiture arising upon the said acts of tunnage & poundage but so as no part of the duties thereby arising to us be lost or lessened & that the charges of recovery be reimbursed to us if any such charges shall be. And we do hereby require and authorize you our said com^{rs} to cause the collectors to pass their accounts upon oath at the end of every year or oftener as you shall see cause which oath we do hereby empower you our said com^{rs} resp̄ly or any three or more of you or so many of you as by law may from time to time to administer. And we do hereby grant unto you our said com^{rs} resp̄ly and every one of you or so many of you as by law may as also to all persons employed by you full power & authority to administer such oaths as by law may be administered to any person for the due execution of the prem̄es. And we do hereby grant unto you our s^d com^{rs} resp̄ly or any three or more of you full power & authority to issue out warrants to our receiver general or cashier for the time being or to any collector or deputy collector or receiver of our said revenue to extend lay out & pay or cause to be paid and allowed to the said officers or any other person or persons whats^r such sums of money for salaries rewards or for incident or contingent charges as shall necessarily arise in or for the management of our said revenues or any of them. And we do hereby grant unto you our said com^{rs} or any three or more of you full power to grant bills of portage to masters of ships according to usage & also bills of stores to merchants to the value of ten shill^s in customs & also powers to compound as to you or any three or more of you shall seem meet any seizures or things forfeited for not paying the duty imposed thereupon so as the duty if it had been paid had not exceeded forty shill^s & the persons finally to acquit. And we do by these presents require & command you our said com^{rs} and governors of our revenue afores^d resp̄ly that you & every of you resp̄ly in manner aforesaid do carefully and diligently attend the execution & discharge of the respective trusts afores^d in & by all things as becometh. And we do hereby direct appoint and empower all our said collectors & subcom^{rs} of our revenue to pay all monies collected by them to our vice treār receiver general or cashier in our said kingdom of Ireland for the time being or otherwise as we or our treasurer or our com^{rs} of our treasury for the time being shall direct except what they shall be ordered by you our said com^{rs} to pay for the several sallaries rewards & incident charges aforesaid according to the true intent and meaning of these presents & that they from time to time to render unto you or any three or more of you our said com^{rs} resp̄ly an account of what they have collected or paid as afores^d. And we do hereby declare and grant that you our said com^{rs} resp̄ly & every of you and those employed by you or under you shall during your continuance in this our service be exempted from serving upon juries or bearing any civill or military office. And whereas we have made sufficient provision for the payment of and answering all the moneys arising by or out of the said revenues hereby committed to

the

the management of you our said com^{rs} resp̃ly as afores^d we do hereby
for us our heirs & succ^{rs} grant and declare that you our said com^{rs} and
every of you and your heirs executors and adm̃iors & every of them
shall be and remain for ever clear free and finally discharged of & from
all sums of money whats^r growing and acrewing as afores^d and of and
from rendering unto us our heirs and succ^{rs} any account for the same
or any part thereof or for any fines penalties or forfeitures compounded
remitted or mittigated or for any excise upon foreign goods imported
and unsold and compounded & for which shall not be rec^d by you
notwithstanding the said moneys shall have been or may be collected
by any person deputed or deriving authority from you our said com^{rs}
resp̃ly or any three or more of you notwithstanding such person shall
not pay or answer the same to our vice treãr or receiver general or to
such receiver or officer as we have or shall appoint to receive the same
and that neither our said com^{rs} resp̃ly nor their heirs executors or
adm̃iors shall be by us or our heirs or succ^{rs} sued prosecuted or any
way molested in their estates persons & goods in any of our courts
whats^r for or by reason of any thing they or any of them shall act or
do by virtue of these our l̃res patents & the powers thereunto resp̃ly
belonging or by any exposition or construction thereupon save for
voluntary or particular misfeazance done or acted by them or any of
them. And we do hereby strictly charge and command all officers of the
admiralty and all persons deriving any authority from the lord high
admiral or com^{rs} of admiralty & all & every justice & justices of the
peace mayors sheriffs bailiffs and constables headborroughs customers
collectors comptrollers clerks of the peace & all other our officers and
ministers whatsoever within every county city burrough or corporation
barony parish or place and all other officers & ministers & all other our
subjects whatsoever that they & every of them from time to time be
aiding and assisting to you our said chief com^{rs} and governors resp̃ly
and to the subcom^{rs} collectors surveyors comptrollers & to all other
officers and ministers whats^r which are or shall be appointed by you
and to all and every person & persons employed in the execution of all
and singular & every other the powers privileges and authorities and
other the prem̃ises to you hereby given or granted or in obeying or
executing such directions or p̃cepts as shall from time to time be
directed unto them for the due execution of this commission as
becometh upon pain of our displeasure and such other penalties
as by the acts or statutes of this realme can or may be inflicted upon
them for their negligence or contempt in that behalf and as they will
answer the contrary at their utmost perils. And further of our special
grace certain knowledge and meer motion by and with the advice and
consent of our said justices and councill & according to the purport
& tenor of the aforesaid l̃res we have given & granted and by these
presents do give & grant unto each of you the said sir Thomas Southwell William Strickland Willm Connolly Horatio Walpole Thomas
Medlicott Phillips Gibbon & Thomas Wylde severally & resp̃ly for
the execution of the said trust hereby committed to your charge the
salary or allowance of one thousand pounds ster^g by the year the
sallaries of them the said sir Thomas Southwell William Strickland
Wm Connolly Horatio Walpole Thomas Medlicott & Phillips Gibbon
to com̃ence from the time to which they were last paid by virtue of
the said last recited commission or l̃res patents & the salary of the
said Thomas Wylde to com̃ence from the date of this our commission
& to be paid unto you & every of you the said sir Thos Southwell
William

Mr. G. Hatcnell.

William Strickland William Conolly Horatio Walpole Thomas Medlicott Phillips Gibbon & Thomas Wylde resp̃ly out of our said revenues
during our pleasure quarterly at the four most usual feasts or times in
the year that is to say at the birth of our Lord Christ the Annunciation
of the Blessed Virgin Mary the Nativity of Saint John the Baptist &
the feast of Saint Michael the archangel by even & equal porc̃ons.
And our further will and pleasure is & we do hereby give & grant to
you our said comr̃s herein & hereby appointed that when & as often
as they or any of them shall happen to dye or to depart this life in our
said service hereby to them committed or shall be removed therefrom
that then & in every such case so much of their and every of their
sallary or sallarys resp̃ly as shall have incurred to the day of such
death or removal shall be paid to them their exŏors and adm̃ors
respectively all and every of which before menc̃oned sallarys allowances
annuities rewards incident and contingent charges to be paid and
allowed out of the said revenues profits and incomes by the orders or
by the order of any three or more of you resp̃ly without your being
charged with the moneys paid in respect of your signing the orders
for the same. And we do hereby fully empower and authorize you our
said comr̃s of the excise and new impost & the comr̃s of our revenues
resp̃ly as aforesaid to proceed and finish all causes & cases whatsoever
which are or shall be left undetermined by virtue of the late or any
former commission or commissions granted by us unto any former
commiss̃rs for managem̃t of our revenues of our said kingdom of
Ireland. Provided always that this our commission be enrolled in the
rolls of our high court of chancery in our said kingdom of Ireland
within the space of six months next ensuing the date. In witness
whereof we have caused these our letters to be made patents. Witness
our aforesaid justices general & general governors of our said kingdom
of Ireland at Dublin the first day of October in the second year of
our reign.

Irrot̃r duodecimo die Octobr̃a anno r. ℞ Georgii secundo.

Do you produce also a Copy of another Patent, of the Date of the
Seventh of George the First ?

I do. (*Producing the same.*)

Will you read it ?

The same was read as follows :

No. 5.

George by the grace of God of Great Britain France & Ireland
king defender of the faith &c. To our trusty & well beloved William
Strickland esqr our right trusty & welbeloved councellor William
Conolly esqr our trusty & well beloved Tho̊s Medlicott Phillips Gybbon
Thomas Wylde Edward Hopkins & William Harrison esqr̃s greeting.
Whereas by our letters patents under the great seal of that our
kingdom of Ireland bearing date the ninth day of June in the second
year of our reign and in the year of our Lord God one thousand seven
hund̃d & sixteen we constituted our trusty and welbeloved councellor
Tho̊s lord Southwell by the name of sir Thomas Southwell kñt now
lately deceased our trusty & welbeloved William Strickland esqr our
trusty and welbeloved councellor William Conolly esqr our trusty and
welbeloved Thomas Medlycott and Thomas Wylde esqr̃s to be comr̃s
of our revenue of excise there & the said Thomas lord Southwell
William Strickland William Conolly Tho̊s Medlicott Phillips Gybbon
Thomas Wylde and Edward Hopkins to be our chief comr̃s and

governors in and throughout our said kingdom of Ireland of and for all and every other our revenues profits and incomes whatsoever due or payable unto us in our said kingdom at a sallary of one thousand pounds per añm to each of them as by the said letters patents relaĉon being thereunto had may more fully appear. And whereas we have thought fit to determine and make void the said letters patents whereby the said Thomas lord Southwell by the name of sir Thomas Southwell kn̄t William Strickland William Conolly Thomas Medlicott and Thomas Wylde were appointed our comᵣˢ of excise in our said kingdom of Ireland and also whereby the said Thomas lord Southwell William Strickland William Conolly Thomas Medlicott Phillips Gibbon Thomas Wylde and Edward Hopkins were constituted our chief comᵣˢ and governors in & throughout our said kingdom of Ireland & for all & every other our revenues profits and incomes whatsᵣ due or payable unto us in our said kingdom of Ireland. Now know ye that we by and with the advice and consent of our right trusty and right entirely beloved cousin and councellor Charles duke of Grafton our lieuᵗ general & general governor of our said kingdom of Ireland and of our right trusty and welbeloved cousin and councellor Alan lord viscount Midleton lord high chancellor of our said kingdom of Ireland and our right trusty and welbeloved councellor William Conolly esqᵣ speaker of our house of commons in that our kingdom of Ireland our justices and general governors of our said kingdom of Ireland according to the tenor and effect of our privy letters under our privy signet and royal sign manual bearing date at our court at Herenhansen the nineteenth day of August O. S. & in the seventh year of our reign and now enrolled in the rolls of our high court of chancery in our said kingdom of Ireland have revoked determined and made void & by these presents we do revoke determine & make void the said letters patent bearing date the said ninth day of June in the second year of our reign and in the year of our Lord God one thousᵈ & sixteen whereby the said Thomas lord Southwell by the name of sir Thomas Southwell William Strickland Wᵐ Conolly Thomas Medlicott and Thomas Wylde were appointed comᵣˢ of our revenue of excise in our said kingdom of Ireland and whereby the said Thomas lord Southwell by the name of sir Thomas Southwell William Strickland William Conolly Thomas Medlycott Phillips Gibbon Thomas Wylde and Edward Hopkins were constituted our chief commissioners and governours in and throughout our said kingdom of Ireland of and for all & every other our revenues profits and incomes whatsoever due or payable unto us in our said kingdom of Ireland. Know ye further that we reposing special trust & confidence in the abilities integrities and fidelities of our right trusty and welbeloved William Strickland esqᵣ our right trusty & well beloved councellor William Connolly esqᵣ our trusty & well beloved Thomas Medlicott Philips Gibbon Thomas Wylde Edward Hopkins & William Harrison esqᵃ of our special grace certain knowlege and meer motion by & with the advice and consent aforesaid & according to the tenor and effect of our aforesaid letters have nominated constituted and appointed and by these presents do nominate constitute and appoint you the said William Strickland William Conolly Thomas Medlicott Thomas Wylde & William Harrison esqᵣˢ to be our commissioners of our revenue of excise within our said kingdom of Ireland and you the said William Strickland William Conolly Thomas Medlicott Thomas Wylde & William Harrison our governors and chief commissioners of and for the office of excise and new impost settled within our city of
Dublin

Dublin within our said kingdom of Ireland during our pleasure   And we do hereby give and grant unto you the said William Strickland William Conolly Thomas Medlicott Thomas Wylde & William Harrison or any three or more of you or so many of you as by the laws and statutes of our said kingdom of Ireland are appointed to be a quorum full power and authority in and throughout our said kingdom of Ireland to exercise execute and put in due execution all and every the powers and authorities that by the act made in the parliament which was holden at Dublin in the fourteenth and fifteenth years of the reign of our late royal brother King Charles the second entitled an act for settling the excise of new impost upon his mat^ie his heirs and successors according to the book of rates therein inserted are given granted and confirmed unto us or which are thereby directed or appointed to be done by us or by any person or persons who by virtue of or in pursuance of the said act are to be constituted and appointed commissioners governors officers and ministers for the execution thereof respectively in as full and ample manner as we they or any others thereunto authorized by the said act may might or ought to do by virtue of and according to the true intent & meaning of the said act.   And we do hereby give and grant unto you William Strickland William Conolly Thomas Medlicott Thomas Wylde and William Harison or any two or more of you full power and authority during our will and pleasure to exercise and execute all other the powers and privileges & authorities whatsoever of right to us belonging or appertaining for the due managing levying ordering and receiving our revenues arising by the said act of excise and new impost and the arrears thereof and all sums of money which are or shall be due and payable to us by virtue of the said Act.   And we do hereby further give and grant unto you the said William Strickland William Conolly Thomas Medlicott Thomas Wylde & William Harison and your deputies substitutes collectors officers and agents full power and authority during our will and pleasure to demand sue for distrain prosecute and recover or cause to be demanded received levied collected sued for distrained prosecuted and recovered & by your deputies substitutes collectors officers and agents to receive levy & collect in the several and respective counties barronies places cities towns corporate within our said kingdom of Ireland all such sum and sums of money due & in arreare or that shall grow due and payable to us by virtue of the aforesaid act of excise and new impost and to perform and execute all and singular the powers given unto us by force and virtue of the aforesaid act & to do all matters and things touching the well ordering governing and receiving levying and collecting the premises as shall be agreeable to law.   And we do hereby give unto you or any three or more of you in manner as aforesaid full power and authority to nominate constitute and appoint in and throughout our said kingdom of Ireland subcommissioners deputies collectors accomptants clerks surveyors waiters searchers gaugers and other inferior officers respectively at or in the several counties cities baronies burroughs towns parishes and places of this kingdom and the islands & territories thereunto belonging from time to time as fully as the late or any former commissioners of the excise or chief governor or chief governors and councel or the lord treasurer of Ireland or any others are by the said act of parliament or by the laws and statutes of this realme directed authorized or empowered or as may lawfully be done or granted by us and any commissioners collectors receivers accomptants clerks surveyors searchers gaugers and other

inferior

inferior officers already appointed or hereafter to be appointed in relation to the said revenue of excise and new impost to suspend remove and displace and to constitute and appoint others in their places respectively according as you our said commissioners or any three or more of you shall think fit or requisite for our service to take receive or cause to be taken and received in our name & to our use such security from the respective collectors & other officers for the faithful discharge of their respective trusts as to you our said commissioners or any three or more of you respectively shall be approved of and thought reasonable & to allow to the said comm^{rs} receivers collectors accomptants clerks surveyors waiters searchers gaugers and other inferior officers such salaries as are already or hereafter shall be allowed or settled by us or by our high treasurer or the comm̃n^{rs} of the treasury for the time being and where no sallarys are or shall be specially by us or by our high treasurer or the comm̃n^{rs} of the treasury for the time being in all such cases your our said comm̃n^{rs} or any three or more of you may allow to the said officers such salaries as to you our said comm̃n^{rs} or any three or more of you upon due consideration of the services performed or to be performed shall be thought reasonable and fitting to be allowed and paid out of our revenue. And we do hereby give and grant unto you our said commissioners or any three or more of you full power and authority if you shall think fit with the approbation of our lord lieu^t or chief governor of our said kingdom of Ireland for the time being first had and obtained from time to time to farm our said revenue of excise upon beer and ale throughout our whole realm of Ireland or arising in any particular place thereof provided the said farm do not exceed the term of one year. And whereas the excise upon foreigne goods imported is not payable by the merchants till the goods are sold and yet in some cases it would be for our service to have the moneys advanced we .do hereby give and grant unto you our said commissioners or any three of you full power and authority if you shall think fit to agree with any such merchant for the excise of such goods imported and unsold and to allow him in the composition such reasonable satisfaction for the advance of his money as to you shall seem reasonable. And we hereby give and grant to you our said commissioners or any three or more of you resp^{ly} or to so many of you as by law may have full power and authority where you shall find reasonable to compound dispence with remitt or mitigate any fine penalty or forfeitures whereunto we shall or may be intitled to by virtue of the said act so as no part of the duties thereby arising to us be lost or lessened & that the charges of recovery be reimbursed to us if any such charges shall be. And furthur of our special grace certain knowlege & meer motion by and with the advice and consent aforesaid & of our privy council of our said kingdom of Ireland & according to the purport and tenor of our aforesaid letters we have nominated constituted and appointed and by these presents do nominate constitute and appoint you the said William Strickland William Conolly Thomas Medlicott Phillips Gibbon Thomas Wylde Edward Hopkins & Wm Harrison our chief commissioners and governors during our pleasure in and throughout our said kingdom of Ireland of and for all and every other our revenues profits and incomes arising or which are or shall be answerable due owing in arrear or payable to us within our said kingdom of Ireland by virtue of all and every the serviceable acts of parliament hereinafter mentioned or any other ways or means whatsoever that is to say one act entitled an act for settling

13

the

the subsidy of poundage & granting a subsidy of tunnage and other sums of money unto his royal mãt^ie his heirs and successors the same to be paid upon the merchandizes imported and exported into or out of the kingdom of Ireland according to a book of rates hereunto annexed and an act entitled an act for the improvement of his mãt^ies revenue upon the granting of benefices for selling of ale & beer and also one other act entitled an act for the better ordering the selling of wines and aqua vite together with all sorts of strong waters by retaile and also one other act entitled an act for establishing an additional revenue upon his mãt^ie his heirs and successors for the support of his and their crown and dignity and also one other act entitled an additional act for the better ordering and collecting the revenue arising by hearth money and also out of and for all and every the quitt rents & other rents and payments arising or which are or shall be due answerable or payable to us by virtue of one other act entitled an act for the better execution of his mãt^ies gracious declaration for the settlement of his kingdom of Ireland and satisfaction of the several interests of adventurers soldiers and other his subjects there & also one other act entitled an act for the explaining some doubts arising upon an act entitled an act for the better execution of his mãt^ies gracious declaration for the settlement of his kingdom of Ireland and satisfaction of the several interests of adventurers soldiers and other his subjects there and for making some alterations of and additions unto the said act for the more speedy & effectual settlement of the said kingdom and also of and for all and all manner of chief rents rents services rents of inheritance rents of assize rents charge and rents seck or dry rents fee farms rents reserved upon leases made or to be made custodiam rents or composition money exchequer rents nomine decime et vicesime assart rents rents due for purprestures arrented coppyhold rents and all other certain antient rents and other crown rents or other rents payable to us our heirs or successors within this our said realme of Ireland which now are or ought to be in charge or in being or existent or which at any time hereafter shall or may grow due or be answerable or payable or of right ought to be paid to us our heirs or successors by any person or persons bodies politick or corporate by reason of any term charter patent lease demise or grant made or to be made of any mannors messuages lands tenements or hereditaments or of any rights royalties offices liberties franchises or immunities whatsoever within this our realme of Ireland and also of and for all and every other the revenues duties incomes profits benefits & advantages of what nature or kind soever which shall or may or ought to happen come arise grow due or be due answerable payable compounded accounted for reserved or appointed to be paid unto us our heirs and successors for our use or uses from any person or persons bodies politic or corporate or for any cause matter or thing whatsoever in our said kingdom of Ireland or whereunto we our heirs and successors shall or may be any ways justly entitled by virtue or in presence of all or any the statutes or acts last before mentioned or by any acts statutes laws or customs now in force in our said kingdom of Ireland or by any outlawry attainder or forfeiture or by any custom usage prescription right progative covenant condition agreement tenure charters patents lease demise or grant made or to be made of any manor messuage lands tenements or hereditaments or of any rights privileges liberties royalties francbises or immunities whatsoever or which we our heirs or successors by any lawful ways or means can or may receive within our said

Mr. G. Hatchell.

said kingdom of Ireland whether the same be great or small branches of our revenue certain or casual ordinary or extraordinary or otherwise whatsoever or howsoever happening or arising within our said kingdom of Ireland. And we do give and grant by these psents unto you the said Wm Strickland William Conolly Thomas Medlicott Phillips Gibbon Thomas Wylde Edward Hopkins & Wm Harrison your deputies substitutes officers & agents full power and authority during our will and pleasure to demand sue for distrain prosecute and recover or cause to be demanded received levied collected sued for distrained prosecuted and recovered and by your deputies substitutes collectors officers & agents to receive levy and collect in the several and respective counties baronies places cities and towns corporate and elsewhere within our said kingdom of Ireland all and every & other our revenues profits and incomes sum & sums of money due and in arrear or that shall grow due and payable to us by virtue of the last before recited acts of parliament or any of them or otherwise howsoever and to do perform and execute and singular the powers & authorities given unto us by force and virtue thereof and to do all matters & things touching & concerning the well ordering governing receiving levying & collecting the premises as shall be agreeable to law & we hereby require and command you our said chief commr^s and governors resply & every of you that you do from time to time observe perform fulfill and keep all and singular the orders rules instructions and directions which now are or which shall from time to time hereafter be made or given you by us or by our lord high treasurer or from the lords commr^s of the treasury for the time being when there is or shall be no lord treasurer touching or concerning the better ordering managing collecting and reserving the revenues herein before mentioned. And we do hereby give unto you our said respective commr^s or any three or more of you in manner aforesaid full power and authority to nominate constitute and appoint such person & persons from time to time as you our said commr^s or any three or more of you shall think fit to be your secretary to be attendant upon you our said respective commr^s in the execution of your said respective commissions & from time to time to do execute & perform all and every the matter and things which to the said office and employment of secretary appertains as you or any three or more of you our said respective commr^s shall think fit. And also we hereby likewise grant unto you our said commr^s or any three or more of you full power & authority from time to time to nominate and appoint such person and persons to be agent and soliciter to & for you our said respective commr^s in all such cases matters and things wherein you our said respective commr^s can or may stand in need of or have occasion to use the assistance or service of any agent or soliciter as you shall think fit and we do likewise give unto you or any three or more of you in manner aforesaid full power and authority to nominate constitute and appoint in and throughout our said kingdom of Ireland subcommr^s deputies receivers collectors accomptants clerks surveyors waiters searchers gaugers or other inferior officers resply at or in the several counties cities baronies burroughs towns parishes and places of this kingdom and the islands and territories thereunto belonging from time to time as fully as the late or any former commr^s chief governor or governors and council of Ireland or the lord treasurer of Ireland or any others are by any act or acts of parliament or by the laws and statutes of this realm directed authorized or empowered as may be lawfully done or granted by us and such respective officers

sub-

subcomm^{nrs} collectors receivers accomptants clerks surveyors waiters searchers gaugers & other inferior officers already appointed or hereafter to be appointed in relation to the said revenues last mentioned to suspend remove or displace & to constitute and appoint others in his and their place and places resp̃ly according as you our said comm̃n^{rs} or any three or more of you resp̃ly shall think fit and requisite for our services and to take and receive & to cause to be taken and received in our names and to our use such securities from the respective collectors and other officers for the faithful discharge of their respective trusts as by you our said comm^{nrs} or any three or more of you resp̃ly shall be approved of and thought reasonable and to allow the said secretary and agent or solicitors or the subcomm^{nrs} collectors receivers accomptants clerks surveyors waiters searchers gaugers and other inferior officers such sallarys as are already or shall be hereafter allowed or settled by us or by the high treasurer or comm^{nrs} of the treasury in Great Britain for the time being and where no sallarys are or shall be resp̃ly settled by us or by our high treasurer or our comm̃n^{rs} of our treasury for the time being in all such cases you our said comm^{nrs} or any three or more of you resp̃ly may allow to such secretary or agent and sol^r and other officers such salary as to you our said comm^{nrs} or any three or more of you resp̃ly upon due consideration of the service pformed or to be performed shall be thought reasonable and fitting to be allowed and paid out of our said revenue and we do likewise give and grant unto you our said comm^{nrs} or any three or more of you full power and authority if you shall think fit with the approbation of our lord lieutenant or chief governor or governors there for the time being first had and obtained from time to time to farme out our hearth money and licenses upon beer ale wine and strong waters throughout our whole realme of Ireland or arising in any particular place thereof provided the said farme do not exceed the term of one year. And we do hereby require you our said comm̃n^{rs} resp̃ly from time to time to give an account to our said lord lieu^t or other chief governor or governors and to our lord high treasurer or lord comm̃n^{rs} of our treasury of Great Britain for the time being of your actings and proceedings in pursuance of this our commission as often as it shall be demanded of you by our lord lieu^t or other chief governor or governors of Ireland or lords comm̃n^{rs} of our treasury or lord treasurer for the time being. And we do hereby give and grant unto you our said comm̃n^{rs} or any three or more of you resp̃l^y or so many of you as by law may have full power and authority where you shall find it reasonable to compound and dispence with remit or mitigate any fine penalty or forfeiture whereunto we shall or may be entitled by virtue of the said acts or any of them so as the same extend not to any forfeiture arising upon the said acts of tunnage and poundage but so as no part of the duties thereby arising to us be lost or lessened and that the charges of recovery be reembursed to us if any such charges shall be. And we do hereby require and authorize you our said comm^{nrs} to cause the collectors to pass their accounts upon oath at the end of every year or oftener as you shall see cause which oath we do hereby empower you our said comm̃n^{rs} resp̃ly or any three or more of you or so many of you as by law may from time to time to administer and we do hereby grant unto you our said comm^{nrs} resp̃ly and every one of you or so many of you as by law may as also to all psons employed by you full power and authority to administer such oaths as by law may be administered to any person

for

Mr. G. Hatchell.

for the due execution of the premises and we do hereby grant unto you our said comm^{rs} resp̄ly or any three or more of you full power and authority to issue out warrants to our receiver general or cashier for the time being or to any collector or deputy collector or receiver of our said revenue to extend lay out & pay or cause to be paid and allowed to the said officers or any other person or persons whats^r such sums of money for salaries rewards or for incident or contingent charges as shall necessarily arise in or for the management of our said revenues or any of them. And we do hereby grant unto you our said comm^{rs} or any three or more of you full power to grant bills of portage to masters of ships according to usage and also bills of stores to merchants to the value of ten shills in customs & also powers to compound as to you or any three or more of you shall seem meet any seizures or things forfeited for not paying the duty imposed thereupon so as the duty if it had been paid had not exceeded forty shillings and the persons finally to acquit. And we do by these presents require & command you our said comm^{rs} and governors of our revenue aforesaid resp̄ly that you and every of you resp̄ly in manner aforesaid do carefully and diligently attend the execution & discharge of the respective trusts aforesaid & by all things as becometh. And we do hereby direct appoint and empower all our said collectors & subcomm^{rs} of our revenue to pay all monies collected by them to our vice tre^r receiver general or cashier in our said kingdom of Ireland for the time being or otherwise as we or our trēr or comm^{rs} of our treasury for the time being shall direct except what they shall be ordered by you our said comm^{rs} to pay for the several sallaries rewards & incident charges aforesaid according to the true intent and meaning of these presents & that they from time to time to render unto you or any three or more of you our said comm^{rs} respectively an account of what they have collected or paid as aforesaid. And we do hereby declare and grant that you our said comm^{rs} resp̄ly and every of you and those employed by you or under you shall during your continuance in this our service be exempted from serving upon juries or bearing any civil or military office. And whereas we have made sufficient provision for the payment of and answering all the moneys arising by or out of the said revenues hereby committed to the management of you our said comm^{rs} resp̄ly as aforesaid we do hereby for us our heirs and successors grant and declare that you our said comm^{rs} and every of you your heirs executors and administrators & every of them shall be and remain for ever clear free and finally discharged of & from all sums whatsoever growing and acrewing as afores^d and of and from rendering unto us our heirs and succ^{rs} any account for the same or any part thereof or for any fines penalties or forfeitures compounded remitted or mitigated or for any excise upon foreign goods imported and unsold and compounded and for which shall not be received by you notwithstanding the said moneys shall have been or may be collected by any person deputed or deriving authority from you our said comm̄n^{rs} resp̄ly or any three or more of you notwithstanding such person shall not pay or answer the same to our vice trēr or receiver general or to such receiver or officer as we have or shall appoint to receive the same and that neither our said comm^{rs} resp̄ly nor their heirs executors or adm̄ors shall be by us or our heirs or successors sued prosecuted or any way molested in their estates persons & goods in any of our courts whatsoever or by reason of any thing they or any of them shall act or do by virtue of these our letters patent and the powers therunto resp̄ly belonging

or

or by any exposition or construction thereupon save for voluntary or particular misfeazance done or acted by them or any of them and we do hereby strictly charge and command all officers of the admiralty and all persons deriving any authority from the lord high admiral or comm^{rs} of admiralty & all and every justice or justice of the peace mayors sheriffs bailiffs and constables headborroughs customers collectors comptrollers clerks of the peace and all other our officers and ministers whatsoever within every county city borrough or corporation barony parish or place and all other officers & ministers & all other our subjects whatsoever that they and every of them from time to time be aiding and assisting to you our said chief comm^{rs} and governors resply and to the subcomm^{rs} collectors surveyors comptrollers and to all other officers and ministers whatsoever which are or shall be appointed by you and to all and every person & persons employed in the execution of all and singular and every other the powers privileges and authorities and other the premises to you hereby given or granted or in obeying or executing such directions or precepts as shall from time to time be directing unto them for the due execution of this commission as becometh upon pain of our displeasure and such other penalties as by the acts or statutes of this realme can or may be inflicted upon them for their negligence or contempt in that behalf and as they will answer the contrary at their utmost perils and further of our special grace certain knowlege and meer motion by and with the advice and consent of our said justices and council & according to the purport and tenor of the aforesaid lres we have given & granted and by these presents do give and grant unto each of you the said William Strickland William Conolly Horatio Walpole Thomas Medlicott Phillips Gibbon & Thomas Wylde Edward Hopkins & William Harrison severally and respectively for the execution of the said trust hereby committed to your charge the salary or allowance of one thousand pounds ster by the year the sallaries of them the said William Strickland Wm Conolly Thomas Medlicott Phillips Gibbon Thomas Wylde & Edward Hopkins to commence from the time to which they were last paid by virtue of the said last recited commission or lres patents & the salary of the said William Harrison to commence from the date of this our commission and to be paid unto you & every of you the said William Strickland William Connolly Thomas Medlicott Phillips Gibbon Thomas Wylde Edward Hopkins & Wm Harrison resply out of our said revenues during our pleasure quarterly at the four most usual feasts or times in the year that is to say at the birth of our Lord Christ the Annunciation of the Blessed Virgin Mary the Nativity of Saint John the Baptist & the feast of Saint Michael the Archangel by even and equal portions. And our further will and pleasure is and we do hereby give and grant to you our said comm^{rs} herein and hereby appointed that when & as often as they or any of them shall happen to dye or to depart this life in our said service hereby to them committed or shall be removed therefrom that then and in every such case so much of their and every of their salary or sallarys resply as shall have incurred to the day of such death or removal shall be paid to them their exors and admors respectively all and every of which before mentioned sallarys allowances annuities rewards incident & contingent charges to be paid and allowed out of the said revenues profits and incomes by the orders or by the order of any three or more of you resply without your being charged with the moneys paid in respect of your signing the orders for the same. And we do hereby finally empower and authorize you our said comm^{rs} of the excise and

Mr. G. Hatchell. new impost and the comm^rs of our revenues resply as aforesaid to proceed and finish all causes and cases whatsoever which are or shall be left undetermined by virtue of the late or any former commission or commissions granted by us unto any former commissioners for management of our revenues of our said kingdom of Ireland. Provided always that this our commission be enrolled in the rolls of our high court of chancery in our said kingdom of Ireland within the space of six months next ensuing the date. In witness whereof we have caused these our letters patent to be made patents. Witness our aforesaid justices general & general governors of our said kingdom of Ireland at Dublin the 4 day of July in the seventh year of our reign.

Irrot quinto die Octobris anno r. R Georgij octavo.

Have you compared both of these with the original Patent Rolls in Ireland?
I have. I have brought the original Rolls here.

Will you produce them?

The same were produced.

Do you produce these from the Records of the Enrolments in Ireland?
Yes.

They are in your Custody as the Clerk of the Enrolments?
Yes.

Mrs. E. B. Lambe. Then Mrs. ELIZABETH BROWNE LAMBE was called in; and having been sworn, was examined as follows:

(*Sir Fitzroy Kelly.*) Do you reside at Cheltenham?
Yes.

How long have you resided there?
Six Years.

May I venture to ask your Age. How old are you?
Seventy-six.

What was your maiden Name?
Elizabeth Wylde.

Do you know if you are descended from Mr. Justice Tracy?
I have always been led to believe so.

Do you know from any of your Family, and can you tell me from which of your Family you have heard it, in what Degree of Relationship you stand to the Judge?
His Great Great Granddaughter, and we inherited Property from him, the Coscombe Property, which we sold to Mr. Hanbury Tracy for 30,000*l.*

You say that you are his Great Great Granddaughter; have you learned that either from your Parents or from any of your Family; tell me from whom?
From my Father and from my Great Aunt Elizabeth Wylde.

Who was your Great Aunt? What was her Name?
Elizabeth Wylde.

Did you know her well?
Very well. She visited my Father's Living every Year. He was in possession of the Family Living Forty Years, and my Aunt came every Summer from Bath to visit him.

Your

Your Father was a Clergyman ?
Yes.
What was his Name ?
Charles Edmund Wylde.
(*By a Lord.*) What was the Living he held ?
Glazeley, in Shropshire.
(*Sir Fitzroy Kelly.*) Is that the Living which you say he held for Forty Years ?
Yes ; the Family Living.
Was it there that your Great Aunt Elizabeth Wylde came to visit him from Bath every Year ?
Yes.
For how many Years. I do not ask you exactly; but about how many Years was it that your Great Aunt came ?
For many Years after I left School, and long before.
Do you remember when your Great Aunt died ; in what Year she died ?
Yes. I was Twenty-one when she died. I was born in 1770.
And she died in 1791 ?
Yes.
Was she a maiden Lady ?
Yes.
She never married ?
No.
You say that she visited your Father for a great Number of Years ; have you had or have you been present at many Conversations with her relating to the Family ?
Yes.
Used she frequently to speak of different Members of the Family ?
Yes.
Have you ever heard her mention a William Tracy ?
Yes, as a beloved Uncle ; she spoke of him with Affection.
You have heard her speak of William Tracy as a beloved Uncle, and you say she spoke of him with Affection ?
He was not recognized by the Family, and she spoke of him with Regret.

Mr. Attorney General submitted, That the Counsel for the Claimant was not entitled in giving Evidence of Declarations of Pedigree to give Evidence of Declarations of Fact.

Sir Fitzroy Kelly was heard against the Objection.

(*Sir Fitzroy Kelly.*) What have you heard your Great Aunt Elizabeth say on the Subject of her Uncle William Tracy's Relationship to the Family ?
I have heard her say that he was not recognized by the Family on account of his Marriage.
With respect to his Marriage, have you heard her speak of the Marriage of her Uncle William ?
Decidedly.

(62.)   Have

Have you heard her speak of whom he married ?

Mary O'Brien.

Have you heard her speak of him with relation to whose Son he was ?

Many Times.

As whose Son have you heard her speak of him ?

As the Son of the Judge.

What have you heard your Great Aunt Elizabeth state regarding this Son William and his Marriage ?

I have heard her state that the Family did not provide for him, and that was the Reason my Great Grandfather Wylde provided for him. He was provided for by him entirely.

You have mentioned that you have heard his Marriage with a Person of the Name of O'Brien spoken of ; what have you heard her say in relation to that ?

I thought I had stated it before. He married Mary O'Brien, and he was not looked upon by the Family after, and not provided for in any way by his Father. That was the Reason why Wylde my Great Grandfather provided for him. I think the Letter states that.

Will you tell me any thing else that you can remember ever having heard your Great Aunt Elizabeth say with respect to the Relationship of William Tracy to the Family ?

No more than I have already stated. He was the Third Son of the Judge ; and we were always taught to look up to the Name of Tracy. We have Five Pictures of him.

Did you come into possession of any Documents belonging to the Family. Just be so good as to look at that Letter and the Paper fastened to it. (*Two Papers being shown to the Witness.*) Those are your Papers ; are they not your Property ?

Yes ; I know it by rote.

When did you come into possession of them ?

When my Sister died.

When was that ?

In 1833.

Do you know in whose Possession they were originally ?

In the Possession of the Mother of my Aunt.

(*By a Lord.*) When did you first see them ?

In my Father's Lifetime.

(*Sir Fitzroy Kelly.*) As nearly as you can say, about how many Years ago did you first see that Letter ?

(*By a Lord.*) Was it after you came from School ?

After I left School ; when I was Sixteen.

In whose Possession was it then ?

My Aunt's it was then. It came from my Aunt to my Father ; she left a Deed of Gift.

Which Aunt are you speaking of ?

My Great Aunt Elizabeth Wylde.

Was that Letter in the Possession of your Great Aunt Elizabeth when you first saw it, being a Girl of Sixteen ?

I would not speak with Certainty. My Father was my Great Aunt's right hand, and she consulted him upon all Occasions, and her Papers were left with him.

When

When were her Papers left with him?
I cannot say in what Year.

About when was it; was it when she died?
When she did not think herself scarcely capable of managing her Papers without consulting my Father.

But you yourself saw the Papers long before your Aunt's Decease?
Yes.

In whose Hands was that Paper when you first saw it? Who showed it to you?
My Father, I suppose.

(*Sir Fitzroy Kelly.*) Have the kindness to try and recollect yourself. You saw it a great many Years ago, before your Aunt's Death. In whose Possession do you recollect to have seen it first? Who showed it to you when you first saw it?
My Father and my Aunt together. I conclude that such Papers as that were not shown to me at Sixteen. It was with my Father and my Aunt.

(*By a Lord.*) What was your Father doing with it when he showed it to you?
Reading it, I suppose.

Was it your Father or your Aunt that had hold of it?
It was in my Aunt's Possession; it was her Paper.

What Room was it in when she shewed it to you?
I am not prepared to reply to such a Question.

Was it in your Father's House or your Aunt's House?
That I know not.

Where did your Aunt live?
At Bath.

Did you often go to her House?
Every Summer.

Did your Father always go with you?
She came to my Father's every Summer.

Then you did not go every Summer to her House, but she came to your House?
She came to our House.

Was it at the Bath House or the Parsonage House that you saw the Paper first?
At my Father's House; Charles Edmund Wylde's.

The Reverend Charles Edmund Wylde?
Yes.

Your Aunt was there too?
Yes.

Was it in the Dining-room or the Drawing-room?
That I am not prepared to say.

You are not prepared to say whether it was in the Bath House or the Parsonage House that you saw it first?
In my Father's House in Shropshire, not at Bath.

That you are sure of?
Yes.

G   But

But not very sure of it. Will you take upon yourself to swear that it was at the Parsonage House that you saw it ?
I will not do any such thing.

When did you next see the Paper ?
Not till it came into my Father's Possession.

When was that ?
At my Aunt's Death.

When did she die ?
I have stated that before ; when I was Twenty-one. I was born in 1770.

And then it came into your Sister's Possession ?
Yes.

Was your Sister married or unmarried ?
Unmarried.

She was living with your Father ?
Yes.

Did your Sister go to Bath to get the Paper at your Aunt's House ?
Certainly not ; it came to her after my Aunt's Death.

Who brought it to you ?
My Sister, I suppose.

Did it come to your Sister or to your Father ?
To my Sister. My Father had been dead long before.

Then did your Sister show it to you when she got it ?
I had seen it in my Sister's Possession, and when she died it came to me, as every other Paper did.

Do you subscribe to the Expenses of supporting this Claim ?
No.

(*Sir Fitzroy Kelly.*) You say that this Paper was originally your Aunt's, and then it came to your Sister, and upon her Death it came to you. Did you during this very long Period of Time frequently see that Letter, or only very rarely ?
We admired the letter ; we were affected by reading the Letter.

Did you frequently look at it ?
We did ; and we remembered " the Dregs of Life," which is very striking.

You remember the Expression " the Dregs of Life ?"
Yes ; we revered the Memory of the Judge always, and every thing that belonged to him.

Have you ever seen any Document or Number of Documents in the Handwriting of the Judge so as to make yourself acquainted with the Character of his Handwriting, or is this the only Signature of the Judge that you have ever seen ?
I could not say what I have not seen in the present Claimant's Possession.

But until a very short Time, till within the last Two or Three Years, you had not seen any Document in the Judge's Handwriting ; you were not then acquainted with the Character of it ?
No.

Take

Take this Letter into your Hand; you see that there is now fastened *Mrs. E. B. Lambe.* to the Letter by Two Wafers this Piece of Paper with some Writing upon it?

This is my Aunt's.

Wait a Moment till I have asked my Question. The Question I wish to put to you is, whether this smaller Paper was fastened to the Letter when you first saw the Letter?

Decidedly not.

It was separate?

Separate.

When then did you first see the other Paper; take it into your Hand, and consider, and tell me as nearly as you can when you first saw that other Paper which you call your Aunt's?

When the Paper came into my Sister's Possession, into Mary Wylde's Possession, which was at the Death of my Aunt.

When you say your Aunt you always mean your Great Aunt Elizabeth?

Yes, Elizabeth.

Then you saw the smaller Paper?

Yes.

Then the smaller Paper was separated from the other at that Time?

No, it was not; I saw them joined together.

Have the goodness to attend to the Question, and the Form in which I put it to you; when you first saw this Letter of the Judge's Writing was this other Paper which is now fastened to it by Wafers fastened to it then?

No; I had seen it in my Father's Possession; when it was left to my Sister this was wafered to it.

Then when you first saw it, before your Father's Death, the Letter was separate; when it came into your Sister's Hands, or rather when you first saw it after it came into your Sister's Hands, the Two were united together?

Yes; and that is my Aunt's Writing.

Was it fastened in the Way in which you see it now?

Yes, exactly; it has never been moved.

During the whole Time then from that Period to the present, as far as you know, it has been fastened in the same Way?

Yes.

There is some pasting, something outside here, that I suppose has been done recently?

Done by a Friend lately to keep it together.

You say that this Linen, or whatever it is, has been put on recently by a Friend; before that Time, and while this Document was in your Possession, was it together, or did the Parts come completely separate?

No; it was beginning to separate.

So that it required something behind to keep it together?

Yes.

But has the Paper been always united together; never completely detached?

Never.

(62.)   Who

Mrs. E. B. Lambe.

Who was it that put it together ? Who was it that fastened on this Canvass or Linen ?

I could not tell ; I do not recollect at all.

(*By a Lord.*) How long has it been done ?

I do not know; my Papers were left to Friends when I was ill, and I was not able to do it myself; it was one of the Times that I went to Clifton and Cleavdon.

(*Sir Fitzroy Kelly.*) How long ago ?

Three or Four Years ago.

Do you know who wafered those together; did you see it done ?

No.

Have the goodness to look at this Paper, and do not answer in a Hurry ; look at this Paper which is added, which contains some Names and Dates ; have the kindness to read it to yourself, and then I am going to put a Question to you about it. (*The Witness read the same.*) Tell me, as nearly as you can remember, when was it that you first saw that Paper?

When it came into my Sister's Possession.

At the Time when it came into your Sister's Possession was it then fastened to the Letter by this Wafer ?

Yes.

And so has continued ever since ?

And so has continued ever since, and never been out of my Possession.

When did it come into your Possession ; you say at your Sister's Death ?

When she died.

When was that ?

In 1833.

Now I must trouble you to open it again, and look at it ; have you ever seen any other Documents and Writings in the same Handwriting as this Paper ?

Many.

What Documents have you seen ?

I am not exactly prepared to say what, but many of my Aunt's Writing that were shown when the first Case was here, and I acknowledge them as my Aunt's Writing, my Great Aunt.

Have you read this Paper ?

Yes.

Whose Writing do you take it to be ?

My Great Aunt's.

(*By a Lord.*) Have you seen your Great Aunt write in her Lifetime ?

Yes ; I corresponded with her for many Years.

Being acquainted with her Handwriting, you say that that Paper is in her Handwriting ?

Yes.

(*Sir Fitzroy Kelly.*) Will you look at that attentively, and say whether you are not making some Mistake, or whether you suppose that to be your Great Aunt's Writing ?

I have seen it so often, and read it often.

Was

Was your Great Aunt married, so that she could have Children ?
No.

Then will you explain how this could be her Writing ?
This was her Mother's Document; that is my Great Aunt, the
" Daughter Elizabeth."

But I am not asking as to whom it refers to, but whose Handwriting
it is ?
This was a Copy of her's from her Mother's.

You suppose it to be a Copy of her's from her Mother's ?
I suppose so, because it is my Aunt's Writing.

Have you ever seen any Writing of your Great Grandmother, Anne
Wylde, the Daughter of the Judge ?
I have got a Bible with her Name in it by her own Hand, and it is
endeavoured to be scratched out ; but there is another.

You have a Bible with her Name in it ?
I have the Bible; it was the Judge's Daughter's Bible.   (*A Bible·
was produced.*)

Is that the Bible ?
That is the Bible.

Where did you get that Bible ?
With my Father's other Effects.

When did you first see it ?
As soon as I could read, I suppose.   We were always taught to look
at the Bible.

Was that Bible in your Father's Possession ?
In my Father's Possession.   .

As long as you remember ?
As long as I remember ; bound in Calf at the Time.   I remember its
being bound.

There is an Entry of " Anne Wylde " here ; do you say that that
is your Great Grandmother's Handwriting ?
I did not know my Great Grandmother.

Have you ever seen any Documents in her Handwriting which
enable you to speak to the Character of her Writing, or is that the
only Piece of her Writing that you know of?
That I could not say positively.

Then all that you know of it is that that Bible has been in your
Family, and was in your Father's Possession, as long back as you can
remember ?
Yes.

You said something about scratching out ; is that the scratching out
that you meant ?   (*An Erasure being pointed out to the Witness.*)
Yes ; that is the very thing that was scratched out.

When was it scratched out ?
That I do not immediately know ; not by me.

How long ago ?
Seven or Eight or Nine or Ten Years ago ; it was scratched out
thinking it was the only Name that was in the Bible, and I found this
other.

H   Do

Mrs. E. B. Lambe.

Do you remember that the Name was there?

Yes, quite well; and extremely displeased I was at its being scratched out " Anne Wylde " from the Book.

Do you know Mr. James Tracy, the Claimant?

Yes.

How long have you known him? When did you first know him?

I cannot tell exactly now; it was since I came to Cheltenham.

(*By a Lord.*) About how long ago is it since you came to Cheltenham?

In 1843 I came to Cheltenham.

(*Sir Fitzroy Kelly.*) What I wish to draw your Attention to is this, what was it that first brought you into communication with Mr. James Tracy respecting this Family and his Claim?

He called upon me.

When?

In June.

In what Year?

I cannot tell the Year.

(*By a Lord.*) How many Years do you think it is ago?

My Sister died in 1833, and I did not see him until after my Sister's Death.

Did he call upon you soon after your Sister died?

No.

How long after?

Not till I came to Cheltenham.

How long have you been living at Cheltenham?

Eight Years.

Was it soon after you came to Cheltenham that Mr. Tracy called upon you?

No; I have been at Cheltenham Three Years before I knew Mr. Tracy.

Then Five Years ago he called upon you?

Yes.

(*Sir Fitzroy Kelly.*) Who was it that introduced you, and made you acquainted with the Claimant?

He introduced himself. He wished to see the Picture of the Judge, which he knew was in my Possession.

Was any one with you when he first came to you?

Yes.

Who was with you?

Ladies of my Acquaintance in Cheltenham.

Will you have the goodness to name any body who was with you at Cheltenham at the Time when he first came, in order that we may get, if we can, at the Date?

A Lady of the Name of Symonds was with me.

She was with you when he first came to you?

Yes.

Where does that Lady live? Does she live at Cheltenham?

She had a House in Cheltenham which has been let some Time; I have not heard any thing of her since; she is the Widow of an Officer.

You

You have spoken of a Picture of the Judge; have you ever seen any Picture of this William Tracy?
Yes.

When did you first see that Picture?
At Coscombe.

When; was it while you were very young or recently?
It was before the Coscombe Property was sold.

About what Period of Time was it; was it Twenty Years ago, or Thirty or Forty, or how many?
No.

Can you give me any Idea of the Time?
I was not prepared to answer that Question. When the Estate came to us it was to be divided, and it was sold and divided.

When that Event took place, then you saw the Picture?
Yes.

Was it the Picture of a grave Man or a Boy?
Decidedly a Man.

What Age should you say, a young Man or middle aged?
A young Man; he wore a Wig, with a Scarlet Coat; it is at my Brother's now.

(*By a Lord.*) Whose Picture was it called?
He was called the Fool of the Family.

It was called the Picture of the Fool of the Family?
Yes.

(*Sir Fitzroy Kelly.*) What was his Name?
William Tracy.

(*By a Lord.*) What Age should you take William Tracy to have been at the Time that Portrait was taken?
I should think perhaps Two or Three and Twenty.

Cross-examined by Mr. Attorney General.

You say that the Papers were in the Custody of some of your Friends for some Time?
No; they were not in the Custody, but they were pasted, and that was pasted and other things arranged and put away when I was going to Cleavdon; I was not equal to do it myself.

Did you leave them with any Person to arrange them for you?
Yes.

Who was it?
I could not possibly tell who pasted it.

Did you leave it with several Persons?
No, I did not leave it with any body; it was in my own Possession.

Did you see it done?
No, I did not see it done.

Can you tell me about how long ago it was done?
No.

Was it before or after James Tracy called upon you at Cheltenham?
That I cannot tell.

Was it Two or Three Years ago?
It was tattered and it was pasted; that is all I can say.

Cannot

Mrs. E. B. Lambe.

Cannot you tell me about when ?
No, I cannot tell about when.

Was it at Cheltenham, or where ?
It might have been done at Cheltenham.

Are you sure ?
No, I would not be sure.

Do you remember this Letter being very much tattered ?
It was torn all to Pieces ; it was put up in a Piece of ruled Paper to keep it together.

Was it torn quite across where the Direction is ?
No, it was not torn right across.

You see it is mended under the Piece of Paper attached to it ; was that done at the same Time that the other Part was mended ; was this mending underneath the Paper here done at the same Time that the Back was mended ?
It was altogether made secure, and it was put into the ruled Paper again.

That was done after your Sister's Death ?
Yes ; since it came into my own Possession.

You say that when the Paper first came into your Sister's Possession upon the Death of your Aunt that Paper was attached ?
Clearly.

Have you had that Paper ever since your Sister's Death ?
Certainly.

In your own keeping ?
Yes.

What did you do with it when you gave it to be mended ?
I did not give it ; it remained with my other Papers, which were arranged, as my other Things were, by my Friends with me ; I was not capable of doing it myself.

I understood you to say that you left your Papers when you went away ?
No, I never left them.

Where did you keep them ?
In a Desk or Bureau.

Cannot you tell me where you were in the habit of keeping that particular Paper ?
Among other Papers.

Where ?
In a Desk or a Bureau, as suited me best ; which I liked best.

Did you change them from Time to Time from one Place to another ?
I sometimes took my Papers with me (when I went) in my Desk ; sometimes I left them in the Bureau.

Did you ever when you went away take those Papers with you in your Desk ?
I cannot say.

(*By a Lord.*)   Did you lock them up ?
Always.

Then

Then how did your Friends get at them to mend them ?
I gave my Friends my Keys when I trusted them to pack up my Things.

Do you know to whom you gave the Keys ?
Yes.

Whom did you give them to ?
That I do not recollect ; whoever was with me packing up.

(*Mr. Attorney General.*) When James Tracy came to you, you say some Time after your Sister's Death, did you show him this Paper?
Yes.

At first ?
No.

When was it tnat you showed it to him first ?
Before the last Case was on ; I think so.

Did you give it to him to take away with him ?
No.

How long before the last Case was it that he was with you ?
I could not say.

Did you tell him then every thing you knew about it ?
Yes.

Did any body else come to you to ask you what you knew besides Mr. Tracy ?
No.

Have you never been examined by any body, by any Attorney ?
As to the Relationship ?

As to what you knew about the Family ?
Yes.

When was that ?
That I do not know.

Was it before the last Case ?
That I cannot tell.

How many Years ago was it ?
That I cannot tell.

Was it shortly after you had first seen Mr. Tracy ?
No, I think not.

Can you tell me how long ?
I could not say.

Who was the Gentleman who examined you ?
Mr. Bourdillon.

(*By a Lord.*) Where did he examine you ?
At my own House.

At Cheltenham ?
Yes.

Has he been more than once to you ?
No.

Then you were never in London to be examined ?
No.

Were you in London last Spring ?
I have been in London some Time.

Mrs. E. B. Lambe.

Did you see the Solicitor then?
No.

(*Mr. Attorney General.*) Did you never see Mr. Bourdillon more than once about it?
No.

And that was at Cheltenham?
Yes.

How many Years ago you cannot say?
I do not know.

Was it Two Years ago?
Before the last Case.

How often have you seen Mr. Tracy at Cheltenham?
Very often.

You said that he had shown you some Writing which he said was the Judge's Writing?
I think I have seen some of the Judge's Writing.

(*By a Lord.*) In his Hands?
I think in his Hands.

(*Mr. Attorney General.*) Mr. Tracy showed you the Judge's Writing?
Yes. I will not say decidedly that he showed it to me, but I have seen the Judge's Writing somewhere.

You spoke to Mr. Tracy about your being a Relation of the Judge?
Of course I did; he would have sought a Quarrel with me if I had not.

And to Mr. Bourdillon?
I told every body; I was proud of it.

(*By a Lord.*) Did you know Mr. James Tracy's Father?
No.

You never saw him?
No.

When did you first hear of Mr. James Tracy having set up a Claim to this Tracy Peerage?
Many Years ago.

Had you shown this Paper to any body before you showed it to Mr. James Tracy, after you heard of the Claim to the Peerage?
To Mr. Bourdillon.

Did you show it to him before the last Case was on?
Yes, when the Case was quashed here.

Did you give Mr. Bourdillon Possession of the Paper?
No.

Did he ever have it in his Possession?
No, it was in my Possession.

Was it in the Summer or the Winter that you first saw Mr. Bourdillon?
In June.

Re-examined by Sir Fitzroy Kelly.

You say that you saw Mr. Bourdillon, and made some Communications to him before the last Case was on; is that so?
Yes.

What

What do you mean by the "last Case;" before what Case was on?
The Case that was before the Lords.

Were you present when that Case was before the Lords?
No, I was not wanted.

Did you make a Deposition, or sign any Paper?
Yes.

Was that for the Purpose of what you call the "Case," for the Case coming on?
I do not understand you.

Was it to Mr. Bourdillon that you gave the Paper?
I gave Mr. Bourdillon what I have given you as far as I could.

You gave to Mr. Bourdillon the Information that you have given me, but did not you make a Deposition or a Declaration before the Magistrates?
Yes.

Was that about the same Time?
Yes, I think it was.

Is there any thing that will enable you to fix the Time at which you say you saw Mr. Bourdillon, and which you say was before "the Case" was on; is there any thing that will enable you to say in what Year it was?
No. .

How long was it after you had first seen Mr. James Tracy on this Subject that you saw Mr. Bourdillon?
A long Time.

How long?
Not till after the Hearing had been here in this House.

I want to know what Hearing you are talking about?
There was the printed Case came out, and I was expected to be called, but I was not called.

Should you know that printed Case again if you saw it?
Yes.

How long after that was it that you saw Mr. Bourdillon?
Years, I think it might be; I do not know. I hope I am giving as clear Evidence as I can; but I am very tired.

Can you give us any thing that will serve us as to the Dates; did you give this Paper to Mr. Bourdillon, or sign a Paper before a Magistrate, before what you call "the last Case" was on?
No; it is Four Years since I signed the Declaration.

Do not hurry yourself; collect yourself as well as you can, and tell me whether that is the Declaration that you suppose it is Four Years ago that you signed? (*A Paper being shown to the Witness.*)
That is my own Name.

You need not read it; just look at it, and see what it is about, and tell me whether that is the Declaration of which you have been speaking?
Yes; that is the only one that I ever signed.

You never signed any other Declaration?
No.

(*By a Lord.*) You expected to be called as a Witness?
Yes.

Will

Mrs. E. B. Lambe. Will you try and recollect, as near you can, how long it was since you first saw James Tracy?
I told you.

Will you state again how long you think it is, because it may be material?
In June 1839.

How many Years ago was it?
Five Years ago.

About June, Five Years ago?
Yes.

Are you sure it is as much as Five Years ago?
I should hesitate rather.

How long after your Sister's Death was it; your Sister died in 1833; how long after your Sister's Death was it?
It may be a Year, or it may be Two Years.

Within a Year or Two Years after your Sister's Death he called upon you?
Yes.

Did you show him this Letter at that Time?
No, I did not.

When did you first show him this Letter?
I cannot tell.

Did you tell him that you had a Letter from Judge Tracy?
No, not then; I did not know him sufficiently.

Did you tell him that you were related to Judge Tracy?
Immediately; that was the Purport of his Call to see the Judge's Picture, and he found I was related.

Did you tell him what your Aunt Elizabeth had told you respecting William the Judge's Son?
When he asked me the Question I did; I told him what I had mentioned, but not on our first Introduction.

How long after your first Introduction was it that you told him about what you had heard from your Aunt Elizabeth respecting William the Judge's Son; when did you first tell that to James Tracy?
I could not say; when the Case was inquired into more minutely I thought it of course proper to give my Attention to it.

You told him from the first that you were descended from the Judge?
I did.

Did not he ask you any thing about the Judge's Son William at that Time?
Yes; he told me that there was no such Person; but I said I knew better, I had heard my Aunt talk of him.

You said that to James Tracy the first Time you saw him?
I do not know the first Time; I said, "If you go to my Brother's you will see his Picture."

What did he say about there being no other Person?
I cannot tell who he heard it from, but that he was forgotten of the Family; that was the thing, that he was forgotten.

Did

Did you tell him that you had heard your Aunt Elizabeth speak about him?
.I did; that I had heard her speak of him with feeling.

How long after your Sister's Death was it? You told us that your Sister died in 1833; how soon after your Sister's Death did you tell Mr. Tracy about your Aunt Elizabeth?
I do not know; when the first Case came on here.

It was a great deal more than One Year after your Sister's Death?
Yes.

About Five Years ago you say?
Yes.

When did you first show that Paper to Mr. Tracy?
That I do not know; but he wished to find the Pedigree of the Wylde's, and I gave him an Introduction to Mrs. Wylde Browne of Bath, and he saw the Pedigree.

Then you showed him that Paper?
Yes.

Did you show him that when first you saw him?
No.

But the second Time?
No; nor the third Time.

But you showed it to him some Years ago?
Yes.

Are you quite sure that that Paper has never been out of your Hands?
Yes; not from me.

You never gave it to Mr. Bourdillon at all?
Never.

Then Mr. Bourdillon never had it in his Keeping?
No.

Where did you bring it from this Morning when you came here?
From the Bible I suppose.

Did you have it in the Bible yesterday?
It has been with my Papers since I came here.

Where have those Papers been since you came here?
In my own Trunk.

Locked up?
Yes.

And you had the Keys?
Yes.

And nobody has had the Trunk but you?
No; it has been in my Possession.

And nobody has had that Paper?
No.

Did you give that Paper to Mr. Bourdillon or his Clerk, or any other Person?
No; I never saw his Clerk.

Did you give it to Mr. Bourdillon himself?
No; I think I gave it to Mr. Tracy.

(62.)   K   When?

Mrs. E. B. Lambe.

When?

I do not know.

Are you sure that it was never out of your Possession?

It has never been with any body but myself.

You said, in answer to a Question, that you were not prepared to answer it. What do you mean by being "prepared to answer it"?

I did not mean to prevaricate, but I could not think.

Did you ever talk over this Case with Mr. Bourdillon?

Yes.

When?

At my own House at Cheltenham.

Did you never see him but at your own House at Cheltenham?

Never.

You never saw him in London?

Never.

(*Sir Fitzroy Kelly.*) I want to know whether I have understood correctly from you, that when you first saw Mr. James Tracy, at whatever Time it may have been, Mrs. Symonds was with you?

Yes.

Was any body with you when you first showed him the Judge's Letter and the Papers?

No, I cannot say.

You say you gave him a Letter of Introduction to Mrs. Wylde Brown?

Yes.

Was that at the Time you first communicated to him this Information?

Yes.

The Witness is directed to withdraw.

Mr. Fleming stated, That, with the Permission of the Committee, he would examine next some Witnesses from Ireland who were anxious to return.

Mr. W. H. Harding.

Then Mr. WILLIAM HENRY HARDING was called in; and having been sworn, was examined as follows:

(*Mr. Fleming.*) Do you hold any Office in Ireland?

I do.

What is it?

Senior Clerk of the Record Office in the Custom House, Dublin.

Do you produce an original Book from that Office?

I do. (*Producing the same.*)

Does it contain any Entry recording a Payment of Money to Thomas Wylde?

It does.

Will you read it?

The Witness read the same as follows:

An

An Establishment
for the Quarter Ending the 24th day of June 1726.

Commissioners and Officers appointed by Patent and Commission for Management of His Majesty's Revenue in Ireland.

		£
William Conolly, Esqr.	Wm Conolly - -	250 — —
	Thomas Medlycott -	250 — —
Thomas Medlycott, Esqr.	Tho. Wylde, by Order	
	ye Money sent by }	250 — —
Thomas Wylde, Esqr.	Bill. K. T. - }	

Have you a correct Copy of that?
I have, written by myself, and compared by myself with the Original.

The same was delivered in.

Then Mr. EDWARD WOODVILLE RICKETTS was called in; and having been sworn, was examined as follows: *Mr. E. W. Ricketts.*

(*Mr. Fleming.*) Do you hold any public Office?
I am a Clerk in Her Majesty's Treasury.
Do you produce one of the Books from the Treasury?
Yes, the Minute Book of the Treasury, dated 1727.
Does it contain any Entry in reference to Mr. Wylde?
It does.
Will you read it?

The same was read as follows:

Whitehall, Treasury Chambers, 24th Oct. 1727.
Present

Mr Chancellor Exchequer.   Mr Dodington.
Sir Charles Turner.   Sir George Oxenden.
Mr Clayton.

Prepare the War^t for renewing the Commⁿ of Excise without Altera^{con} other than inserting Thos Wylde instead of Patrick Haldane.

Have you got a Copy of that?
I have got a correct Copy which I made myself, and compared it myself.

The same was delivered in.

Then the Reverend GEORGE LARDNER FOXTON was called in; and having been sworn, was examined as follows: *Rev. G. L. Foxton.*

(*Mr. Fleming.*) Are you a Clergyman?
Yes.
Are you Vicar of Saint Peter's Church, Worcester?
Yes.
Do you produce the Register Book of that Parish for the Year 1726?
I do. (*Producing the same.*)

(62.)

Do

Rev. G. L. Foxton.
Mr. B. Clubb.

Do you find in that Year an Entry of the Christening of the Son of Thomas Wylde and Anne his Wife?
Yes.

Will you have the kindness to read it?

The same was read as follows:

No. 8.

Christenings in the Year 1726.

Jan. 3^d. Tracy, Son of Tho. Wylde, Esqr, & Anne his Wife.

(*To Mr. Clubb.*) Have you got a Copy of that?
Yes.

Is it a true Copy?
It is.

The same was delivered in.

(*To Mr. Foxton.*) Now will you refer to the Burials of 1727. Have you an Entry of the Burial of Tracy, the Son of Thomas Wylde, Esquire, in 1727?
Yes.

What is the Entry?

The same was read as follows:

No. 9.

Burials in the Year 1727.

April ye 9th. Tracy, Son of Thomas Wylde, Esqr.

(*To Mr. Clubb.*) Have you a true and correct Copy of that?
I have.

The same was delivered in.

Mr. J. Ford.

Then Mr. JAMES FORD was called in; and having been sworn, was examined as follows:

(*Mr. Fleming.*) Do you hold any Office in Doctors Commons?
I am a Clerk in the Prerogative Office.

Have you got the original Will of Anne Wylde?
I have. (*Producing the same.*)

Will you read it?

The same was read as follows:

No. 10.

Original so.

In the name of God amen. I Anne Wylde of the parish of St Michael Bedwardine in the county of Worcester widow of Thomas Wylde esq^r late of the Commandry in the city of Worcester dec^{ed} do make my last will and testament in manner following. First I will and direct my body to be buried in the most decent private manner possible without pomp and without bearers. Secondly I give and bequeath to my dear daughter Ann Wylde widow the sum of one hundred guineas also to each of her six children ten pounds apiece also I give and bequeath to my nephew Robert Pratt esq^r the sum of one hundred pounds also I give to my maid servant Penelope Bruton the sum of five pounds and all my wearing apparel provided she be in my service at the time of
my

my decease.   Lastly I give and bequeath to my dear daughter Elizabeth Wylde all my ready money moneys in the public funds or upon
any other securitys or by any ways due and owing to me and all and
singular my real and personal estate goods chattels and credits whatsoever and wheresoever and do make and constitute my said daughter
Elizabeth sole executrix of this my last will and testament hereby
revoking all former wills by me at any time made.   In witness whereof
I have hereunto set my hand and seal this thirtieth day of November
in the year of our Lord one thousand seven hundred fifty nine.

ANN WYLDE.   (L. S.)

> Signed sealed published and declared by the testatrix
> as and for her last will and testament in the pre-
> sence of us who in her sight and at her request
> have subscribed our names as witnesses.
> EDWARD GRIFFIN.   WILL^x OLIVER.

> Proved at London the 13th day of June 1761 before the Judge
> by the oath of Elizabeth Wylde spinster the sole executrix to
> whom administration was granted having been first sworn by
> commission duly to administer.

Have you got a Copy of that Will?
I have.

Is it a true and correct Copy?
It is.

Did you compare it yourself?
I examined it myself.

The same was delivered in.

Then SAMUEL ROGERS was called in; and having been sworn,
was examined as follows:

(*Mr. Fleming.*)   Are you Sexton of the Abbey Church at Bath?
Yes.

Are you acquainted with the Abbey Church at Bath?
Yes.

Have you been long acquainted with it?
Thirty Years and more.

Do you know a Tombstone there erected to the Memory of Anne
Wylde, the Relict of Thomas Wylde?
Yes.

How long have you known that Tombstone?
Thirty Years.

Has it, during those Thirty Years, been in the same State as it is
now in?
The flat Stone has, but the Monument is removed.   This is the
flat Stone.

Is the flat Stone in the same State as it was when you first knew it?
Yes.

(*Mr. Attorney General.*)   Whereabouts is it?
Before the Screen.

(62.)   L   Has

Mr. S. Rogers. Has it been there all the Time?
Mr. B. Clubb. Yes. No one would touch a Stone there except myself.

(*To Mr. Clubb.*) Have you got a Copy of that Inscription upon the Tombstone?
Yes. (*Producing the same.*)

Is it a true and correct Copy?
Yes.

(*To Mr. Rogers.*) Do you know this to be a true and correct Copy?
Yes.

The same was delivered in, and read as follows:

No. 11.

Underneath
are deposited the Remains of
Ann Wylde
Relict of Thomas Wylde, Esqr
of the Commandry Worcester
First Married to
Charles Dowdeswell, Esqr
of Forthampton, Gloucestershire
and Daughter of the Honorable
Mr. Justice Tracy
of Coscombe, Gloucestershire
She departed this Life
May the 12th 1761
aged 75 Years.

Rev.
W. E. L. Faulkner. Then the Reverend WILLIAM ELISHA LAW FAULKNER was
called in; and having been sworn, was examined as follows:

(*Mr. Fleming.*) Are you Incumbent of St. James's, Clerkenwell?
Yes.

Have you got the original Register of that Parish?
Yes.

Does it contain an Entry of the Burial of Thomas Wylde?
It does.

Will you read it?

The same was read as follows:

No. 12.

1740.   Burials.
April 14.   Th^s Wilde Esq.
70, Lincoln inn feilds.

(*To Mr. Clubb.*) Have you got a Copy of that Entry?
I have.

Is it a true and correct Copy?
It is.

The same was delivered in.

Then

Then Mr. JAMES FORD was again called in ; and was further examined as follows :

(*Mr. Fleming.*)   Do you produce the original Book of Administrations of the Prerogative Court in the Year 1791 ?
I do.

Do you find an Administration under the Date of 1791 of the Goods of Elizabeth Wylde, deceased ?
I do.

(*Mr. Attorney General.*)   To whom was it granted ?
To Charles Edmund Wylde, Nephew, and only next of Kin of the Deceased.

Will you read it ?

The same was read as follows :

Extracted from the Registry of the Prerogative Court of Canterbury.
June 1791.

Elizabeth Wylde.   On the First Day Admͦon of the Goods, Chattels, and Credits of Elizabeth Wylde, late of the Parish of Walcot in the County of Somerset, Spinster, dec̆ed, was granted to Charles Edmund Wylde the Nephew only next of Kin of the said dec̆ed, having been first sworn by Com̆on duly to adm'.

No. 13.

Chas. Dyneley   ⎱
John Iggulden ⎰ Deputy
W. F. Gostling ⎰ Registers.

Have you got a true and correct Copy of it ?
I have.

The same was delivered in.

(*To Mr. Rogers.*)   Do you know another Monument in the Abbey Church at Bath to the Memory of Anne, the Relict of Thomas Wylde ?
Yes.

How long have you known that Tombstone ?
Thirty Years.

Has that Tombstone been altered during that Period ?
It has not been altered ; it has been moved from one Part of the Church to another Part of the Church.

Has the Inscription upon it been altered ?
Not at all.

Then is the Monument in precisely the same State, save that it has been moved from one Part of the Church to another ?
Precisely.

(*Mr. Attorney General.*)   Have you examined this Copy of it ?
Yes ; I went through it Letter by Letter.

The same was delivered in, and read as follows :

Near to this Place are deposited the Remains of Ann, Wife of Robert Wylde, Esqʳ. of the Commandry in the County of Worcester, and Daughter of Charles Dowdeswell, Esqʳ. and Anne his Wife, of Forthampton Court in the County of Gloucester.

No. 14.

(62.)

She

Mr. J. Ford.
Mr. B. Clubb.

She died May 12th 1764, aged 52 Years, and left Issue Four Sons and Four Daughters.

In the same Vault rests in Peace

Elizabeth, Daughter of Thomas Wylde Esqr, and Anne his Wife, of Lincoln's Inn Fields, London, and Sister to the above named Robert Wylde.

She died a Spinster, May 17th 1791, aged 65 Years.

This Monument was erected by the Revd C. Wylde, Rector of Glaseley in the County of Salop, only surviving Son of the said Robert Wylde, as a lively Memorial of his filial Affection and grateful Tribute of his tender Regard.

Rev. G. L. Foxton. Then the Reverend GEORGE LARDNER FOXTON was called in, and further examined as follows:

(*Mr. Fleming.*) Will you turn to the Year 1732 in the Register of the Parish of St. Peter, Worcester. Do you find an Entry under the Date of 1732 of the Baptism of Charles Edmond, Son of Robert Wylde and Anne his Wife?

Yes.

Will you read it?

The same was read as follows:

No. 15.   Christenings for the Year 1732.

Decemb ye 31. Charles Edmond, Son of Robert Wylde Esqr and Anne his Wife.

(*To Mr. Clubb.*) Have you got a Copy of that?
I have.

Did you compare it with the original Entry?
I did.

Is it a true Copy?
It is.

The same was delivered in.

(*To Mr. Foxton.*) Will you have the kindness to look at the Entry of Burials for the Year 1741?
Yes.

Do you find an Entry in that Year of the Burial of Thomas Wylde, Esquire?
Yes.

What is the Date of it?
The 26th of October 1741.

Will you read it?

The same was read as follows:

No. 16.   Burials for the Year 1741.

Octob^r 26th. Robert Wylde Esqr.

(*To Mr. Clubb.*) Do you produce a true Copy of that Entry?
I do.

The same was delivered in.

Then

Then the Reverend GEORGE BELLATT was called in ; and having been sworn, was examined as follows :

(*Mr. Fleming.*) Are you Incumbent of the Parish Church of Saint Leonard's, Bridgnorth ?
Yes.

Do you produce the original Register of that Church ?
I do. (*Producing the same.*)

Do you find in it an Entry of the Marriage of Charles Wylde, Clerk, under the Date of 1765 ?
I do.

Will you read the Entry ?

The same was read as follows :

Banns of Marriage between
(No. 185.)   Charles Wylde, Clerk of the Parish of S⁺ Leonard's in Bridgnorth, and Mʳˢ Mary Fewtrel of the Parish of S⁺ Leonard's in Bridgnorth, were married in this Church by Licence this Fourth Day of September in the Year One thousand seven hundred and sixty five by me,

No. 17.

Thoˢ Littleton, Minʳ.

This Marriage was solemnized between us {C. Wylde.
{Mary Fewtrell.

In the Presence of Charles Fewtrell.
Ann Phillips.

Mr. Attorney General asked, Whether it was proposed to apply this Entry to prove the Marriage of Charles Edmond Wylde ; and Mr. Fleming stated, that it was.

(*To Mr. Clubb.*)   Have you a Copy of that ?
I have.

Is it a true Copy ?
It is.

The same was delivered in.

Then the Reverend JOHN WILLIAM BROMLEY was called in ; and having been sworn, was examined as follows :

(*Mr. Fleming.*)   Are you in Holy Orders ?
Yes.

Are you Curate of Deuxhill and Glazeley near Bridgnorth ?
Yes.

Do you produce the original Register of that Parish ?
I do.   (*Producing the same.*)

Is it in your Custody as Curate of the Parish ?
Yes.

Do you find in the Year 1798 an Entry of the Burial of Charles Edmond Wylde ?
I do.

Will you read it ?

The same was read as follows :

(62.)   M   1798.

1798.

Buried. Charles Edmund Wylde,
Rector, January 25th.

No. 18.

(*To Mr. Clubb.*) Have you a Copy of that Entry?
I have.

Have you examined it yourself with the original Entry?
I have.

Is it a correct Copy?
It is.

The same was delivered in.

(*To Mr. Bromley.*) Do you find an Entry of the Baptism of
Elizabeth Brown, the Daughter of Charles Edmund Wylde, Rector,
and Mary his Wife?
I do.

Will you have the goodness to read it to their Lordships?

The same was read as follows:

No.19.
1770.

Elizabeth Browne, the Daughter of Charles Edmund Wylde, Rector,
& Mary his Wife, was baptised at Glaseley.
Oct.r 16th.

(*To Mr. Clubb.*) Have you got a Copy of that?
I have.

Is it a true Copy?
Yes.

Have you compared it yourself with the Original?
I have.

The same was delivered in.

Rev. G. Bellatt. Then the Reverend GEORGE BELLATT was called in, and further
examined as follows:

(*Mr. Fleming.*) Do you produce the original Register of the Parish
of Saint Leonard's, Bridgnorth, for the Year 1811?
Yes. (*Producing the same.*)

Do you find an Entry of the Marriage of William Lamb and
Elizabeth Browne Wylde?
I do.

Will you read it to their Lordships?

The same was read as follows:

No.20. [The Year 1811.] Page 43.

No 532. William Lamb, Bac.r, of the Parish of Alberbury & Co.
of Salop, and Elizabeth Browne Wylde, Spin.r, of the same, were
married in this Church, by Licence, this Fifteenth Day of September in
the Year One thousand eight hundred and eleven by me, E. H. Payne,
Curate.

This Marriage was solemnized between us { William Lamb.
{ Eliz. Browne Wylde.

In the Presence of { Harriet Harding.
{ Samuel Higgins.

(*To*

(*To Mr. Clubb.*) Have you a true Copy of the Entry just read by the Witness ?
I have.

You examined it yourself, and you know it to be a true Copy ?
Yes.

The same was delivered in.

Then the Reverend GEORGE LARDNER FOXTON was called in, and further examined :

(*Mr. Fleming.*) Do you find in the Register Book of Saint Peter's, Worcester, an Entry of the Baptism of Thomas Wylde in the Year 1731 ?
I do.

Will you have the kindness to read it to their Lordships ?

The same was read as follows :

Christenings for the Year 1731.

No. 21.

Decemb^r ye 21st.   Thomas, Son of Robert Wylde, Esqr, & Anne his Wife.

(*To Mr. Clubb.*) Have you a Copy of that which you have compared with the original Entry ?
I have.

Is it a true Copy ?
It is.

The same was delivered in.

The Witnesses were directed to withdraw.

The Counsel were directed to withdraw.

Proposed to adjourn this Committee sine Die,

Accordingly,

Adjourned *sine Die.*

Die Martis, 4° Maii 1847.

The EARL OF SHAFTESBURY in the Chair.

THE Order of Adjournment was read.

The Minutes of the last Committee were read.

The Counsel and Parties were ordered to be called in ;

And Sir Fitzroy Kelly, Mr. Serjeant Shee, Mr. Fleming, Mr. Charles Bourdillon, and Mr. Hudson appearing as Counsel for the Petitioner ;

And Mr. Attorney General and Mr. Solicitor General for Ireland appearing on behalf of the Crown ;

Sir Fitzroy Kelly stated, That he proposed first to put in a Letter with the Paper annexed to it which had been produced at the last Meeting of the Committee, when Evidence had been given with respect to the Custody and Handswriting.

The same were delivered in, and read as follows :

No. 22.

Dear daughter,   Coscombe, Jan. 29, 173$\frac{3}{2}$.

I received the favour of your very obligeing letter of the 20th wherein you are pleased to express so great and affectionate a concern for my health.   I am upon the very dregs of life and the best I can say of myself is that I live without pain which is reckoned by some to be the pleasure of an old man but I cannot say I take delight in any thing in this world therefore shure it is time to leave it but as for that I must resign to the will of Allmighty God and hope of his infinite mercy he will prepare me for it.   I am glad to hear that you and your family are got over the generall complaint of colds without any partickler mischief I thank God wee have escaped them here very well.   I design to go to Bath this next season which will be the latter end of March or the beginning of April tho I cannot expect much benefit from the waters. But wherever I am or whatever befalls me I shall as long as I have breath wish you all the happiness in the world.   I am with all service to Mr Wylde to whom I am very much obliged your very affectionate father.

Your letter came free.   R. TRACY.

To Thos Wylde Esq. at the Excise Office in London.

My Bro Tracy was born Augst 30, 1684.
My Self was born March 22, 1686.
My Bro Richard was born Oct. 24, 1691.
My Bro W^m was born Feb. 16, 1692.
My Sister was born Oct. 22, 1697.

My Daugter Ann was born July 6, 1712, of a Sunday Evening.
My Daughter Elizabeth was born Augst 3, 1725, of a Tuesday Morning.
My Son Tracy was born Dec. 28, 1726, Wednesday Morning.

(62.2.)   N   The

The Counsel being asked whether Mrs. Lambe was in attendance, stated that she was not.

The Counsel was informed, That the Attendance of Mrs. Lambe would be required at the next Sitting of the Committee.

Hannah Perry.

Then HANNAH PERRY was called in ; and having been sworn, was examined as follows :

(*Sir Fitzroy Kelly.*)   Where do you live ?
In my Father's House at Bridgenorth.

Were you in the Service of any of the Wylde Family ?
Yes.

In whose Service were you ?
In Miss Mary Wylde's.

Was she a Sister of Mrs. Lambe ?
Yes.

How long were you in her Service ?
Twenty-six Years within a few Months.

When did you cease to be in her Service ?
At her Death.

When was that ?
About Ten Years since to the best of my Knowledge.

Have you brought with you a Picture ?
Yes.

[A Picture was produced.]

Look at that Picture ; you know that Picture ?
Yes.

How long ago was it that you happened first to see that Picture ?
In 1807 to the best of my Recollection.

In whose Possession was it then ?
It was brought up from Coscombe in Gloucestershire with some more.

Family Pictures ?
Yes, the Family Pictures of the Judge Tracy.

Brought from Coscombe to what Place ?
To Kidderminster, to the Reverend Robert Wylde's.

What Relation was he of the Family ?
He was a Brother of Miss Wylde.

And, consequently, Brother to Mrs. Lambe ?
Yes.

He lived at Kidderminster ?
Yes ; in the Vicarage at Kidderminster.

You say that this Picture was brought to Kidderminster with some other Family Pictures ?
Yes.

From whom did you hear any thing about this Matter ?
From living in the Wylde Family.

Which of the Family ?
Miss Mary Wylde.

(*By*

(*By a Lord.*)   Is she dead ?
Yes.

She is the Person who died about Ten Years ago ?
Yes.

Did you hear from Miss Mary Wylde whose Son the Person represented in that Picture was ?

Mr. Solicitor General for Ireland objected, That this Question was not admissible.

Sir Fitzroy Kelly submitted, That it having been proved that Miss Wylde was a Member of the Tracy Family, the Question was admissible.

The Counsel was informed, That the Committee were of opinion that this Question could not be put.

(*Sir Fitzroy Kelly.*)   Did you ever hear Miss Wylde say any thing as to whose Son William Tracy was ?
Judge Tracy's.

Have you heard any Statement made by Miss Wylde relative to William Tracy as connected with that Picture ?

Mr. Solicitor General for Ireland objected to the Question.

The Counsel was informed, That the Question was inadmissible.

(*Sir Fitzroy Kelly.*)   Did you ever hear Miss Wylde say whose Son the Original of that Picture was ?

Mr. Solicitor General for Ireland objected to the Question.

Sir Fitzroy Kelly was heard in support of the Question.

The Counsel was informed, That this Question was open to the same Objection as the former one.

(*Sir Fitzroy Kelly.*)   You say that you have heard from Miss Wylde that William Tracy was the Son of Judge Tracy ?
Yes.

Did you ever hear from Miss Wylde any thing concerning William Tracy's Descent in reference to that Picture when the Picture was alluded to ?

Mr. Solicitor General for Ireland objected to the Question.

Sir Fitzroy Kelly was heard against the Objection, and stated, That he proposed to ask the following Question.   " Have you heard from Miss Wylde of whose Son that was the Picture ? "

The Counsel was informed, That the Committee were of opinion that that Question could not be put.

(*Sir Fitzroy Kelly.*)   You say that you lived Twenty-six Years in the Family ?
Yes.

(62.2.)

Did

Hannah Perry.

Did you know various other Members of the Family besides Miss Wylde?

I knew Miss Wylde's Mother, Mrs. Charles Edmund Wylde, of Glazeley, and the Mother of Mrs. Browne Lambe, and the Mother of Mr. John Fewtrill Wylde.

Do you remember about when that Mrs. Wylde died?

I cannot speak exactly to the Year.

I want to know whether she was an old Lady?

Yes; she was Seventy-four when she died.

About how long ago did she die?

I dare say she has been dead Twenty Years.

Did you ever hear from her of a William Tracy, whose Son he was?

Yes.

Whose Son?

The Son of Judge Tracy.

Have you heard the same thing from all the Members of this Family with whom you lived, or whom you have heard talk about the Family?

The Counsel was informed, That the Persons must be named to whom the Question was intended to refer.

You have heard this, you say, from Miss Wylde, who is dead, and from Mrs. Wylde her Mother, who is dead; is there any other Member of the Family whom you knew that is dead?

There is Mr. Hincksman and Mr. Purton.

Are they dead?

Yes.

What Relation was Mr. Hincksman?

I cannot say; he was a distant Relation.

Was he an old Man or a young Man?

An old Gentleman when he died; he was about Eighty-two, I think, when he died. Mr. Purton was not so much.

What was Mr. Purton?

I think he was a Relation through Marriage, but I cannot say exactly what.

Cross-examined by Mr. Solicitor General for Ireland.

You say that you were about Twenty Years living with Miss Wylde?

I was Twenty-six Years all but a few Months.

Did you ever live with other Members of her Family?

I lived with her Mother; with Miss Wylde in her Mother's House. I was not a hired Servant to her Mother, but I was to Miss Wylde; they lived together.

Did Miss Wylde live with her Mother up to her Mother's Death?

She lived with her Mother about Three Years, I think, and then she took a House and went to it, she and Mrs. Browne Lambe, till Mrs. Browne Lambe was married, and she went to live with her Mother again.

Was she living with her Mother at the Time of her Mother's Death?

She was.

And

And you were living in the same House?
I was.

Where did the Mother die?
At Bridgenorth in Shropshire.

(*By a Lord.*) Were you living with them when the Family were at Coscombe?
Yes.

When was that?
I cannot exactly say; they went down to see it.

They only went to see it?
No.

You cannot tell when it was?
I cannot say in what Year it was.

Can you tell any thing like when it was?
I cannot say what Year it was.

About how many Years ago?
I cannot say.

Was it Forty Years ago?
I dare say it was.

Was it more?
I cannot say.

Was it before or after they got the Picture?
I think it was after, but I cannot speak for Truth.

Was the House inhabited when they went to Coscombe?
I cannot say.

Was there a House at Coscombe when they went there?
Oh yes.

Was the House inhabited?
I cannot say.

Did they stay there?
They were at Cheltenham and went to see it; I have heard them say that.

Were you at Cheltenham with them?
No.

Did not you say that you went with them to Coscombe?
I did not say any such thing.

And you never were at Coscombe?
No.

(*Mr. Solicitor General for Ireland.*) From the Time that you first went into the Service of Miss Wylde you remained with her till her Death?
Yes.

You never left her Service at all?
No.

You have already stated that you were never yourself at Coscombe?
No.

(*By a Lord.*) Was it after or before you went to live with Miss Wylde that they paid this visit to Coscombe?
I do not know.

Hannah Perry.

All you know is that you heard that they had once been there in their Lives ?
Yes.

Were you at Kidderminster when the Pictures came ?
Yes.

When was that?
In 1827 to the best of my Knowledge.

Are you sure of that ?
To the best of my Knowledge it was that Year.

Were you in the Service of Miss Wylde at the Time ?
Yes.

And you were living at Kidderminster with Miss Wylde ?
I went with her to her Brother's—to the Vicarage.

You were there when the Pictures came ?
Yes.

And that was in the Year 1827 ?
To the best of my Knowledge.

Do you mean to say that it was about that Time ?
Yes.

You are not sure whether it was in 1827, or 1826, or 1828 ; but it was about that Time ?
It was about that Time.

Where did the Pictures come from ?
They came from Coscombe in Gloucestershire.

Upon what Occasion did they come from Coscombe ; how came they to be brought from Coscombe ?
I cannot say.

There were a Parcel of Pictures brought from Coscombe ?
Yes.

And that Picture was amongst them ?
Yes.

Do you know where this Picture has been ever since ?
They were at the Reverend Robert Wylde's for some Years, hung up, at Kidderminster.

Have you ever seen them there ?
All the Time in the course of going there with my Mistress.

How long did you stay at Kidderminster ; you were only on a Visit ?
Yes.

Have you seen this Picture since ?
Yes.

When did you see it ?
It was taken to Claverdon in Warwickshire ; they were removed from there after Mr. Robert Wylde lost his first Wife to Claverdon in Warwickshire after he married his present Lady.

Were the Pictures moved ?
Yes, to Claverdon.

Have you ever seen them at Claverdon ?
No.

You

You have not seen this Picture since 1826 have you?
Yes.

When was the last Time that you saw this Picture at Kidderminster?
The Year that Mr. Wylde went to Claverdon.

Do you know how long ago that was?
I cannot say.

Have you ever seen this Picture since that?
Yes; it was brought by Mr. Robert Wylde's Widow from Claverdon when she went to live at Bridgenorth.

When was that?
I cannot exactly say when.

You saw it at that Time?
Yes.

Are you sure that it is the same Picture?
Yes.

How do you know it?
I remember it perfectly well because it was represented to be one of the Judge's Sons.

And you can swear that it is the same Picture?
Yes.

When did you see it last before you saw it here To-day?
I saw it at Uplands.

When was that?
I am in the habit of going there very often.

Whose is Uplands?
Mr. John Fewtrill Wylde's.

This Picture has been there?
Yes.

Was it brought from there now?
Yes.

You know it do you?
Yes.

You are confident that it was about the Year 1826 that this Picture was brought to Kidderminster from Coscombe?
It was about 1826 or 1827.

You were at Coscombe yourself were you?
No.

When you talk of about 1827 are you sure that it was not many Years before that that those Pictures were brought there; are you sure that it was not more than Twenty Years ago?
To the best of my Recollection it was the first Year I went to live with Miss Wylde.

In what Year was that?
In 1827.

Who brought these Pictures?
They were brought by the Waggon.

How do you know where they came from?
I heard Mr. Hincksman and Mr. Purton say that they came up from Coscombe.

(62.2.)   Re examined

Re-examined by Sir Fitzroy Kelly.

You have mentioned Two different Times at which you say. these Pictures were brought from Coscombe; how long do you say that you lived with Miss Wylde?
Twenty-six Years.

Do you say that it was the first Year you lived with her?
To the best of my Recollection.

Now reflect a little, and tell me when it was, because you have given us Two different Dates; how long has Miss Wylde been dead?
About Ten Years.

Do you know what Year this is now?
Yes, 1847.

Do you know what Year she died in?
She has been dead about Ten Years.

Do you know or not; are you sure it was not 1833 when she died?
I cannot say.

She died, you say, about Ten Years ago, and you lived with her Twenty-six Years before that?
Yes, before her Death.

These Pictures were brought the first Year you lived with her?
Yes. I had not lived with Miss Wylde before the Year I went to Kidderminster.

Then do you still say that it was the first Year that you lived with Miss Wylde?
Yes.

And do you mean that after that Time you lived with her for Twenty-six Years?
I did.

You say that it was the first Year that you lived with Miss Wylde that these Pictures came up to Kidderminster; was that Twenty-six Years before Miss Wylde's Death?
Yes.

Then will you state how you make it out to be 1827; was not it 1807?
1807.

Then what did you mean by saying 1827; was it a Mistake?
Yes, it was 1807.

(*By a Lord.*) How old may you be?
Fifty-seven.

How old were you when you first went to live with Miss Wylde?
About Thirteen.

At what Period in 1807 did these Pictures come to Kidderminster?
I cannot say exactly, but I think it was some time in the Summer Months.

Sir Fitzroy Kelly stated, That the Fragments of the Tombstone were ready to be produced.

The Counsel was informed, That the Fragments might be produced and laid upon the Floor of the House, which was done accordingly.

Then

Then SAMUEL SHEANE Esquire was called in ; and having been sworn, was examined as follows :

(*Mr. Serjeant Shee.*) I believe you reside at Mountmelick in the Queen's County ?
I do.

Are you a Magistrate of the Queen's County ?
I am.

How long have you been resident in the Neighbourhood ?
For about Twenty-seven Years.

Do you know the Churchyard of Castlebrack ?
I do.

Is there any Church in the Churchyard ?
There is the Ruin of a Church, but no Church.

Have you had occasion frequently to go there ?
I have been there, I think, Five Times altogether within the last Ten Years.

Do you remember any respectable Persons in that Neighbourhood in the Rank of Gentlemen being buried there ?
I was aware of the Names of one Family, a Family of the Name of Dunn, who, I suppose, are the only Persons in the Rank of Gentry buried there ; I mean that have Tombstones over them.

Do you know of the Burial Service having been performed there on the Funeral of any Person ?
No.

When you first recollect the Churchyard was it enclosed ?
It is enclosed partially with a Ditch, but no sufficient Enclosure.

How was it used when you first remember it ; did Cattle graze upon it ?
It was surrounded by other Land, and the Fence was of that Nature that Cattle could pass through and repass. The Place was grazed by Cattle.

Was it a Place of Resort for the Peasantry of the District ?
It is a Place very much resorted to ; there is a great annual Fair held there on the 12th of August.

Do you remember whether it was the Custom of the Peasantry to have rural Sports there ?
I have always heard so the last Twenty Years.

Have you ever seen them amusing themselves there ?
I have never been there at such Amusements.

Do you remember a House close to the Churchyard ?
I do.

Who occupied that House when you first remember it ?
A Person of the Name of Dunn, a Widow Woman.

Did she carry on any Business there ?
Yes, she kept an Alehouse, a very poor wretched Cabin.

Was there a large Room at the Back of that House ?
The House at present consists of Two Apartments, and there appears to be a little narrow Entrance into the Graveyard ; and adjoining that Entrance there appears to have been a Room which is in a State of Dilapidation.

Is there a Room at the Back of the House ?
It is at one End.

Now without a Roof?
Now without a Roof.

And I believe that was larger than any other Room in the House ?
It appears to be so.

Have you any Recollection of how that Room was used when you first remember the House occupied by the Widow Dunn ?
No.

Have you seen the Stone called the Tracy Stone, which is now lying at the Feet of their Lordships ?
I have seen it upon Two Occasions, not as it now is.

There are several Fragments lying there. When did you first see any Portion of that Stone ?
On the 28th of October 1844.

Which Portion did you see ?
There were then only Four Pieces, the Four upper Pieces ; there were not Five then ; the smaller Piece in the Centre has broken off since.

Where did you see them ?
In the Churchyard of Castlebrack.

In what Condition were they when you saw them ?
They were lying on the Grass in the Churchyard pretty much in the same Way as they are now lying there.

In what Part of the Churchyard ?
Near to the Entrance Gate as they went in, a little rude Wicket Doorway.

Nearer to that than to the Ruins of the Church ?
Yes.

Who were there when you first saw these Fragments ?
There was a considerable Number of Persons there, several Magistrates and surrounding People living in the Neighbourhood ; they were then in the Possession of Mr. Digby Baynham.

Some of the Magistrates who were there I believe are now in Attendance ?
They are.

Who is Mr. Digby Baynham ?
He is a respectable Person in some Kind of Trade in the Village of Killeigh in King's County, and within Two or Three Miles of the Burial Place.

Did you examine the Stones particularly on that Occasion ?
Very carefully.

Did you remain there all the Time the Stones were there on that Day ?
I did.

Did you see them removed from the Place where you first saw them ?
I saw them packed up to be brought back again in the Custody of Mr. Baynham.

I believe there are other Fragments to which you have not yet spoken ; when did you first see them ?
On the 22d of March in the present Year.

Where

Where did you first see them ?
In the Churchyard of Castlebrack.

In what Part of the Churchyard ?
I think about the same Place that I saw the Stones originally, about the same Position.

But they had not been there at all when you first saw the others in October 1844 ?
No ; there were only the Four Parts I mentioned before.

When you first saw those Two last Fragments were they lying upon the Ground or were they embedded in the Ground ?
They were lying altogether pretty much the same as they are at present.

Did it appear to you that they had been placed there to be looked at, or were they where they had been previously found ?
They had been previously found, and had been placed there, as I understood, to be viewed by the Magistrates who then attended.

Were the other Four Fragments there upon that Occasion ?
Yes ; Five.

(*By a Lord.*)   Had that little Bit been broken off then ?
Yes ; it was broken between the Time I saw it first and the second Time.

(*Mr. Serjeant Shee.*)   Were a great many Persons present upon that Occasion ?
A considerable Number.

Several Magistrates of the County ?
Yes.

And humbler Persons ?
Yes.

How long did your Examination in the Churchyard of the Stones last upon that Occasion ?
Two or Three Hours.

Were you there the whole of the Time that the Stones were there upon the Ground ?
I was there the whole of the Time.

Do you remember any thing being done with the Stones while they continued in the Churchyard ?
I do.

Will you state what it was ?
I recollect that to satisfy myself of the Genuineness of the Parts, at my Suggestion, the Stones were all turned up that I might examine the Back of the Stone ; that was done.   An old Witness was there, and I spoke to him.

What was his Name ?
John Delany.

Had you known him any Time ?
Upwards of Twenty Years.

What is he ?
A small Farmer.

What Age is he ?
I suppose over Eighty Years old.

(62.2.)

———

Where does he live ?   How far from the Graveyard ?

I suppose about a Mile.

Was he among those who were examining the Stone on the second Occasion ?

He was.

Was any thing done to the Stone, or with it, by him, in your Presence ?

At my Suggestion the Stone was carried to the other Side of the Ruin—the South Side of the Ruin.

When they had carried it was it placed upon the Ground ?

It was placed upon the Grass.

At what Distance from the Ruin ?

I did not measure it ; it was very convenient ; perhaps near Three Paces, I think.

Did it remain there any Time ?

No ; for a few Minutes.

After that had been done was any thing else done with the Stone in your Presence ?

Yes.

What was done ?

A wooden Case had been prepared, and all the Parts of that Stone that were there were carefully packed in my Presence and that of the other Magistrates, and nailed down and sealed with our Seals.

Before it was put into the Box did you personally make any Examination of the Edges of the several Fragments ?

I did.

Can you state to their Lordships the Names of any Gentlemen who were there present and who assisted you in that Examination ?

I can.   Captain Warburton of Garyhinch.

Is he here ?

He is ; and Captain Tibeaudo, a Magistrate of King's County.

From your own personal Examination of the Edges of the Stone generally can you state to their Lordships whether it is now in the same Plight that it was when you first saw it ?

Precisely so.

(*By a Lord.*)   Have you examined the Edges this Morning ?

I saw them put together in the Hall, and I saw them last Night when they were opened.

(*Mr. Serjeant Shee.*)   You say that they were packed up in a Box, and that that Box was sealed ?

It was sealed with the Seals of the Magistrates present, Five or Six ?

Was that Box produced last Night in your Presence at the Chambers of Sir Fitzroy Kelly, in the Temple ?

It was.

Did you examine the Seal which you had affixed to it at Castlebrack ?

I did.

And you were present when the other Gentlemen did the same ?

I was.

Are you satisfied that the Stone which was taken out of the Box at Sir Fitzroy Kelly's Chambers is the Stone that was sealed up at Castlebrack ?

I am positive of it.

Have

Have you any Doubt of it?
No Doubt in the World.

(*By a Lord.*) Did you observe at Castlebrack a great Difference in the Thickness of Two of the large Pieces, that one is nearly double the Thickness of the other?
Yes; it was for that Purpose I got the Stone turned up to examine the Back of it.

(*Mr. Serjeant Shee.*) Do you know the Locality where those different Pieces of Stone were found?
Not of my own Knowledge.

Have you examined particularly the Inscription upon the Stone?
I have examined the Cutting.

Are you able to inform their Lordships whether it has occasionally happened in that Neighbourhood that Portions of Tombstones have been found in the Dwellings of Individuals? Do you know a Person of the Name of Deverell at Mountmelick?
I do.

Did you ever see a Tombstone at his House?
I saw Portions of a Tombstone; I was present when they were raised out of the Floor of his Kitchen.

What Tombstone is that?
It is a Tombstone that purports to bear the Name of Mr. Swill.

How long ago was it?
It was on the Morning of the Day that I went to Castlebrack; the 28th of October 1844.

Do you know of any other Tombstone or Portion of a Tombstone being found in a private Dwelling previously to that Time?
I do.

In what Year?
As nearly as I can recollect about Six Years ago.

In whose House was that?
It was in the House of a Person of the Name of Doyle, a Carpenter.

Are the Fragments which were then found now upon the Floor of their Lordships House?
The same.

Whose Tombstone was it?
A Person of the Name of Croasdaile. They are a very respectable Family in the Neighbourhood.

Did you see it taken up?
I did.

In what Part of the House was it before it was moved?
When I first saw it Six Years ago merely by Accident it formed Part of the Flooring of the House which was then undergoing Repair.

Was that at Mountmelick?
Yes.

How far is that from Castlebrack?
I suppose Five or Six Miles.

Cross-examined by Mr. Solicitor General for Ireland.

How far do you live from the Churchyard of Castlebrack?
Five or Six Miles.

Samuel Sheane,
Esq.

Is Castlebrack a Parish?

It is.

Where is the Parish Church?

It is Part of the Union of O'Regan composed of Rosanallis, Rary, Castlebrack, and Killmanmon.

Is there a Burying Place belonging to the Union different from Castlebrack?

Several.

How many?

There is One at Mountmellick and there are Three others.

What Roman Catholic Chapel is the nearest to Castlebrack?

The Chapel of Clonahadoo.

How far is that from Castlebrack?

About a Mile.

Are the Tracy Family Catholics or Protestants?

The Name is not an uncommon one in the Neighbourhood. A Portion of the Family are Protestants and a Portion Roman Catholics.

Do you know which the Claimant is?

I am not aware of my own Knowledge.

How long have you known the present Claimant?

I never saw him till Saturday last.

Do you know any of his Family in the Neighbourhood?

I know that a Brother of his lived in the Neighbourhood about Five Miles from Maryborough.

Do you know a Place called Ross in that Neighbourhood?

I know a Place called Ross in the Neighbourhood of Maryborough; but I have heard that there is a Ross in King's County, of which I know nothing.

How far from Castlebrack is either of those Ross's?

I know a Village near which Ross in King's County is situated; it is not far from the Village of Mountbolus. I suppose it is about Seven or Eight Miles from Castlebrack.

Is this Ross in King's County a Village or merely a Country Place?

Merely a Country Place.

Is it a Farm?

A Townland.

You know nothing of the Extent of it?

No, nothing whatever.

Your own Family were not buried in this Churchyard of Castlebrack?

No, certainly not.

And you knew nothing of this Tombstone until you saw it in October 1844?

Not till I saw it in October 1844.

You were sent for to view this Tombstone?

I was the Magistrate who took all the Depositions in the Case.

There was a Meeting of Gentlemen and some of the Country People upon the 28th of October?

I do not know whether I should be at liberty to tell you how it was that my Attention was drawn to the Case. I knew nothing about it before.

You

You were sent for by some Friend of Mr. Tracy's?
I can hardly say that.

Who sent for you upon the second Occasion?
I think I got Notice from the Solicitor of the Claimant to request that I would go to take some more Depositions, and to view the Tombstone which would then be produced.

The small Piece in the Centre was not broken when you saw it on the first Occasion?
It was not broken when I saw it on the first Occasion. It was in Four Pieces on the first Occasion.

Was a Person of the Name of Heagney present upon that Occasion?
I think not.

Examined by the Committee.

Do you say that the Name of Tracy is common in this Neighbourhood?
There are several Families of Tracy.

Some Protestant and some Catholic?
Yes.

Have they been long settled in that Neighbourhood?
I understand that they have been. I know a very old Man of that Name.

Is he any Relation of the Claimant?
I believe he is not; he is a Solicitor; a very old Man, upwards of Eighty Years old.

Do you know whether the Tracy's have been long settled in that Country?
I believe they have some Time.

Can you say how long?
I should certainly say for more than a Century.

There are a good many Families of the Name of Tracy there, both Roman Catholics and Protestants?
Yes; but those professing the Roman Catholic Religion are more numerous.

How do the Tracy's in that Country call their Name?
They pronounce the Word Tracy in the same Way, but the Name is spelt differently from what it is on this Tombstone.

How is it spelt?
T-r-e-c-y.

In Ireland *e* is pronounced like *a*?
It is.

Trecy?
There is the *a* broad; *Tracy.*

In the District round Castlebrack within what Radius are these Tracy's?
There are Three or Four Families at Mountmellick; there are others within the Parish of Castlebrack, or in the immediate Neighbourhood of it.

There are more than could well have sprung from One Tracy who went there a Hundred Years ago?
I never understood that the Tracy Family ever resided in that Neighbourhood.

(62.2.)   Then

Then JOHN TIBEANDO Esquire was called in; and having been sworn, was examined as follows:

(*Mr. Serjeant Shee.*)   Where do you reside?
At Portnahinch, in the Queen's County.
Are you a Magistrate of that County?
I am.

The Counsel being asked, Whether the Evidence of this Witness would carry the Case further back than that of the last Witness, stated that he was not aware that it would do so.

The Counsel was informed, That the Committee considered it unnecessary to call any more Witnesses to prove the Facts stated by the last Witness, as the Committee entertained no Doubt that those Facts had been correctly stated.

Mr. Serjeant Shee stated, That he would abstain from repeating the same Questions.

(*Mr. Serjeant Shee to the Witness.*)   Did it happen to you to know Instances of Stones being removed from the Churchyard of Castlebrack by Persons living in the Neighbourhood?
Not in Castlebrack.
In any other Churchyard in that Neighbourhood?
I have prevented Stones from being carried away.   I have prevented my own Mason from taking them.
How often?
I could not call to mind; probably more than once or twice.
Have you ever seen Fragments of Tombstones in private Dwellings used as Hearthstones in that Neighbourhood?
I have, near Castlebrack.
How often do you remember having seen Tombstones so used?
I think in Two or Three Instances; I went to the Houses and raised them, and looked at them.

Then Mr. JOHN WRAFTER was called in; and having been sworn, was examined as follows:

(*Sir Fitzroy Kelly.*)   What are you by Trade?
A Stonecutter.

How long have you been engaged in that Business?
Since 1807.   I was bound an Apprentice to it.

Where do you carry on your Business?
At Tullamore and different Parts of Queen's County; that is the principal Place now.

Is that far from Castlebrack?
It is about Six Miles.

Are you conversant with the Sort of Gravestones that are to be found in the Neighbourhood?
Yes; I constantly put up Tombstones.

Have

Have you had Opportunities of observing the Sort of Stones that Gravestones have been erected of in that Neighbourhood before your own Time ?

Yes.

Have you seen those Fragments of a Gravestone which lie there ?

Yes, I have seen them.

Have you examined them ?

Yes.

Attentively ?

Yes, if those be the ones.

Look at them, and let us understand which you have seen of them, and which you have examined ?

I think those Four Pieces. (*The Four upper Pieces.*)

Have your examined the Fragments of a Tombstone purporting to be to the Memory of a Person of the Name of William the Son of Judge Tracy ?

Yes.

Does that appear to you from your Experience to be a Tombstone of the Date of towards the Middle of the last Century ?

It does ; it corresponds with the rest of them.

Do you yourself inscribe upon Tombstones ?

I do.

Have you examined the Inscription—the Cutting ?

I have.

Does that appear to you to be a Cutting of the Time at which it purports to bear Date ?

It does.

Have you also looked at the Edges where it is broken ?

Yes.

Does your Examination into the Edges lead you to believe that the Stone is of that Date ?

It does.

As you are a Cutter of Stones and Maker of Inscriptions yourself can you tell me would it be easy to make an Inscription of that Kind and that Appearance ?

It would ; but it would not be easy to make it like that ; it could not be cut in that kind of way that it appeared to me with Part of the Letters chipped.

(*By a Lord.*) Should you have any Difficulty in carving Letters of that Sort ?

No, not a bit ; but to put the Letters in the Places where they are broken across would not be easy.

But supposing they had been altogether in One Piece would there have been any Difficulty in carving all that ?

No.

And then there would not have been any Difficulty in taking a Mallet and breaking it into Five Pieces ?

A Person would not know how many Pieces that Stone would break into.

Supposing you had the Original in One Piece, would you have any Difficulty in breaking it into Four or Five ?

No.

Mr. John Wrafter.

(*Sir Fitzroy Kelly.*) Does that Stone present to your Eye the Appearance of a Stone the Date of which it purports to bear, and is the Cutting of that Date likewise?
It does.

(*Mr. Solicitor General for Ireland.*) You are speaking of these Four Pieces?
Yes.

What are the other Two?
I know nothing of those.

You never examined the others at all?
I think not.

(*Sir Fitzroy Kelly.*) Where a Tombstone is wanted to be laid flat on the Earth do you work it on both Sides, do you smooth both Sides or merely the Side which is to be uppermost, and upon which you have got the Inscription?
Only the uppermost Side.

The under Side is left as the Stone is taken?
Just as it comes up from the Mountains. The Flags on the Top of the Mountains are taken in that Way.

Does it happen with Stones containing Inscriptions that although the upper Surface is smooth and flat the varying Surface underneath will prevent its being the same Thickness throughout?
It does.

Have you examined that Stone?
I have.

Is there any thing in the Difference in Thickness between one Part and another which is otherwise than what is found in Tombstones?
That Stone has shelved away; it has slided off the same as Slates.

(*By a Lord.*) Did it shelve off equally?
There is no knowing where they shelve and where they break; when it comes to a hard veiny Flint it will break.

There will be a sudden Dip after the Thickness?
Yes; perhaps it may turn across the whole Face of it.

(*Sir Fitzroy Kelly.*) Have you any Experience which enables you to judge of the real Age of a Stone from its Appearance?
No, I do not think I could.

(*By a Lord.*) Have you examined those Two Stones?
I do not think I ever saw them; I cannot bring to my Recollection that I ever did.

Have you been accustomed to work in Quarries, and to get Stone which you afterwards worked?
Yes.

You have quarried different Stones which you afterwards covered with Inscriptions?
Yes.

Will you look at these? (*Two of the Fragments being handed to the Witness.*) You see that Fracture?
Yes.

Now attend to the Grain of that Stone; now turn it round; is not that what you call Sandstone?
Yes; Mountain Grit.

Now

Now look at the Grain of the other Piece ; does that appear to you
to be the very same ?

Part and Parcel of the same.

You think that it is Part and Parcel of the same ?

Yes ; my Opinion is that it is.

That it is Mountain Grit as well as the other ?

Yes ; I am sure that it is out of the same Quarry or Bed.

Now look at those Letters ; look at the O B E N here, and now look at these (*the Letters on the other Piece*) ; does it seem to you to be the same Sort of Writing ?

These seem to be cleaned out, scraped out.

More than the others ?

Yes.

Are not these Letters deeper than those ?

I think not if those were scraped out.

You think that it is the same Sort of Writing ; you see no material Difference between the Kind of Writing here and there ; take that D for instance ?

That is very like the other.

Look at A ?

It is very much the same as the other.

Look if there is an R or a P ? (*The Witness compared the Two R's.*) Is not that better made than this ?

No, this is the best made in my Opinion, but on these Stones I often see them with the wrong Part of the Letter turned first.

You do not see any material Difference in the Kind of Cutting or the Handwriting ?

I think there is no Difference if this was scraped out like the other.

Which upon the whole seems the best written ?

This (*the smaller Fragment*).

Which of those Two Stones is the hardest ?

I think that is the hardest (*the larger Fragment*) ; they are from the same Place.

You know that Stones differ coming from the same Quarry ?

From the same Quarry they do.

(*Sir Fitzroy Kelly.*) You say that they appear to you to be Stones of the Date of about a Century ago ; is it the same Sort of Stone that is generally used in the Churchyards in this Neighbourhood in Queen's County ?

Yes ; there are some Sixty or Eighty of the same Description in the same Churchyard. About Twenty Years ago there was a Family of the Name of Dunn who formerly had Stone of that Kind, and they got me to make a Limestone Monument for the whole of the Family, and I broke up Part of the old Grit Stone and threw it down to make a Foundation for the other.

Do you know that Bits of Gravestones are sometimes taken from the Churchyards and used in Houses for Hearths, and other Purposes of that Sort ?

They are frequently carried away by Persons to make Rubstones to sharpen Carpenters Tools and Stonecutters Tools ; those are thought nothing about now-a-days in Churchyards.

(62.2.)   Have

Mr. John Wrafter.

Have you examined the Back of the Stone to see if there is any Ridge or Line formed in the Stone that goes from one Side to the other?
I did at the Time.

Has any Part of any of those Stones been used for sharpening; have you observed that?
No, I did not see that there was.

Cross-examined by Mr. Solicitor General for Ireland.

You say that these Stones are taken from a Mountain in the Neighbourhood?
Yes.

How far is the Mountain you speak of from the Churchyard of Castlebrack?
About Four Miles, Five Miles, or Six Miles.

(*By a Lord.*) Is there any other Stonecutter in the Neighbourhood besides yourself?
Yes, plenty.

How many more?
I suppose I have Forty working for me.

Any Master Stonecutters?
Yes.

(*Mr Solicitor General for Ireland.*) How far do you live from Castlebrack?
About Six Miles.

(*By a Lord.*) You have Forty Stonecutters working for you?
Yes, frequently.

Could all of those carve upon Stone?
No.

How many of them could?
About Five.

Is there another Stonecutter besides yourself in that Neighbourhood?
Yes.

How many more?
I suppose in a Circle of Ten Miles there are Ten or Twelve.

Each of those has Workmen under them?
No, they work themselves.

And they can carve?
Yes.

How many Quarries are open in that Neighbourhood?
According as we take Employments. We opened a Quarry lately to build a Church near there.

You take the Quarry that is nearest to the Work?
Yes.

(*Mr. Solicitor General for Ireland.*) On this Mountain are there a great Number of broad Flagstones with the Surface exposed?
Yes.

There would be no Difficulty in getting one of those old Stones?
No; there is One Mountain there that is covered with them.

And

And you would not have to quarry them except from the Surface of the Earth; they lie on the Surface of the Mountain?
Yes.

You would have no Difficulty in going to the Mountain To-morrow and getting an old Stone like that?
I think you would.

Would you not be able to get one?
I think not.

I do not mean a broken one, I mean a whole one. Would there be any Difficulty in getting a large Stone like that on the Face of the Mountain?
Not at all.

Are they not employed in fact for cutting for common Grave-stones?
They are not used now at all. Persons that have had them in their Families put them away and get more durable ones; they get a Marble Kind.

(*By a Lord.*) Do you know the Churchyard of Castlebrack?
Perfectly.

Are there many old Stones of this Character which are so worn that all the Inscription would be worn off?
They are broken in Bits.

Are some so broken and worn that all Traces of the Letters are gone?
Not the whole; you find Parts of Letters.

You do not think that it would be easy to find a Gravestone in the Churchyard of this Character which could have this Inscription put upon it?
No such Stone could be found in the Churchyard.

We have had Evidence that the Stones in the Churchyard are very much worn and injured, that the Churchyard has been used for Cock-fighting and all Sorts of Purposes; if the People collected there and stood upon the Stones the Inscriptions would probably get worn off. Now would it not be easy to find a Stone where the Inscription has gone altogether?
They are of a far harder Kind than these.

Do you call this a soft Stone or a hard Stone?
A hard Stone.

Not likely to wear in Channels?
It might wear in Channels.

If it were a Hearth Stone would it wear in Channels?
It would.

Do not they play such a Game as shoving Stones in Castlebrack Churchyard?
Yes.

Are not the Stones very frequently rubbed and broken in that Game?
I never saw that Game played with them, but I saw a Game where they put up Stones, and they break them into Bits, and pitch them for Quoits.

Suppose that a Gravestone had stood for a Century in Castlebrack Churchyard, and had been trod upon by the People coming to the

Mr. John Wrafter. various Games, and upon various Occasions, do you think the Letters would remain as sharp and fresh as these appear to you to be ?
I do not think they would.

Is there any thing in this Inscription that would induce you to say that it was impossible that those Letters could have been carved within the last Year or Two ?
There is nothing that would induce me to say that they could not. It could be done.

Do you think that the Appearances on the Back of those Two Stones are the same ?
Yes, they split in the same kind of way. There is where the Flint Vein dips down in the soft Sand, the whole Face is smoothed, and the Face would come off about Half an Inch thick.

Re-examined by Sir Fitzroy Kelly.

You say that a Stone might be found now like that which is produced, not a Tombstone, but a Stone of that Description ; do you mean that it might be cut from the Quarry, or do you think that it would be possible to find one uninscribed lying about ?
It would be possible that it could be found upon the Mountain.

Do you mean that you could find such a Stone in a Quarry cut like that ? Do you mean that such Stones are to be found by looking for, of that Size, ready cut ?
You could not find it now without quarrying it.

If you wanted such a Stone as that of that particular Description you could get it, but it must be quarried ?
It must be quarried.

(*By a Lord.*) You do not meet with them upon the Surface of the Ground ?
No, not now-a-days.

Nor anywhere except by quarrying for them. Do you mean to say that you can get Stones of this Sort lying about without quarrying ?
There are Parts of the Mountains where you can.

There are Parts of the Mountains where there are Veins of Stones— Masses of Stone ?
Yes.

In order to get a Piece of this Size and Shape must not you go with Pickaxes and quarry for it ?
There are some of them on the Ground.

On the Outside of the Ground ?
Yes.

On the Surface ?
Yes.

Of that Size and Shape ?
Yes ; they would be thicker than that.

Did you ever see any one that was not a great deal thicker than that ?
Yes ; I have seen them thinner.

Did you ever see any of the same Size as that lying about ?
Yes.

In what Part of the Ground ?
Upon the Side of the Mountains.

Was

Was not there a Quarry there ?
Yes.

Were those Stones that you saw lying there near the Quarry ?
Not a Quarry that is worked.

Is it an old Quarry that is not worked near which you saw them ?
No.

Then what Sort of Quarry is it ?
It is a Place that they are thrown on, on the Side of the Mountain.

Who threw them there ?
I cannot tell.

They had been there for ever ?
I think they had.

Do you mean to say that they were not originally quarried ?
I do not know that they were not originally quarried.

Did they look as if they had been originally quarried out ?
No.

Do you mean to say that they had slipped out of the Mountain of
that oblong Shape, with the opposite Sides parallel ?
Some of them would.

And square ?
Yes.

With the opposite Sides parallel and equal ?
Yes.

And without any body shaping them ?
Yes.

(*Sir Fitzroy Kelly.*) You have examined that Stone ; do you
mean to say that it appears to you to be in a State of Nature as it was
found upon the Surface of the Earth in the Quarry, or does it appear
to have been fashioned by the human Hand ?
I know that Stone, and on examining it I should say that it was
formerly thicker Stone than it is now, but it is of a reedy Nature, and
Time and pitching about made it slip asunder.

You see that this Stone now has even Sides, it is apparently cut to
make the Two Sides parallel ; am I to understand it to be your
Opinion that it was found in that State either in the Quarry or on the
Surface of the Earth, or has it been cut into that State ?
It has been cut into that State, I think ; but there are Stones at the
Sides in Places in the Quarry that run parallel all along in that Way
with perpendicular Joints to them and horizontal Joints, and you might
take them off.

But to bring it into that Shape it would have to be cut at the Edges ?
It would.

(*By a Lord.*) You do not find them with Inscriptions upon them ?
I never saw one of them with an Inscription upon it.

(*Sir Fitzroy Kelly.*) You say that a Gravestone lying flat upon the
Earth and trodden on for a Century would probably have the Letters
more effaced than these Letters are. Tell me whether in your
Experience Inscriptions on different Stones do not within the same
Time disappear in different Degrees ? Do not you find that one Stone
keeps its Inscription quite fresh for a great many Years, while upon

(62.2.)   another

Mr. John Wrafter. another the Inscription will be very considerably, if not altogether, effaced?
Yes.

You find that Inscriptions disappear more or less according to Accident and Time upon one Stone than upon another?
Yes, according to the Grit that the Stone is composed of. If it is a soft Grit like the Portland or like the Welsh the Inscription would disappear by walking over it in a few Years.

Do you sometimes find that upon the same Tombstone one Part of the Inscription remains perfectly legible while the other has got nearly effaced?
Yes, because there might be Shelves in it, and it dries up, and Part of the Letters go away with it.

You say that that Stone might have been cut as we now see it within the last few Years; does it appear to you to be a recent Cutting or an old Cutting?
It appears to be an old Cutting.

John Delany. Then JOHN DELANY was called in; and having been sworn, was examined as follows:

(*Mr. Serjeant Shee.*) How old are you?
Eighty-six.

Where do you reside?
In the Parish of Castlebrack.

How long have you lived in the Parish of Castlebrack?
Since I was born.

What Occupation do you carry on?
A Farmer.

You have lived in Castlebrack all your Life; how near to the Churchyard?
Within Two Fields. I had for Fifty-seven Years a Farm that was not over a Mile from it.

When you first remember Castlebrack Churchyard in what Condition was it? Was it well enclosed?
It was badly enclosed.

We understand that there is a Ruin in that Churchyard?
There is.

Was that Church in Ruins when you first remember it?
Yes; it was always in Ruins in my Memory.

Do you remember a School close to the Churchyard?
I do.

Did you go to that School?
I did.

Can you tell us about what Age you were when you went there first?
I was about Ten Years old, I think.

By whom was that School kept?
It was a Man of the Name of Dempsey.

When

When you attended the School did you go there every Day ?   *John Delany.*
Every Day for a good many Years.   I stopped in Castlebrack at my Uncle's.

And that was near to the Churchyard ?
Within a few Perches of the Churchyard.   I stopped with him a Quarter of a Year.

Did the Boys play in the Churchyard ?
They did.

You have done so frequently ?
Frequently I was there.

Do you remember at that early Period of your Life an old Tombstone in the Churchyard ?
I do.

Do you remember the Inscription upon it ?
I think I do remember some.

Will you endeavour to recollect what you remember to have seen written or cut upon that Stone ?
Here lieth the Body of William Tracy, of Ross, in the King's County, the Third Son, I think, of an English Judge.   I think that is what was on it.

Is that all you recollect to have read upon it at that Time ?
Yes.

Can you tell their Lordships how many Years you remained at the School ?
Something about Fourteen Years.

In what Part of the Churchyard do you remember that Stone to have been ?
It laid the South Side of the Church.

How far from the Church ?
About Four or Five Yards.

Do you remember any thing particular being done to that Stone while you were at School ?
I do.

Will you state all you remember ?
There was a Parcel of People about it reading it, looking over it.   It was common when a Funeral came there, or on Sundays when great Meetings would be there, for the People to be looking at it, and there was a wicked Fellow in the Churchyard.   " I will soon settle that," said he, taking up a big Stone and throwing it on the Top of it, and cracked it in some Parts ; I could not recollect how many.

Have you a distinct Recollection of having seen it before it was cracked or injured at all ?
Yes, I have.

Can you tell when that Circumstance occurred into how many Pieces it was cracked or broken ?
I do not recollect how many.

Do you remember afterwards seeing it when it was more broken than it was upon that Occasion ?
I did, but I did not take much Notice of it till it disappeared from me some Length of Time after.

(62.2.)   T   During

John Delany.

During the Time that you remember Castlebrack Churchyard has it been used for Games and Amusements by the Country People?

Frequently.

Is there a Game called "Shoving Stones" that the People play there?

Yes.

What Sort of a Game is that?

Playing Ball.

I ask you about shoving Stones, throwing Stones; is that a common Game with the People?

It was at that Time.

Used they to play at that Game in the Churchyard?

Sometimes I have seen it; often indeed.

And I believe all Sorts of Games were played there?

Cock-fighting, Fives-playing, and so on.

Was there an annual Fair held in the Neighbourhood of the Churchyard?

There was, round the Churchyard.

Do you remember at any Time having gone through the Churchyard and observed that the Stone was no longer there?

I do, but I cannot remember the Date of it.

Can you tell us about how long ago it was when you first observed that the Stone was gone?

I think about Five or Six-and-twenty Years ago, or something thereaway.

Will you look at the Stone that is on the Floor; did you ever see within the last Two or Three Years any of those Pieces of Stone at the House of a Man called Digby Baynham?

I did.

Will you point out to their Lordships which of those Fragments you saw at the House of Digby Baynham?

Those Two, and those (*Nos.* 1, 2, 3, *and* 4).

When did you first see them at the House of Digby Baynham?

I saw them at the House of Mr. Baynham in Killeigh.

When was that?

Two or Three Years ago.

Did you at that Time see the other Fragments?

No, not till I saw them at Castlebrack Churchyard.

When you first saw those that you saw at Mr. Baynham's did you know them again?

I did look over them at the Time.

Can you now state whether you had ever seen them before at an earlier Period of your Life?

I have, in Castlebrack Churchyard.

Have you any Doubt about it?

Not the smallest.

You say that you afterwards saw the Two other Fragments in Castlebrack Churchyard?

I saw the whole before it was broken, and I saw those Four at the Time when I saw them at Mr. Baynham's.

You

You say that after you had seen the Four Fragments at Mr. Baynham's you saw the Two other Fragments at Castlebrack Churchyard?
I did, when they were brought there by other People.

Do you know whether in the earlier Period of your Life, when you were a young Man, you had seen those Two other Fragments before?
I had; I had seen the whole Stone.

Have you any Doubt that that is the Stone which you saw when you were a young Man in Castlebrack Churchyard?
I have not the smallest Doubt of it.

Do you happen to know of Tombstones ever having been found in the Houses of the People in that Neighbourhood?
I heard tell they were.

(*By a Lord.*) Did you ever see any yourself?
I did see some of them in some of the Houses in Castlebrack.

How long ago?
It is a good while ago.

How many Years?
I think it is Seventeen or Eighteen or Twenty Years ago.

You say that a wicked Fellow took a Stone; why did he take a Stone and break this?
I could not tell his Reason for it.

Had there been a Quarrel?
No, there was not.

No breaking of Heads?
No; he did not like to see a Crowd in the Way, and he took a Stone and broke it.

You told us the Inscription that you saw upon the Stone when you were a Lad; how did it run; let us hear what was written upon it?
Here lieth the Body of William Tracy, of Ross, King's County, being Third Son of an English Judge.

Did it say any thing more about the English Judge?
No.

When did you first tell any body that you remembered having seen those Words upon the Stone; how long ago?
I cannot recollect whether it is Four or Five Years ago since I first told the People.

Who did you tell it to?
I told it to one of the Mr. Tracy's.

You told him what you had seen when you were a Lad?
I did.

You told him the Words you have told us now?
I did.

When did you last hear those Words spoken by any body else? When has any body lately read over those Words to you that you have told us To-day?
I do not recollect when.

Was it a Month ago or Two Months?
I do not recollect what Time it was at all.

(62.2.)

(*Mr.*

John Delany.

(*Mr. Serjeant Shee.*)   Do you remember the House close to the Gate of the old Churchyard at Castlebrack ?
I do.

Was that House in your Recollection Thirty or Forty Years ago kept by a Person called James Dunn ?
It was.

And Poll Dunn, his Wife ?
Yes.

It was a Public House was it not ?
They sold Liquor in it.

It was what they called a Tap and Dance House ?
It was.

Used they to dance in a large Room on one Side of the House ?
There was a large Room in it where they used to dance.

Is that House occupied now ?
It is.

Is the Room in which they used to dance existing now ?
That Room is gone to Ruins.

Do you remember at any Time seeing in the Floor of that Room a Portion of a Tombstone ?
I do.

When ? How long ago ?
About Thirty Years ago.

Do you mean any Portion of the Stones now upon the Floor, or other Stones ?
I did not make any Remark of that.

Did you see more than One Fragment of a Tombstone, or only One ?
I think I saw more.

Can you say in what Part of the Room ?
One Part near the Fire and another Part near the Wall.

When James and Poll Dunn lived in the House had they Charge of the Churchyard of Castlebrack ?
They had.

Were there many Houses near their's ?
There were Four or Five Public Houses in the Place.

But further off from the Churchyard than their's ?
No, they were all very near it, just facing the Churchyard.

Do you remember a Person of the Name of James Tracy living in that Neighbourhood?
I do.

Do you remember where he lived ?
At a Place called Gurteen in King's County,

How far is Gurteen from Castlebrack ?
Between Three and Four Miles.

When you first remember him what aged Man was he ?
I cannot tell.

About what Age ? Was he a Youth or a grown-up Man ?
He was a grown-up Man.

Had he a Family ?
I do not remember any of his Family other than a Son.

What

What was his Name ?
Joe.

Do you remember where Joe lived ?
He lived in Geashill.

How far is Geashill from Castlebrack ?
Between Three and Four Miles.

Do you remember the Death of James Tracy ?
I do.

Can you tell me about when he died ?
I think about Fifty-two or Fifty-three Years ago.

Were you present at his Funeral ?
I was.

Where did you see him laid ?
By this Tombstone which I see here, by the Side of it.

In Castlebrack Churchyard close to this Stone ?
Yes.

Did you at any Time hear him say who his Father was?
I have heard him tell an Uncle of mine in the Fair of Castlebrack,
I heard him say, that his Father was buried yonder, the Son of an
English Judge.

Do you remember his mentioning his Father's Name ?
I do.

What was his Father's Name ?
William Tracy.

Cross-examined by Mr. Attorney General.

What Business are you ?   How do you get your Living ?
I am a Farmer.

What Quantity of Land do you hold ?
I hold Twenty-five Acres.

Within Two Fields of the Churchyard ?
Yes.

How long have you held that Farm ?
About Fifty-six Years.

Who is your Landlord ?
Mr. Sands.

How long have you known the Tracy's in that Neighbourhood ?
I have known the Tracy's these Sixty or Seventy Years.

Are there many of them about there ?
None of this Family ; none of the Tracy's that lay Claim to this.

How long have you known what you call "this Family " ?
I have known them these Seventy Years.

Have you known them well ?
I have known Joe Tracy, these People's Father ; I have known him
to live in Geashill a good while.

Have you been on good Terms with them ?
Yes.

John Delany.

Have you frequently spoken about this Claim with them? Have they ever talked to you about this Claim?
No.

They never spoke to you upon the Subject?
No.

Nor asked you any Question about it?
No.

When did you first tell them what you have mentioned to their Lordships?
Three or Four Years ago.

Or more; is it not more than that?
No.

Do you remember People coming up here some Years ago; Persons coming from Castlebrack to London some Years back?
Yes, I think it was after their coming.

Did you speak to Mr. Tracy about it then?
No, I did not.

How was that?
I was engaged in my Business; I did not mind.

You were living at the Time Two Fields from the Churchyard?
Yes.

Did not you know that Persons were coming constantly to the Churchyard to make Inquiries?
I did not know it till afterwards.

Had not you heard that there were Inquiries upon the Subject?
They never inquired of me.

Did you see Mr. Tracy from Time to Time while the thing was going on?
No, I was not there.

Did you see him before that while the Case was going on?
I did not; I did not mind it.

How far does he live from you?
I live Three or Four Miles from where Joe Tracy lived, but I live Seven Miles from the other Brother.

Were you in the habit of seeing him at Markets and Fairs about?
Sometimes I was.

And he never spoke to you upon the Matter?
No, not until he came home from this Mission the first Time.

Did he speak to you immediately after he had been on this Mission the first Time?
It was I spoke to him first.

To which of the Tracy's did you speak?
I spoke to Tim Tracy and Joe Tracy.

Is that the Claimant?
The Brother.

How long is that ago?
I think it is Three Years ago.

Where was it that you heard this Talk between your Uncle and James?
It is a long Time ago.

How

How long?
I think it is nearly Sixty Years.

Whereabouts were they?
In the Fair of Castlebrack.

In the Churchyard?
Close to the Churchyard. They were talking about Sheep; whether they had bought them or sold them I do not know.

What led to the Talk?
My Uncle was a Neighbour to them; they were talking in the Churchyard, and I heard him mention that this Man was buried up yonder, William Tracy, the Son of an English Judge.

Have you frequently talked about the Conversation between James Tracy and your Uncle since it took place?
No, I have never heard any thing of it between them since.

Did you ever mention to any Person what you heard James Tracy tell your Uncle?
Not for a long Time after, till this Matter came up.

You never mentioned it till Three or Four Years ago?
Never that I can recollect.

You never talked of it at all?
I do not remember that I did.

You say that you were at School there. Was the old Stone which you have talked about in Memory of Mr. Tracy close to the Church?
Yes, within Four or Five Yards of the Back of the Church.

Was there a Footpath going by it?
No, there was not; there was a Door of the Church on one Side of it a little.

Was this Part much frequented by People walking upon it and playing there?
Yes, it was.

Were there great Meetings in the Churchyard at Fair Times?
Yes; Cock Fights on Sundays and Dancings in the Summer Time.

Were the Cock Fights and the Meetings held about the Place where the Stone was?
They were on the Boundary of the Churchyard.

Were they in the Churchyard?
On one Side of it.

Were there large Numbers of Persons meeting in the Churchyard?
There used to be.

About the Part where this Stone was?
When there were Meetings some of them would go to read this.

You read the Inscription often to yourself?
I did.

When did you first talk of having read the Inscription latterly?
I talked of it to James Tracy at the Time that he was speaking to my Uncle; I said that I had read that Inscription.

You say that some Time ago People were inquiring for the Tomb-stone?
Yes.

(62.2.)   Did

John Delany.

Did not you say any thing about it at the Time ?
No, I did not, to any body, not that I think of.

When you first remember the Stone was it a square Stone ?
It was.

No Part broken off?
No Part broken off.

Did the Inscription cover the whole Stone, or was there a Space left at the Bottom ?
I think there was some little Space at the Bottom.

In that Space was there Room enough for another Inscription ?
I think not.

Was it plain to read ?
Yes.

Was it as clean and as plain as it is now ?
Yes.

Quite plain ?
Yes.

Quite as clean as it is now ?
Yes.

In your Opinion nothing has been done to clean the Stone ; it was always quite as clean as it is now ?
No, I do not think it has been.

Was the whole of the Inscription upon the Stone to be read as it is now, quite plain ?
It was.

Any body could read it ?
They could.

You recollect dancing in this Dancing-room ; you say there were Pieces of Tombstone there ?
I do ; I do not know what Tombstone that belonged to.

Was one of them in a Place where great Numbers of People would be ? One of them was near the Fireplace, was not it ?
Yes.

And the other in another Part of the Room ?
I noticed Two or Three of the Pieces.

Was the Inscription up or down ?
I do not know, but I noticed Letters.

The Letters were on the upper Side ?
Yes, that is all I know.

You say that both Pieces had Letters upon them ?
Both Pieces had Letters.

Was the Part which was nearest the Fire a Place where People would stand near the Fire, so that the Stone would be under their Feet ?
Yes, it would.

If the People sat lounging by the Fire they would sit with their Feet upon the Stone ?
Yes.

The other Part was close against the Wall ?
Yes.

There

There would not be so much treading upon that ? *John Delany.*
No.

Therefore, as far as you saw, the Part by the Fire would be more trodden upon than the Part by the Wall ?
I cannot tell.

Would it not be so ; would not the Part by the Fire be more trodden upon than the Part by the Wall ?
I did not notice that.

Was it not more exposed to be worn near the Fire ?
I could not tell you.

When were you last in this old Room, or the Ruins of it ?
It is a great while ago.

Did you see the Stones then ?
I did.

How many Years ago was that after you missed the Stones from the Churchyard ? When was it you first saw those Pieces of Tombstone in that Room ?
It was more than Forty Years ago.

You missed the Tombstone from the Churchyard Twenty-five Years ago, and you saw those Pieces of Tombstone in the Dancing-room more than Forty Years ago?
I did.

When was it that you first remember to have seen those Pieces of Stone with the Writing upon them in the Dancing-room ; how long ago think you ?
It is nearly Forty Years ago.

Are you sure of that ?
Something about that.

I am speaking now of the Pieces of Tombstone that you saw in the Dancing-room with the Letters upwards ; when do you first remember to have seen those in the Dancing-room ?
It is nearly Fifty Years ago since I saw them there.

You are quite sure of that ?
It is.

Then when did you last see this Stone in the Churchyard ?
It is not very long since I have seen it.

I do not mean when it was lately taken there, but when you saw it on the Grave ?
It is about Twenty-five Years since I have seen it lying on the Grave in the Churchyard.

How long ago was it that that wicked Fellow broke it ?
It is beyond Sixty Years, near Seventy.

Was it one of the Boys of the School, or a Man?
He was a Man ; he was a Relation of an Uncle of mine.

Was he playing with the Boys, or what brought him there?
He lived just close to the Place ; he had a Farm just near.

What brought you there ?
I was like the others in the Churchyard, because I was there almost every Sunday to play ; I lived so near it.

John Delany.

You were there playing on Sunday?
Yes.

Were you a Man grown up then?
I was grown up.

Did he say why he did it, why he broke the Stone?
I cannot tell his Meaning, but he broke it; he said he would soon put it aside, and then they would not torment him with looking at it and leaping over it; he would not have them torment him.

Did they torment him about any other Stone?
I do not know; but they had a Practice of leaping over that more than other Stones; it was nearly worn smooth.

Had they a Practice of playing upon that Stone more than any other?
They had.

So that the Stone would be the most worn Stone of any in the Churchyard?
It was not worn, the Letters were not worn over it at all; they would be leaping over it.

They leaped over that Stone more than any other Stone in the Churchyard?
More than any other that I saw.

Was that the Reason the Man broke it?
Yes.

How came you to go there in October, when you saw the Stones lying in the Churchyard?
There was a Meeting to be in Castlebrack to inspect them.

Who called the Meeting?
Mr. Tracy I suppose; one of the Mr. Tracy's desired me to attend there.

He asked you to attend there?
He did.

Was the Inscription read out aloud to the People?
It was.

Read over several Times?
Yes.

I suppose the People kneeled down upon it, and saw how far they could make out the Writing?
They leant down to look at the Letters.

Did they compare different Stones in the Neighbourhood to see if it was like them?
They read several Stones, and looked for Dates that could be compared to it.

When did you first hear that any Part of it was found?
About Three or Four Years ago.

Did you go over at once?
No, I did not, till I was brought by Mr. Tracy.

How long after you heard of it was it that the Meeting was held in the Churchyard?
It was nearly a Year before I was brought to look at it at Mr. Baynham's.

Did

Did Mr. Baynham bring it himself?

He brought me in and showed it me there; he brought me at Night from my own Place; he wanted me to reach at a certain Time, and the Night came on before I could reach there, and I stopped at Mr. Baynham's.

You knew the Stone directly?
I knew it directly as soon as I saw it.

How many Pieces were there when you first saw it?
Four.

You remembered that you had seen it, and you remembered that it had been broken in Pieces when you were young?
I knew it was the Stone that I saw.

You knew it was the Stone that was broken many Years ago?
I think that Stone was broken Sixty Years ago or Sixty-five Years ago.

As it is now?
As it is now.

Broken in the same Pieces?
Yes.

Into how many Pieces was it broken; do you think that it was broken into more than Four Pieces when you recollect it?
I could not tell till I saw it in Castlebrack afterwards.

You do not know whether it was broken across Half, or into Four Pieces or more?
I think it was across at that Time, but I was not particular in knowing in what Way.

What Religion were those Tracy's you have talked of; was the Man that spoke to your Uncle many Years ago a Catholic or a Protestant?
A Protestant James Tracy was.

Are there many of them Protestants in that Neighbourhood?
No.

How many?
There was no other that I know of of the Tracy's that were Protestants but Doctor Tracy, but he was not any thing to that Family.

Where did he live?
At Mountmellick.

He lives close by?
That Man is dead many Years ago.

Do you know a Place called Ross?
I do not know where Ross is.

You never saw the Place?
No.

(*By a Lord.*) How was the Stone broken by that wicked Fellow?
By a big Stone thrown upon it.

It must have been a very large Stone to break it?
It was.

Are there many of those large Stones lying about there?
There are, belonging to our Castle there.

Was this Stone level with the Ground when it was broken?
It was lying flat on the Ground.

(62.2.)

Was

John Delany.

Was there any Masonry underneath it?

No, there was not; it was lying flat on the Earth.

Do you know the Name of the Man that broke it?

I do.

What was his Name?

A Man of the Name of Brian Dunn, he went to America since, and I suppose died there.

Was he a young Man or a middle aged Man?

He was a young Man.

You say you cannot recollect how many Pieces he broke it into?

I cannot say; at that Time I did not mind how many Pieces it was till I saw it come back.

Did he throw the Stone once or twice?

He threw the Stone once on it, and cracked it; I do not know how many Pieces he made of it.

You remember the Shape of the Stone, that it was perfectly square?

I do.

There is a Piece still wanting?

Yes.

Does any Person live nearer to Castlebrack Church than you do?

Yes, there are a good many People.

You say that you live about Two Fields from it?

Yes, but not upon the same Concern.

Are there many Houses near the Church?

There are a good many.

Re-examined by Mr. Serjeant Shee.

About those Stones that you saw Forty Years ago in the Dancing-room, you say that these Stones had an Inscription upon them?

There was, but I cannot tell what it was.

Are you quite sure that when you saw them there the whole of this Stone was in the Churchyard?

It was.

So that they could not be the same?

Not at all.

Allow me to call your Attention to the breaking by that Man. You say that there was a Stone thrown down upon this one in the Church-yard, and that it was broken. Did you blame the Man for doing it?

I had nothing to do with it, but my Uncle was Brother-in-law to the Man that broke the Stone. He called " Shame !" at him for doing so ; and he said " What matter about it? I broke it, and they will not be tormenting me with looking at it and reading it every Day."

Did he say who or what the Person was who was buried there?

No, he did not make mention of any such thing.

Or as to what Religion he was?

No, I did not hear any such thing.

Just endeavour to recollect. Was the Man who threw the Stone a Catholic?

He was.

Did

Did he say what Religion the Person was who was buried there?
I did not hear him make mention of any such thing.

(*By a Lord.*) Have you never at any Time told any body that the Man said something about the Religion that the Person was of who was buried there?
I do not recollect that I have.

You will not be sure that you did not say so?
I am sure I did not.

Are you sure that you have never said any thing of that Sort?
Yes.

Were you examined by the Gentleman who is Solicitor for the Party here?
Yes. I think they asked me whether I knew that that was the Stone, and I said that it was.

Was that all?
That was all. I said that that was the Stone.

And then they read to you the Inscription, did not they?
They did.

(*Mr. Serjeant Shee.*) You say that you knew James Tracy of Gurteen and Joseph Tracy of Geashill?
Yes.

Was Joseph Tracy a Protestant or a Catholic?
He was a Protestant.

You do not know of what Religion the present Claimant is?
No.

You say that there were no other Protestants at the Time, besides James Tracy, of the Name of Tracy, except Dr. Tracy?
James and Joe were Protestants; Joe the Son of James.

And there was Dr. Tracy a Protestant?
He was nothing at all to them; he was of another Family.

All the other Tracy's about there were Roman Catholics, were not they?
Yes.

Then Mr. PATRICK BOYNE was called in; and having been sworn, was examined as follows:

(*Mr. Serjeant Shee.*) Where do you reside?
At Dureen, in King's County.

I believe you are not a Magistrate?
No.

But you are one of the Grand Jurors of the Quarter Sessions?
Yes, a very old one.

How long have you resided in that Neighbourhood?
About Twenty-six Years.

Did you marry the Daughter of a Gentleman of the Name of Wyer?
I did.

About when did you marry that Lady?
At the latter End of May or the Beginning of June 1813.

Y I believe

Mr. Patrick Boyne.   I believe you were examined before a Committee of this House in the Year 1843 upon this Claim ?

I had that Honour.

Do you remember being asked upon that Occasion respecting a Tombstone in the Churchyard at Castlebrack which you had seen at the Time of your Marriage ?

I was asked about a Stone, but I did not see it at the Time of my Marriage, but shortly after ; some Months after my Marriage.

Do you remember being asked whether you recollected the Inscription upon that Stone ?

I do.

Will you state what your Recollection was ?

That I did.

Do you remember being asked by a noble Lord whether you had taken a Minute of that Inscription ?

I do.

Do you remember saying that you had no distinct Recollection of your having done so, but that you thought you might have done so ?

It was something to that Effect.

I believe it was in the Month of May 1843 that you were examined upon that Occasion ?

It was.

Did you shortly after return to Ireland ?

Yes, immediately after.

On your Return to Ireland did you examine some Papers which had been connected with the Affairs of your Father-in-law, the late Mr. Wyer ?

I did.

A Bundle of Papers ?

Yes, a great deal of Papers.

Where were those Papers when you returned to Ireland after your Examination in this House ?

They were in my Desk, formerly my Father-in-law's Desk, at the House where I now reside.

At Dureen ?

Yes.

In a Desk which your Father-in-law used ?

Yes.

When did Mr. Wyer die ?

I think about August 1818.

Having searched among those Papers did you find any Minute or any Paper connected with Castlebrack Churchyard ?

I did.

Have you it here now ?

The Agent has got it from me.

Is this the Paper ?   (*A Paper being shown to the Witness.*)

That is my Writing.

Read what you say is your Writing ?

The Writing is this : " Virazel v. Tuthill. Decree in this Cause made absolute the 3d April 1802. Lord Redesdale, Chancellor."

Is

Is there any other Minute upon that Paper in your own Handwriting?

I think there is.

Will you look for it?
There is.

Will you read it?
" Old Tomb, C. Brack. William Tracy of Ross, Son of the Honorable Tracy, an English Judge, 1734. 3d October 1813."

Do you state positively that when you found that Paper in what had been your Father-in-law's Desk that Minute was upon it?
Yes.

It is in Pencil?
It is in Pencil.

In your own Handwriting?
Yes.

When was it written?
On the 3d of October 1813.

You remember going to the Churchyard about that Time, do not you?
I do.

I think in your former Examination you said it was after Prayers. I presume you mean after Mass in some Chapel in the Neighbourhood?
Yes.

Then you went with your Wife and your Sister-in-law to Castlebrack Churchyard?
Yes.

Can you recollect what interested you in the Inscription on a Tombstone to the Memory of a Man of the Family of Tracy?
I do.

Tell us what it was?
The old Tracy Tomb was quite near my Family Tomb. I was a good deal struck, being a Stranger in the Country, and never having been in Castlebrack before, to see an Inscription on it to " The Honorable Tracy." Along with that my Father-in-law's Mother was of the same Name. I took out my Pencil, and on, I think, my own Family Tomb I made this Minute or Pencil Mark in order to show it to my Father-in-law, and ask who this Mr. Tracy was, or what Connexion he was.

Do you remember calling Mr. Wyer's Attention to the Circumstance when you went home?
I did.

You have read to their Lordships that upon the Paper there is a Memorandum of your own " Virazel v. Tuthill. Decree in this Cause made absolute the 3d April 1802. Lord Redesdale, Chancellor "?
So it appears from what I see there.

Was Mr. Wyer connected with a Family of the Name of Virazel?
He was.

Had his Wife been a Lady of that Name?
One of his Wives was; his first Wife was.

(62.2.)

After

After her Death did he enjoy some of the Property which had come to him by his Marriage with Miss Virazel?
He did.

Did you ever hear of a Person of the Name of Tuthill?
I did.

Had there been Two Ladies of the Name of Virazel who had possessed that Estate before your Father-in-law?
I understood that there were.

After your Marriage had you any Reason to apprehend any Proceedings at the Suit of a Person of the Name of Tuthill?
I had.

You had by your Marriage become interested in the Property which Mr. Wyer derived from the Virazel's?
Yes; I got One Half.

And you were alarmed by Rumours about it?
I was a good deal concerned.

You were interested and anxious to be informed?
Yes.

In consequence of what you had heard had you any Conversation with your Father-in-law, Mr. Wyer, upon the Subject of what you had heard?
I had.

Do you remember his telling you any thing about it?
I do.

At the Time he told you whatever he said did you write any thing?
Yes.

At the Time of the Conversation did you write upon any thing at the Time?
I took this Minute or Extract from a Paper of Mr. Wyer's, which he gave me to satisfy me that there should be no Recourse afterwards by Mr. Tuthill.

You then wrote upon the Paper " Decree made absolute by Lord Redesdale "?
I did.

Do you remember upon the Occasion of your taking that Minute who produced the Paper?
My Father-in-law. .

Do you remember where he took the Paper from?
He took it from a Desk in his Room.

Did he separate this from another Part of the same Sheet?
I. think it was a Letter that was addressed to him on the Chimney-piece. He said, " Take the Back of this and take an Extract here;" and this is in my Hand.

Are you quite certain that at the Time when you wrote this Memorandum about the Decree of my Lord Redesdale the Address " To Mr. Weir, Cottage, Clonagoun," was upon the Paper?
Quite certain.

When next did you see the Stone that you have seen in 1813 in the Churchyard?
I think it was about 1816.

Was

Was it still in the Churchyard ?
In 1816 it was.

Have you seen it recently ?
I saw it on a late Occasion at Killeigh.

Was it under the Care of Mr. Digby Baynham ?
Yes.

Who showed it to you then?
I was requested to attend there by the Agent in Dublin, and I attended at Mr. Baynham's House to see the Stone.

Did you see there all the Fragments now produced, or only a Portion of them ?
Only a Portion.

Which of them did you see ?
These which are next the Bar.

Did you see the Pieces marked 1, 2, 3, and 4 ?
I did.

When you saw them at Mr. Baynham's upon that Occasion did you know them again ?
Yes, I immediately knew that they were the old Tomb that I took the Memorandum of, with this Exception, that the Appearance of them was dryer than when I saw them in the Graveyard.

Cross-examined by Mr. Attorney General.

You were examined here in 1843 ?
I was.

At that Time you stated that when you saw this Tombstone first you were living at Dublin ?
Yes.

Was Mr. Wyer living at Dublin likewise ?
No.

Where was he living?
Where I now live ; I was at his House on a Visit.

How far was that from Castlebrack ?
About Four Miles.

When was it that you wrote this Piece of Pen and Ink Writing ?
It was some Days previous to the Sunday that I went to Castlebrack.

It was a Piece of Paper which Mr. Wyer gave you, and you wrote from his Dictation ?
Not from his Dictation ; I wrote from an Extract he had.

What did you do with it?
I had it in my Pocket.

Did you carry it in your Pocket ?
I think it was lying in my Pocket previous to the Sunday ; I had it in my Waistcoat Pocket, and I took my Pencil out and made the Memorandum.

Was Mr. Wyer with you when you went to the Churchyard ?
No.

Who was with you ?
My Wife and her Sister.

Mr. Patrick Boyne.

Was the Inscription on the old Tombstone quite legible then?
Partly legible.

Was there any Difficulty in reading it?
Yes; I have some Recollection that there was some Grass or something over it, and I got out my Knife so that I could decipher the thing properly.

Was it necessary for you to do something with your Knife or otherwise before you could make out the Inscription?
There was a great Portion of it visible I recollect, but I have also a Recollection, I think, that there was some Grass growing over it.

Could you make it out without picking it out with your Knife?
I dare say I could, but I wanted not to lose Time.

Could you read it well enough without picking it out with your Knife?
I think I might if I took Time, but I have a Recollection that I took out my Knife.

Did it appear to be the same Colour as this, the same Sort of Stone?
It was blacker with the Weather from lying on the Grass.

Was it Green from the Effect of the Weather?
No, it was rather blacker; I think something like that Fragment there. (*Pointing to the lower Fragment.*)

Something like the End of it?
Yes.

Did you observe whether the whole Stone was there?
In 1813 the whole Stone was perfect.

Not broken?
Yes.

Into how many Pieces?
I should only say cracked across it in 1813.

In 1813 it was cracked across?
Yes.

Was it in the same State in 1816 when you saw it?
I think there was a greater Portion of it broken in the Year 1816.

How many Cracks were there then?
I have no Recollection.

You wanted to show it to your Father-in-law?
That was my Object in taking the Memorandum.

Your Father-in-law at that Time lived close by?
Yes, where I now live, Four Miles off.

Did it occur to you that he might as well go to see it himself, and satisfy his Curiosity?
He was a very old Man.

How old?
I dare say he was beyond Fifty; a very delicate Man, very asthmatic.

Was he in the habit of going out?
He was.

Did you not take him to the Tombstone to satisfy his Curiosity?
No; I do not think he knew that I was going.

Did not you tell him afterwards?
Not till I returned.

Why

Why did not you make a Copy of it, instead of merely taking the *Mr. Patrick Boyne.* Substance ?

I had no Purpose to serve by it ; I took the Memorandum to show to him who this Honourable Mr. Tracy was.

" Old Tomb, Castlebrack, William Tracy of Ross, Son of the Honourable Tracy, an English Judge." If you had no Object, except to satisfy your Father-in-law, why did you put a Date to that Memorandum when you made it ?

I cannot tell ; I dated it according to the Date.

The Memorandum which you had taken for your own Satisfaction about Lord Redesdale's Decree is not dated, but the Memorandum about the Tombstone is dated ; why is that ?

I cannot tell ; I am clear that I dated it, and gave it to my Father-in-law.

Was it your Habit to put Dates to every thing ?
No.

Why did you put a Date to the Note about the Tombstone ?

I have no Idea, but that the Date was that Sunday ; this was to satisfy myself ; it did not require a Date.

But as your Father-in-law knew that the Day you came back was Sunday, that did not require a Date. Did it require a Date to satisfy him that you had been there ?

No, I do not think that it did.

Why did you put a Date ?
I cannot tell Thirty Years ago.

Was it your Habit in taking Notes of Things to put Dates ?

In any thing important in my own Business I was generally systematic, and I put down Dates, and I did so in this Minute here. I do not know the Reason.

Can you tell why you put the Date ?
I cannot tell why I did.

You have put the Year as well as the Date of the Month when you made your Memorandum, can you account for that ?

I had no Purpose to serve but to show it to my Father-in-law. I put the Date of the Stone and I put the Day I was there. I had no Purpose to serve.

Did you leave the Paper with your Father-in-law ?
I did.

Did you copy the Memorandum in Ink from the Paper which he had ?

I told you so before.

Then why did you leave that Copy, with the Original, with your Father-in-law, when you had taken it for your own Satisfaction ?

I had no Interest in the Circumstance of the Tomb, and I was satisfied that I was right with regard to the Suit, and I left the thing altogether with him.

For the Purpose of quieting your Mind you took a Copy from a Paper which your Father-in-law had in his Possession relating to this Suit, and you left it with your Father-in-law ?

I left it with him.

You gave him the Copy and he had the Original ?
Yes.

I ask

Mr. Patrick Boyne.

I ask you how you came to do that?
I cannot tell.

You say that you carried it in your Pocket till you got to the Church-yard, and then you gave it to your Father-in-law, and left it with him; why did you do that; was it for better Security? Explain it if you can?
I gave it to the old Gentleman, and I got it in his Papers some Time after his Death.

Why did you leave it with him as you made it for your own Satis-faction, and the Original being with your Father-in-law?
I gave it to him to keep it, I did not require it, and I was satisfied with regard to the Decree. I took no Trouble to ask him for it, and he kept it.

You cannot give any other Reason?
No, I do not think I can.

When did you see the Tombstone?
I have stated in 1813, and I have stated in 1816.

When next?
I think next it was about Four Years ago.

Where did you see it?
At Killeigh.

In Mr. Baynham's Possession?
Yes.

How much of it did you see then?
I have answered that Question.

Answer it again. How many Pieces did you see?
Four.

Did you afterwards see it in the Churchyard?
I did.

Were there many Persons there?
There were a great many.

Was the Inscription read aloud?
No.

Did any body read it when the People were congregating in the Churchyard?
I did not hear them.

Were you close by?
I was.

Did you go to the Churchyard a second Time to see the Tomb-stone?
I did, in consequence of a Communication from the Law Agent in Dublin, Mr. Burke.

Was the Inscription on the Tombstone then read out?
No, it was not read at all; I saw it.

Nobody read it?
I did not hear any one read it.

You did not read it yourself?
I had a Recollection that it was the old Tomb that I took a Memorandum of.

You

You stated before that you were some Connexion of the Tracy *Mr. Patrick Boyne.* Family?
No, I never did.

How long have you known the Claimant?
I have known the Claimant a good many Years by Countenance; I knew him as a Merchant in Dublin.

How long?
I think Twenty Years ago.

You knew him well?
I cannot say that I knew him well. If I met him I saluted him as a Countryman of mine.

You knew his Father before?
I recollect seeing him.

Has not the Claimant been frequently at your House?
No.

Do you state that positively?
Yes.

Have you met together upon this Business frequently?
Not often.

When did you first communicate to him that you had found this Paper?
I never communicated it to him.

How did he first know it?
I mentioned it to his Brother.

Did you ever mention to him, or to any Person previously to your coming before this House upon the former Occasion, that you had taken a Note of the Tombstone?
I mentioned it to the Brother of the Claimant. I met him at an Hotel. We talked over the Matter.

Did you ever tell him before you were last examined that you had taken a Note of the Inscription?
I did; I told his Brother that I had some Recollection of taking a Memorandum.

Did you mention that before you were examined here?
I did.

How was it that you did not mention that in your Examination?
I think I mentioned to some of the noble Lords that I had some Recollection of taking a Memorandum.

Did you mention it to the Solicitor of the Claimant?
I think I did.

Are you sure of that?
I think I did.

Are you sure of it?
I have no Doubt that I mentioned that I took the Memorandum. I mentioned to the Brother of the Claimant that I thought I had taken a Memorandum of the old Tomb. I was not quite clear, it being so many Years ago; but I had some indistinct Recollection of taking a Minute.

Did you search for it?
I did previously to 1843.

(62.2.)   A a   Did

Mr. Patrick Boyne.

Did you search all the Papers that you have now?

I searched the loose Papers, but where I found it was in an old Pocket Book with other Papers.

Whose Pocket Book?

An old Pocket Book of some of the Family, Mr. Wyer's Family, an old Red Pocket Book.

Was it a Pocket Book that Mr. Wyer had used?

He had used it occasionally, and it was in his Desk with other old Books.

Have you got it here?

It is in my Trunk at the Terminus. My Trunk has been mislaid. I was there this Morning to see whether it had come in from Birmingham. It contains that Pocket Book and some old Papers. It was placed among some Papers in the outer Division of the Desk.

How was it folded?

It was in that Way (*describing it*). It was among other old Papers.

I see there is something written in the Corner; what is that? It seems to have been erased lately; it looks as if it had been scratched out with a Penknife?

I do not know what it is.

Hold it up, and you will see that something has been scratched out with a Penknife?

Yes, there is something here; it is something like " Mr. Merton."

If it be the Corner torn off a Letter I do not understand Part of it being scratched out with a Penknife?

Nor I either.

You do not know how that is?

No.

Re-examined by Mr. Serjeant Shee.

Was Mr. Wyer at all related to any of these Tracy's?

Not at all.

(*By a Lord.*)   Do you know Joseph Tracy?

I do.

Were you in the habit of going to Mass with him?

No; he lives in another County from me.

Did you not say so in the Year 1843 when you were before the House?

Do you mean Joseph Tracy the elder or Joseph Tracy the younger?

Joseph Tracy the Father of the present Claimant?

I saw him at our Chapel. I thought you meant Joseph Tracy the younger.

You went to Mass with him?

He attended the same Chapel.

You are a Roman Catholic yourself?

I am.

When you went back from being here before you searched to see whether you had made a Memorandum or not?

I went back to see whether I could get the Memorandum.

Did

Did you think of looking into this Desk ?
It was there that I found it, but I did not think of it till after I was examined here.

Did you find it immediately afterwards ?
I think some Months.   I think that this Memorandum was got either in July or August.

You have stated that you mentioned to the Claimant a little before you were examined here that you were in doubt whether you had made a Memorandum ?
If I did so the noble Lord might have hurried me, but I think I was ultimately clear that I took a Memorandum.

You were understood to say, in answer to a Question from the learned Counsel, that you had mentioned to Mr. Tracy before you were examined here that you were in doubt whether you had made a Memorandum ?
No ; I recollect stating that to the Brother of the Claimant, not to the Claimant at all ; I had no Connexion with the Claimant.

The Subject having been so far stirred by your Conversation with the Brother of the Claimant, did not you think of making a Search in the Repositories, or in the Desk, or in any other way, to find if you had a Memorandum ?
I did, but the Time was exceedingly short.   I have a Recollection of going through a great Mass of Papers, and I could not find it.

But in the course of your Examination you did not think of going to the Desk ?
Previously to the last Examination I searched for the Memorandum.
Did you search the Desk ?
I did.

How happened it that you did not see it ?
It was placed with other Papers in an old Pocket Book detached from the loose Papers.   There were some valuable Matters belonging to the Virazel Family, and this was put with them as a Matter of Safety having this Copy of the Decree on it.

Then when you were searching for this particular Memorandum you did not think of examining the Papers in the Pocket Book ?
No ; the Pocket Book was in the upper Part of the Desk.

(*Mr. Serjeant Shee.*)   You stated that you knew Joseph Tracy the Father of the Claimant, and that he was a Catholic ?
Yes.

How long is it since you first knew him ?
They have been in the Country, I think, Six or Seven-and-twenty Years.

You did not know him longer than Thirty Years ago ?
No.

Have they always been Catholics since you knew them ?
Yes.

You have seen them go to Chapel ?
Yes.

Then

Mr. James Burke. Then Mr. JAMES BURKE was called in; and having been sworn, was examined as follows:

(*Sir Fitzroy Kelly.*)   Are you a Solicitor practising in Dublin?
I am.

Do you produce an attested Copy of the Minutes of a Decree in the Cause of Verazell against Tuthill?
I do.

Did you compare it with the original Register Book?
I did.

Is it a true Copy?
It is.   It is attested by the proper Officer.

What is the Date?
The Date is the 3d of April 1802.

The same was delivered in, and read as follows:

No. 23.   KING.

Saturday, 3d April 1802.

Present, His Honor the Master of the Rolls.

Verazell v. Tuthill. } Cause called on for Judgment.   Mr. Williams for Plaintiff prays the Remainder of the Proofs of the Parties may be entered as read.

Administration to Gabrail Verazell granted to Issabella Maria Verazel, dated Third May One thousand seven hundred and fifty-one, read. Administration to Hariott Verazall granted to same, dated Third Day of May One thousand seven hundred and fifty-one, read. Like to Vatable Verazal granted to same, dated the Third Day of May One thousand seven hundred and fifty-one, read. Like to Catherine Verazal granted to same, dated the Third Day of May One thousand seven hundred and fifty-one, read. Like to Jane Verazel granted to same, dated the Twenty-sixth Day of February One thousand seven hundred and fifty-two, read. Probate of the Will of Peter Verazel granted to Marianna Sarah Verazel, dated the Second Day of November One thousand seven hundred and fifty-seven, read. Exemplification of Probate of Will of Isabella Maria Verazel granted to Elizabeth Verazel, dated the Fourth Day of January One thousand eight hundred and two, read. Administration to Peter Vatable granted to Joseph Mason, dated the Seventh Day of November One thousand eight hundred and one, read. The like with Will annexed to Mary Vatable granted to Joseph Mason, dated the Twenty-eighth Day of July One thousand eight hundred and one, read. Administration with the Will of Catherine Verazel annexed granted to Joseph Mason, dated   One thousand eight hundred and one, read. Daniel Verazel to Isabella Maria Verazel, Bond of Penalty Six hundred and sixty-six Pounds Thirteen Shillings and Four-pence, dated the Ninth Day of March One thousand seven hundred and forty-three, read. The like to Elizabeth Verazel, read. John M'Daniel to the First, Second, and Third Cross Interrogatories, read. Elizabeth Mooney to the First, Second, and Third Cross Interrogatories, read. Original Account of Assetts of Peter Vatable, drawn up by Daniel Verazel, read.

Let said conditional Decree be }
varied by the Register.   }

COURT.

COURT. Make conditional Decree absolute against Defendants *Mr. James Burke.* therein, and let the Will of said Mary Vatable, dated the Thirteenth Day of June One thousand seven hundred and sixteen, and the Articles of the Eleventh Day of March One thousand seven hundred and five, in the Pleadings mentioned, be carried into execution, and let the Will of said Daniel Verazel, dated the Tenth Day of May One thousand seven hundred and forty-four, be decreed to be well proved, and that the Trust thereof be carried into execution, and let it be referred to one of the Masters to take an Account of the Assetts of Peter and Mary Vatable in the Pleadings named at the Times of their Deaths respectively, into whose Hands same came, and how disposed of, and what Debts they, or either of them, owed at the Time of their Deaths ; also an Account of the Real and Personal Fortune of said Daniel Verazel on the Execution of said Deed of Appointment of the Twenty-first Day of June One thousand seven hundred and thirty-five, and at his Death, and also the Time of his Death respectively, into whose Hands same came, and how disposed of; and also an Account of the Debts due by him on said Twenty-first Day of June One thousand seven hundred and thirty-five, and at his Death, and let said Master report the Time of the Deaths of the several Children of said Daniel and Catherine Verazel in the Peadings mentioned to have died ; and let an Account be taken of the several Sums due to said Catherine Verazel under said Articles of the Eleventh Day of March One thousand seven hundred and five, and under the Will of said. Daniel Verazel ; and also an Account of the several Sums due to the several Children of said Daniel and Catherine Verazel under said Will of said Mary Vatable, and under said Will of said Daniel Verazel ; and also an Account of the Debts of said Catherine Verazel, and of the several Children of said Daniel and Catherine, and of the Legacies of such of said several Persons as made Wills ; and let an Account be also taken of the Real and Personal Fortune of Peter Verazel in the Pleadings named, into whose Hands the same came, and how disposed of ; and let an Account be taken of what is due to the Plaintiff as personal Representative of said Catherine Verazel, and of her several Brothers and Sisters deceased; and let an Account be taken of the several Debts and Incumbrances affecting the Lands and Premises in the Pleadings mentioned, and let said Decree to an Account of One thousand seven hundred and fifty-two, and said Order of the Thirteenth Day of May One thousand seven hundred and fifty-six, be carried into execution, and let all proper Accounts be decreed, and let said Freehold Estate of said Daniel Verazel and Peter Verazel be sold under the Decree of this Court, and let the Monies arising therefrom be paid and applied towards the Discharge and Satisfaction of the several Demands and Incumbrances affecting the same, and let all Persons having Debts, Charges, and Incumbrances affecting said Premises be at liberty to come in before said Master to prove and ascertain their respective Demands, Master first publishing an Advertizment. And as to the Defendant John Tuthill, let the Bill stand dismissed without Costs.

FRAN. PRENDERGAST.

Then MARTIN HEAGNEY was called in ; and having been sworn, *Martin Heagney.* was examined as follows :

(*Sir Fitzroy Kelly.*) What are you by Business ?
A Farmer.

Martin Heagney.

How old are you?
Nearly Fifty.

Where do you live?
I live at Kilcaven.

Did you ever see that Tombstone which you see there now while it was lying on the Ground?
Yes, I did.

How often did you see it?
I have seen Fragments of it in the Churchyard of Castlebrack.

About what Time did you first see it lying on the Ground?
I saw it about Thirty Years ago.

About how long ago did you last see it?
About Thirty Years.

I believe you gave Evidence here at the Bar of the House of Lords in the Year 1843?
I did.

You gave Evidence that you had seen the Tombstone some considerable Number of Years before?
I did.

Upon your Return to Ireland did you proceed to search for this Tombstone or for any Portion of it?
I did.

Where did you first search?
In the Churchyard.

Did you search there once or more than once?
I searched more than once.

For a considerable Time together?
Yes.

Were you able to find any Portion of the Tombstone in the Churchyard?
I was not.

Did you afterward search anywhere else?
Yes.

Where?
In the Floor of an old House near the Churchyard.

At the House we have head of? Mrs. Dunn's?
Yes.

Where Poll Dunn lived?
Yes.

The Floor of what Room was it that you searched?
It was the Taproom.

Were there several Stones or Fragments of Stones in that Room?
There were.

Did they form Part of the Floor or the Hearth, or for what Purpose did they seem to have been applied?
They formed Part of the Floor.

Having searched this Room did you at last find any Portions of that Stone which lies there?
I did.

How many Pieces did you find?
Two Pieces.

Tell

Tell me as nearly as you can when you found those Two Pieces?
I found them the 13th of August 1843.

You see that Stone as it lies upon the Floor?
I do.

Are you able to say whether they are the Two Pieces that you found?
The First and Second I found.

Those are the nearest this Way which appears to have formed one Piece of the Stone which was cut in Two vertically?
Yes.

When you had found those Two Pieces of Stone what did you do with them?
I brought them into the Churchyard and put them under a Tombstone that was raised off the Ground.

How long did you leave them there?
Till Morning.

Till the next Morning?
Yes.

What did you do with them further?
I brought them home.

To your own House?
Yes.

Where is that?
About Two Miles or a Mile and a Half from the Churchyard.

What is the Name of the Place you live in?
Kilcaven.

Did you keep them at your own House till you afterwards took them to Mr. Baynham's?
Yes.

They were in your own Care?
Yes.

Was it while you kept those Two Pieces of Stone in your own House that you afterwards found any more Pieces?
It was.

How soon after this 13th of August did you find the other Pieces?
It was, I think, in October.

Then did you continue your Searches from Time to Time after you had found the first Two Pieces in Dunn's Room?
I did.

Where did you find any more of the Pieces?
I found the other Two Pieces in another old Ruin.

Where was that?
Near where I live; about Half a Mile from where I live.

How far from Castlebrack Churchyard?
Two Miles.

Had you searched any other Places before you went there?
Yes, a great many Places.

What made you go there? Was it in consequence of something that somebody told you?
Yes.

Then

Martin Heagney.

Then you found Two more Pieces?
Yes.

Point out which were those Pieces?
The Fourth and Fifth.

At that Time did that little triangular Piece form a Part of Number Four?
It did.

Numbers One and Two were as they are now in Two Pieces when you found them at Dunn's?
Yes.

And Four and Five were in Two Pieces also?
Yes.

The little Bit was not broken off?
Yes.

What was the Name of the Person on whose Premises Pieces Four and Five were found?
Delany.

His Christian Name?
Edward Delany.

Not the old Man we have seen here?
No.

Then you found those Two Pieces Four and Five, you say, in October; what did you do with them?
I brought them home.

Then you had Four Pieces?
I had.

How long did you keep them yourself?
About Two Weeks or Three Weeks.

Where did you take them to then?
I took them to Mr. Baynham of Killeigh.

What is he?
A Shopkeeper.

Who desired you to take them there?
Mr. Timothy Tracy bid me take them there.

Do you remember the Date when you took them to Killeigh?
No, I do not recollect the Date.

Did you then deliver them to Mr. Baynham himself?
I did.

Did you leave them with him?
Yes.

And from that Time you have not had them at all in your Custody?
No.

Were you present at a later Period when those Pieces which you had found amongst others were produced and laid down in Castlebrack Churchyard when several Magistrates were present?
I was.

Did you then again see the Four Pieces?
Yes.

Are

Are you sure that those are the Four Pieces which you had found and delivered to Mr. Baynham ?

Quite sure.

Have you looked at them carefully and attentively since ?

I have.

Are you able now to speak positively as to whether those Pieces which are now lying there did form that very Tombstone which, you say, you saw some Thirty Years ago ?

The very ones.

I omitted to ask you when you found those Two Pieces Numbers One and Two in the Taproom at Dunn's was the Part containing the Inscription uppermost or the other Side ?

The other Side was uppermost.

The Inscription was downward ?

Yes.

With respect to those that you afterwards found at Edward Delany's, how were they ?

They were amongst a Heap of Stones ; it was himself got them out. He removed them out of the Hearth-place or Fire-place.

You say that you found them at Delany's ; did you take them from Delany's yourself ?

Yes.

When you first saw them at Delany's where and in what Condition did you see them ?

Among a Heap of Stones and Rubbish.

In what Part of Delany's Premises ?

In the Yard.

You say they were among a Heap of Stones and Rubbish ; were any of the other Stones there any thing like Stones of the same Description as if they had been Pieces of Tombstones, or were they Stones of a different Character ?

They were of a different Character.

Edward Delany and you were together ?

He was not with me.

You went to Delany's, Delany was not with you, but there you saw a Heap of Stones and Rubbish. Then did you search in that Heap yourself ?

Yes.

Were you alone ?

Yes.

Was it in the course of that Search that you found those Two Pieces of Stone ?

Yes.

And you took them to your own House ?

Yes.

Cross-examined by Mr. Attorney General.

You stated when you were examined in 1843 that you were no Relation of the Tracy's ?

Yes, I did.

C c And

And that they found you by mere Accident?
Yes.

How came you to devote your Time to the Object of searching for these Stones? Are you paid for your Services for that Purpose?
No, I was not.

Did any body employ you to occupy a great Portion of your Time in hunting about the Country for these Stones?
No, they did not.

How came you to do it?
I wished to establish the Truth.

Then was it purely from a Love of Truth which must succeed that you occupied your Time for a long Period in searching for those Stones?
It was that; and every Person that came to give Evidence here before was accused. The Country People would throw some Ridicule on the Person.

Did the People who lived about the District and near the Churchyard say that you had told what was not true when you said that you had seen the Tombstones?
Some People said that.

Were they People who lived close on the Spot?
I think some of them did.

People that were in the Churchyard a good deal?
The People in the Churchyard did not say it.

Did you hear it said by the People that lived in the Neighbourhood that you had been up to London saying what was not true?
I heard People say so.

How long were you engaged in searching for the Stones?
Not very long, not many Days.

Where did you first go?
To the Churchyard at Castlebrack.

Did that take you long?
I spent Two or Three Hours every Time.

Where did you go then?
I went to Mike Dunn's.

Was he alive?
He is.

Was he in the Dancing-room when you found the Stones?
No, he was not there when I found the Stones.

Was he in the Place?
Yes, he is living in the Place.

Was any body by when you found this Tombstone in the old Room at Dunn's?
No.

What Time of the Day was it that you found it?
In the Night.

You went by yourself in the Night to make this Search?
Yes.

Had you your Lantern with you?
Yes.

What

What Time in the Night?
I dare say it was Twelve o'Clock or One o'Clock.

Did you take any body with you?
No.

Did any body know that you were going?
No.

You went of your own Head at Twelve at Night to hunt for the Tombstone?
Yes.

Did you find the Pieces at once?
I saw them before I went at Night.

You knew where these Stones were?
No; I knew that there were some Stones there, but I pulled up Three or Four Pieces before I found the right ones. I pulled up Three Pieces besides those Two.

You pulled up Three Pieces and they were wrong?
Yes.

And you were lucky enough to find the other Two together?
Yes.

Where were they lying?
Just inside the Door.

They were just in the Tread of the Door?
Yes.

Were the Letters up or down?
The Letters were down.

Do you remember the Room when it was standing?
Yes.

It was very much used, was not it?
Yes.

Mr. Attorney General desired that the Pieces of Stone should be turned over, which was done accordingly.

Upon your solemn Oath do you mean to say that in the Tread of the Door of a Room which was greatly frequented you found those Two Pieces of Stone?
I do.

Do you know much of the Nature of the Stone in the Neighbourhood?
No, I am not acquainted with the Nature of the Stone.

But you found them close in the Tread of the Door lying in that Way?
A Piece inside of the Door.

Just where the People would tread coming in?
They would tread over all the Room.

Did you not find them in a Place which all the People coming into the Dancing-room must have passed over?
Yes.

And they were in the State in which they are now?
Only they were dirty then.

(62.2.)

But

Martin Heagney.

But they have not been cut or chiselled since?
No.

You are sure that they were in that State?
Yes.

Where did you go to search after you had made this Discovery?
I went to several Places.

Tell me where?
I went to a Man's House where I heard that there was a Piece of a Tombstone.

Whose House was that?
I think it was a Man of the Name of Frost Grady; there was no Person living in it then.

Did you find it then?
No.

How many Days were you before you were successful in finding those Two other Pieces?
About Two Months.

Did you always search at Night?
No; sometimes in the Day.

Tell me any Place where you went in the Day to find it?
I went to every Place where I thought I might find it.

Tell me the Name of any Person that you saw in your first Search?
Several Persons.

Tell me the Name of any one?
Edward Delany.

Is he here?
He is.

He was the Man that told you where the Stones were to be found?
He searched with me Two or Three Times.

Was he the Man that told you that in the Ruins you would find Two or Three more?
No, another Man of the same Name, Edward Delany.

Do you believe that those Stones had been used as a Flooring?
I could not see whether they were on the Floor or in the Dirt.

You do not know whether the Letters were up or down?
No.

Have you looked at the Bottom to see how they were?
I have looked to see whether they were worn underneath.

Do you find that they have the Appearance of having been used for a Fire, or that they have been trodden upon at all?
I could not tell.

You do not know?
No.

From their Appearance do you suppose that they have lain upper Side uppermost?
I could not judge, but I am certain that I got the first with the Letters down.

Did you find the second Lot in the Night?
No.

Was

Was any one with you ?
No.

The Owner of the House was not with you ?
Nobody.

You took them to Mr. Baynham's. Why did you take them to Mr. Baynham's ?
Mr. Tracy bid me take them there.

Is Mr. Baynham any Relation of Mr. Tracy ?
Not to my Knowledge.

Why could he not trust you to keep them ?
I could not give you any Reason for that.

Where did you find the other Pieces ?
I found only Four Pieces.

Where did the others come from ?
I do not know.

Have you been paid at all for your Trouble ?
No.

How long have you been in Town this Time ?
On Friday Night last I came.

(*By a Lord.*) What Colour do you call that Stone ?
I call it a Whiteish or Greyish Stone.

You call it a White Stone do you ?
Yes.

(*Mr. Attorney General.*) Was it when you saw it in the Church-yard many Years ago of the same Colour that it is now ?
I think not quite the same, it looked darker then.

Was it Black then ?
No.

Was it Greenish from the Weather ?
Yes.

When you saw it many Years ago in the Churchyard it was Greenish ?
I think it was nearly the same Colour as now.

Were those Two Pieces you found at Delany's in a Heap of Rubbish exposed to the Weather?
Not when I found them.

Were the Pieces that you found at Poll Dunn's exposed to the Weather.
They were not.   There was a great deal of Clay over them.

You had to shovel off the Clay to find them ?
Yes.

Then you were exceedingly lucky in finding them at the fourth Trial after uncovering only Three others.   I thought that the Surface was exposed, but you say that it was all covered with Earth ?
Not all, there were Part of the Stones covered.

Were these covered ?
They were.

Did you not consider it great Luck to find them so soon ?
No one could have discovered that they were in the Floor.

Martin Heagney.

Re-examined by Sir Fitzroy Kelly.

You were asked why you took the Trouble to make all these Searches; did you give Evidence upon Oath here that you had actually seen this Tombstone when it was in the Earth?
I did.

When you got back home you found from the Results of the Case that there were some People that doubted the Truth of your Statement?
Yes, there were Stories set going that prejudiced People against us.

Did that induce you to prosecute your Search till you had found the Fragments?
Yes.

You say that you searched at Night in Dunn's Premises; is Dunn at all favourable to this Claim?
I do not know.

Is Mr. Dunn a Tenant; does he hold either the Churchyard or the House or something under a Gentleman of the Name of Kemmis, who is the Brother of the Crown Solicitor?
He holds a House and Garden.

With regard to those Two Pieces which were found at Dunn's you say they were near the Doorway?
About Two Feet.

Do you know how long that Place has been a Ruin?
I do not exactly know; a good many Years.

How many should you say; is it Ten or Twelve Years since it was used as a Dancing-room?
More.

Of course you do not know when those Stones were put there. Do you remember them during the Time that the House was frequented?
I do not.

Were they very much covered with the Earth?
I think there was an Inch of Clay at least or more.

Were they so far covered by the Earth as to be in some Degree protected on the upper Surface?
Yes.

Are those earthen Floors common in Ireland?
There are earthen Floors generally in poor People's Houses.

Was it after Edward Delany had said something to you that you went and searched in that Place?
Yes.

(*By a Lord.*) When you found the Stones in Dunn's House did you see first some other Stone which was uncovered?
Yes.

You saw some Stone uncovered, and then you thought that there might be other Stones, and you removed the Earth to look for other Stones?
Yes.

And those were let into the Floor?
Yes.

Had

Had you some Difficulty in getting them up?
Yes; I put a Piece of Iron under them and raised them up.

They were not only let in but covered up?
Yes.

The Earth which was upon them was an Accumulation of Rubbish.
It was not an earthen Floor which had been laid upon them?
I think not.

When the Room was used as a Dancing-room the Stones made the
Floor of the Room?
They were in the Floor, but there might be Clay over them.

(*Sir Fitzroy Kelly.*) Are there Stones left there now in the
Dancing-room?
No, there are none there now.

(*By a Lord.*) Do you recollect what was the Inscription upon the
Tombstone when it was in the Churchyard?
Yes.

What was it?
" Here lieth the Body of William Tracy, Esquire, late of Ross in the
Queen's County, Son of the Honourable Robert Tracy, one of the Judges
in England," or something to that Effect.

You have a clear Recollection of that?
I have.

In the Year 1845 you had likewise a Recollection of seeing the
Tombstone and the Inscription upon it?
Yes.

Was your Recollection then in conformity with your Recollection
now?
It was in Substance but not entirely in Words.

It appears here that you recollected seeing " Erected by Mary Tracy
to the Memory of her Husband William Tracy, late of Ross in the
King's County, Son to Judge Tracy of England." That was your
Recollection in 1843?
Yes.

You observe that that is different from your Recollection now?
It is.

Which do you think is the correct Recollection?
The last I gave ; " Here lieth the Body of William Tracy."

Then you were incorrect in your Recollection on the former Occasion?
I was as far as that.

How came you to think of Mary Tracy?
I recollected that there was something about Mary Tracy on the
Tomb.

Do you recollect now that there was something about Mary Tracy?
I do.

What was it?
There are two Words that I think have a Meaning for Mary Tracy.
Two Letters. I recollect seeing the whole of it on the Tomb.

What Part of the Tomb was it?
On the lower Part.

The

Martin Heagney.

The Part that is wanting now?
There is some of it here now.
Which Part?
On either of those Two (*pointing to Pieces Six and Seven*).
Which are the Words that are like Mary Tracy? (*The Pieces being handed to the Witness.*)
[The Witness pointed them out.]

Did you ever hear a Paper read which said any thing about William Tracy, Son of Judge Tracy, one of the Judges of England, or something to that Effect?
I think not.

Did you never hear a Paper read about the Honourable Robert Tracy, a Judge of England?
Not to my Recollection.

Never at all?
No.

Did you never hear Words to that Effect spoken, whether they were read from a Paper or not?
I cannot recollect. I think I did not.

Who examined you before you were brought over as a Witness last Time?
Mr. Burke.

Where did he examine you?
At Castlebrack.

Did he take down what you said?
He did.

Did he read any thing to you?
No.

Did he say any thing about an Inscription to you?
No.

He did not ask you any Questions about an Inscription?
No.

He did not ask you whether you recollected having seen any thing upon the Stone?
Oh yes, he did.

Then he did examine you about the Inscription?
He asked me did I recollect the Inscription on the Tomb.

And you said you did?
Yes.

Did he ask you whether you recollected such and such Words about William Tracy?
No, he asked me what was it.

And you told him?
Yes.

And he never told you any Words?
Never.

Has he examined you since that?
No.

Has

Has any body examined you here since that ?
No.

You have not seen any body to ask you any Question before you came here To-day ?
No.

Has nobody asked you any Questions about the Things you have now been telling us, about finding the Stones and taking them to your House, and then taking them to Mr. Baynham's, and finding the others afterwards ?
No, only what I told Mr. Burke in Ireland.

You told all to Mr. Burke in Ireland that you have told To-day ?
Yes.

Then did he tell you any thing about the Inscription, about William Tracy, the Son of the Honourable Robert Tracy, one of the Judges of England ?
No.

Did he ask you any Question about that Inscription ?
He asked me what was it.

But never told you any Words ?
No.

That you are quite sure of ?
That I am quite sure of.

Were you at the Meeting at the Churchyard when several Gentlemen were there ?
Yes, I was.

Did you hear the Inscription read at that Time ?
I did not hear any one reading it, but I looked at it.

You did not hear any one read it to the Company in general ?
No, I did not.

(*Sir Fitzroy Kelly.*) Did Mr. Burke suggest any thing to you, or did you merely give him your Evidence to the best of your Recollection ?
I gave him my Evidence ; he never suggested any thing to me.

Then EDWARD DELANY was called in ; and having been sworn, was examined as follows :

(*Mr. Serjeant Shee.*) What Age are you ?
Forty-seven.

Where do you live ?
In the Parish of Castlebrack.

What are you ?
A Carpenter by Trade.

How long have you lived in the Parish of Castlebrack ?
Since I was born.

Do you remember at any Time when you were a Lad seeing a Tombstone at Castlebrack ?
Yes.

Do you remember the Inscription upon it, or the Substance of it ?
I remember some of it.

E e   How

Edward Delany.

How much do you remember?

Just Two or Three odd Words. I well remember that I used to hear People read it.

What was the Name?

Judge Tracy and William Tracy.

But you do not remember the Words exactly?

No, I do not; but I recollect seeing People reading it.

Did you know James and Poll Dunn who kept the House close by when it was a Dancing and Tap House?

I did.

Do you recollect seeing any Pieces of a Tombstone at that House?

I do.

I believe you were not examined in the Year 1843 before a Committee of this House. This is your first Appearance here?

This is my first.

In the Month of June 1843 did you in consequence of any thing you had heard make Search for a Tombstone which you had seen long ago in the Churchyard at Castlebrack?

I did.

Where did you first make Search for it?

Along and round the Ditches where there were Stones and Ruins thrown up.

Among other Places you searched did you search in the Floor of what had been the Tap and Dancing Room of Poll and James Dunn's?

Yes.

Was that about the Month of June?

It was.

Was it by Day or by Night?

Just at Daylight.

Very early in the Morning?

Yes.

Were you long at it?

Not long.

How long?

About Twenty Minutes. The Roof was off the House and the Floor all full of Thatch and Dirt.

Had you any thing with you?

A Stake.

After you had searched some Time did you find any thing?

I found Two Pieces of Flags in the Floor.

Was there much Dirt over them?

About that deep down (*several Inches*).

Did it appear to you to be Dirt that had been placed there on purpose to cover the Stone, or that it had accumulated in course of Time?

No, it was Part of the Ruins of the Thatch of the old House that fell in.

When

When you first saw those Stones was there any Inscription on them ?

There were some Letters on them, but I could not tell what was on them.

Was there any Inscription on the upper Part of them, or was the Inscription underneath ?
It was uppermost.

Did you remove them ?
No.

Did you take them up at all ?
I did not.

Did you cover them up again ?
I did.

Some Time after that did you see the last Witness, Heagney ?
I did.

And you spoke to him ?
I did.

Did you know at the Time that he was searching for Tombstones ?
I did.

Did you afterwards search anywhere else for Tombstones ?
I did.

Where ?
In the Churchyard.

About when was that ?
About the 15th of March.

In this Year ?
Yes.

At what Time of the Day or the Night ?
It was at Night.

At what Time of the Night ?
Between Ten and Eleven.

Had you a Lantern with you ?
No, it was a Starlight Night.

In what Part of the Churchyard did you search ?
Inside the Walls of the old Church in a large Heap of Stones.

Inside the Walls of the old ruined Church ?
Yes, in the Body of it.

There was a Heap of Stones there ?
Yes.

Were you long before you found any Stone that attracted your Attention ?
About Two Hours.

Did you at last come to Stones which had Inscriptions on them ?
Yes.

How many did you find with Inscriptions on them ?
I found Four Pieces.

How many of those Four are here ?
Two.

(62.2.)

Which

Edward Delany.

Which are the Two?

   [The Witness pointed out Pieces Six and Seven.]

Did you remove them from the Churchyard that Night?
I did.

Where did you bring them to?
I brought them to my House.

Did you examine them that Night?
No, I got them examined the following Morning.

Can you read?
No; I got them examined.

After the Examination did you take them to Mr. Digby Baynham's at Killeigh?
I went home and told him that I had found Two Pieces of Tombstone.

Was it he that examined them for you?
No, a Nephew of my own.

In consequence of what passed between you and Mr. Baynham did you afterwards take them to his House?
No; he himself and Mr. Burke came. Mr. Burke came first.

After this Mr. Baynham came, did you deliver them to Mr. Baynham?
I did to Mr. Burke.

Did you afterwards see those Fragments together?
I did.

Where?
In the Churchyard.

Upon what Occasion was that? Was it when the Magistrates were examining them?
Yes.

In your Belief is that which you saw on that Occasion, and what is now before their Lordships, the same Stone that you remember Years ago there?
It is.

Have you any Doubt about it?
To the best of my Knowledge it is.

I understood you to say that you could not read; do you know your Letters?
Yes, I know my Letters, but I could not tell any thing about Figures and Writing.

Could you make out the Names with a little Trouble?
Yes.

    Cross-examined by Mr. Attorney General.

What Business are you?
A Carpenter.

Where do you live now?
In the Parish of Castlebrack.

How far from the Churchyard?
About Three Quarters of a Mile.

               Have

Have you known the Tracy's long ?
Not a great while.

How many Years ?
I do not recollect how many Years.

Have you known them Twenty Years ?
No.

Ten Years ?
I cannot exactly tell you how long I have known them.

Did you know them before this Matter came up about the Claim ?
Perhaps I might.

Have they ever spoken to you upon the Subject ?
No.

Have they ever talked to you about this Matter ?
No, not till now.

When did they first speak to you about it ?
Since I came over here.

That is the first Time ?
Yes.

How came you to be searching for these Stones ?
Because I heard that it was a valuable Thing to get them.

What is that to you ?
I will tell you how I came to search for them. A Man came and told me to call at Mr. Tracy's at Maryborough.

Did you go to him ?
I did not see him when I went to Maryborough.

When was this ?
Three or Four Years ago.

How long was it before you began to search ?
About Twelve Months after that I began to search myself.

Why did you begin to search if you did not expect to get any Money for it ?
I did not.

How long were so engaged ?
Different Starts of Days and Nights.

You did not expect to get any thing ?
I looked for nothing.

You do not expect to get any thing now ?
Nothing but my Hire for my Loss of Time.

For coming here ?
Yes.

Had nobody told you to search ?
No.

Your Search was from mere Curiosity ?
Yes.

How long had you known this Poll Dunn's House ?
Near Thirty Years.

When was it last used as a Dancing Shop ?
Between Ten and Twelve Years ago.

Edward Delany.

Was the Floor always in the same State when you knew it?
Always.

There was no Alteration in the Floor at the Time you knew it?
It was sometimes repaired.

When did you know it repaired?
I cannot tell the Day and Month.

How long before it fell down?
Three or Four Years.

Who repaired it?
The Family in the House.

The old Man himself?
The old Man was not alive at this Time, but his Son was and his Wife.

Are the Son and the Wife alive now?
Yes.

Pretty well I hope?
Middling.

Where are they?
At the House in Castlebrack.

Those are the People that repaired it?
Yes.

They have been there many Years?
They have.

What Time of the Day did you go into Poll Dunn's Dancing Shop to look after these Stones?
Just at Daylight.

What Time in the Morning?
Before the Sun rises.

Could you see?
I could.

Did you take any Lantern with you?
No.

Did you know where to look?
I knew where the Floor used to be flagged in the Dancing Time.

Was that the Place they danced upon?
Yes.

And then you looked and found those Stones?
Yes.

Were the Letters up or down?
The Letters were up.

Did you afterwards tell Heagney that if he went there he would find them?
I told him that there were Pieces of Tombstones in Poll Dunn's Floor.

Can you tell me whether those are the Pieces that you saw in the Floor the Morning you went (*Numbers One and Two*); are those the Two that you saw at Poll Dunn's Shop that Morning?
I think they are.

They

They were lying in that Way ?

Not together.

With the Letters up ?

Yes.

I understand you to say that you can follow Letters ?

I could follow odd ones, odd printed Letters.

When you saw those " printed Letters" that induced you to believe that those were what you were looking for ?

Yes, but I did not tell Heagney that I had seen Letters on it.

Where were they lying ; they were not together, were they ?

No.

You are sure of that ?

Yes.

Where were they ?

One was partly in the Centre of the Floor, the other close up to the Fire.

Those marked One and Two are the Two you saw there ?

I think they are.

Have you any Doubt about it ?

To the best of my Knowledge they are.

Having satisfied yourself that those were the Stones you told Heagney where to go and find them ?

I told him that there were those Two Pieces of Tombstone.

Did you tell him that those were the Things he wanted ?

I did not.

You knew that he was searching ?

I did know that he was searching because he and I searched the Churchyard together.

You said that in Poll Dunn's Dancing Shop he would find Two of them ?

Yes, but I searched there by myself.

You did not take them up ?

No, I did not, because I could not take them up in the Daytime. The Man that lived there would not have let me take them up.

Did Heagney tell you afterwards that he had found them ?

No.

Did not he say " It is all right," and tell you that he found the Stones?

No.

How long after did you hear that he had found them ?

I do not remember how long it was.

Tell me about ?

It was a good while.

You have danced there yourself ?

I have.

Was the Floor sanded or cleaned before they began ? Did you dance upon the Flag partly ?

Yes ; the Flags used to be danced upon.

They were flagged I suppose for the Purpose of being danced upon ?

Pieces of Tombstones used to be put in the Fire-places ; several other Tombstones besides Mr. Tracy's.

(62.2.)

But

Edward Delany.

But you danced upon the Flags partly?
I do not say, but I might.

The People did?
The People did.

You do not know any thing about the second Finding at your Namesake Delany's?
No.

You found the rest at the third Finding?
I found those Two Pieces myself.

At what Time was it that you went into the Ruins of the Church to find them?
Between Ten and Eleven o'Clock at Night.

Only by Starlight?
That was all.

Was any body with you?
Not one.

How many Pieces did you take away with you?
I took Four.

Two of them upon Examination turned out to be the Pieces you wanted?
Yes.

Were there many Pieces of Tombstone besides the Four?
Several Pieces.

A great many?
Yes.

Where did you take those Four Pieces that you took away?
To my own House.

How far off?
About Three Quarters of a Mile.

(*By a Lord.*) Did you take them all at once?
I took them in One Night, I could not carry them all together; I used to move them on a Distance, and come back for the others.

(*Mr. Attorney General.*) Did you move them all at once out of the Churchyard?
Yes, and left them, and came back and fetched them.

It gave you a long Job?
It was a long Job.

Who saw them first?
A Nephew of mine.

What is his Name?
James Delany.

Is he here?
No.

What has become of him?
He is a young Boy.

How old?
Fifteen or Sixteen Years of Age.

What has become of the other Two Pieces that you found?
I left them at home.

How

How did you find out that these Two Pieces belonged to the Tombstone?
I did not know till Mr. Burke saw them.

You kept the Four Pieces till Mr. Burke came?
Yes. I did not know that they belonged to the Tombstone till Mr. Burke came and examined them.

Why did you not take away all the others that were there? Why did you select the Four out of the Lot? There is nothing upon them but " Widow " and " M.A." Why did you select those out of the whole Lot that you found in the Church?

(The Witness did not answer.)

(*By a Lord.*) What made you fix upon those Four Pieces of Stone more than any other Pieces of Stone which you found there?
I took those Four away. I went to the Heap Two or Three Days afterwards and I found a great many Pieces.

Then why did you take away those Four in preference to the others?
I went Two or Three Days afterwards and got a great many Pieces.

When you took away those Four first there were a great many besides?
There were.

Why did you choose out those Four to take away rather than any other Four?
Because I did not stir the Heap well first when I took away what I found first.

They were all lying together were not they?
No, they were not.

Then others were mixed up with them?
Not with those. I had to toss a great many Stones and Rubbish before I found those.

You tossed a great many others out of the Way before you found those Four?
Other Kind of Stones.

Why did you not take any others besides those Four?
Because they were round Stones, Building Stones.

Were there no other Stones of that Kind besides those Four?
I could feel no Letters on them.

Were those the only Stones that had any Letters?
That was all. Four Pieces had Letters on them.

At what Hour of the Night was it?
Between Ten and Eleven at Night.

There was no Moon?
No.

No Starlight?
No.

Had you a Candle in your Hand?
No.

Any Lantern?
No.

Edward Delany.

You had not your dark Lantern there?
No.

How could you read the Letters?
I did not read them.

Could you feel the Difference between M and A?
No, I could not tell what was on them; I got them home and got them examined.

Who sent you there?
Nobody; I went out of my Head.

To choose a Grave?
It is Time enough to do that when I want it.

However you took a Walk in the Churchyard?
I did.

Do you often walk in the Churchyard?
I do often.

And always find Stones?
Not always.

Did you ever bring home any Stones except those Four?
I did.

Where were they?
In the Churchyard.

What did you do with the other Stones?
Some of them are at home and some of them are here.

And nobody told you to go and get them?
No.

Re-examined by Mr. Serjeant Shee.

When you first went to look for this Tombstone in the old Dancing House you found that the Floor had been covered with Stones?
With Dirt and Thatch.

Under the Dirt was the Floor covered with Stones?
There was a good deal up and down.

Did you see that there were some Stones with Inscriptions and some without?
Yes.

You could not read them?
No.

After that you spoke to Heagney?
Yes.

Some of the Stones were without Inscriptions and some with Inscriptions?
Yes.

Afterwards Heagney got them away without your knowing any thing about it?
Yes.

As to the Stones in the Churchyard you seem to have had some little Difficulty in getting away the Four you did take that Night?
It was not easy to carry them.

Perhaps that was one Reason why you did not take any more?
Yes, it was.

You

You did take Four?

I did.

Are all those Four here?

No, only Two out of the Four.

What did you do with the other Two?

They are at home.

(*By a Lord.*) They did not fit these Stones?

No.

You say that you found these Two Pieces inside the old Church?

Yes.

Covered up with a great many other Stones?

Yes.

Those Stones must have been brought there at some Time?

They were pitched up from one Time to another; there was a Ball Alley there, and there were some that were broken and smashed.

But I suppose the Ball Alley would be as clear of Rubbish as the Church; nobody would have brought Stones out of the Churchyard to the Ball Alley, would they?

Yes, they would, to make a Floor to the Ball Alley.

But this was not laid in any way like a Flooring, was it? Was it laid like a Flooring?

No, the Ball Alley was taken up again. The Parish Minister when he heard of it had it all ripped up again, and he had the Stones flung up into a Heap.

(*Mr. Serjeant Shee.*) You stated that you thought that the other Two Pieces of Stone which you took along with those which you have here were at home; did you give them to Mr. Baynham at any Time?

I showed them to him, I did not bring them.

Would you know them again if you saw them here?

Yes.

(*Mr. Attorney General.*) Are you sure that they are at your House?

They are.

(*By a Lord.*) Why did you take the dead Hour of the Night to make this Search when there was neither Sun nor Moon? Why could you not have gone when it was broad Daylight?

I would not be allowed to go into the Churchyard to search at Daylight; the People in the Yard would not allow me to go into the Yard to break the Fence.

Did you ask Leave to go there?

I did not. I was ordered away some Time before when I was going to search.

Are the Dunn's alive now?

The old Man and his Wife are dead.

How old are the Dunn's that are alive now?

The Dunn that is alive now is about my own Age.

(*Mr. Serjeant Shee.*) Did you ever use a Tombstone for any Purpose in your Trade or Business?

I have.

(62.2.)

For

Edward Delany.

For what Purpose?
For Whetstones, sharpening Tools.
Often?
Yes.

Have you known other People do it in the Neighbourhood?
Yes, plenty.

And use them for other Purposes?
Yes; the Smiths bring them home for grinding Wheels.

Have you known them used as Hearthstones in the Neighbourhood?
Yes.

(*By a Lord.*) Are there any Tombstones remaining in the Grave-yard?
There are some remaining, but a great deal are carried away for that Purpose.

They are favourite Stones for Whetstones?
Yes, they are.

(*Mr. Attorney General.*) Does that Sort of Stone come from that Neighbourhood near the Place?
No, only from the Quarry it belongs to.

How far off from the Churchyard?
There are some Parts of it Four Miles, Part of it Ten Miles.

How near can you get Stone of that Sort off the Mountain?
Not less than Four Miles.

Mr. D. Baynham.

Then Mr. DIGBY BAYNHAM was called in; and having been sworn, was examined as follows:

(*Mr. Serjeant Shee.*) Where do you reside?
At Killeigh.

Is that in the King's County?
Yes.

Do you carry on any Business there?
I keep a Shop.

Have you done so for a long Time?
About Twenty Years.

Do you remember in December 1843 Martin Heagney bringing any thing to you?
I do.

What did he bring you?
He brought me an old Tombstone in Pieces—in Four Pieces.

Do you see them upon the Floor there?
The Four nearest Pieces with a little Piece in the Middle.

Was that little Piece detached at that Time?
No, it was broken on a subsequent Day when the Magistrates were looking at it.

Did you keep them at your House?
I kept them ever since.

Did you attend a Meeting of the Magistrates early in 1844?
I did.

Where

Where was that?

At Castlebrack.

Did you take the Pieces of the Tombstone which Heagney had conveyed to you to that Meeting?

I did.

They were then examined by the Magistrates?

They were.

Did you attend at any other Time at Castlebrack?

I did, at another Meeting.

Was that about the Month of October?

I do not recollect.

But later in that Year?

Yes.

Were there upon that Occasion more Stones than those Four which you had first received from Heagney?

Not at the Second Meeting.

Was there a Third Meeting?

There was a Third Meeting previous to their being sent up.

Were there then Six Stones?

Yes; Two more had been discovered since.

Had those Two others been brought to you by any Person?

They were brought by a Man of the Name of Edward Delany.

About when did he give them to you?

I think it was about a Week before I came up here, before I had Notice to come here.

Did you keep them at your House for any Time?

I kept them from that Time to the Meeting of the Magistrates; they had been sealed up at Castlebrack.

Do you happen to know that Tombstones are used in that Neighbourhood for domestic Purposes?

Indeed I do.

Often?

I have often seen them, and known them to be so used.

Cross-examined by Mr. Attorney General.

Were you employed by Mr. Tracy to keep them?

They were left at my Place.

How came they to bring them to you?

I cannot say.

Were you led to expect that they would come?

I did not know it till the Evening they came.

You had received no Instructions from Mr. Tracy, or any body on his Behalf, to employ those Persons?

Not the slightest.

Have you any Connexion with the Parties?

No Connexion, but I know a Brother of Mr. Tracy's.

You were on Terms of Business with him?

He does Business in Dublin.

Mr. D. Baynham.   Why was your House selected as a Place of Deposit?

I ~~could not say~~; it might be that the Magistrates might see them near Castlebrack.

Did you go to Castlebrack on ~~each Occasion~~?
I conveyed them there; they told me that it ~~was necessary to go~~ with them.

You were there yourself Three Times?
At the Three Meetings of the Magistrates.

I presume that they are in the same State in which you received them?
They are.

Mr. John Dunn.   Then Mr. JOHN DUNN was called in; and having been sworn, was examined as follows:

(*Mr. Serjeant Shee.*)   Where do you reside?
In the City of Dublin.

Did you ever live at Castlebrack or in that Neighbourhood?
In the Neighbourhood.

Where did you live?
I lived within about Six Miles of it.

Was that at a Place called Derrylakeen?
At Derrylakeen.

What are you?
An Inspector in the City of Dublin Police.

I believe you had a Relation living at this Derrylakeen?
Yes.

Was it your Father or your Uncle?
No, my Grandmother.

You recollect Castlebrack Churchyard?
Perfectly well.

How long is it since you first remember it?
Upwards of Thirty Years.

Do you recollect seeing a Tombstone which attracted your Attention there?
I do.

What attracted your Attention upon it?
A Person noticed it to me, an old Man who was a Tenant of my Grandmother's; he remarked it particularly to me.

Do you recollect what the Inscription was upon it?
What attracted my Attention and Notice particularly was the Word "Ross," for the Townland that belonged to my Grandmother was adjoining Ross.

That having attracted your Attention, do you recollect the Name you read upon it?
I do.

Just tell their Lordships what it was?
I recollect reading the Name of Tracy, a Judge. There was the Name of "Tracy" on it and of "Ross," and this Ross adjoins a Townland

Townland that belonged to my Family; and knowing the Gentleman that lived there perfectly well, Mr. Briscoe, I was inquiring from my Grandmother how it was that he was from that Part.

Do you recollect any thing else besides " Tracy" and " Ross ;" you said something about the Word " Judge"?
An English Peer.

Do you recollect what the Word was that you saw?
Nothing more than that he was an English Judge or Peer.

(*By a Lord.*) Was there any thing about " Peer " upon this Tombstone?
A Judge. It is a long Time back.

(*Mr. Serjeant Shee.*) Which Part of the Churchyard did you see it in?
It was within a Couple of Yards of the old Church.

Do you remember upon which Side of it?
I cannot say particularly now.

(*By a Lord.*) Was it whole or broken?
To the best of my Knowledge it was cracked.

Standing up?
No, lying flat.

Was it fixed in the Ground?
It lay on the Ground flat.

Was it fixed in the Ground?
Clay was about it.

Was it much cracked?
I did not take particular Notice of it at that Time; there was a little Crack; the Centre was sunk.

What called your Attention particularly to it?
This old Man that I mentioned noticed it to me. I went to his Brother's Funeral. He was an old Schoolmaster. He had lived at Castlebrack, and he was interred in the Churchyard. He had been originally from the Neighbourhood of Castlebrack.

Cross-examined by Mr. Attorney General.

How old are you?
I am Forty-eight Years of Age.

You were about Seventeen or Eighteen at that Time?
Yes.

Have you known the Tracy's any Time?
I know a Family of Tracy's near a Place called Gurteen.

Do you know the Family of the Claimant?
Not till lately.

When did you first know them?
Between Three and Four Years back.

How was it that the Matter was recalled to your Recollection?
I had seen it frequently in the Newspapers, and knowing this Tracy, I have always been given to understand that they were the same Family.

(62.2.) When

When did you communicate with them ?
About Three or Four Years ago.

Before or after the last Inquiry ?
I do not know that I knew any thing about the former Inquiry.

You think it is as much as Four Years ago that you first communicated with them ?
I think it is about Four Years.

Do any of the Tracy's live in Dublin where you are now ?
No.

Have you been in the habit of seeing them ?
I have been in the habit of seeing Mr. Tracy at Kilmainham.

Have you seen him often ?
Three or Four Times.

Did he find you out ?
I have seen him at Kilmainham.

Did you tell him all that you recollected ?
Yes.

Do you now recollect what was on the Tombstone ?
I recollect perfectly the Circumstance of " Ross."

Have you seen the Tombstone since ?
I saw it about Two Years and a Half ago in Castlebrack.

How could the Word " Ross " be connected with the Tracy's or with
this Claim in your Mind ?
What drew my Attention particularly to it was this : Mr. Briscoe
of Ross in the King's County where my Family has Property was a
particular Friend of my Family. I asked my Grandmother how it
was that the Gentleman lived at Ross.

I understand you to say that you particularly remarked this Word
" Ross." I want to know what Connexion the Word " Ross " had
with the Claimant ?
I cannot say for that.

I presume you have never had any Conversation about it with any
body since you were Eighteen Years of Age ?
I recollect to have heard my Family speak of it. I had an Uncle
that lived in a Place called Clonaslee, in Queen's County, under
General Dunn, and I have been frequently there, and have heard him
and his Family speak of this English Gentleman being interred in
Castlebrack Churchyard.

When was it that you first talked of it after having read it Thirty
Years ago ?
Frequently after that I have been asked Questions about it.

Was that because you say it was near the Place of your Grandmother ?
Yes.

What Sort of a Place is Ross ?
It was the Estate of this Mr. Briscoe.

Is it a Farm or a Townland ?
A Townland.

Is

Is it split into several Farms or held by one Occupant ?
It was held by Mr. Briscoe himself then, but he is dead.

It is a large Place, is it ?
It is.

How far from Castlebrack Church ?
I dare say about Eight Miles.

Is there any other Church nearer ?
There is.

What ?
Tullamore is nearer to it, and there is a Place called Killogbey.

There are several Places nearer ?
Yes.

Protestant Churches ?
Yes.

(*By a Lord.*) At the Time that you first knew Ross it was occupied altogether by Mr. Briscoe ?
Yes.

The whole of the Townland ?
Yes.

Was there a House upon it ?
His House.

No other House?
Yes.

Was it an old House ?
It was a very old House.

How long had it been in the Family of Mr. Briscoe ?
I cannot say, but that was my Reason for asking the Questions.

But you do not know how long Ross was in the Possession of the Briscoe Family ?
I believe a considerable Time ; I cannot say how long.

Did the Forefathers of Mr. Briscoe possess the old House and Townland ?
I cannot say as for that.

When did you first hear of this Claim made to the Tracy Peerage by this Family ?
I think I read it in the Newspapers Three or Four Years back.

Not more than Three or Four Years back ?
I think it is about that Time.

Between the Time when you were a Lad of Eighteen and that Time had you told any body what you had read upon the Tombstone ?
I frequently had Conversation about it. I have various Relatives in King's and Queen's County ; I have heard them speak about it.

Had you conversed about it before you heard of the Claim made by the Irish Tracy's to this Peerage ?
I do not know that I had.

The first Time that you heard of this Claim was Three or Four Years ago ?
I heard of it in the Papers before that.

Is it more than Three or Four Years ago?
I think so.

After you first heard of that Claim made by the Tracy's to whom did you first mention what you had read upon the Tombstone?
I have conversed with a Variety of Persons.

To whom did you first mention it?
A Grandmother of mine.

It came into your Head that it might be material upon the Inquiry?
I never thought of such a thing; my Reason for asking was in consequence of this Mr. Briscoe.

It was to your Grandmother that you mentioned it?
It was.

Within the last Three or Four Years to whom did you first mention what you had seen upon the Tombstone?
I mentioned it to a Variety of People whom I knew from the King's County; I mentioned it to some of the Southern Family in the Queen's County.

You mentioned it to a great many People?
I did.

Do you know many Families of the Name of Tracy in that Country?
I never knew them, except One Family that lived at a Place called Gurteen.

Why did you happen to mention this to your Grandmother?
In consequence of this Townland of Ross which joins our Property.

When were you first called upon to give Evidence as a Witness in this Case?
I believe about Two Years and a Half ago. I was down in Killeigh near this Churchyard.

This is the first Time of your being examined here?
Yes.

When were you first asked to become a Witness to prove what you knew about the Tombstone?
A Gentleman, Mr. Burke, asked me some Questions about it?

How long ago?
It is going on Three Years; Two Years and a Half ago.

Did he take down in Writing what you told him?
He did.

Did he tell you what was upon the Tombstone?
No, he did not.

Did he say any thing to you about the Words that were upon it?
No.

Did he ask you about the Words?
He asked me what I knew, and I then gave him as far as I could think.

He did not ask you Questions respecting particular Words?
No, he did not.

He showed you nothing in Writing?
No.

He

He read you nothing?
No.

(*Mr. Attorney General.*) You saw the Tombstone in Castlebrack Churchyard when it was found and put together there in the Presence of the Magistrates?
Yes.

(*By a Lord.*) You told Mr. Burke what you recollected of it before you saw the Tombstone in Castlebrack Churchyard?
Yes.

Re-examined by Mr. Serjeant Shee.

You have no Doubt that this is the Stone you saw originally?
No.

(*By a Lord.*) You have no Doubt that those Four Pieces are the original Stone?
To the best of my Opinion I believe it is.

Was that the Shape of it as far as you recollect?
As far as I can recollect.

When the Magistrates were there you saw nothing of those Two lower Parts?
No, I do not think I did.

When you saw it when you were a Lad of Seventeen or Eighteen did the Letters appear to you to be as fresh and sharp as they are now?
I think they did.

They appeared to you to be of a plain and legible Nature?
Yes, as far as I could read it.

You found those Four Stones lying in the Churchyard indented in the Ground?
I cannot say that it was as much broken as it is now.

Did you read the Inscription with any Care?
My Attention was drawn to it by that old Man, who was a Schoolmaster.

Did you look over it with Care and Attention?
I did.

Did you observe the Omission of Letters in any Word?
I do not know as to that; I do not remember that.

Was it exposed to be trodden upon by People who were walking when it lay in the Churchyard?
It was there exposed for any Person to walk on.

To walk upon it with their Shoes?
Yes.

Was it as clean as it is now?
I do not know for that, that it was as clean as it is at present.

It had not any faded Appearance, there was no Moss upon it?
As well as I can recollect Grass was growing about it.

Was there any Green upon it, on the Letters?
I could not positively say as to that.

(62.2.)

Do

Mr. John Dunn.

Do you recollect any thing in the lower Part of the Inscription about the Widow?
I do not remember that Part.

Did you ever see those Two lower Stones? (*Nos.* 6 *and* 7 *being shown to the Witness.*) Did you ever see them before?
I cannot say whether I have.

What was the Shape of the Stone when you saw it lying in the Churchyard?
It was a regular Square, something more long than broad.

Was it like that? (*Nos.* 1, 2, 3, 4, *and* 5.)
It was something like that.

Something like those Five Pieces?
Like the Five Pieces.

When you saw it first you saw it in its original Position as a Gravestone in the Churchyard, only broken?
Yes.

Do you say in looking at it as it appears now that you recollect it as the same Stone that you saw in the Churchyard; do you recognize it by any particular Features or Appearances as the same Stone that you saw before?
I am almost positive that it is the same Stone.

What is it that you now recollect to have seen in the Churchyard?
I have not read that.

Cast your Eye over it, and state what it is that you saw lying in the Churchyard?
[The Witness examined the Stone, and read the Inscription upon it.]
I recollect the Words I saw at Castlebrack.

Is it the Shape and Size of the Stone that you saw; how much of the Stone that you see lying there have you formerly seen in Castlebrack Churchyard; what Part of it?
I consider that it is something larger than the present Stone that is here.

But not so long as that?
I cannot say as to that.

Something longer than it was broad?
Yes.

(*Mr. Attorney General.*) Do you remember how many Pieces it was broken into?
I do not.

B. L. Tarlton.

Then BARRAKIA LOWE TARLTON was then called in; and having been sworn, was examined as follows:

(*Mr. Serjeant Shee.*) Where do you live?
At Killeigh.

Is that in the King's County?
Yes.

What are you?
I am a Farmer; I hold Situations under Lord Digby.

You

You were examined here before the Committee for this Claim in the Month of May 1843?
I was.

You stated upon that Occasion that you had gone with your Uncle in the Year 1812 to the Churchyard of Castlebrack?
Yes.

Do you remember seeing a Tombstone?
Yes.

You stated what your Recollection of the Inscription upon it was?
I did.

Have you since seen some Fragments of a Tombstone in the Possession of Mr. Digby Baynham?
I have.

When did you see them?
In December 1843, I think.

Did you see them afterwards in 1844?
Yes, I saw them Three Times in Castlebrack afterwards.

You were present at the Examination by the Magistrates?
Yes.

Did you form an Opinion whether the Fragments that you saw upon those Occasions are the same Tombstone you saw before?
I believe them to be the same.

Have you seen them since you have been in Town?
Yes, I saw them last Night.

Do you know them again upon the Floor?
Yes.

Have you any Doubt that that is the same which you saw in the Churchyard in 1812?
Not the smallest; the centre Break was not in it when I saw it.

Cross-examined by Mr. Attorney General.

It is in the same State now, with the Exception of the centre Break, as when you saw it?
Yes.

And the same Colour?
I think rather a darker Colour.

Was the Inscription at the Time as legible as it is now?
I think it was more legible.

You said that you had to clean the Stone before you could read it?
Yes; it was then grown over with a Kind of Grass, and filled with Clay.

Was it legible in 1812 before you cleaned it?
Not before I cleaned it.

Had it been in that State long?
I could not say.

Did you see it afterwards?
I did.

When?
About a Year or Two after.

(62.2.)   K k   Was

Was it then again covered over with Dirt ?
No, it was clean.

Was it as clean as it is now ?
No.

According to your Recollection what was the Inscription upon it ?
It mentioned that the Stone was erected by Mary the beloved Wife,
whether on the Top or the Bottom I could not say. Now I know that
it must have been on the Bottom, but at first my Recollection led me
to believe that it was on the Top.

What else ?
That he was the Third Son of an English Judge, and that he was
late of Ross in the King's County.

Was it broken when you saw it ?
It was.

Into how many Pieces ?
Into Four ; then there was a centre Piece, and the centre Piece was
broken, Fragments off it.

Whereabouts was the centre Piece ; was that the Top or the Bottom
of the Stone ?
The Bottom of the Stone.

It was broken into Four Pieces when you recollect it ?
Yes.

Cracked as it is now ?
Yes, Four Cracks, but the small Crack was not there.

(*By a Lord.*) Was there a Corner off ?
At the Bottom.

The Word " Tracy " was upon it ?
Yes.

The Word " Tracy " was not off it ?
No.

So that if any body has said that the Word " Tracy " was off it he
has said that which is not true ?
The Word " Tracy " was on the Stone.

Was the greater Part of the Inscription upon it gone ?
Not the greater Part ; I should imagine not.

You have no Doubt that the greater Part was not gone ?
By the Length of the Stone I judge that the greater Part was not
gone.

You have no Doubt now that the greater Part of the Inscription was
not gone ?
Yes ; I think from the Length of the Stone that the greater Part
was there.

So that if any body has said that the greater Part of the Inscription
was gone he has said what was not true ?
I think the greater Part of it was there from the Length of the
Stone.

The greater Part of the Inscription remained upon it ?
Yes, from the Length of the Stone.

What

What Part was broken off?

The Bottom, which contained other Names, though I cannot recollect what they were.

But the Part of the Stone that had the Inscription upon it was not gone?

Certainly not.

The greater Part of the Stone that had the Inscription was not gone?
I think not.

(*Mr. Attorney General.*) The Bottom Part and not the Top was broken?

The Bottom Part and not the Top.

(*By a Lord.*) Some Part of the Inscription remained?
Yes.

Something about an English Judge?
Yes.

Following after the Word " Tracy " ?
Yes.

You have no Doubt about that?
I have no Doubt about that.

Where did you see it last?
In the Churchyard of Castlebrack.   Last Night was the last Time I saw it, but I did not read it.

Re-examined by Mr. Serjeant Shee.

You stated upon the former Occasion that you had some Recollection that the Tombstone was erected to the Memory of William, the Son of a Judge, by Mary his Wife?

Yes, and other Inscriptions after that, but I could not remember the Names.

(*By a Lord.*) Did you ever hear any body read the Inscription?
I cannot say that I did.

Or show it to you written?
I saw many People read it.

Did you ever hear any body away from the Tombstone read the Inscription to you?
No.

Or tell you the Words?
No, I had no Occasion for that, because any thing that I knew about the Stone I had explained Years ago to other People.

There were other People looking at this Stone on account of some Claim, were there?

Not at the Stone, but making Inquiries for it.

For the Purpose of setting up this Claim?
Setting up a Claim on their own Account.

You told it to a Person of the Name of Tracy?
Yes.

Was that a Person in any way connected with the present Claimant?
No.

How does he spell his Name?
T.-r-a-c-y.

(62.2.)

There

There are a good many Tracy's in that Neighbourhood?
Yes.

How do they spell their Names?
I think in that Way, T-r-a-c-y.

Not T-r-e-a-c-y?
No, I think not.

There are Tracy's living in the immediate Neighbourhood?
There are.

In the Parish?
There are not in the Parish that I know at present; there were many, but the Tracy's that I know live in an adjoining Parish.

Are there any People of that Name living in the Parish of Castle-brack?
I do not know that there are.

There have been?
Yes.

Do they spell their Names the same Way?
Yes.

There are none now?
I do not know any body, only Mr. Tracy of ———.

Does he claim any Relationship with the Claimant?
No.

Is he a Protestant or a Catholic?
A Catholic.

Is the Claimant a Catholic or a Protestant?
I cannot say. I believe his Brother is a Roman Catholic.

Are there a great many Catholic Tracy's in that Part?
I have known Families of the Tracy's to be Catholics.

There are more Catholic Tracy's than Protestants, are not there?
Yes, I think there are. I have known Families of Tracy's, Two to be Protestant and Two Roman Catholic.

You never saw this Tombstone after 1813?
Never till I saw it in Mr. Baynham's Possession.

This Tombstone seems to have been a Matter of considerable Conversation and Wonderment?
For many Years it has been talked of.

The Witnesses were directed to withdraw.

The Counsel were directed to withdraw.

Proposed to adjourn this Committee *sine Die;*

Accordingly,

Adjourned *sine Die.*

3.

Die Martis, 15° *Junii* 1847.

The EARL OF SHAFTESBURY·in the Chair.

THE Order of Adjournment was read.

The Minutes of the last Committee were read.

The Counsel and Parties were ordered to be called in;

And Sir Fitzroy Kelly, Mr. Serjeant Shee, Mr. Fleming, Mr. Charles Bourdillon, and Mr. Hudson appearing as Counsel for the Petitioner;

And Mr. Attorney General and Mr. Solicitor General for Ireland appearing on behalf of the Crown.

Then JOHN ROTHERHAM was called in; and having been sworn, was examined as follows:

Evidence on the Tracy Claim of Peerage.

John Rotherham.

(*Mr. Serjeant Shee.*)   Where do you reside?
At Killeigh.
Is that in the King's County?
Yes.
May I ask what Age you are?
I am Fifty-three.
What is your Position in Life?
A Farmer.
Do you know the Churchyard at Castlebrack?
I do.
How long have you known it?
I suppose I have known it these Forty Years.
Do you remember in the Years 1809 and 1810 being there?
I do, perfectly well.
When you were there in those Years did you observe more than once a Tombstone in the Churchyard?
I did in the Year 1809.
Was that the first Time you saw it?
That was the first Time I saw it.
Did you discover it yourself, or was it pointed out to you?
It was pointed out to me by a Man of the Name of James Dunn.
(*By a Lord.*)   Was he any Connexion of the Tracy Family?
No, I do not think he was.
(*Mr. Serjeant Shee.*)   Do you know who he was?
He kept a Public House close by on the Spot just by the Churchyard.

(62.3.)   L l   Was

John Rotherham.

Was there a Ruin in the Churchyard, an old Church?
Yes, there was.

How near to that Ruin was the Tombstone to which your Attention was called upon that Occasion?
I think within Three or Four Yards.

On which Side?
On the South Side.

Do you remember at any Time about 1809 or 1810 being there when Boys were playing in the Churchyard?
I have been there at Cock-fights.

Do you remember particularly being there upon an Occasion when any thing happened?
I do.

Did any thing happen to the Stone?
There were Boys leaping over it, and my Attention was called to look at the leaping, being a Boy. One Boy leaped it cleverly, a Boy of the Name of Rourke, and another Boy of the Name of Dunn leaped with his Shoes on and leaped on the Stone. This James Dunn minded the Churchyard, and he came over with a Pole he had and drove the Boys away; he said they broke the Tracy Stone.

Did you see the Stone after that?
I did; I went and looked at the Stone.

Was it broken?
The Stone was cracked in the Middle.

Upon that Occasion did you read the Inscription upon that Stone?
I read Two Lines.

What do you recollect to have read upon it?
I think it was to the Memory of William Tracy, Esquire, of Ross in the King's County.

Any thing more?
No. I did not see any thing more. William Tracy, Esquire, of Ross in the King's County.

(*By a Lord.*) Did you take a Note of it?
No, but I have a perfect Recollection of it.

How many Lines were there altogether?
I cannot say, because the Stone was rather down in the Middle.

Were there Four Lines or Forty?
I cannot say.

And yet you remember the Word " Esquire "?
I do.

Was " Esq." with a Dot, or " Esquire "?
I think it was " Eqs."

And that you call Esquire?
Yes. We were called away; there were Cocks going to be fought, and we were called away. I think it was " Eqs " upon the Stone. I only saw the Two Lines.

(*Mr. Serjeant Shee.*) That is all you remember of the Inscription?
Yes.

(*By a Lord.*) When did you first tell this to any body about " Esquire "?
I told this at the Time that Mr. Bourdillon was in the Country, about

about Three or Four Years ago. I was not at home at that Time. I told Mr. Baynham in Killeigh. I had not been at home. I was up in Dublin at the Time, and I was not called upon afterwards till some Time back ; then Mr. Burke took me.

You are not in any way connected with Mr. Tracy ?
Not by any means. I never saw the Claimant till I saw him a Day or Two ago.

You say there were Boys jumping upon the Stone. Up to what Age do you call People " Boys " in Ireland ?
We call them " Boys " up to Sixteen or Eighteen.

Do not you call them a little older ?
We call them young Men or Boys up to Sixteen or Eighteen, perhaps a little more.

(By a Lord.) What is a " Gossoon " ?
Gossoon is neither a Man nor a Boy.

(Mr. Serjeant Shee.) Do not they sometimes call a Man a Boy if he is Twenty-six Years of Age, if he is unmarried ?
Yes.

And Thirty-five or Forty sometimes ?
Yes.

At the Time you are speaking of, Forty Years ago, did you occupy a Farm in the Neighbourhood of Castlebrack ?
I did not at that Time.

Did you afterwards ?
I did in 1814.

What was it called ? Lacken Farm ?
Yes.

How far was that from Castlebrack ?
Across Two small Fields.

Have you since left your Farm ?
I had it under the Court for Sixteen Years during a Minority.

Under the Court of Chancery ?
Yes ; and when the Lease expired I gave it up to the Minor.

While you were there had you an Opportunity of knowing whether Tombstones were ever used in private Houses for any Purposes, such as the flooring of Rooms or any thing ?
No, but the Tenant that was there before my Father got the Farm in the Year 1814 made Two large Corn Frames which had Flags covering the Pillars, and there was a great deal of them composed of Tombstones.

Was there any Inscription upon them ?
Some little, but they were fluted round in Parts.

They appeared to you to be old Tombstones ?
They appeared to me to be old Tombstones.

Have you at any Time lately seen Fragments of a Tombstone at the House of a Person of the Name of Baynham ?
I have seen it in the Churchyard of Castlebrack ; it was brought there.

Was Baynham there then ?
He was.

(62.3.)   Can

John Rotherham. Can you state whether that was the same Stone you had seen Forty Years ago?

To the best of my Belief it is.

I am speaking now of the Tracy Stone?

I know.

You saw Two Pieces of Stone in the Churchyard when Baynham was there?

Four Pieces of Stone; Five Pieces.

Can you form any Opinion whether the Pieces of Stone you saw on that Occasion were Pieces of the same Stone that you had seen Forty Years ago?

To the best of my Belief the Two Pieces that I read are the same Stone.

Did you see the Word "Esquire" on them?

I did. I did not take particular Notice, but I think it was there.

Cross-examined by Mr. Attorney General.

Where were you living in the Year 1809?

At Craigue near Killeigh.

How far is that from Castlebrack?

Two Miles.

What Occasion took you to Castlebrack in the Year 1809 when you first saw this Stone?

We had Cock-fights and rural Sports very often, generally every Holiday; People came Ten Miles.

Were you in the habit of going as a Boy to this Churchyard?

Not unless there were those Cock-fights. I was at that Time fond of having fighting Cocks, and I used to fight.

How old were you then?

About Fifteen or Sixteen Years of Age.

Was your Father a Farmer?

He was.

What Farm did he hold?

The Farm of Craigue.

Was it of any Extent?

It is 142 Acres. I hold that, and I hold another Farm Two Miles from that.

Who is your Landlord?

Earl Digby.

You say that this Stone was pointed out to you by Dunn; was he in the habit of pointing out Stones to Persons who went there?

No. The Reason that he pointed it out was that the Boys injured the Stone.

I am talking now of 1809; you are speaking of 1810 when the Injury took place?

No, it was in 1809 when the Injury took place. It was on the 24th of June, on a Holiday.

Can you mention some Persons who were there with you?

There were different People there; People of the Name of Dunn, and People of the Name of Burke; a Man of the Name of Mickleduff. Many Men went from Killeigh.

Was

Was it upon that Occasion that the Boys were leaping over the Stone ?
While the Cocks were heeling the Boys went to divert themselves.

They were jumping over the Stone?
Over different Stones.

Where was the Stone broken ?
It was broken in the Middle.

Was it broken while you were there, or was it broken when you first saw it ?
When I first saw it the Stone was broken, and down in the Middle, and there was Grass upon it.

Are you quite sure that the Boy that jumped upon it did not break it ?
He might have broken some out of the off Side ; he came with his Shoes upon it.

You think that by jumping upon it with his Shoes he broke the Stone ?
I think he did crack it ; it made a great Noise, and Dunn said that he did crack it.

The Crack that you saw was occasioned by the Boy jumping upon it, which you heard make a Noise ?
So Dunn said.

You heard the Crack ?
I heard the Crack.

Whereabouts was the Crack made that you heard ?
I think it was rather upon the off Side.   I did not take particular Notice because the Cracks were coming out.

Was it towards the Head or the Tail of the Stone ?
I think it was partly towards the Tail.

Upon the Stone being cracked in this Way Dunn interposed with his Pole and drove the Boys away ?
Yes.

Did he then point out what the Stone was ?
He mentioned it ; he said " you Blackguards you come here to sport and you have done Mischief; you have broken the Tracy Stone."

There is no Doubt that the Boy that jumped upon the Stone broke it ?
The Stone from its Position must have been broken in the Middle before because it was down in the Middle, but I think the Boy broke off the Side.

How did the Inscription begin ?
I think it began " To the Memory of William Tracy, Esquire," as nearly as I can guess, " of Ross in King's County."

Is that all that you read of it ?
All that I could read of it without taking the Dirt off it.

Was it covered over with Clay and Grass ?
It was covered over in the Centre with Dirt.   The Centre was lower than the Ends.

It was difficult to make it out ?
It was.

Was the next Time that you saw it in 1810 ?
I did not say that I was there in 1810.

(62.3.)   M m   You

John Rotherham.; You said before that you observed the Tombstone in 1809, and that the Boys were leaping over it in 1810 ?

No, it was in 1809 that I saw the Boys leap over it.

Did you see the Stone more than once ?

I do not think I did see it ? I had not been in the Churchyard till I got a Farm near it in 1814.

Did you see the Stone then ?

I did not.

Did you look for it ?

I did not.

You never looked for it afterwards ?

I never did.

Did you talk about this to any body ?

No, I recollected it perfectly well. The first Time that I spoke of it was to Mr. Baynham.

When was that ?

Three or Four Years ago.

Was that before or after Mr. Bourdillon called at your House ?

Mr. Bourdillon did not call at my House.

Was it before Mr. Bourdillon was in the Country ?

It was.

How long ago ?

I think Three or Four Years ago.

Do you remember this Case having been heard before ?

I do.

Was it before or after that ?

Before that.

How long before ?

I think a Year or Two.

A Year before the Case was heard upon the former Occasion you mentioned this to Mr. Baynham ?

I did.

When Mr. Bourdillon was in the Country you were not living in that Country ?

No, I was in Dublin at that Time ; when I came home I mentioned to Mr. Baynham what I knew about it.

When were you applied to upon this Occasion ?

I was applied to by Mr. Burke afterwards.

When were you applied to for this Occasion ?

Two Years ago.

When did you come to Town to be examined ?

On Thursday last.

For the first Time ?

For the first Time.

You say that you think you should recognize the Stone again which you saw in the Churchyard with Baynham ; what Part of it was it you recognized ?

I should recognize what I have seen.

What Part ?

The Two upper Lines which I have seen.

Only

Only the Two upper Lines?

Only the Two upper Lines which I have seen; I saw it exposed upon that Day.

Have you seen the Stone recently?
I have.

Tell me what is upon it now?
I think it is "To the Memory of William Tracy, Esquire, of Ross in King's County."

What else?
Son of Robert Tracy, one of the Lords of ——————, one of the Barons of ——————.

When was it that you read it last? You say that you saw it in the Churchyard; how long ago?
I think it is since I saw it in the Churchyard; it is nearly Three Years ago.

Did you read it attentively?
No, I did not.

Did you read it?
I did read it.

Now tell me what was upon it?
I think it is "To the Memory of William Tracy of Ross in the the King's County, Son to Robert Tracy, one of the Judges of England," or something like that.

Was that all?
There is much more of it, but a Part of it is not legible.

Is that to the best of your Recollection what was upon it?
That is partly my Recollection.

Have you no more Recollection of what you read Three Years ago than that?
No, I never took a Note of it.

How often did you see it in the Churchyard?
Never but once.

Did you not see it with Baynham?
Yes, at that Time.

You say that you saw it in 1809?
I only saw Two Lines of it.

Did you see it more than once with Baynham recently?
No.

Did you read it more than once?
No.

There are a good many Tracy's living in the Country?
Yes.

How many do you know?
I know Two Families. There is the Family of Mountmelick and there is the Family at Ard.

Which is the Claimant's Family?
The Claimant's Family do not live any of them about us now.

How far off?
I do not think there are any of them about our Neighbourhood any where.

What

What is the Religion of the Family at Mountmelick?
I think the Family at Mountmelick is Catholic.

And the other Family?
Protestant.

How far is that from Castlebrack?
Ard is Five Miles, and Mountmelick is Six Miles.

Do you know the Family well?
I know the Ard Family well; he is a Solicitor, and he has done Business for me.

How many Years have you employed him?
It is Twelve or Fourteen Years since I employed him.

Where do you live yourself?
Where my Father and Grandfather lived, at Craigue near Killeigh.

Re-examined by Mr. Serjeant Shee.

Upon the last Occasion when this Case was before their Lordships you were unwell, you were obliged to have an Operation performed upon your Face?
I was.

(*By a Lord.*) You said first that when you saw the Boy break the Stone it was the Tail of the Stone?
I think it was the Tail.

Did you read what was upon the Stone?
I read nothing but the Two Lines. The Stone was covered with Clay and Dirt.

What Part did you read?
The Beginning.

Why did not you read to the Bottom?
I could not; I had not Time to clean it.

It was covered with Gravel?
It was covered with Clay and Grass.

How could a Boy jumping upon it break the lower Part of it if it was under Ground?
One Boy leaped with his Shoes, and leaped upon the Edge of the Stone.

You say that the lower Part was under Ground; you have said that the upper Part was exposed, and that the lower Part of it was covered with Grass and Clay?
The Middle of it. Both Ends of the Stone were rather up, and it rather sunk in the Middle as if it was broken.

You did not see the Boy use any Stone to break it?
No, it was for Sport the Boys leaped.

If it was broken it was broken merely by the Boy jumping?
The old Man said that he had broken the Tracy Stone.

You saw the Boy jump upon it?
Yes, I saw Two leap; One leaped over it, and One leaped upon it.

You are sure that he threw no Stone upon it?
Yes.

You

You are quite sure that you heard the Sound of its breaking ?
Yes. That was it that called the Attention of the old Man to put them away.

That was in 1809 ?
Yes.

Then Mr. JOSEPH LANGFORD was called in ; and having been sworn, was examined as follows : *Mr. J. Langford.*

(*Mr. Serjeant Shee.*) How old are you ?
Indeed I am a pretty good Age. I am beyond Seventy, Seventy-six, and I believe more.

Where do you live ?
When at home I live in Queen's County in a Place called Rearybeg Town Land.

Is that in the Parish of Rosenallis ?
It is a Parish of itself ; the Parish of Reary ; but it is included in the Parish of Rosenallis.

Are you a Farmer ?
Yes.

How far is the Place where you live from Castlebrack Churchyard ?
I think it is nearly Two Miles.

How long do you remember Castlebrack Churchyard ?
From Youth to old Age.

Do you remember a Person of the Name of James Tracy who lived at Gurteen ?
Right well.

How long is it since you first became acquainted with James Tracy of Gurteen ?
It is a good while now. I knew him by Eyesight before I knew his Name, or had any personal Interview with him.

How long is it since you first knew him by Eyesight ?
In the Year 1792 I first became acquainted with him.

How long before that had you known him by seeing him ?
Perhaps a Year, in the Market of Tullamore.

Can you judge about what Age he was when you first became acquainted with him in 1792 ?
From his Appearance he appeared to me to be a Man advanced in Years. I am sure he was a good deal beyond Fifty, and I think nearer Sixty than Fifty ; he might be more than Sixty.

Was he then living at Gurteen ?
Yes.

Do you remember about that Time meeting him at Cock-fights in the Neighbourhood ?
Indeed I do.

At Killeigh did you meet him at a Cock-fight ?
I did.

Did you meet him at Geashill ?
Yes.

At a Cock-fight ?
Yes.

(62.s.) N n Do

Mr. J. Langford. Do you remember on one Occasion after the Cock-fights going with him to a Tent hard by for Refreshment?

I do, in Killeigh.

Did you take Refreshment together?

Yes, there did Four or Five of us go in together.

Was there a Man of the Name of Green there too?

Yes, John Green and Charles Green, Two Brothers.

Do you recollect the Names of any other Persons who were there at that Time?

There were Two Men of the Name of Gibbs, but they are all dead; I am the last surviving Person of the whole.

When you were all together in that Tent did Conversation arise respecting the Family of that Tracy of Gurteen?

Some Conversation arose respecting the Tracy Family.

Did he say who his Father was?

He did.

What did he say of him?

He said that he was the Son of a Gentleman.

Any thing more? Do you recollect what he said about it?

He said that he was the Son of an English Judge.

Who did he say was the Son of an English Judge, himself or his Father?

His Father.

Did he say any thing more about his Father that you recollect?

He said that he was buried in Castlebrack.

I believe you had some Doubt about what he said at the Time?

I really had.

Did any further Conversation take place about it? Did you speak to the Greens about it?

John Green was sitting by my Side, and I turned to him and asked him——

You spoke to John Green about it, but in consequence of something that John Green said, did you go to Castlebrack Churchyard?

The next Funeral I went to.

The next Funeral you attended at Castlebrack Churchyard; did you look about the Yard?

I did look about the Yard; I bethought of the Conversation that passed.

What did you look for?

I looked for the Stone to try was his Statement true.

Did you find the Tombstone?

I found the Tomb quite ready.

What Year was this in?

This was in the latter End of the Year 1792 or the Beginning of 1793 to the best of my Recollection; I cannot swear to a Month.

You found the Stone?

I found the Stone quite ready.

Do you remember what Inscription there was upon the Stone?

I do remember that it was " William Tracy."

What

What else ?
Several Things.

Endeavour to recollect generally ; you may not be able to recollect the very Words ?
The very Words I could not.

As near as you recollect what was the Inscription upon that Stone ?
" William Tracy, Son of Judge Tracy of England, Judge of the Common Pleas." I can remember that much of it.

After that Time, in the latter End of 1792 or the Beginning of 1793, did you see the Stone again ? When did you see it after that ?
It was nearly Half a Year, or it may be the next Funeral that I went to. Curiosity invited me to go and look again at the Tomb.

You did go ?
I did go.

Was it in the same Place as it was before ?
In the very same Place.

On the first Occasion was it injured at all ? Had it been broken ?
It was broken.

Where ?
Broken partly across the Middle, a Kind of a crooked Break.

Are you sure that was there the first Time you saw it ?
That was the very first Time I saw it.

You say you saw it again Half a Year or a Year afterwards at the next Funeral ; did you see it again after that at any Time ?
I will not take upon me to swear, but I can swear I saw it Twice, and to the best of my Knowledge I did Three Times.

Do you know how long it is ago since James Tracy died ?
I will go as near as I can to it ; the Time is easy to calculate it.

Did he die long after your first Acquaintance with him ?
No, a short Time after that. I was married in the Year 1796, the 9th Day of May, and to the best of my Knowledge and Recollection James Tracy was dead a Year or perhaps Two before that Time.

Did you know his Son, Joseph Tracy ?
Yes.

Did he live at Geashill ?
He did live at Geashill as a married Man.

Have you seen any Portion of this Tracy Stone lately ?
The Day the Meeting of Magistrates and Gentlemen was in Castlebrack I heard of it, and I went there to try whether it was Part of the Ruins of the Stone that I saw.

On the Day of the Meeting of the Magistrates you went to the Churchyard to see whether the Stone that was there was Part of the Stone that you had seen before ?
Yes.

Did you see the Stone that was there upon the Occasion of the Meeting of the Magistrates ?
Yes ; there was Part of the Tomb there. I believe Three or Four Pieces.

What

Mr. J. Langford.

What is your Belief? Was the Stone you saw when the Magistrates were assembled the same Stone you had seen in the Years 1792 and 1798?
It is my firm Belief that what I saw was Part of this Stone that I saw then.

Cross-examined by Mr. Solicitor General for Ireland.

You said that all the Persons present at this Conversation in the Tent, except yourself, are dead?
I think they are.

Are you sure?
I am not really sure, but to the best of my Knowledge and Belief they are,

Which of them is it that you are not quite sure of being dead? Will you mention the Names of those Persons?
I mentioned the Names of the Two Gibbs's. I am sure both those are dead.

Who else was present besides the Two Gibbs's?
There was John Green and Charles Green.

Are they dead?
Both long since.

Who else?
I do not recollect any other.

There were a great many more in the Tent?
Yes, but not in the Company.

Were there only Six of you in Company?
I will not positively say that there were no more, but those formed the Company.

Did you tell who your Father was that Day?
I had no Occasion.

Nobody talked of his Father except Tracy?
No.

You said that you had known him a short Time before then?
I knew him by Sight before I knew his Name.

How far did you live from him?
Beyond Three Miles; nearer Four than Three, I think.

What Circumstances was he in at that Time?
A Farmer.

What Quantity of Land did he hold?
I do not know; I never saw the Survey,

Did you ever see his House?
Yes.

What Sort of a House had he?
A thatched House, the same Sort that the Irish generally have.

All the Irish have thatched Houses?
Not all, but Persons in Country Places.

What Circumstances did he appear in?
He appeared to be a very genteel Man.

But you could not say about what Quantity of Land he held?
Indeed I could not; how could I when I never inquired.

Was

Was he a well dressed Man, having the Appearance of a Gentleman ?
Yes, genteelly dressed ; he had the Appearance of a Gentleman.

Do you know what Religion he was ? Was he a Catholic or a Protestant ?
I believe him to belong to the Established Church.

Did you ever see him at Church ?
Once.

At what Church ?
Killeigh.

Are you yourself of the Established Church ?
Yes. I was there that Day.

Are there any Tracy's in that Neighbourhood Catholics ?
Several.

What Family of the Tracy's are Catholics ?
There are Families of the Tracy's about Mountmelick and in other Places who are Catholics.

You know the present Claimant ?
I saw him twice, I believe, since I came to Town.

His Father was a Protestant ?
He was.

And his Grandfather ?
Yes.

And all his Family ?
You are going too far in the Story now.

Do you know whether all his Family were Protestants ?
I am not speaking for any one but himself.

You speak positively of James Tracy ?
I speak positively. I have seen him in the Church of Killeigh, and I was there myself.

This House of his, how long had you known him to live in that House which you have spoken of ?
I dare say about Two Years.

Were you ever in the House ?
Indeed I will not positively say that I was, but I was very often in John Green's, his Neighbour, because he and I were out upon Shooting Parties continually.

Were you in the habit of shooting much ?
Yes.

At that Time ?
At that Time.

How old were you at that Time, in the Year 1792 or 1793 ?
Suppose I am Seventy-six now it is easily calculated.

Were you at that Time the Owner of a House yourself?
No ; I was Owner of good Property.

What Property ?
Landed Property.

To what Amount ?
About 40*l.* a Year.

(62,3.)   O o   I suppose

Mr. J. Langford.
———

I suppose Mr. Tracy was a Man apparently in about your Circumstances?

I do not know; he might.

Or better or worse?

I made no Inquiry about it.

Was he apparently of the Class of a labouring Man, or was he above a labouring Man?

He was a Man genteelly dressed, with a genteel Appearance.

Did you ever meet him out shooting?

Never.

It was only with Green you were in the habit of shooting?

Only with Green.

When did you first tell this Conversation you had with Mr. Tracy to any one about who his Father was and his Grandfather? When were you first found out by the Claimant?

I spoke of it at different Times.

When and to whom?

I could not tell who I spoke to in public Company.

How long ago did you first begin to speak of it?

I do not recollect.

Do you recollect hearing of the Trial that was in the House of Lords about it before?

I recollect hear Talk of it.

Did not you talk of this before then?

I think I did.

To whom?

I spoke of it openly in public Company.

But you were not brought here before?

No.

Did you ever speak to Mr. Bourdillon, the Attorney, about it, the English Gentleman that was going over making Inquiries?

I do not think I did.

Or to any Gentleman, an Attorney, making Inquiries about it?

I do not think I did.

To whom did you tell all you knew about it?

To a Gentleman of the Name of Mr. Burke.

When first did you speak to Mr. Burke about it?

Mr. Burke came and spoke to me because I was on my sick Bed.

When did Mr. Burke come to you?

I do not remember. If Mr. Burke was here he could tell better, because I was in Bed at the Time in a very sick and weak State.

But you do not recollect how many Years ago it was?

I believe it is between Two and Three Years.

Was it before or after the Meeting of the Magistrates at the Church-yard?

It was after.

Did you talk to any one about it before the Meeting in the Church-yard?

To several. I spoke in public Company, and said that I thought I
knew

knew as much about the Tracy Family as any one that was taken over to the Trial.

Did you tell that to Mr. Tracy himself or any of his Family?
No, they never spoke to me upon the Subject.
Nor you to them?
No.

You said that when first you knew Mr. Tracy he was about Fifty or Sixty Years of Age?
I think so from his Appearance then; he might be more.

Are you sure that he was not near Seventy at the Time?
Indeed I am not. I never saw any Entry of his Age.

Was he an older Man than yourself?
Yes, a good deal.

About what Age were you when you first knew Mr. Tracy?
About One or Two-and-twenty.

Mr. Tracy appeared to be Fifty at all events?
He did, more.

Nearer Sixty?
Nearer Sixty; he may have been older.

You have no Doubt that he was beyond Fifty, and probably near Sixty?
I have not the least Doubt that he was beyond Fifty, and might have been near Sixty.

He had a Son at the Time?
Yes, he had.

What Age was his Son?
I never asked him.

Was the Son a grown up Man at the Time?
He was grown up.

Was he married at the Time?
I do not think he was.

Was he living in his Father's House, or had he a House of his own?
I think he was living with his Father.

But he was a grown up young Man?
Yes; but he did not associate with Gamblers at all.

You did not yourself associate with Gamblers, did you?
I had a Hand in all those Cock-fights and Horse-racing, every one of them.

Did Mr. Tracy associate with Gamblers?
He did.

But not his Son?
No.

You never saw this Tombstone till you heard Mr. Tracy talking of his Family?
I never took notice of it.

You say that you saw it twice after this Conversation?
Yes.

Did you ever see it more than on those Two Occasions?
To the best of my Recollection I saw it Three Times, but I am sure of twice.

(62.3.)

Have

Have you been at many Funerals since that at this Church ?
A great many.

And you never looked for it except those Three Times ?
Never.

Never thought of it ?
Never thought of it.

And never missed it from the Churchyard ?
I do not say that I did not miss it.

When did you miss it, that is what I want to know ?
I think it is about Fifteen Years ago since I missed it.

How long before the Time you missed it had you seen it ? What Interval was there between the Time when you saw it and when you missed it ?
I had no particular liking to go and look for the Stone, only walking about the Churchyard and looking at the Place where the Stone lay.

The Churchyard is not a very large one ?
It is a good large Churchyard.

How many Acres in it ?
I have never seen it surveyed. I think it would be easy to count the Acres.

About an Acre ?
I think there is one, it may be something more.

You missed it Fifteen Years ago, and you cannot say how long before that it was you had seen it ?
I tell you exactly the Time I saw it ; I saw it in 1792 or 1793.

Did you ever see it from 1792 or 1793 except once before you missed it Fifteen Years ago ?
Never, I was not interested in it, except Curiosity. Curiosity led me to look at it.

It was broken the first Time you saw it ?
It was.

How many Cracks were there in it the first Time you saw it ?
There were Two Cracks across the Middle of it ; there might be small Cracks in it. I only went to try whether what Mr. Tracy alluded to was true or not.

You read Part of the Inscription ?
Yes.

There was nobody with you ?
Indeed there was ; there was a young Man of the Name of Thompson went with me.

Is he alive ?
He is dead in America.

Was there any one with you the second Time you saw it ?
I do not recollect that any one was with me.

You recollect quite well the Inscription that was upon it ?
I recollect Part of it.

You have mentioned it already ?
Yes, I have.

Do you know New Ross in King's County ?
Yes,

How

How far is it from this Churchyard of Castlebrack ?
I believe about Four Miles.

Was there a Dwelling House at Ross ?
Yes, many.

Who lived in Ross when you first knew it ?
I never was much acquainted with many of the Inhabitants of Ross.
Mr. Briscoe lived there.

Did you ever know any of the Tracy's to live in Ross ?
I cannot say that I have.

(*By a Lord.*) How many Years were you acquainted with James
Tracy ?
Two or Three.

The Witness is directed to withdraw.

Then Mr. JAMES BURKE was called in ; and having been sworn,
was examined as follows :

(*Mr. Serjeant Shee.*) I believe you are Solicitor to the Claimant?
Yes.

You have been engaged in Ireland in preparing this Case ?
Yes.

Do you remember being shown some Pieces of Stone at the House of
Edward Delany ?
I do.

When was that ?
It was previously to last May. I think it was about the latter End
of March or the Beginning of April.

Was there any Inscription upon those Pieces of Stone ?
There was.

Not sufficient I believe to enable you to judge what they were ?
No.

Did you afterwards compare them with some other Pieces of Tombstone ?
I did.

Where did you find those other Pieces of Tombstone ?
With Mr. Baynham of Killeigh.

Did they correspond with the Fragments that Mr. Baynham showed
you ?
They did.

Are those Two Pieces of Stone now in the House here ?
The Two lower Pieces of the Tracy Stone that are there are the
Two Pieces.

I believe that you left them in the Care of Mr. Baynham ?
I did.

Cross-examined by Mr. Attorney General.

Are those the Pieces that were produced the other Day ?
They are.

[The Pieces of Stone were again produced and placed upon the Floor
of the House.]

(62.3.)   P p   Which

Mr. James Burke.

Which were the Pieces that you saw at the House of Delany?
Those Two lower Pieces.

You left them with him?
I left them with him until I went down in the Evening for them to see whether they would correspond with the Pieces which Mr. Baynham had.

And then you brought them to Mr. Baynham's?
I did.

You say that at the Time that you first saw them the Inscriptions were not legible?
They were.

I thought you said that you could not read them?
I could read them, but I could not connect the Subject.

Sir Fitzroy Kelly stated, That in obedience to the Direction of the Committee an Order of the House had been served upon Mrs. Lambe requiring her Attendance To-day, but that from the State of her Health she was unable to appear, and that he was prepared with Evidence to prove that Fact.

Mr. J. B. Cotter.

Then Mr. JOHN BERKELY COTTER was called in; and having been sworn, was examined as follows:

(*Sir Fitzroy Kelly.*) Did you proceed to Cheltenham with the Order of this House for the Attendance of Mrs. Lambe upon this Occasion?
I did.

What are you?
I am a Gentleman.

Of any Profession?
No.

When did you go to Cheltenham?
I went on the 10th of this Month.

Did you wait on Mrs. Lambe?
I did.

Did you inform her that her Attendance was required upon this Occasion?
I did.

Was she in a Condition to appear pursuant to their Lordships Order?
Decidedly not.

In what State of Health did you find her?
I found her in a very tottering State of Health.

Did you feel it your Duty to ask her who was her Medical Man in order to communicate with him?
I did.

You learnt, I believe, that a Gentleman of the Name of Salt was in attendance upon her?
I did.

Did she in fact herself decline to appear upon the Ground of her being unable to come?
She did distinctly.

You

You were prepared to pay her Expences, and to do all that you could do to procure her Attendance?

Decidedly; those were my Instructions, and I was determined to carry them out.

Then Mr. CHARLES SALT was called in; and having been sworn, was examined as follows:

(*Sir Fitzroy Kelly.*)   You are a Surgeon?
Yes.

And you practise at Cheltenham?
Yes.

I believe you have been in Practice a great many Years?
I have.

Do you attend a Lady of the Name of Lambe at Cheltenham?
I do.

Did you understand that an Order of the House had been obtained for her Attendance here upon this Occasion?
I did.

Is she in a Condition to appear in obedience to that Order?
Decidedly not; it would have been at the imminent Risk of her Life if she had attended.   She was not in a State to attend.

What is the Description of the Complaint which renders her unable to attend?
I believe her to have a Disease at the Heart and a Determination of Blood to the Head, and Two or Three other Complaints besides; the Gout for example.

In fact is she in such a Condition as would render it consistent with your Duty to permit her to come?
Most decidedly I considered it my Duty to protect her, and to prevent her coming.

You say that it would be attended with imminent Hazard to her Life?
Yes.

(*By a Lord.*)   How long has she laboured under these Maladies?
I have attended her between Three and Four Years.   She had got at the Commencement Palpitations at the Heart, but they have increased very much of late.

How long is it since she was examined here?
I cannot say.

Sir Fitzroy Kelly stated, That it appeared from the Minutes that Mrs. Lambe was examined on the 23d of March.

Have these organic Complaints come on since the 23d of March last?
Certainly not.

Was she well enough to attend then?
She did attend then, but it was contrary to my Wish at the Time.

If you had been asked then whether it was dangerous for her to attend would you not have said that it was dangerous?
I certainly should have said so then.

(62.3.)   But

Mr. Charles Salt.

But she attended ?
She did attend.

At a Risk ?
At a Risk. She herself was determined to do so.

But this Time she was not herself determined to do so?
No, she said she was incapable.

How long has she been at Cheltenham under your Care this last Time ?
She has been under my Care Three Years and a Half.

You say that she was at Cheltenham since she left London after the Cause was heard in this House ?
She went from London to Brighton, and there she remained some Weeks. The precise Time I cannot say.

How long has she been at Cheltenham since her Return from Brighton ?
I cannot recollect the precise Date.

How long have you attended her since her Return from Brighton ?
I cannot exactly say.

Did you attend her before she came up the first Time here ?
Yes.

(*Sir Fitzroy Kelly.*) Do you think that she was, on the 23d of March when she attended at the Bar, in such a Condition as that her Attendance might then be productive of Injury to her Health ?
Certainly ; but not to the Extent that it would be now.

Mr. J. B. Cotter.

Then Mr. JOHN BERKELY COTTER was again called in, and further examined as follows :

(*Sir Fitzroy Kelly.*) Did you see this Lady, Mrs. Lambe, on the Evening of her Attendance here on the 23d of March ?
On the Evening after I did.

In what State did she appear to you to be ?
I was sent for about Twelve o'Clock at Night, I think. The Messenger stated to me that she was dying. She had got Palpitation of the Heart, or something of that Kind. By the Time I arrived there was a Surgeon with her. She was excessively bad, and I remained with her till Three in the Morning, when she was better.

Did she appear to you to be in a very alarming Condition ?
She could hardly speak. She was breathing very hard, and all that Kind of Thing. I really thought she was dying.

(*By a Lord.*) Are you a Medical Man ?
No, I am not.

(*Sir Fitzroy Kelly.*) A Medical Man was sent for, and attended her ?
Yes, and remained with her after I went away.

(*By a Lord.*) Are you a Relation of Mrs. Lambe's ?
None whatever.

Sir Fitzroy Kelly stated, That if after this Evidence the Committee were of opinion that any further Steps should be taken with respect to the Attendance of Mrs. Lambe the Claimant was ready to obey the Directions of the Committee.

(*By*

(*By a Lord to the Witness.*) In what Capacity were you sent for to attend Mrs. Lambe at Twelve o'Clock at Night?

As a Friend of her's. I was living immediately opposite; and the only Friend she had near her was myself. I went over to her to render any Assistance that I could.

How long have you been acquainted with her?
About Four Months.

How long did she stay in Town after that?
She remained in Town Eight or Nine Days after that.

Do you mean that you had been acquainted with her Four Months before March?
No; Four Months up to this Time.

You did not know her before March last?
No.

Then why were you sent for more than any other Person?
I was sent down by the Solicitor to conduct Mrs. Lambe up. I am a Client of Mr. Bourdillon's.

Does Mr. Bourdillon employ his Clients to conduct his Witnesses?
No, he does not.

Then Mr. JOSEPH LANGFORD was again called in, and further examined as follows:

(*Mr. Serjeant Shee.*) Will you have the goodness to look at that Stone which is before you?
That was the first Break. (*Pointing to the Break across the Middle.*) That is the very identical Stone; that is Part of the Stone that I saw.

Which Part do you mean?
I saw the whole; this Break was in it. (*The horizontal Crack across the Centre.*) There might be some other Side Cracks in it.

Have you any Doubt that that is the same Stone that you saw?
I have not the slightest Doubt of it; that is the very identical Stone.

(*Mr. Attorney General.*) Am I to understand you to say that there were more Breaks than that one?
I did not look at the Time, but I saw that main Break across the Middle; there might be slight Cracks besides.

Could there be Cracks without your perceiving them?
I was not interested in it, only to see whether what Mr. Tracy said was true.

Was it cracked downwards as well as across?
It was hollow in the Middle, and there was Grass growing up through the Crack.

Up through the Crack?
Yes.

Was it cracked downwards towards the Tail of the Stone? You see a Crack there now. Was it cracked in that Way down from the cross Crack?
I do not know. I took no Pains except just to look at the Inscription.

Was it very much covered over with Mud and Dirt?
It was lying on the Surface, and there was Grass growing in it. It

(62.3.)   Q q   was

(156)

Mr. J. Langford.
was partly sunk in the Middle of the Stone, and the Grass was growing
in here. I had to take the Grass off the Edge of it before I could read
the Inscription.

You read the whole Inscription?
At that Time I did.

You cleaned the Stone for the Purpose?
Yes. The Stone did not want any cleaning.

Was the Inscription perfectly plain and clean?
The Inscription was plain enough.

You read it without any Difficulty?
Without any Difficulty.

How many Lines were there?
Indeed I do not keep in my Memory how many Lines there were.

You can tell me whether there were Two or Ten or more?
I did not count the Lines or the Letters either. I was not interested
in it. I thought that there was no Occasion to make an Almanack in
my Head.

Did you read more than the first Two or Three Lines?
To the best of my Recollection I read the whole.

Do you recollect what was at the Bottom of the Stone?
Not the Particulars, I do not.

Do you recollect any thing about it?
I recollect nothing, but to the best of my Recollection that this Stone
was erected by his Wife; and I think the Name was Mary.

That was all?
That was all.

Mr. D. Baynham.
Then Mr. DIGBY BAYNHAM was again called in, and further
examined as follows :

(*Mr. Serjeant Shee.*) Will you read the Inscription upon the Stone?
" Here lyeth the Body
of William Tracy, Esq.,
late of Ross in the Kin
g's County, the Third
Son of the Honourab e
Robert Tracy, late
one of the Judges of
the Common Place " ——

(*Mr. Attorney General.*) How is the " Place " spelt?
PLACE.

Will you look at it again; is not it an E? Is not it PEACE? Do
not you see the middle Stroke of the E?
It looks like a Chip. I do not think it is long enough for an E.

Is not there a top Stroke?
There is a top Stroke that appears something longer than the Stroke
of an L.

Is not there in the Middle, between the Top and the Bottom, a Stroke
something like the middle Stroke of an E?
There is a small Mark appearing here; it is like a Spot. It is too
short for a Stroke.

Could

Could you take upon yourself to say whether that is an L or an E ?
I could not.

(*Mr. Serjeant Shee.*) Will you read on ?
" Place in ngland, who depa ted
the 15ᵗʰ October 1734 in
42ⁿᵈ Year "——— A Piece of Stone is wanting there.

There is only the Letter O there ?
That is all.

Go to the next Line ?
" Ving his." Then in the next Line " Widow Ma "; and in the
next Line " ted."

Then Mr. CHARLES HARRIOT SMITH was called in ; and
having been sworn, was examined as follows :

(*Mr. Serjeant Shee.*) You reside in London ?
I do.

What is your Profession ?
A Mason.

Were you appointed by the Government to select Stone for the
Houses of Parliament ?
I was.

Did you in the Month of May last, at the Request of Mr. Maule of
the Treasury, examine this Tracy Stone ?
I did.

You, no doubt, examined it carefully ?
Certainly.

What Description of Stone is it ?
Laminated Sandstone.

Is it a Stone of considerable Hardness ?
It is.

Did you examine particularly the Inscription upon it ?
I did.

Can you form an Opinion as to the Antiquity of the Inscription ; as
to the Time when it was made upon that Stone ?
It appeared to me to be certainly from Seventy to One hundred
Years old.

Do you see any thing about the Stone or the Inscription which would
lead you to doubt its being a genuine Tombstone ?
I examined it with that View, and it did not occur to me that there
was any Doubt upon that Point.

Have other Stones been shown to you from the Churchyard of
Castlebrack ?
I examined Three Stones recently which I was told were from the
same Churchyard.

Were any of those about the same Date as to the Inscription ?
Rather later.

Did they appear to you to have the same general Character as this
Stone ?
Yes, precisely.

I believe they are now within the House ?
I think they are.

(62.3.)

Is

Is it at all an unusual Thing for Flags of this Description of Stone to be cut unevenly, thicker at one Part than at another?

That is very common of an earlier Date.

Does it sometimes happen within your Experience that on Stones of that Age the Formation of the same Letters is different in different Parts of the Stone?

Yes; it is a very common Thing with Stones of that Date.

Of what Date?

Say from Seventy to One hundred Years since.

You have said that you have examined the Letters of the Inscription upon this Stone; have you examined the Breaks of the Stone?

Yes, I have.

Do they appear to you to be Breaks which have been made by Accident?

I should think so.

Can you form any Opinion as to how long those Breaks had been in that Stone?

Some of them appear to have been a considerable Time since. I judge so from the Appearance; some of the Pieces being much more worn than others, although evidently broken from the same Pieces.

Cross-examined by Mr. Solicitor General for Ireland.

Is there any thing in the Appearance of this Stone which would lead you to know whether it was originally taken from the Quarry, or whether it may not have been got upon the Surface of the Mountain? Have you sometimes seen Flags lying upon the Surface of the Mountain?

I have not been to that Part of the World, and therefore I cannot judge from Circumstances of that Kind, but from the Nature of the Stone I should say that it had been taken from some greater Depth than the Surface of the Mountain.

Is there any thing upon the Surface of the Stone which would lead you to that Conclusion?

Only with Allusion to other Stones of similar Character in this Country.

You have never been in the Part of Ireland from whence it is alleged that this Stone is taken?

No.

Have you in the Quarries in England or in the Mountains about them seen large Flag Stones lying upon the Surface which have been there Time out of Mind?

Certainly.

Is there any thing in the Appearance of that Stone which would prevent your coming to the Conclusion that it may have been originally a Stone got lying upon the Surface in that Way?

I think not.

Why not?

Because in Stones which have been lying a considerable Time near the Surface there is a certain Amount of Weathering in them which is very conspicuous to Persons who have paid Attention to it.

In

In the Case of a Stone originally taken out of the Quarry, after what Length of Time does it assume that weathering Appearance?
I do not think that it ever assumes the same Appearance; not in the Memory of Man.

Not even in a Century?
No.

There is none of that weathering Appearance about this Stone?
Not of that Description.

What is the Difference between the Two?
Generally speaking, the Stones nearer the Surface contain a great Quantity of Clay in their Composition. They are, generally speaking, more decomposable when exposed to the Weather. The Stones taken from a great Depth in the Ground are generally more durable.

(*By a Lord.*) But that is not always the Case; sometimes the upper Stratum is the best?
Not of Sandstone.

Do you see the upper Part there, the left Part, where there is a little chipping?
Yes.

Has that at all the Appearance of a Stone exposed upon the Surface, and remaining a great Length of Time?
Not longer, I think, than the Stone appears to be by the Date of it.

About a Century?
About a Century.

(*Mr. Solicitor General for Ireland.*) Has it the Appearance of being an old Stone lying on the Surface?
I think not. That is my Impression.

Of course that can be only Matter of Opinion?
Certainly.

You have never been in Ireland?
I have not.

Are you able to say, from the Appearance of these Creaks, and the Examination which you have made, which of them appears to have been made the longest?
I can hardly speak to that Point, but I should say the cross ones, the transverse.

Do you mean at the Top or at the Bottom?
In all probability it would be the Middle of the Stone that would be broken first.

I am asking your Opinion from the Examination of the Stone?
I cannot say with Certainty.

Have you examined it with that View?
I have.

As far as the mere Examination of the Stone goes you cannot point out which of those appears to be of the longer Date?
I cannot.

Nor do you see any Difference between the smaller Break there in the Centre and the others? That appears just as ancient as any of the others?
I think it is very likely to be.

(62.3.)   R r   Will

Mr. C. H. Smith

Mr. C. H. Smith.   Will you just look at that again? Will you just go close to the Stone, and examine the small Piece in the Centre? Try and replace it, and examine the Portion of Stone from which it has been detached?

[The Witness applied the small Fragment to the vacant Space.]

I cannot see that this Piece belongs to that Place at all. This other thin Piece is a Piece from the under Side of the Stone.

Will you try the other Piece?

I cannot see that this Piece belongs to this Place at all.

The Conclusion in your Mind is that it does not belong to that Place at all?

I think not.

Will you examine the Sides of that Aperture on the larger Piece of Stone? Will you raise up the large Piece of Stone? Just examine the Edges of it on all Sides, and state whether, as far as you can judge, there is any Difference?

No, it does not fit any of those Parts.

Will you examine that Piece from the very Commencement, (No. 3.) Examine the Nature of that from this Point to the very Extremity all the Way down. Does not the entire of that Crack all the Way round appear to be made at the same Time, or is there any Difference in any Portion of it from the Beginning to the End?

There is some Appearance of this transverse Crack being rather older than the other, but those Appearances are exceedingly slight.

Is not that from handling?

No, not from handling.

But those Cracks all the Way round appear ancient Cracks?

They are certainly of considerable Date?

And there is no Difference between the upper and the lower Part?

I do not see any.

As far as you can judge you would suppose them to have been made at about the same Time?

I think so. This transverse Crack certainly has little the Appearance of being rather older.

When you say "a little" what do you mean?

A very short Period compared to the whole.

Say some Ten or Twenty Years?

Yes, that would be Abundance.

Would that on the Right Hand appear to be an old Crack?

Yes, of considerable Date.

As far as you can judge at least Half a Century. It could not have been made for the Purpose of this Examination?

Certainly not.

No Portion of that Crack could have been made within the last few Years for the Purposes of this Trial?

I think not.

That applies to the entire of these Breaks?

All these Fragments.

It applies to every Particle of those Fragments?

Yes.

Some

Some of the Irish People are very handy People?
They are.

Is there any thing in those Letters which it would be very difficult to copy? If a Man wanted to copy Letters of that Description would there be any Difficulty in doing it?
I think it would be very difficult, because there is a certain Appearance in the Angles of those Letters which I think would not be very well accomplished by any Workmen of the present Day. There might be great Resemblance given to the Letters.

Would it be more difficult to give them the Colouring, so as to give them the Appearance of Antiquity, than it would be to give to a modern Crack the Appearance of an old one? Supposing a Man was base enough to manufacture a Tombstone, would he have greater Difficulty in manufacturing the Cracks than he would the Letters?
I do not know whether it would be greater or not; in both Cases I think it would be difficult.

About the same Difficulty?
About the same Difficulty.

There would not be a bit more Difficulty in the one than in the other?
No, I think not. I should not know how to set about it.

(By a Lord.) Are you a Stonemason?
I am.

And you think that you could not copy that Inscription?
Not to give it the same Appearance to the Eyes of an intelligent Person.

(Mr. Solicitor General for Ireland.) An experienced Person?
An experienced Person.

(By a Lord.) You observe a different Colour in those Two lower Pieces?
Yes.

How do you account for that?
That Stone has evidently been worn much more than the other, as if it had been placed in some Position to be subject to be more exposed to Wear and Weather.

To the Weather or to being worn?
Being worn.

Worn by People's treading or what?
People's treading upon it would produce that Effect.

Making it darker?
Not precisely making it darker, but the Letters would be worn.

The Question refers to the Colour?
The Colour might be produced in a short Time; for example, if this had been in a Fireplace where it had been washed frequently with dirty Water.

In how long a Time?
Probably in a few Years.

(Mr. Solicitor General for Ireland.) Do not you think that a few Months would smoke it?
It would; but a few Years would do it more effectually.

(62.s.)   Re-examined

Re-examined by Mr. Serjeant Shee.

In your Opinion about how many Years have the most recent of those Fractures been made, as far as you can form an Opinion?
I should say certainly Ten Years.

With regard to the different Degrees of Clearness; supposing Part of the Stone had been covered for a considerable Time with Earth and Grass, would not that protect the Inscription, and when the Grass was cleaned off would it not be much clearer than another Part which had not been so covered?
Certainly.

You do not undertake to state an Opinion that all these Cracks took place at the same Time?
I should think not. That is only a Matter of Opinion.

It would consist with your Opinion that one of them is Twenty Years old and another Thirty?
Yes.

Still all of considerable Age?
All of considerable Age.

When you first saw this Tracy Stone was there a small Piece that fitted that Space in the Middle?
I think there was. I think there was a small Piece that fitted, and my Recollection is to that Effect, that that Piece fitted tolerably well there; and this little Bit, as well as my Memory serves me, I tried to fit in in some other Place, and I could not find that it would fit. I think there was a Bit that very nearly fitted that triangular Hole. After I had examined it I packed up the Fragments again, and I well recollect putting that Piece in. I am certain of it. (*A small Piece was produced out of the Box and shown to the Witness.*) This is the Piece. I recollect perfectly well the Letters upon it. (*The Witness put the Piece into its Place.*) That is the Piece I am confident.

(*Mr. Solicitor General for Ireland.*) Can you form any Opinion as to the Age of that Break?
It seems one of the most recent; I judge from the Sharpness of the Edges of it.

But still a good many Years?
Certainly.

Certainly Thirty or Forty Years?
Twenty or Thirty.

At least Twenty or Thirty?
Yes.

Then Mr. DANIEL TROY was called in; and having been sworn, was examined as follows:

(*Mr. Serjeant Shee.*) I believe you are a Stonecutter and Builder?
I was a Stonecutter.

Where do you carry on your Business?
I carry on no Business as a Stonecutter now.

Where do you live?
In Queen's County in Ireland.

How

How far from Castlebrack?
Something about Four Miles and a Half or Five Miles.

You did carry on the Business of a Stonecutter for some Time?
I worked at the Trade Seven Years.

In the Neighbourhood of Castlebrack?
More than Four Miles and a Half or Five.

Are you acquainted with the different Quarries in the Neighbourhood of Castlebrack?
Very well acquainted with them.

Have you seen this Tracy Stone?
I have.

Can you judge from your Experience of Stones in the Neighbourhood from what Quarry it comes?
I can.

Where do you think it comes from?
From the Quarry in Tinnehinch, called the Mill Quarter Quarry.

When you say you were a Stonecutter was it Part of your Business to cut Inscriptions upon Stones?
No.

Only to shape the Stone?
I have carved the Stone, and cut it into different Shapes, but not Letters.

You have ornamented it?
Yes.

From your Experience in your Business could you form an Opinion as to the Date of that Stone, how long it has been inscribed?
I considered it to be beyond 100 Years of Age from the Appearance of it when I saw it first.

When did you see it first?
I think it is about Four Years ago.

Have you examined particularly the Letters?
Most particularly.

Do you think it would be possible for a Person accustomed to inscribe Stones of that Description to take a Stone, and cut it in such a Manner as to give it, to the Eye of an experienced Person like yourself, the Appearance of an old Stone?
I think he could not.

Why not? What would be the Difficulty?
The Edges of the Letters have a sharp Edge on them. These are worn away apparently by Time.

Would it not be possible with Tools, with some Dexterity, to give it that Appearance of Smoothness which Time gives?
It gives a rough Appearance, not a smooth one.

Would it be possible to give it the rough Appearance that Time gives it?
I think by no means.

Not so as to deceive you?
Not so as to deceive me.

Mr. Doniel Troy.

Is it usual in your Part of the Country to find Tombstones of unequal Thickness in different Parts of them?

I never knew an Instance yet of equal Thickness, that the whole Stone was equal.

Is it usual to find Tombstones rough on one Side in that Part of the Country?

Nothing more common; they have what the Tradesmen call a Face and a Back.

Is it consistent with your Experience that the same Letter will sometimes be formed differently upon the same Stone?

Certainly.

That sometimes happens?

It generally happens on Tombstones at that Date.

Have you formed an Opinion, after examining those Fragments, whether or not they were originally Part of one Stone?

It is my firm Belief that they are Parts of one Stone.

On what do you form that Opinion?

From the Texture of the Stone, and the gritty Appearance of it.

Are there any Lines in the Structure of the Stone which enable you to judge whether all those Fragments were originally Part of one Stone?

There are on the Back of it, but I do not think I should require any such Thing; I should know it by the Appearance of the Stone.

What is it which you observe in the Stone which satisfies you that all those Fragments were originally one Stone?

The same Texture; and on the Back of it there are some Channels and some Rises on the Stone.

Are there any Rises on the Back of the Stone?

There are.

Do they run through the different Fragments?

They do; not through all the Fragments, but through the next one to them.

They are to be seen on Two Fragments which are next to each other?

Just so.

Do you agree with the last Witness, that if a Stone was covered up partly by Dirt or by Grass for some Years one Part of the Inscription when the Dirt was washed off would be clearer than another?

It would give it a newer Appearance; it would be clearer.

Can you account for the Circumstance that some Part of this Stone appears darker than the other?

Part of it appears to have been more exposed to the Action of the Air, to have been covered with Vegetation caused by the Action of the Air.

Which Part of it do you think has been most exposed?

The bottom Part of it appears to me to have been the most exposed.

Is it a hard Stone to cut?

That is the Second Quality of hard Stone; I think not the very hardest.

You mean the Second Quality of hard Stone in your Neighbourhood?

Yes.

Cross-

Cross-examined by Mr. Attorney General.

Is it what you call Sandstone?
Sandstone or Grit; it is generally called Grit.

Is it a Stone which is liable to wear by the Tread?
That is according to the Quality of the Stone; that Quality is not; it would wear, but not so much as other Stones.

If it were to be used as a Hearthstone or a Paving Stone would it wear much by the Tread?
It would wear a good deal. If it was used as a Hearthstone it would wear less than if it was used as a Paving Stone; the Heat of the Fire would make the Stone harder.

If used as a Paving Stone it would be liable to be worn very much?
It would.

Have you looked at the Back of the Stone?
I have.

Does there appear to be any Wear at all upon the Back of the Stone?
Not any.

Is not it a perfectly unhewn or undressed Stone, as it appears to have come originally from the Quarry, on the Back?
It is.

And there is no wearing or smoothing at all upon it?
Not that I perceive.

I understand you to say that as far as the Back of the Stone or the undressed Part of it is concerned there appears to have been no Wear upon it?
I do not consider that there is any Wear upon it.

Then on the Front does there seem to have been a great deal of Wear?
The Front has the Appearance of a great deal of Wear.

Which Part?
Every Part of it.

Is this a Stone which from its Structure will wear more in one Place than another?
It may or it may not. There are what are called Flints in these Stones which will not wear so much as other Parts.

Do you perceive upon that Stone any Portions that are softer than the rest of the Stone?
I do not see any Appearance of it.

How far is the Quarry from whence you think that Stone came from Castlebrack?
I consider it to be about Four and a Half Miles in a straight Line from Castlebrack.

Is that the Place from whence they get the Tombstones used in Castlebrack?
They get them from several Places, but I consider that is the Place where that Stone was got.

Are there other Stones of that Quality in Castlebrack Churchyard?
There are a great Number.

(62.3.)

Were

Were any of those produced in London of the same Quality?
There are.

Are they thicker or thinner than that?
Some thicker.

Is not it unusual to have a Tombstone in Ireland of so thin a Stone as this?
Not at all.

You say that there is an Appearance of Wearing, and that it would be difficult to give that Appearance of Sharpness or Wearing to the Cracks?
The Front of the Stone appears to be worn; the Cracks appear to be worn.

They are not sharp?
They are not sharp.

Which should you say is the oldest Crack, the Top or the Bottom?
[The Witness examined the Stone.]
I could not say which was the oldest.

Are they about the same Date, think you?
This is the oldest. (*Pointing to the lower one.*)

What Date should you ascribe to that?
That is very old.

Does it appear to have been taken to Pieces and worn so that the Edges are rounded off; are the Edges rounded or sharp?
They are rounded on this Edge, and they are sharp on the Back.

You think from the Appearance of Wear upon them that they must have been lying with the Inscription uppermost?
I am sure they must.

And the bottom Crack you say is the oldest; about how much older than the other?
I could not form an Opinion.

It is difficult to form an Opinion?
It is after the Stone has been covered with Vegetation.

To what do you ascribe the Discoloration of those Two bottom Stones?
The Action of the Air.

Not to Fire?
Not to Fire.

In your Judgment they have not been used as Hearthstones?
I could not say.

Could you tell from the Appearance of the Stones if they had been so used?
You might have seen it at the Time, but then the Colouring might wear away afterwards.

Is your Knowledge of Stone so inadequate that you cannot tell whether this has been exposed to the Action of Fire or not?
It does not appear to have been exposed to the Action of Fire.

Turn to the Back?
There is less Appearance there.

Turn

Turn the smaller Piece ; does that appear to have been exposed to the Action of Fire ?

No.

Does any one of those Pieces appear to have been exposed to the Action of Fire ?

[The Witness turned another Piece over.]

That is a little blacker.

I ask whether it has been exposed to the Action of Fire ?

I think the Fire could not act on the Back of it with the Face of it uppermost.

Has it been exposed to the Action of Fire, any Part of it ?

I could not say that it was.

In your Judgment it has not been so exposed ?

Not that I could say.

Do not some of the Letters in the upper Stone appear to have been picked out again ?

They appear to have been rubbed.

Do not they appear to have been tooled out or cleaned, and with some sharp Instrument. Do not you see a Freshness in the Appearance ?

They appear to have been rubbed over or cleaned, or else the Vegetation has passed away from the Stone.

Do you say that it is impossible at this Day to have made a Stone with that Appearance ?

I think it would be impossible to give it that old Appearance.

Did you ever know any Person try ?

I never knew a Person try.

Then from what are you speaking ?

From the Appearance of the Stone.

But you have never known it tried ?

I think I could not be deceived.

Is it not possible to wear off the rough Edge, or to rub off the rough Edge ?

It would give a new Appearance to the Stone.

Do you know a Man of the Name of Mr. Guinness who was a Stonecutter in the Neighbourhood ?

Yes.

What has become of him ?

I think he has gone to America.

When did he go ?

Three or Four Years ago.

How was that ?

Because he could not live at home.

Why not ?

He was so poor that he could not pay his Rent. He paid no Rent for Four or Five Years.

How long had he lived in that Neighbourhood ?

As long as I recollect.

Was he a practised Stonemason ?

He worked at the Stonecutting Trade.

(62.3.)   T t   Had

Mr. Daniel Troy.

Had he been in the habit of cutting Stone?

I never knew him cut a Gravestone. Such Gravestones as these are not in Use in my Time.

Had he been in the habit of engraving upon Stones?

He never engraved upon Stones.

What did he do?

He worked all Kinds of rough Work.

When he did leave the Country?

Three or Four Years ago.

Where did he live?

At a Place called Longford.

How far from this Churchyard?

Four and a Half Miles or Five.

Did he work at that Quarry called Mill Quarter Quarry?

He lived about a Mile and a Half from that.

Was he in the habit of working upon those Stones?

No Man that I ever knew was in the habit of working upon those Stones. I never knew a Stone to be taken out of that Quarry within my Time.

Have you ever been there?

I have.

Have you seen Stones lying about there?

I saw Fragments of Stones.

You saw no large Flagstones?

No.

Is it usual to find Flags upon the Surface of a Mountain by a Quarry?

A most unusual Thing.

You never heard of such a Thing?

I might hear of it, but I never saw such a Thing.

Are you sure that no such Things are found there?

Not that I ever saw there.

What has your Experience been as a Mason?

I was a Cutter of Stone; I served my Time to it.

Do you mean a Hewer or a Letter Cutter?

I never cut any Letters.

You never tried your Hand at Letters in your Life?

I might at Figures, but not at Letters.

What was your principal Department, was it the dressing of Stone or the raising of Stone?

I assisted in the Quarries. I assisted at the cutting of geometrical Steps.

Then you lent your Hand first in getting the Stone from the Quarry, and then in dressing it?

Yes, and all those Things.

How many Years were you in it?

Seven; beyond Seven.

Did you give it up then?

I gave it up for Building.

How

How long have you been out of Business?
Ten Years.   My Brother has a Quarry there now, and I assist when I go home.   I use Stone in building.

You are now a Builder?
Yes.

You have had no practical Experience of Stonecutting in the last Ten Years?
No, except to get my Works done.

Overlooking as a Master Builder?
Yes.

That is all?
Yes.

Have you many Stonecutters living about there?
Very few.   My Brother is the only Man that carries on much Business there now.

Are there no other Persons that practise lettering there now?
He does not practise lettering.

Who is the Man that does the lettering?
There is no Man that does lettering there.

Since Mr. Guinness left?
Mr. Guinness never did lettering.

(*By a Lord.*)   What are those Stones used now for?
They are not used at all.   Limestone is generally used in place of these Gritstones.

Do they put Inscriptions upon the Tombstones?
Yes.

Then who makes the Inscriptions?
The Tullamore Men.

The Witness was directed to withdraw.

Then Mr. EDWARD RICHARDSON was called in; and having been sworn, was examined as follows :

(*Mr. Serjeant Shee.*)   What are you by Business?
Sculptor.

Are you a Member of the Archæological Society?
I am.

You were recently employed in repairing and beautifying the Monuments in the Temple Church?
Yes.

Have you seen the Stone which is lying on the Floor of the House?
I saw it last Friday.

Where?
At the Offices of the House.

Did you examine it particularly?
I looked closely at it.

What is your Opinion as to the Antiquity of the Inscription upon that Stone?
It struck me altogether as being genuine.

(62.s.)   Did

Did you observe any thing about it which could raise a Doubt in your Mind as to its being genuine?
No.

Have you looked at the cutting of the Letters?
I have.

Did they appear to you upon careful Examination to have been cut about that Date of that Stone according to the Inscription?
As far as I could judge.

Can you form an Opinion whether they could have been cut within a recent Period?
I do not think so to give them that Appearance.

Do you think it would be impossible to impose upon a practised Man like yourself by cutting a Stone with the Intention of making it look like an old Stone?
I think so.

Have you looked at the Breaks in the Stone?
I have.

Of what Date do you think those Breaks must be, take the most recent one, in your Opinion?
In my Opinion the first Fracture was right across the Middle, and then a subsequent Fracture possibly occurred afterwards, and then the next Fracture might have occurred from a Blow.

Have you any Doubt, looking at the Nature of the Stone itself, that those Fragments were all originally one Stone?
Looking at them the other Day I could not discern any Difference. There is a Difference in the Colour of those Two lower Pieces and of the Two upper Pieces, and I account for that by the Difference of Wear.

In your Opinion, supposing it was one large Stone of the same Description of Stone as that, would it be easy for a Person to break it in that Way so as to give the Edges of the Fragments the same Appearance that those Edges present now?
If a Person broke a Stone of that Size and Age the Stone would break in all Ways. It might break in that Way, or it might break in other Ways.

Would it be possible to take that whole Stone and break it in such a Manner as to give to the Edges of the Fragments the Appearance of Age which you now observe in them?
I think not.

Is it a hard Stone?
It is.

I believe you saw other Stones at the Office of the House of Lords at the same Time that you saw this?
I saw Fragments of Stones.

Did they appear to you to be of the same Character?
The same Description of Stone.

Were there any with Inscriptions upon them?
With Parts of Inscriptions.

About the same Date as this?
About the same Date.

Did

Did the Inscriptions appear to you to be of the same Sort of Character as the Inscription upon this?

They did; some were deeper cut, others were more shallow.

Cross-examined by Mr. Solicitor General for Ireland.

Your Opinion as to the Antiquity of those Fractures is formed more from the Position of them than from the Appearance of the Edges?

I look at the Breaks as occurring from the Circumstance of a Stone falling upon them.

You say that cross one appears to be the first?

The lower cross one. I think the Breaks would have gone in a continuous Line unless this had been the first.

Therefore your Judgment as to this being the first Break is formed more from the Appearance of the Breaks themselves than from the Examination of the Edges?

Certainly.

Is there any thing in the Appearance of the Edges of this lower Fracture that would lead you to suppose that it was earlier made than the one in the upper Part?

Not any great Difference. I cannot see any Difference.

Can you see any Difference in that very small Break? Did you examine it?

No, I did not.

Will you look at it; examine it all the Way round; does it not appear all of the same Age?

No, I think not. I think that this and that appear rather older. (*Pointing out the Parts.*)

Does not this appear fresher than the rest?

This little Hollow is rather darker.

And therefore has the Appearance of being older?

As regards the Colour.

So that you would say that the smaller Fracture is rather older than the other?

Yes, I should think so.

You never before saw any Stones from the Quarry that this came from?

No.

You have no Knowledge of the Quarry, or of the Description of Stone in that Part of the Country?

No. It accords very much with the Stone from the Northern Districts—the Yorkshire Stone.

You see those White Spots on the lower Stone, to what do you attribute those Spots?

I do not know what it is; something has been rubbed against it.

Have not those Spots the Appearance of Stone found on the Surface of a Mountain, not taken from the Quarry. You have seen Quarries of this Description on mountainous Ground. Have you not found Stones lying on the Mountain?

I cannot say that I have; I am more in Town.

(62.3.)   U u   You

Mr. E. Richardson.

You know very little of the State of the Quarry yourself?
Very little.

You know very little about getting Stone out of the Quarry?
Very little.

Your Knowledge would not enable you to say whether the Stone was taken from the Surface of the Quarry, or from a great Depth, or whether it was taken from the Surface of the Earth?
Certainly not.

These Letters are apparently very old?
They have that Appearance.

But apparently all made at the same Time?
All made at the same Time, I think.

There is nothing in the Letters that would lead you to suppose that they were not all written at the same Time?
No; I scraped it out with a Pencil, and it immediately came to that Appearance which lead me at once to suppose that these had been cleaned out in the same Way; the Four upper Pieces; I wished to satisfy myself upon that.

You are not yourself in the habit of engraving or cutting Letters of this Description upon Stone?
No.

You know nothing of that Trade?
No.

Would there be any great Difficulty in restoring those Letters?
There would be great Difficulty in imitating the Appearance of Age comparing it with other Stones that I saw.

There is nothing in the Formation of the Letters that a Man could not imitate?
The Letters run differently according to the Period.

Of course if you got a Man now to make a new Stone he would not make it in this Shape; but would there be any thing to prevent a handy Man imitating those Letters?
A Man might imitate it, but its general Appearance gives me the Impression of its being correct.

Re-examined by Mr. Serjeant Shee.

I understand you to say that comparing the Appearance of the Inscription upon this Stone with other Stones which you have seen in the Office of the House of Lords it would be difficult to give to new Inscriptions the Appearance of old ones?
I allude to perfect Stones; there is one very much of the Character of this.

Of what Date?
There is one of 1786. There is a Peculiarity in the lettering of One Stone; the lettering is not deeply cut; it is cut shallow but very much of the same Character. The Stone of earlier Date is decidedly more deeply cut than this.

(*By a Lord.*) Some of those Stones from Castlebrack have more the Appearance of Marble?
It is a very coarse Grit.

(*Mr.*

(*Mr. Serjeant Shee.*)   Is there Marble in that Neighbourhood?
I do not know.

Mr. Serjeant Shee stated, That the Stones to which the Witness had referred had been brought for the Purpose of showing the Character of other Inscriptions in the same Neighbourhood and about the same Date, and that they were now in the Neighbourhood of the House, but that they were too large and cumbrous to bring in.

Then GEORGE NEWCOME Esquire was called in ; and having been sworn, was examined as follows :

(*Mr. Serjeant Shee.*)   You reside at Clonygown in the King's County?
I do.

Are you a Magistrate of that County?
I am.

Do you know the Neighbourhood of Castlebrack?
I do.

Do you know the Ruins of a House formerly occupied by a Person of the Name of Dunn?
I do.

Did you at any Time see some Stones taken out of the Garden of that House?
I did, in Company with other Gentlemen.

How many Gentlemen were there there?
There were Six Magistrates and a Number of other Persons present.

Upon that Occasion did you see Pieces of Stones with Inscriptions upon them, which appeared to be Fragments of Tombstones, taken out of the Earth at the Back of the House there?
I did.

Was that in Part of the Premises where a large Room had formerly been?
Yes.

And I believe some in a Garden close to it?
Yes.

Were the Inscriptions upon those Pieces of Stone legible?
Yes.

Do you remember any Portions of them?
I do not remember.

Was there sufficient of them legible to enable you to judge whether they were Fragments of old Tombstones?
We all considered they were.

Did you examine the Premises of any other Persons in the Neighbourhood ; Michael Connell's for instance?
We did ; as well as I remember we entered Three or Four Houses.

Did you find Tombstones or Pieces of Tombstones in those Houses?
Yes.

In how many of those Houses?
Three, I think.

(62.3.)   With

G. Newcome, Esq.

With Inscriptions upon them ?
Yes.

Applied to what Purposes?
There was one that I remember at the Back of the Hearthstone. There was another that the Fire was placed on. The Fire was removed in order to exhibit it to our View.

Before you made those Observations at Castlebrack did you know the Fact that Tombstones were taken out of old Churchyards to be used for domestic Purposes in that Way?
I had heard it.

But you did not know it of your own Knowledge ?
No.

Did you examine the Tombstones generally in the Churchyard of Castlebrack ?
I did.

Did you observe whether any of the Stones you saw there were irregular in point of Thickness, thicker at one Part than another ?
Yes.

Was that frequently the Case ?
Almost always.

Did it appear that they were smoothly worked in Front, but rough at the Back ?
I found that the Stones of a particular Character from the Rosenallis Mountains were all rough at the Back.

Is that the same Description of Stone as this Grit ?
Yes, the same.

Do they use Limestone more frequently now for Tombstones ?
Yes.

Did you observe, on examining the Tombstones at Castlebrack Churchyard, whether the same Letters on the same Stone were sometimes of a different Shape ?
I did. I took a Memorandum of some Peculiarities, particularly the Letter A. I observed it in one Line made quite differently from another. I have a Fac-simile in my Pocket if I may refer to it.

You mean the First Letter of the Alphabet ?
Yes.

That on the same Stone it would appear in Two different Forms ?
Yes.

(*By a Lord.*) When did you make this Visit ?
I made Three or Four Visits.

When you went to this House of Dunn's ?
It was as well as I remember in the Month of March 1844.

How long have you heard of Tombstones being taken for domestic Purposes ?
Long previous to that.

Cross-examined by Mr. Solicitor General for Ireland.

Had those Stones been found long previous to your Visit ?
I heard they were.

You were not present when they were found in Dunn's House ?
No.

When

G. *Newcome, Esq.*

When you say that those Stones were found in a Portion of Dunn's House you mean in the Taproom?
Yes.

Is any Portion of the House still standing?
There is.

Who is living in the House still?
I think it is a Person of the Name of Connell.

At all events there is somebody living in the Portion of the House of which this Taproom was originally Part?
Yes.

And there has been so for a Number of Years?
Yes.

But you yourself do not know the Name of that Person?
As well as I remember it is Connell. There is a Person of the Name of Connell there and a Person of the Name of Dunn; it is either the one or the other.

When for the first Time did you see the "Tracy Stone" as it is called?
I saw it, I think, in the Month of October 1844, only a Portion of it.

How long before or after the Month of October 1844 was it that you went into the Taproom and found the other Fragments of Stones?
I have been in the Taproom in January 1844; and I was again there in October 1844; as well as I remember I was there in March and in October.

That is Three Times in 1844?
Yes.

You did not know whether any Portion of those Stones had been at that Time found?
I heard of them, but I did not see them till October 1844.

Then until October 1844 you had not heard that they had been found?
I had heard previously to October 1844.

But in January 1844, when you were in Dunn's House, had you heard that they had been found?
I heard that they had been found then, but they were not exhibited to the Magistrates.

What brought you to Dunn's House at that Time?
I was requested to attend with some Gentlemen.

But the Stone that had been found was not then exhibited?
Not till October.

Who were the Gentlemen who attended in January when you went to the Place, but the Stone was not shown to you?
I think nearly the same; there was Captain Warburton of Garryhinch, and there was Captain Tibeaudo, and other Gentlemen.

At that Time this Tracy Stone was not exhibited to you?
I do not recollect that it was.

Did you inquire upon that Occasion to see this Tracy Stone?
We were informed that it was at Killeigh at Mr. Baynham's.

And you did not go to look at it?
No.

(62.3.)   X x   How

How far from Castlebrack do you live yourself?
Three Miles to Three and a Half.

How long have you lived in the Neighbourhood?
Since I was a Boy.

There are Two Families of the Name of Tracy in that Neighbourhood?
There are.

How many different Families of the Name of Tracy do you know in that Neighbourhood?
I know Three; there is one Family in Mountmelick, another in Ard in King's County, and the Family of the Claimant.

How far is Ard from Castlebrack?
About Three Miles.

How far is the Claimant's Residence from the Church at Castlebrack?
About the same.

Is it in the same Direction as Ard?
You leave Ard to the right in going to it. I do not think there is a Quarter of a Mile Difference.

Did you know the Father of the Claimant?
I did.

Do you recollect his Grandfather?
No.

Where did the Father live?
At Geashill.

Is that where the present Claimant lives?
I believe not now.

Did you ever know the present Claimant to live there?
I did.

Are there any Tracy's who are Catholics?
Yes; some of the Claimant's Connexions are Catholics.

Do you know what Religion his Father was?
I heard that his Father was a Protestant.

You did not know it?
I did not know it.

You never knew the Grandfather?
No.

Re-examined by Mr. Serjeant Shee.

I think you made some slight Mistake as to the Date; perhaps you will have the goodness to look at a Paper which you signed at the Time?
I have a Memorandum, but I unfortunately left it at my Hotel.

It is as to whether you saw the Stone in January 1844? (*A Paper was shown to the Witness.*) Perhaps you will have the goodness to look at your Signature to that; perhaps that will enable you to state whether you were accurate in saying that you had not seen it in January 1844?
This is dated the 28th of October, the Day that I stated I saw it.

Had you not seen it before that Date? How many Times have you seen it altogether at Castlebrack?
Three Times.

Were

Were any of those Times previous to October 1844 ?
I am endeavouring to recollect. I know the first Time I saw it I observed that the Inscription ended with " England."

But you cannot tell me the Date exactly ?
I cannot. If you allow me to refer to my Memorandum Book perhaps I can.

You may refer to any thing you made at the Time ?

[The Witness referred to a Memorandum Book.]

Unfortunately the Memorandum I took I left at the Hotel.

You stated that you knew the Father of the present Claimant ?
I did.

Was he acquainted with your Father ?
He was.

What Station of Life was he in ?
He was a Man very much respected in the County, always called " Lord Tracy " as long as I can remember ; he was always designated as such in my Memory between Forty and Fifty Years ago.

(By a Lord.) On what Ground was he called Lord Tracy ?
Under the Impression that he was entitled to a Peerage.

Did you ever hear that he was entitled to any Property that was left to the right Heirs of Lord Tracy ?
I always heard that he was not placed in his proper Position in the Country.

The Witness was directed to withdraw.

Then the Reverend JOHN DIGBY WINGFIELD was called in ; and having been sworn, was examined as follows :

(Mr. Serjeant Shee.) I believe you are Rector of Geashill in the King's County ?
I am.

Did you know the Father of the Claimant ?
I did.

In what Condition of Life was he ?
When I knew him he was very low ; in Need.

Low in point of Circumstances ?
Yes.

What was he ?
He lived in one of the small Cottages in Geashill.

Was he received at all in the Society of Gentlemen ?
Not that I know.

Do you know whether he was a Man of Education ?
I should say not.

(By a Lord.) You are speaking of the Father of the Claimant ?
The Father of the Claimant.

(62.s.)   Joseph

Joseph Tracy ?
Yes.

(*Mr. Serjeant Shee.*) Do you know any thing of Tombstones being taken out of Churches and used for domestic Purposes ?
I do. I have seen Fragments of them. I have seen them in Two Houses.

In the Neighbourhood of Castlebrack ?
Two in the Neighbourhood of Castlebrack, the other in Geashill ; but I do not think the Stone at Geashill so decidedly a Gravestone as those in Castlebrack.

(*By a Lord.*) When did you first see them ?
On the 5th of June last as well as I remember.

Last Week ?
Yes.

Where was it you saw them ?
In Cabins close to Castlebrack ; One near my own Churchyard.

You said that the Claimant's Father was a Man in low Circumstances ; did you ever hear him called " Lord Tracy " ?
I never heard him called " Lord Tracy."

Have you ever heard that he was called so ?
No ; but I heard always that he was of good Family.

But you never heard him called " Lord Tracy " ?
Never.

(*Mr. Serjeant Shee.*) Have you ever heard the Father of the Claimant say any thing of his Family or his Descent ?
No, never.

Or any Relation of the Claimant ?
No ; I have heard them say that they were of good Family. I heard the Mother to the best of my Recollection, once say that, and that was all I ever heard.

Cross-examined by Mr. Attorney General.

Who directed your Attention to the Fragments of Tombstones on the Fifth of this Month ?
I can hardly say whether it was Mr. Newcome or Mr. Burke, but they came to me.

They took you for the Purpose of seeing some Stones ?
Yes.

You proceeded to the Cabin where you saw the Stones ?
Yes.

Before that Time you had not observed such a thing taking place ?
No, I had not.

The Witness was directed to withdraw.

Mr. Serjeant Shee stated, That he proposed to proceed now to another Branch of Evidence, as to the Reputation of the Portion of the Tracy Family resident in Dublin with relation to their Connexion with the English Family.

Then

Then Mr. JAMES FORD MARTIN was called in ; and having been sworn, was examined as follows :

(*Mr. Serjeant Shee.*) You now live in Clarendon Place, Vassal Road, Brixton ?
I do.

Are you in any Business ?
No.

Did you formerly live in Dublin ?
I did.

How long is it since you left Dublin ?
The last Time I left Dublin was in the Year 1798.

You ceased to reside there then ?
I have not been there since.

Do you remember an old Lady of the Name of Tracy living in Dublin ?
I do.

Where did she live in Dublin ?
In Exchequer Street.

How long ago is it that you first remember her ?
My first Remembrance of her was when I was about Nine Years old.

What is your Age now ?
Seventy-six ; past that.

In what Condition was Mrs. Tracy of Exchequer Street when you remember her ?
She was nothing.

You do not know that she followed any Occupation ?
She did not.

Do you remember her Brother ?
I have seen him.

What was his Name ?
His Name was James Tracy.

The Brother of Mrs. Tracy ?
That was James O'Brien.

What was James O'Brien ?
At that Time I was told that he conducted his late Father's Business, a Woollen Draper, Wholesale and Retail.

Do you remember the Street he lived in ?
Yes ; Francis Street.

Were you in the habit of frequently seeing old Mrs. Tracy ?
Yes.

Have you heard her at any Time speak of her Family ?
Yes.

Have you ever heard her speak of her Husband ?
I have.

What have you heard her say of her Husband ?
Lamenting the Difference that there was between his Family and himself and her Family.

(62.s.)   Y y   What

Mr. J. F. Martin.

What particularly do you remember her to have said?

I cannot immediately charge my Memory, but the general Tenor of her Remarks was of that Nature.

Do you remember her saying what he was by Family, what his Family were, and who his Relations were?

Yes, I do.

Endeavour to recollect what she said?

That he was of a high Family in England, and she lamented that she was not able to give her Children the Education she wanted. To the best of my Recollection that Remark occurred between her and my Mother.

In your Presence?

In my Presence; that she could not give her Children the Education she wanted in consequence of her Circumstances.

She said that he was of a high Family in England?

Yes.

Did she go more into Particulars?

I cannot recollect, though I was in the habit of seeing her for Five Years afterwards.

Do you remember her saying who the Father of her Husband was?

Yes, that he was entitled to some Title; but I cannot charge my Memory with the Words she uttered or the Thoughts.

Did she say who her Husband's Father was, independently of the Title; what he was; what Office he held?

I do not know whether I heard that from her Lips or no.

You must not tell me what you heard any other Person say; but will you recollect if you ever heard Mrs. Tracy say who or what the Father of her Husband was?

The very Words I do not think it possible to remember, but I was given to understand from what she uttered that her Father-in-law was one of the Judges in England.

You have stated that she spoke of Differences which existed between the Relations of her Husband in England and her own Family. Do you know to what those Differences were ascribed?

No, I cannot say that I ever heard her say what the Difference was.

Do you remember her Sons?

I have seen them, her Son and Grandson.

Do you remember what was the Name of her Son?

I understood it to be James.

Do you know where he lived?

In King's County I understood.

Do you remember what the Name of his Son was?

Joseph.

Were they often at their Mother's in Dublin?

Yes; I have seen them repeatedly in the course of the Five Years that I was accustomed to see her.

How did it happen that your Knowledge upon this Matter was ascertained by Mr. Tracy, the present Claimant?

I read an Advertisement in the Paper, and I communicated, according to the Address of that Advertisement, my Recollections that I knew something, and accordingly the Claimant called upon me.

Cross-

Cross-examined by Mr. Attorney General.

You say that you now live in England?
I do.

Do you carry on any Business?
No.

What Business did you carry on in Dublin?
I did not carry on any Business, but my Father did.

In what Business was he?
A Watchmaker and Jeweller.

Are you now living upon your own Property?
I am.

Have you never been in any Business?
I have, as a Watchmaker and Jeweller.

Where?
In High Street, Marylebone, but a great Number of Years ago.

You have retired from Business how many Years?
These Fifteen Years.

You are now Seventy-six.
I am.

I understand that you were found by an Advertisement for Witnesses?
So I understand.

It was an Advertisement asking if Persons knew any thing upon the Subject to which you answered?
Yes.

When was that?
I think it is about Three Years ago.

Or more?
It may be more. I have not the Particulars about me.

Were you referred to the Office of Mr. Bourdillon?
No, it was a Cypher at some Coffee House, and I wrote my Answer to the Advertisement.

You say that the Claimant called upon you?
He called upon me a Day or Two afterwards.

Did I rightly understand you to say that you were Nine Years of Age when you first saw old Mrs. Tracy?
Yes.

How old did she appear to be at that Time?
She was very antique according to my Recollection.

About what Age?
I should estimate her about Eighty; she looked it in Appearance.

How many Years were you in Communication with her?
Five Years and upwards.

Up to the Time of her Death?
No; my Family went to reside in Limerick.

When you left Dublin for Limerick she was living?
Yes.

(*By a Lord.*) When was that?
That was about the Year 1786.

(*Mr. Attorney General.*) She carried on no Business?
No.

(62.s.)

Had

Mr. J. F. Martin.

Had she a House of her own?

No, she was in Lodgings.

Living in a humble Way?

Middling.

Keeping no Servants?

I did not see any.

Did she lodge in a single Room, or more than One Room?

Two Rooms; she might have had more.

How often do you think you saw her?

Hundreds of Times.

Was your Mother constantly going there?

Yes.

You were between Nine and Twelve Years of Age?

Between Nine and Fourteen.

Were you in the habit of sitting with her frequently with your Mother?

My Mother was in the habit of sitting with her, and I used to run up and down.

Was your Mother a Friend of hers?

She had got acquainted with her at a Place of Worship called the Round Church—St. Andrew's in Dublin.

You say that her Brother was a Gentleman of the Name of O'Brien?

Yes.

What has become of all those O'Briens?

I do not know.

Are any of them living?

I cannot tell.

Were they living when you left the Neighbourhood?

Yes, her Brother was living, and conducting the Business.

Was he a married Man?

I do not know.

Have you learnt whether any of them are living or not?

Not about the O'Briens. When I returned from residing in Limerick with my Father and Mother, after residing there Eight Years, my Mother's Curiosity induced her to inquire about the old Lady, and she found that she had died the Year after we left Dublin.

Did you ascertain whether any of the O'Briens were living at that Time?

I did not. The last Time I saw Mrs. Tracy, or a little Time before the last, her Brother was there with her.

The last Time that you saw her was in 1786?

Yes.

You say that you saw about that Time her Son James?

Yes.

How old was he?

He seemed to be turned Fifty; an elderly Man.

Was not he more than that?

Yes, he might have been, but not being interested in scrutinizing it I could not say; I should say that it must have been about Fifty.

Or better?

Or more.

How

How old was his Son Joseph?
He seemed to be from Eighteen to Twenty; a Slip of a Lad.

Were they there frequently?
Yes, I used to see them there very frequently.

Most Days when you went?
Not most Days, but I have seen them in the course of the Five Years several Times.

You saw them occasionally?
Yes.

You say that Mrs. Tracy lodged in Exchequer Street?
Yes.

Whereabouts?
A Dozen Houses from Grafton Street.

Whose House was it?
I do not know.

She lived on the First or Second Floor?
Yes.

What Business was carried on below?
A Pastrycook's.

You know that she had nothing to do with the Business?
I never understood that she had.

Who carried on the Business?
A Person of the same Name.

Of the Name of Tracy?
Of the Name of Tracy.

Any Relation?
I do not know.

The Name of Tracy was over the Door?
Yes.

You have seen that Person?
Yes, I have seen that Person in the Shop.

And you knew her as a different Person from the Person who is supposed to be the Great Grandmother of the Claimant?
The Mrs. Tracy I speak of is a different Person from the Person that kept the Shop.

You say that she regretted the Difference between her Husband and his Family. What did you understand her to mean; was it Difference in Position or Difference from having quarrelled?
Both.

In the same Word?
No.

What did she say?
She regretted not being able to give her Children Education because she had not the Means in consequence of that Difference there; that he was nominally discarded; I understood it in that Light.

You have not now a sufficient Recollection to tell us the Words she used?
No, but the Impression only I can describe.

(62.3.)   Z z   Did

Mr. J. F. Martin.

Did you ever hear her speak of her Husband by Name?
Yes, several Times.

To your Mother?
Yes.

I presume that till your Attention was directed to this Subject by the Advertisement, having little to care about it, you thought but little of it?
I thought nothing of it.

Have you had many Interviews with Mr. Tracy, the Claimant?
Several.

How many should you say?
I cannot enumerate them; a good many.

I presume that when you answered the Advertisement he told you the Nature of the Claim before you explained to him what you knew?
I told him all I knew, and where I was born, and where I lived, and my Opportunities.

In order to ascertain whether your Evidence would be useful to him did not he begin by explaining to you the Nature of his Claim, and who he was?
He did not enter into the Claim; Mr. Bourdillon explained the Nature of his Claim.

But the Claimant told you who his Great Grandmother was, through whom he claimed?
Yes.

And all those Circumstances?
Yes.

Has he done so more than once?
No; I knew more than he did about it.

Have you talked together upon the Subject?
Yes, repeatedly.

Mr. Bourdillon likewise has explained to you more in Detail the Nature of Mr. Tracy's Claim?
Rather different from that; he asked me to recollect myself, and by Degrees I did.

I presume that in doing his Duty as a Solicitor he pointed out to you the Points that would be important in the Case?
He recalled my Recollection.

First with respect to any Connexion between Mr. Tracy and the Judge's Family; did he ask you if you could say any thing upon that Subject?
I did not hear any thing upon that Subject till the first Time I had the Honour of waiting upon the House.

You never heard any thing about it?
Not particularly; I did not understand it so as to be able to speak about it.

You did not understand it sufficiently to be able to speak about it till you heard the Evidence given at this Bar?
In respect of his English Connexion.

I presume

I presume from your Age and the long Interval that has elapsed the
Circumstance of this Matter having been talked of has rather brushed
up your Mind upon the Subject?
No doubt of it.

And your Recollection being faint in the first instance became
revived after Conversations?
Yes.

Both with Mr. Tracy, the Claimant, and Mr. Bourdillon, and subsequently by hearing the Evidence here?
Yes, certainly ; and I had a better Opportunity of my own, for I had
a Sister Five or Six Years older than me.

And you talked to her about it?
I did, and she refreshed my Memory.

She brushed you up about it?
Yes.

Then are you able now to say what you distinctly recollect yourself,
and what has been revived in your Mind by Conversation, and what you
heard from your Sister?
It brought to my Recollection the Facts I came here to verify.

A good deal was obscure before you were refreshed by your Sister?
Not having any Idea that I should be called upon to stand here it
did not interest me, but the Circumstances recurred to me immediately,
the Circumstances of seeing the old Lady and hearing her Remarks.

You remember seeing the old Lady, and hearing her talk to your
Mother?
Yes.

Then from Time to Time as you thought upon the Subject and
talked about it the particular Circumstances all came again to your
Mind?
They did.

And the more you have talked with other People the fresher you
have been?
Yes.

The Witness was directed to withdraw.

Then GEORGE NEWCOME Esquire was again called in, and further
examined as follows :

(*By a Lord.*) You were acquainted with the Claimant's Father?
I was.

He was a Friend of yours?
I was acquainted with him.

What Situation of Life was he in?
In humble Circumstances.

How did he gain his Livelihood? Did he live upon his Means, or
was he in any Business? Was he a Day Labourer?
Indeed I cannot say. I did not know him as such.

How did he earn his Livelihood?
I imagine that he had a Piece of Land.

(62.3.)   3 A   A Quarter

A Quarter of an Acre of Potatoes ?

He must have had more than that.

How much more ?

I do not know. I knew him as Mr. Tracy, without any Reference to this Matter.

Was he an Associate of yours ? Did he live in the same Line of Life as you did yourself ?

Not at all.

In very inferior Circumstances ?

Yes.

How near was his Property to yours ?

About Four Miles.

But you cannot state the Extent, whether it was a Quarter of an Acre or Twenty Acres ?

No.

You would be sure that it was not Fifty Acres ?

Yes, I do not think it was.

Had he any Servant ?

I am not aware.

Did he keep a Horse ?

No. I was a very young Lad when I was first acquainted with him.

(*Mr. Serjeant Shee.*) I asked you just now whether you were quite correct in saying that you had not seen this Stone in the Month of January 1844. Have you since referred to some Memorandum that you have kept ?

I stated before that I have left a Pocket Book at my Hotel. I have since found it, and I find an Entry here of an Inspection which I made of a Variety of Stones on the 25th of January 1844.

Does it appear whether you examined this particular Stone upon that Occasion ?

It does appear that I did.

I believe you copied Part of the Inscription ?

I did.

And you have it now in your Hand ?

I have.

(*By a Lord.*) At whose Request did you make that Inspection ?

At the Request of Mr. Burke.

The Solicitor ?

Yes.

In consequence of your being so requested you made a Memorandum of having inspected it ?

I attended with other Magistrates and we took Memorandums of what occurred.

Sir Fitzroy Kelly stated, That for the Purpose of meeting any Objection which might be made to the Entry of the Date in the Prayer Book which had been produced on a former Day he purposed to show that previously to the Alteration of the Style it was usual during the first Three Months of the Year to date Letters and Memoranda as of the new Year as well as of the past Year, and that with

that

that View he would offer in Evidence a Collection of Parliamentary Debates of the Years 1680 and 1681.

After some Discussion Sir Fitzroy Kelly stated, That understanding that no Objection would be raised to the Entry upon this Ground he would not press this Evidence at present, but that he trusted that if this Point should be raised he should be allowed to have an Opportunity of giving Evidence upon it.

Sir Fitzroy Kelly further stated, That the only remaining Evidence he should have to produce consisted of Two or Three Documents which he had not been able yet to procure, and that at the next Sitting of the Committee he should be prepared to lay before the Committee those additional Documents, and to sum up the Case on behalf of the Claimant.

The Witnesses were directed to withdraw.

The Counsel were directed to withdraw.

Proposed to adjourn this Committee *sine Die ;*

Accordingly,

Adjourned *sine Die.*

TRACY PEERAGE.

CASE on the part of MATTHEW TRACY, of No. 40, Kensington Gardens Square, in the County of Middlesex, Esquire, Claimant to the Titles, Honors, and Dignities of Viscount and Baron Tracy of Rathcoole, in the County of Dublin and Kingdom of Ireland.

King Charles I, in the 18th year of his reign, by Letters Patent, dated the 12th day of January, 1642-3, granted to Sir John Tracy, of Toddington, in the County of Gloucester, Knight, and to his heirs male, the degree, dignity, and honour of a Viscount and Baron of the Kingdom of Ireland, by the style and title of Viscount and Baron Tracy, of Rathcoole, in the County of Dublin, in the Kingdom of Ireland. Letters Patent of that date.

The Claimant, Matthew Tracy, hopes to satisfy your Lordships that he is entitled to this Peerage. as now filling the character of heir male of the person to whom the Peerage was granted.

John, Lord Viscount Tracy, the grantee of the peerage, was succeeded in his title and estates by his son and heir Robert, the second Viscount. It is from a younger son of the second Viscount that the Claimant traces his descent. Appendix Prop. I.

Robert, the second Viscount, was twice married.

By his *first* wife he had seven sons, of whom only John, his eldest, left any issue. By his *second* wife he had two sons, of whom the eldest, Robert, is the ancestor of the Claimant. This gentleman went to the bar, and was a Judge of the Court of Common Pleas in England, from the year 1700 to the year 1726.

The Claimant traces his descent through William, the third son of Judge Tracy, of whom more hereafter.

On the death of the second Viscount, in 1662, the Peerage devolved on his eldest son, John. It descended regularly from father to son to Thomas Charles, the sixth Viscount, who succeeded in 1756, and died without issue in 1792. The title then devolved on his half brother, the Reverend John Tracy, D.D., Warden of All Souls' College, Oxford; he died without issue within six months after he succeeded to the title, which then devolved upon his only surviving brother, Henry, the eighth and last Lord Viscount Tracy.

Henry, the eighth Viscount, died in 1797 without male issue; his only daughter, the Honourable Henrietta Susannah, entered into possession of the family estates, and married Charles Hanbury, Esq., of Pontypool, who assumed the name of Tracy, and was subsequently created Baron Sudeley, in the Peerage of the United Kingdom.

Since the death of the eighth Viscount, in 1793, the Peerage has been dormant, no person having established his right to it. The present Claimant has petitioned Her Majesty, and Her Majesty has been graciously pleased to refer his Petition to your Lordships.

The Claimant, as has been already stated, traces his title through the Honourable Robert Tracy, the eldest son of the *second* marriage of John, the second Lord Viscount Tracy. His title, therefore, depends upon two general propositions.

1st. That all descendants of the *first* marriage of the second Lord Viscount Tracy in the male line are extinct.

2nd. That the Claimant now fills the character of the heir male of Judge Tracy, the eldest son of the second Viscount by his *second* marriage

Upon the first proposition no difficulty is apprehended. In a former inquiry as to the right to this Peerage, it was established, to the satisfaction of a Committee of Privileges, that, with the death of the eighth Viscount, the male line of the second Viscount by his *first* marriage became extinct, and that, consequently, the title to the Peerage is vested in the person who can prove himself to be the heir male of Judge Tracy; and the same evidence, which is entirely of a documentary character, will, it is hoped, now be satisfactory to your Lordships. The following are the facts which the Claimant is prepared to prove, with references to the proofs by which they are severally sustained:—

ROBERT, second Viscount Tracy, who succeeded his father, married,

First, Bridget, daughter of John Lyttleton, of Frankley Court, in the County of Worcester, Esquire, who died in the year 1632, leaving issue seven sons.

  1. John, afterwards Lord Viscount Tracy.

  2. Robert, who died before 1665 without issue.

  3. Thomas, who died an infant.

  4. Thomas, died in 1669 without issue.

  5. Horace, died an infant in May, 1619.

  6. William, admitted a Member of the Middle Temple, December, 1649, died, without issue, June, 1706.

  7. Henry, who died after 1662, without issue.

Secondly, Dorothy, daughter of Thomas Cocks, Esquire, by whom he had two sons.

  1. ROBERT, afterwards Judge of the Common Pleas, the Claimant's ancestor. *Appendix Prop. 2.*

  2. BENJAMIN, whose descendants it is not necessary to trace.

His Lordship died in 1662, and was succeeded by *Appendix Prop. 3.*

JOHN, third Lord Viscount Tracy; he married, Elizabeth, daughter of Thomas, Lord Leigh, and had issue three sons.

  1. William, his son and heir. *Appendix Prop. 4.*

  2. Charles, who died unmarried in 1676.

  3. Ferdinando, who succeeded to the estates of Sir John Tracy, of Stanway, and was the ancestor of the Stanway branch of the family. His descendants will afterwards be traced.

The third Viscount died in March, 1686-7, and was succeeded by his eldest son, *Appendix Prop. 5.*

WILLIAM, fourth Viscount Tracy; he married,

 First, Frances, daughter of Leicester, Viscount Hereford, and had issue one son,

   John, died an infant. *Prop. 6.*

 Secondly, Jane, daughter of Sir Thomas Leigh, and had issue an only son,

   Thomas Charles, born in 1690. *Prop. 7.*

The fourth Viscount died in 1712, and was succeeded by his only son,

THOMAS CHARLES, fifth Viscount Tracy; he married, *Prop. 8.*

 First, Elizabeth, daughter of William Keyt, Esquire, who died in October, 1711, leaving two sons.

  1. William, born August 25th, 1715: he died in April, 1752, in his father's lifetime, without issue. *Prop. 9.*

2. Thomas Charles, afterwards sixth Lord Viscount Tracy; he married,

Prop. 11. *Secondly*, Frances, daughter of Sir John Packington, Baronet, and had issue three sons.

1. John, afterwards seventh Lord Tracy; he was in Holy Orders, and Warden of All Souls' College, Oxford.

Prop. 14. 2. Robert Packington, born in September, 1725; died in India, unmarried, in 1743.

3 Henry Leigh, afterwards the eighth and last Viscount Tracy.

The fifth Viscount died in June, 1756, and was succeeded by his son,

Prop. 10. THOMAS CHARLES, sixth Lord Viscount Tracy; he married, in 1755, Harriette, daughter of Peter Bathurst. Esquire of Clarendon Park, in the County of Wilts, and died in August, 1792, without issue, whereupon the title devolved upon his next brother,

Prop. 12. THE REVEREND JOHN, seventh Lord Viscount Tracy: he died, without issue, in February, 1793, upon which the title devolved upon his only surviving brother,

Prop. 13. HENRY LEIGH, eighth Viscount Tracy; he married, on the 12th of September, 1767, Susanna, daughter of Anthony Weaver, Esquire, and had an only child,

Prop. 15. Henrietta Susannah, married to Charles Hanbury, Esquire, who assumed the name of Tracy, and was afterwards created Lord Sudeley.

Prop. 16. His Lordship, the eighth Viscount Tracy, died on the 27th of April, 1797, without issue male.

Upon his death the title would have reverted to the male issue of the Honourable Ferdinando Tracy, of Stanway, the third son of the third Viscount. It will, however, be seen that this branch of the family had then (1797) become extinct in the male line, and that the Stanway estates had passed away to the female heirs.

STATEMENT as to the descendants of FERDINANDO TRACY, third son of JOHN, the third Lord Viscount TRACY.

The Honourable FERDINANDO TRACY, third son of John, third Lord Viscount Tracy, succeeded in 1678 to the Stanway estates under the Will of Sir John

Tracy, of Stanway, in the County of Gloucester, Baronet. The Honourable Ferdinando Tracy married Katharine, daughter of Sir Anthony Keck, and had issue two sons.

Prop. 23.

    1.   Ferdinando Tracy.

    2.   John Tracy.

The Honourable Ferdinando Tracy died in February, 1682.

FERDINANDO TRACY, his eldest son, died unmarried a few days after his father, Prop. 24. whereupon

JOHN TRACY, Esquire, his brother, succeeded to the Stanway estates: he married Ann, daughter of Sir Robert Atkyns, Lord Chief Baron of the Exchequer, and by her had male issue.

    1.   John, died an infant in 1704.

    2.   Robert of whom hereafter.   Prop. 25.

    3.   JOHN, of whom hereafter.

    4.   Ferdinando, who died unmarried in 1792.   Prop. 28.

    5.   ANTHONY, of whom hereafter.

    6.   THOMAS, of whom hereafter.

    7.   William, born in January, 1721; died in May, 1729.

    8.   Edward, died an infant, June, 1723.

    9.   Charles Richard, died an infant, March, 1725-6.

Mr. Tracy died in April, 1735, and was succeeded by his *second* son,

ROBERT TRACY, of Stanway, Esquire; he married Ann Maria, daughter of Sir Prop. 26. Robert Hudson, and died without issue in August, 1767. The Stanway estates then devolved on his next brother,

JOHN TRACY, of Stanway, Esquire, who was cursitor Baron of the Exchequer, and Prop. 27. had assumed the name of Atkyns, but reassumed his family name on inheriting the Stanway estates; he was married to Katharine, daughter of — Lindsay, Esquire, but died without issue in 1773. The Stanway estates then devolved on the daughters of his next brother,

ANTHONY TRACY, who had assumed the name of Keck in compliance with the Prop. 29. Will of his maternal grand-uncle, Francis Keck, Esquire; he married Susan, sister of James, Duke of Hamilton, and died in 1767, leaving no son, but two daughters.

    1.   Henrietta Charlotte.

    2.   Susan.

Henrietta Charlotte assumed the name of Tracy by a private Act of Parliament passed in 1794 ; she had married, in 1774, Edward, twelfth Viscount Hereford, and died without issue.

Susan married, in July, 1771, Lord Elcho, the eldest son of Earl Wemyss; and, on the death of her sister, she inherited the Stanway estates, and assumed the name of Tracy by the provisions of a private Act of Parliament passed in 1818; she died in February, 1835.

'rop. 30. THOMAS TRACY, the 6th son of John Tracy and Ann Atkyns, settled at Sandywell, in Gloucestershire. He married Mary, daughter and heiress of Sir William Dodwell, and had one son —

Dodwell Tracy,

Who died unmarried, in February, 1768. Thomas Tracy himself died in 1770, without surviving issue.

It is therefore shewn, that on the death of John Tracy (Atkyns), the cursitor Baron in 1773, all the male line of Ferdinando, the third son of the third Viscount Tracy, became extinct, and that on the death of Henry Leigh, the eighth Viscount, in 1797, all the male line of the second Viscount, in the descendants of his first marriage, also became extinct.

In order to establish the second proposition, and to complete the title of the Claimant, it now remains for him to shew that he is the heir male of the Honourable Robert Tracy, the eighth son of the second Viscount, the Judge of the Court of Common Pleas.

STATEMENT as to the descendants of the Honourable ROBERT TRACY, Judge of the Common Pleas, in England, eighth son of ROBERT, the second Viscount TRACY, by Dorothy, his second wife.

Prop. 31. The Honourable ROBERT TRACY, son of Robert, second Viscount Tracy, by Dorothy, his second wife, was born in or about the year 1665. He was admitted a member of the Inner Temple, in April, 1673—enrolled Sergeant at Law, 1st of October, 1700—was appointed a Judge of the Common Pleas, November 24th, 1700 ; retired from the Bench in 1726, and died, November, 1735.

He married Anne, daughter of William Dowdeswell, of Pool Court, in the County of Worcester, Esquire, and by her had issue three sons and two daughters.

1. Robert Tracy, a member of the Inner Temple, who died in his father's lifetime, in 1732, unmarried. Prop. 32.

2. Richard Tracy, who married Margaret, daughter of Owen Salusbury, Esquire, by whom he had issue an only son,
Robert Tracy, of whom hereafter.

3. *William Tracy*, Ancestor of the Claimant, of whom hereafter.

4. Anne Tracy, married, *first*, to Charles Dowdeswell, of Forthampton Court in the County of Worcester, Esquire; *secondly*, to Thomas Wylde, Esquire, sometime M.P. for the City of Worcester, and for many years Commissioner of the Revenue, Ireland.

5. Dorothy, who married John, eldest son of Sir John Pratt, Lord Chief Justice of the King's Bench, and half-brother to Charles, Earl Camden.

RICHARD TRACY (second son of the Judge) died in his father's lifetime, in 1734, Prop. 33. leaving his only son,

ROBERT TRACY, of Coscombe, in the County of Gloucester, Esquire; Prop. 34. he died, unmarried, in May, 1756.

William Tracy (third son of the Judge), born 16th of February, 1692, at Prop. 35. Tucks or Tooks Court, in the Parish of St. Andrew's, Holborn. He appears to have been estranged from his family, and to have gone to Ireland, where he married Mary, the daughter of Mr. James O'Brien, a Merchant, or Woollen Draper, of Dublin. By her he had issue one son.

John Tracy, born in 1727.

William Tracy, settled at Ross, in the King's County, Ireland. He died, 15th October, 1734, and was buried in the Church-yard of Castlebrack, in the Queen's County. He left an only son, the before-mentioned

JOHN TRACY, who settled in the County Mayo, where he married Catherine, Prop. 36. daughter of John Treston, Esquire, of that County, by whom he had issue an only son,
Edward Tracy, born in 1735.

John Tracy died in 1799, leaving his only son,

EDWARD TRACY, who married,

Prop. 37.   *First.* Mary, daughter of John Treston, Esquire, of Cottage, in the County of Mayo, by her he had issue —

           Luke, born in 1786, of whom hereafter

Prop. 38.   *Secondly* Margaret, daughter of Martin Mc Hale, Esq., of Cloonkeash, in the parish of Turlough, county of Mayo, and by her had issue :

    1.   Catharine, who married Mr. Patrick Owens.

    2.   *Martin*, the father of the Claimant

    3.   Mary, married to Mr. Mullawney

    4.   John, born in 1804, died in 1848, leaving issue.

Prop. 39.   LUKE TRACY, the eldest son of Edward by his first wife, died in 1834, having married the widow of Captain Hill, but died without issue.

Prop. 40.   MARTIN, his second son (and child of the second marriage), was born in 1800, and died in 1847, having married Catherine, daughter of Matthew Toole, Esq., of Tuam, in the county Galway, and by her he left issue :

    1.   Edward, born in 1828.

Prop. 41   2.   *Matthew*, the Claimant, born in 1829.

    3.   Marian.

    4.   Luke Charles.

    5.   Robert Alfred Martin.

    6.   Arthur Walter.

    7.   Constantine Henry.

    8.   Augusta Mary.

Prop. 42.   EDWARD, the eldest son, died at Bombay in the East Indies, unmarried, where upon the title to the Peerage devolved upon the Claimant,

MATTHEW TRACY, as the eldest male descendant of the Honourable Judge Tracy, son of Robert, second Viscount and Baron Tracy, and therefore, on the extinction of all elder branches in the male line, heir male of the first Lord Viscount Tracy to whom the Peerage was granted

A Pedigree accompanies this case, shewing in the ordinary form the descent of the Claimant from the Grantee of the Patent of 1642, and the course of descent and extinction of the different branches of the family, tracing also some collateral branches from members of whom, on proving their relationship, it may be important to adduce evidence of family reputation.

A great part of this case has already received a very full investigation by the Committee of Privileges of your Lordships' House in the sessions of 1839, and 1843, and afterwards in 1847 and 1848. It will be necessary for the present Claimant to advert to these proceedings, as Mr. James Tracy, the Claimant upon those occasions, relied to a certain extent upon the same title as is now presented to your Lordships. He alleged, and with truth, that the title to the Peerage was, by the extinction of all the elder branches in the male line, now in the heir male of Judge Tracy. He alleged further, as the present Claimant now does, that William Tracy, the third son of Judge Tracy, was married to Miss Mary O'Brien, daughter of Mr. James O'Brien, of Dublin. So far his case was common with that which the present Claimant makes, but in proceeding further to allege that he was the descendant of William Tracy and Mary O'Brien his wife, he made an allegation entirely inconsistent with the title of the present Claimant, an allegation which the Claimant humbly submits is inconsistent with the fact, and which is in truth unsupported by any evidence upon which the slightest reliance could be placed.

In 1836 the former Claimant presented his Petition to his late Majesty, claiming the dignities and titles of Viscount and Baron Tracy of Rathcoole. That Petition was referred to your Lordships' House, and the case was heard by a Committee of Privileges in the sessions of 1839 and 1843, and on the 9th of June, 1843, it was resolved that the Claimant had not made out his claim to the title, honour, and dignity of Viscount Tracy of Rathcoole, in the kingdom of Ireland.

Upon the hearing of the claim in 1843, the Committee of Privileges declared themselves perfectly satisfied with the proof that all the elder branches of the family were extinct in the male line, and intimated to the counsel for the Claimant at the close of the case that he need only address the Committee upon the question of the descent of the Claimant from Judge Tracy.

The decisions of the Committee upon the points of law involved in the case are reported in the tenth volume of " Clarke and Finnelly's Reports," page

Subsequently in 1845 a further Petition was presented to her Majesty by James Tracy, and that Petition her Majesty was also graciously pleased to refer to your Lordships' House. The case was heard in the sessions of 1847 and 1848, but no determination upon the matter of such Petitition has since been come to by your Lordships' House.

Upon the occasion of the first hearing of the Petition of James Tracy, in addition to the evidence shewing the extinction of the elder branches of the family, the then Claimant offered evidence to prove that the William Tracy who married Miss O'Brien was the third son of Judge Tracy, and that he himself was descended from that William Tracy. This evidence principally consisted, *first*, of an entry in a Prayer-book, said to have been in the possession of Mary, the widow of William Tracy, and *secondly* of evidence that there had been in Castlebrack Churchyard a Tombstone to the memory of William Tracy, with an inscription that he was the son of an English Judge.

The Lords of the Committee of Privileges declared their opinion that the entry in the Prayer-book was a fabrication, as the present Claimant humbly submits it was.

Upon the occasion of the hearing of the second Petition, further evidence was adduced on behalf of the then Claimant as follows :

1st. The evidence of Mrs. Sarah Elizabeth Lambe, who was proved to be a near relation of Mrs. Wylde (who was the eldest daughter of Mr. Justice Tracy), that she had heard from deceased members of the Wylde family, that William Tracy, the third son of the Judge, had gone to Ireland, and had married Miss Mary O'Brien. This lady (Mrs. Lambe) who was then 76 years of age, deposed to some details of this family reputation, and she corroborated it by producing a family portrait of William Tracy, and a letter from Judge Tracy, dated the 29th of January, 1732, addressed to his daughter, Mrs. Wylde, and annexed to which letter was a memorandum, alleged to be in the handwriting of Mrs. Wylde, containing, among other entries, that of the birth of William Tracy on the 16th of February, 1692.

Mrs. Lambe has since died, and both the picture and the letter, and the memorandum attached, are now in the possession of the Officers of your Lordships' House.

2nd. He produced the fragments of a stone which he alleged were found in a house near the burial-place of Castlebrack, and which, when put together, bore an inscription corresponding to that to which the witnesses on the former occasion had deposed.

This inscription is as follows :

"Here lyeth the body of William Tracy, Esq., late of Ross, in the King's County, the third son of the Honourable Robert Tracy, late one of the Judges of the Common Pleas in England."

With some further letters, stating it was erected by his widow.

The fragments of this stone were produced before the Committee of Privileges, and are still in the custody of the Officers of your Lordships' House.

The genuineness of this stone was strongly impeached by the Attorney General, and also by the Attorney General for Ireland, who appeared on behalf of Her Majesty, and on the 18th of July, 1848, a witness, named Patrick Holton, was produced, who deposed, that in conjunction with a man named Patrick Magennis (who had employed him for the purpose), he had cut the inscription upon the stone a short time before, for the purposes of the Claimant's case, and in this he was corroborated by a witness named John Egan. Patrick Magennis was then, as he still is, in America.

After this evidence, the counsel for the then Claimant, on 3rd of August, 1848, applied for an adjournment, to enable the latter to bring Patrick Magennis from America, to which application the Committee were pleased to accede.

On the 8th of May, 1849, the Committee again met, when it was stated, that since the former hearing, the then Claimant had died, but had left a son, who would immediately present a Petition to Her Majesty; and the Committee adjourned to the 18th May.

On the 18th May, it was stated to the Committee, that two days before, a Petition had been left with the Secretary of State, and the Committee adjourned to the 7th of June, when it was stated, that a solicitor had been retained for the son of the then late Claimant, and that the Petition of the son had been presented to Her Majesty, and referred to the Attorney General.

No further proceedings appear ever to have been taken on this Petition, and no decision was ever pronounced, either by a Committee of Privileges, or by your Lordships' House.

Claimant has been informed that, on 2nd August, 1854, a Petition was presented to Her Majesty by Benjamin Wheatley Tracy, Esq., a Lieutenant in in the Royal Navy, claiming this Peerage; and this Petition having been referred to your Lordships' House, and on 7th August, 1854, an application was made to the Committee of Privileges, on behalf of Lieutenant Tracy, that he might be at liberty to avail himself of the evidence given on behalf of Mr. James Tracy, which application the Lords of the Committee informed his counsel they would consider at the time when his Case would come before them; but it does not appear that any proceedings have since been taken in reference to Lieutenant Tracy's claim,

Under these circumstances, the present Claimant's claim comes before your Lordships.

On the 17th of January, 1859, he presented his humble Petition to Her Majesty, claiming the titles, honors, and dignities of Viscount and Baron Tracy, and Her Majesty was graciously pleased to refer that Petition to her Attorney General. The Claimant laid before him documents and proofs referring to these former proceedings, and shewing that he was prepared to support, by evidence, the genuineness of the tombstone, and refute the impeachment endeavoured to be cast upon it by the evidence of Patrick Holton.

Her Majesty having been graciously pleased, on the Report of her Attorney General, to refer this claim to your Lordships' House, the Claimant is ready to sustain the case made in his Petition to Her Majesty, and to shew to your Lordships that he is entitled to the Peerage which he claimed by that Petition.

The evidence by which the first proposition, viz., the extinction of the elder branch of the family, will be sustained, is fully stated in the early part of this case, and in the Appendix of Proofs annexed. It is the same which was offered on the hearing of the claim of James Tracy.

The Claimant is quite ready to produce that evidence again, but inasmuch as all that evidence has been submitted to full investigation before your Lordships, in the presence of the English and Irish Attorney General, and was he alleges pronounced satisfactory by the Committee of Privileges, he humbly hopes, that in order to save the expense and the delay consequent upon the reproduction of that evidence, he may be permitted to take it from the Minutes of the Committee of Privileges, who investigated the claim of James Tracy.

In making out the second proposition, viz., the descent of the Claimant from Judge Tracy, the evidence must be directed to two points, which the nature of the case makes quite distinct.

First, the descent of the Claimant, as stated in his Pedigree, from William Tracy of Ross, the husband of Mary O'Brien.

Second, the identity of that William Tracy, with William Tracy, the third son of the Judge.

The first point, which is peculiar to the present Claimant's case and which is now for the first time presented to your Lordships, the Claimant will sustain, by evidence which, he expects, will be perfectly satisfactory to your Lordships. In Ireland, the country in which, from William Tracy downwards, the family of the Claimant has resided, perfect registers of births, deaths, and marriages, are rarely to be met with. John Tracy, the son of William, having married into a Roman Catholic family, appears to have adopted their religious profession. The want of any registers among Roman Catholic families in Ireland is notorious. Every possible attempt to find such registers has been and will be pursued, but although deprived of this most authentic species of evidence, it is humbly hoped, that the evidence of living witnesses, and of family reputation, which will be laid before your Lordships, will conclusively establish the proposition that the Claimant is descended, in the manner stated in his pedigree, from William Tracy of Ross, the husband of Mary O'Brien.

Upon the question of the identity of this William Tracy with the third son of the Judge, the Claimant humbly hopes that he will be permitted to adduce from the minutes of the Committee of Privileges the evidence already given by Mrs. Elizabeth Lambe before the former Committee of Privileges, and that Mrs. Lambe being now dead, her evidence, together with such other evidence as he may be able to offer of the same nature, may be taken to establish a family reputation, in the English branch of the Tracy family, of the marriage of William Tracy, the third son of the Judge, with Miss O'Brien.

He will also rely on the Certificate of Baptism of William Tracy, the letter of Judge Tracy to his daughter Mrs. Wylde, and the memorandum annexed to such letter.

He purposes also to produce evidence of a reputation always existing in the Treston family, that the John Tracy who married Catherine Treston, was the grandson or descendant of an English Judge, and that he and his descendants were the heirs to this Peerage. This evidence will be given by members of the Treston family, occupying a most respectable social position, and will be carried back by other witnesses to a period cotemporaneous with John Tracy himself.

Similar evidence will be adduced, of a reputation existing in the O'Brien family, that the William Tracy who was married to Miss Mary O'Brien, was the son of an English Judge, and of the family of Lord Viscount Tracy.

Assuming this testimony to be satisfactory, Claimant will thus establish the concurrent existence of a tradition to this fact in three families remote from each other

In addition to the above, the Claimant, after the fullest investigation in his power, believes that he can satisfy your Lordships that there did exist, very many years ago, in the burial-place of Castlebrack, an ancient tombstone, over the grave of William Tracy, with an inscription, stating him to be the son of an English Judge,—and also that the fragments now in the custody of the Officers of your Lordships' House are the genuine fragments of that ancient tombstone.

He hopes also to satisfy your Lordships, by unimpeachable testimony, that the stone with the inscription, was seen by living witnesses, in the burial-place at Castlebrack long before the year 1839.

If it is impeached by the evidence of Patrick Holten. who since his former examination has died, the Claimant is prepared to meet this by the evidence of a gentleman, who went to America, for the late Claimant, James Tracy. to see Patrick Magennis ; this gentlemen failed to bring him back as a witness, but will be ready to state the result of the enquiries he made, and of his interviews with Magennis

The Claimant will also be prepared to prove that the character of Patrick Holton was such that he was not worthy of credit on his oath, and to prove circumstances shewing that the account given by him with reference to the Tombstone could not be true.

And to prove by several witnesses that Patrick Holton acknowledged that the evidence which he gave in your Lordships' House was not the truth, and that he made statements before he gave that evidence entirely inconsistent with the supposition that his evidence was true.

The Claimant therefore humbly hopes that upon making these proofs he will satisfy your Lordships that he is now entitled to the Irish Peerage of Tracy, of Rathcoole, and that he will obtain a Report that he has made out his claim to the dignities and titles which he claims by his Petition to her Majesty the Queen

ISAAC BUTT.

July, 1862,

APPENDIX.

I.   To Prove that JOHN, 1st VISCOUNT TRACY, had issue, Sir Robert Tracy his Son and Heir, who succeeded his Father as second Viscount Tracy.

   1.   Pedigree entered in the Herald's Visitation of the County of Gloucester, in the year 1623.
   2.   Will of the said Sir Robert Tracy, then Viscount Tracy, dated 3rd May, 1662.

II   To Prove that the said ROBERT, 2nd VISCOUNT TRACY, had issue by his first Wife, Bridget, seven sons; viz., John Tracy, afterwards third Viscount Tracy,—Robert Tracy,—Thomas Tracy, who died young, before 1623,—another Thomas Tracy,—Horace Tracy, who also died young before 1623, (a)—William Tracy, and Henry Tracy.   And that he had issue by his second Wife, Dorothy, two other sons; viz., Robert Tracy, and Benjamin Tracy.

   1.   The Pedigree entered in the Herald's Visitation of the County of Gloucester, 1623, shews that the said Sir Robert Tracy had issue by Bridget, his first wife, John, his eldest son, Robert, his second son, and Thomas, his third son; and that he had had two other sons, viz., Thomas, and Horace, both of whom were then dead without issue.
   2.   Will of the said Robert, second Viscount Tracy, dated 3rd May, and proved 25th June, 1662. wherein he mentions Dame Dorothy, his wife, and bequeaths " unto each of my *three* sons, viz., " *Thomas, William, and Henry*, and unto my daughter, Frances, severally, the yearly sum or " annuity of three score pounds apiece, during their respective lives, and *unto my sons, Robert* " *and Benjamin*, and unto my daughter, Mary, the yearly sum of twenty pounds apiece, to be " paid unto my dear wife, Dorothy, their mother, for and towards their maintenance."   He also mentions *John Tracy, his eldest son and heir apparent*, whom he appoints his sole executor.
   3.   Will of Dorothy, Viscountess Tracy, dated 11th September, 1684, and proved on the 3rd October, 1685, wherein she mentions *her son, Benjamin Tracy*, and *her son, Robert Tracy, Esq.*

III.   To Prove that the said ROBERT, 2nd VISCOUNT TRACY, died in May, 1662, and left issue, John Tracy, his eldest son, who succeeded as third Viscount Tracy.

   1.   Extract from the transcript of the Register of the Parish Church of Toddington, in the County of Gloucester; whereby it appears, that the said Robert Viscount Tracy, was buried the 11th of May, 1662.
   2.   Will of the said Robert second Viscount Tracy, dated 3rd of May, 1662, and proved 25th of June following, in which he mentions " *John Tracy, his sonne and heyre apparent*," to whom probate of the said Will was granted, by the description of " *Johannis domini Tracy, modo domini vicecomitis Tracy de Rathcule, filii naturalis legitimi dicti defuncti.*"

IV.   To Prove that the said JOHN, 3rd VISCOUNT TRACY, had issue, three sons, viz., Willam Tracy, afterwards 4th Viscount Tracy, Charles Tracy, and Ferdinando Tracy.

   1.   Will of the said John, third Viscount Tracy, dated 3rd of March, 1682-3, and proved 11th of June, 1687, wherein he mentions *his son William Tracy*, on whom and the heirs male of his body, he settled his estates in the County of Gloucester, whom failing, to " *John Tracy, my* " *grandson*," and the heirs male of his body.
   2.   Extract from the Register of Matriculations of the University of Oxford.
        " Coll. Reg. Vice Canc. Dn'e Bathurst.
        " Term S. Mich. 1674.
        " Decr. 4, D. Guilh.: Tracy, a. n. 17 Honmi. Viri Joh. Tracy, Vice-Comitis, Rhogul de
        " Toddington, in Agro Gloc. filius.
        " D. Carolus Tracy, a. n. 16 ejusdem D'ni filius.
        " D. Ferdinandus Tracy, a. n. 15 ejusdem D'ni filius."
   3.   Will of Sir John Tracy, of Stanway, in the County of Gloucester, Baronet, dated 12th of June, 1673, and proved 10th of May, 1678: whereby, after certain previous limitations, he devised his estates of Stanway, &c., " *to Charles Tracy, Esq., second son of the Right Honourable* " *John Lord Viscount Tracy.*" and the heirs male of his body, whom failing, " *to Ferdinando* " *Tracy, third son of the said John, Lord Viscount Tracy, and to the heirs male of his body.*"
   4.   Will of Elizabeth Viscountess Tracy, dated 30th January, 1687-8.

   (a) This Horace Tracy was baptized at Isleworth, in Middlesex, on 28th June, 1618, and was buried there on 20th May, 1619.

V. To Prove that the said JOHN, 3rd VISCOUNT TRACY, died in March, 1687, and was succeeded by his eldest son, William, 4th Viscount Tracy.

    1. "Anno Domini, 1686. The Right Honourable John, Lord Viscount Tracy, died March y^e 8th "and was buried March y_e 11th."—*Toddington Register.*

    2. Will of the said John, the third Viscount Tracy, dated 3rd March, 1682, and proved by his widow and executrix on the 11th of June, 1687, whereby he devised all his estates "*to William Tracy,* "*my son,*" for life, with remainder to the heirs male of his body.

       Note.—At the date of the said Will, the said William Tracy was the testator's only *surviving son.*

    3. Will of Sir John Tracy, Baronet, of Stanway, dated 12th June, 1673, whereby he devised his estates, after divers limitations, "to the use and behoof of *William Tracy, Esq.,* *eldest son of* "*the said John,* Lord Viscount Tracy, for and during the term of his natural life."

    4. The entry of the baptism of Thomas Charles, eldest son of the said William Tracy, on the 3rd August, 1690, shows that the said William was then Viscount Tracy.—*Toddington Registry.*

VI. To Prove that the said WILLIAM, 4th VISCOUNT TRACY, had issue by his first Wife, Frances, an only son, John Tracy, and that the said John Tracy died (in his Father's lifetime), in April, 1684, being then an infant.

    "Anno Dom.: 1684. *John, the son of William Tracy, Esq., and Frances his wife,* was bap- "tized April ye 30th. Anno prædicto."

    "Anno Dom.: 1684. John, the son of William Tracy, Esq., and Frances, his wife, was buried "May the first."—*Toddington Registry.*

VII. To Prove that the said WILLIAM, 4th VISCOUNT TRACY, had issue by his second Wife Jane, an only son, Thomas Charles Tracy; and that the said William, 4th Viscount Tracy, died in April, 1712, and was succeeded by his said son and heir, Thomas Charles, who became 5th Viscount Tracy.

    1. "1690,—Thomas Charles, the son and heir of ye Rt. Honble. William Lord Viscount Tracy. and the Rt. Honble. the Lady Jane Tracy, was born on Sunday ye 27th day of July, about halfe an hour after seaven in ye evening, and was baptized Aug. 3."

    "Anno Domini 1712, the Rt. Honble. William Lord Viscount Tracy died April 18, and buried "April 19."—*Toddington Registry.*

    2. The Will of William, fourth Viscount Tracy, dated 23rd November, 1710, and proved 2nd July, 1712, wherein he mentions "*My son Thomas Charles Tracy,*" and appoints him sole executor, and mentions no other child. And Grant of Probate of the said Will on the 2nd July, 1712, on the oath, "prænobilis et honorandi viri Thomæ Caroli Vicecomitis Tracy filii dicti defuncti et executoris unici," &c.

VIII. To Prove that THOMAS CHARLES, 5th VISCOUNT TRACY, had issue by his first wife Elizabeth, two sons, viz.:—William Tracy, his eldest son, and Thomas Charles Tracy, his second son, afterwards 6th Viscount Tracy.

    1. "William, son of ye Rt. Honble. Thomas Charles Lord Viscount Tracy, was born at Stratford-upon-Avon, August 25, 1715, and baptized there."

    2. Enrollment of a Deed of Bargain and Sale, dated 4th of April, 1748, to which "The Right Ho-"norable Thomas Charles Lord Viscount and Baron Tracy, of Rathcoole, in the County of Dublin, "in the Kingdom of Ireland, and *the Honourable William Tracy, Esquire, eldest son and heir* "*apparent* of the said Thomas Charles Lord Viscount Tracy," were parties.

    3. "1719—Thomas Charles, son of ye Rt. Honble. Thomas Charles Viscount Tracy, was born June 15 "and baptized July the 12th."—*Toddington Registry.*

IX. To Prove that the said WILLIAM TRACY, eldest son and heir apparent of Thomas Charles, 5th Viscount Tracy, died in 1752 (in his father's life-time), without issue male.

    1. "1752.—The Honble. William Tracy, Esqre., son to the Right Honble. Thomas Charles Lord "Viscount Tracy by Lady Elizabeth, was buried April the 15th."—*Toddington Registry.*

    2. Will of the said Thomas Charles, fifth Viscount Tracy, dated 22nd of April, 1756, and proved 25th of June in the same year, wherein he refers to a settlement made on the 16th of September, 1748, between himself and the "*Honourable William Tracy my son, since deceased.*"

X. To Prove that the said THOMAS CHARLES, 5th VISCOUNT TRACY, died in 1756, and was succeeded by his eldest surviving son and heir, Thomas Charles Tracy, who became 6th Viscount Tracy.

    1. "1756.—The Right Honble. Thomas Charles Lord Viscount Tracy was buried June 7th."

2. The entry of the burial of Thomas Charles, eldest son of the said Thomas Charles, 5th Viscount Tracy, on the 18th August, 1792, shows his succession to his father in the Viscountcy.

XI. To Prove that THOMAS CHARLES, 5th VISCOUNT TRACY, had issue by his second wife, Frances, three sons, viz.:—John Tracy, afterwards 7th Viscount Tracy ; Robert Packington Tracy ; and Henry Leigh Tracy, afterwards 8th Viscount Tracy.

1. Enrollment of the Bargain and Sale (before referred to), dated 4th April, 1748, by which certain common recoveries to be suffered, were declared to be intended to enure, in the first place, for corroborating and confirming the estate limited to the Right Honble. *Frances, Lady Viscountess Tracy, wife of the said Thomas Charles Lord Viscount Tracy, for her life, and wherein mention is made of Elizabeth Viscountess Tracy his first wife.*

2. "1722.—John, the son of ye Rt. Honourable Thomas Charles Lord Viscount Tracy by ye " Lady Frances, was born August 8, and baptized August 26."

3. "1725.—Robert Packington, son of ye Rt. Honble. Thomas Charles Lord Viscount Tracy by " the Lady Frances, was born August 28, and baptized September 21, 1725."

4. "1732.—Henry, son of ye Rt. Honble the Lord Viscount Tracy by the Lady Frances, was born January 25th, and baptized February 8th.

5. Will of the said Thomas Charles, 5th Viscount Tracy, dated 22nd April, 1756, and proved 25th June following, wherein he devised estates to his sons, *John and Henry*, and refers to a settlement made between him *and his deceased son William*, dated 16th September, 1748.

XII. To Prove that THOMAS CHARLES, 6th VISCOUNT TRACY, died without male issue in August, 1792, and was succeeded by his half-brother, John Tracy, 7th Viscount Tracy.

1. "1792—August 18th. The Right Honble Thomas Charles Leigh, Lord Viscount Tracy, was " buried."—*Toddington Registry.*

Note.—The succession of the said John Tracy to his half-brother, Thomas Charles, 6th Viscount Tracy, is shewn by the Register of the burial of the said John Tracy, as John Lord Viscount Tracy, on the 10th February, 1793.

XIII. To Prove that JOHN, 7th VISCOUNT TRACY, died in February, 1793, without issue male.

1. "1793—February 10th. The Right Honble and Reverend John Lord Viscount Tracy, D.D., " Warden of All Souls' College, Oxford," was buried.

2. Will of the said John, 7th Viscount Tracy, dated 19th January, 1792, and proved 6th March, 1793, wherein he does not mention any child, which Will was proved by the oath of the *Right Hon. Henry, Lord Viscount Tracy (formerly the Honble. Henry Tracy), the brother of the deceased and sole executor.*

3. His death without issue male is shown by the succession of his brother Henry Tracy, as 8th Viscount Tracy.—*Toddington Registry.*

XIV. To Prove that ROBERT PACKINGTON TRACY, second son of Thomas Charles, 5th Lord Viscount Tracy, by his second wife, died in 1748, in his father's lifetime, without issue male.

1. Will of the said Robert Packington Tracy, dated at Bombay, 29th July, 1748, wherein he bequeathed to his father all that he was possessed of, or might belong to him in any shape whatsoever, and appointed his said father his sole executor, by the name of " Thomas *George* " Lord Tracy," which error is rectified in the Probate granted in London, 15th June, 1749, " by " the oath of the Right Honble. Thomas Charles, Lord Viscount Tracy, the natural and lawful " father of the deceased, and sole executor named in the said Will by the names and title of " Thomas George Lord Tracy, to whom administration was granted."

2. The succession of his younger brother, Henry Leigh Tracy, to the title of Viscount Tracy, in February, 1793.

XV. To Prove that HENRY LEIGH TRACY, third son of Thomas Charles, 5th Viscount Tracy, by his second wife, succeeded his brother John, 7th Viscount Tracy, and became 8th Viscount Tracy.

1. Probate Act of the Will of the Revd. Dr. John Tracy, 7th Viscount Tracy, dated 19th January, 1792, by which it appears that the said Will was proved by the oath of " *the Right Honble* " *Henry Lord Viscount Tracy*, of the Kingdom of Ireland (formerly the Honble Henry Tracy), " the brother of the deceased, and sole executor, &c.

XVI. To Prove that the said HENRY LEIGH, 8th LORD VISCOUNT TRACY, died in 1797, without male issue.

1. "1797, May 11th. The Right Honourable Henry Leigh, Lord Viscount Tracy, was buried Æt. 64."—*Toddington Register*.
2. Will of the said Henry, 8th Viscount Tracy (then the Honourable Henry Tracy), dated 3rd December, 1783, wherein he styled himself "The Honourable Henry Tracy," and appointed his "*brother, the Honourable and Reverend John Tracy*, Warden of All Souls College," one of the guardians to his "*dear daughter, Henrietta Susanna Tracy*," and mentions no other child. The said Will is signed "Hen. Tracy," but a Codicil annexed thereto, dated 2nd May, 1796, containing bequests of Legacies to some of his servants, is signed "Tracy."—The Will with Codicil annexed was proved on the 3rd June, 1797, by the oath of "*the Right Honble. Henrietta Susanna Tracy, Spinster, the daughter and sole executrix*, she having attained her age of "twenty-one years."
3. Parole evidence of the Reverend Francis Edward Witts, who knew the family of the said Henry, 8th Viscount Tracy.

XVII. To Prove that ROBERT TRACY, second son of Robert, 2nd VISCOUNT TRACY, died young and unmarried.

1. The entry of his younger brother William in the books of the Middle Temple, 8th December, 1649, wherein he is described as the *third* son of Robert Viscount Tracy.
2. Will of Sir John Tracy of Stanway.

XVIII To prove that THOMAS TRACY, third son of Robert, 2nd VISCOUNT TRACY, died without issue.

1. Entry of the burial of Mr. Thomas Tracy, on the 3rd of September, 1669.
2. Will of Sir John Tracy of Stanway.

XIX. To Prove that THOMAS and HORACE, the fourth and fifth sons of Robert, 2nd VISCOUNT TRACY, died infants.

Visitation Pedigree.

XX. To Prove that WILLIAM TRACY, sixth son of Robert, 2nd VISCOUNT TRACY, was admitted a Member of the Society of the Middle Temple, on the 8th of December 1649, and that he died without issue male.

1. "8th Dec. 1649. Die et Anno Predict.
"Magister Willielmus Tracy, filius 3ius. Roberti Vicecomitis Tracy admissus est in Societatem "Medii Templi Specialiter et obligatur una cum. Et dat pro fine 4*li*.
2. Said Will of Sir John Tracy of Stanway.
3. "Anno 1706. The Honourable William Tracy, Esq., of the Parish of St. Andrew, Holborn, "London, was buried June 21st. Certified in due time."

XXI. To Prove that HENRY TRACY, seventh son of Robert, 2nd VISCOUNT TRACY, died without issue Male.

Said Will of Sir John Tracy of Stanway.

XXII. To Prove that CHARLES TRACY, second son of JOHN, 3rd VISCOUNT TRACY, died young, without leaving issue Male.

1. "1676. Mr. Charles Tracy was buried May ye 6th Anno Predicto."
2. Entry in the Books of the University of Oxford of the matriculation and subscription of Charles Tracy, second son of John, Viscount Tracy, then aged 16, in the year 1674.

XXIII. To Prove that FERDINANDO TRACY, third son of JOHN, 3rd VISCOUNT TRACY, died in February, 1682, leaving issue by Katherine, daughter of Sir Anthony Keck, two sons, viz. Ferdinando Tracy and John Tracy.

1. "Anno Domini 1682, Ferdinando Tracy, Esq., was buried February the 10th Anno predicto."
2. Said Will of Sir John Tracy, of Stanway.
3. Will of John, third Viscount Tracy, dated 3rd March, 1682.

XXIV. To Prove that FERDINANDO TRACY, eldest son of Ferdinando Tracy, died in 1682, an Infant.

1. "Anno Domini, 1683. Ferdinando, the son of Ferdinando Tracy, Esq., and Katharine his wife, "was buried, Feb. ye 19 Anno predict."
2. Letters of Administration granted on the 7th June, 1683, to the Honourable Katharine Tracy' the mother of Ferdinando Tracy, *an infant*.

XXV. To Prove that JOHN TRACY, Esq., of Stanway, died in April, having had issue nine sons, viz., John Tracy, who died an Infant, in October, 1704, Robert Tracy, John Tracy, Ferdinando Tracy, Anthony Tracy, Thomas Tracy, William Tracy, who died in childhood, in May, 1729, Edward Tracy, who died an Infant, in January, 1723-4, and Charles Richard Tracy, who died an Infant, in March, 1725-6.

1. " 1735. April, Johannes Tracy de Stanway, Armigerii Sepultus xxiiii°

2. " 1704, Octob, Johannes Tracy, filius Johannes Tracy, Armigerii Sepultus iiij'

3. Will of Francis Keck, of Great Tew, in the county of Oxford, Esquire, dated 29th June, 1728, and proved 27th January, 1729, whereby he devised his reversion in certain estates, to *Ferdinando, third son, Anthony, fourth son, Thomas Tracy, fifth son, William Tracy, sixth son, John Tracy, second son, and Robert Tracy, eldest son of his (the testator's) nephew, John Tracy, Esquire,* successively, and to the heirs male of their bodies, provided that such of the devisees, as for the time being, should be entitled to his estates, should take and bear the surname of Keck.

4. " 1712, Anno Dom. Maij. Antonius filius Johannis Tracy, Armigeri baptizatus, 9° "

4. " 1716, Mar. Thomas filius Johannis Tracy, Armigeri, baptizatus, xii° "

6. " 1721, Jan. Gulielmus filius Johannis Tracy, Armigeri baptizatus, viii."

7. " 1729, Maij. Gulielmus filius Johannis et Annæ Tracy, Armigᵗ sepultus xvij ' "

8. " 1723, Janij. Edwardus filius Johannis Tracy de Stanway, Armigeri sepultus."

9. " 1724, Dec. Carolus Richardus filius Johannis Tracy, Armigeri baptizatus, xiiij° "

10. " 1725, Martii. Carolus Richardus filius, Johannis Tracy, Armigeri sepultus, xxij' "

11. " Will of Ann Tracy, of Coscombe, in the County of Gloucester, widow, dated 12th June, 1746 and proved 29th March, 1762, wherein she says, that her late husband, John Tracy Esq., had died intestate, and mentions *her sons, Thomas Tracy and her son Keck* (i. e., *Anthony Tracy*, who assumed the name of *Keck*). In a Codicil she also mentions *her son*, Robert Tracy, Esq.

XXVI. To Prove that ROBERT TRACY, eldest surviving son of John Tracy of Stanway, died in 1767, without issue Male.

1. " 1767.—Robert Tracy Esq., was buried September 6th."

2. Will of the said Robert Tracy of Stanway, in the County of Gloucester, Esq., dated 16th October 1766, and proved on the 4th February, 1768, whereby he devised all his estates to trustees, upon trust, in case he (the said testator) and his brothers, " *John Tracy Atkyns, Thomas Tracy*, and *Anthony Keck*," should all of them *die without issue male*, to the use and behoof of *Henrietta Charlotte Keck*, " eldest daughter of my said brother, Anthony Keck, for and during the term of " her natural life," with remainder to her first and every other son in tail male, and in default of such issue, *to the use of Susan Keck, second daughter of his said brother, Anthony Keck*, for her life, remainder to the first and every other son of the said Susan Keck in tail male, with divers remainders over, with a proviso, that all and every the person and persons who should become entitled to the estates of the testator under the limitations of his Will, should take and use the surname of *Tracy*, and for that purpose procure one or more Act or Acts of Parliament to effect that object.

Note.—The succession of his brother, John Tracy, to the estates of Stanway, shews that the said Robert Tracy died without issue male.

XXVII. To Prove that JOHN TRACY, who assumed the name of Atkyns, but afterwards resumed the name of Tracy, and who was Cursitor Baron of the Exchequer, second surviving son of John Tracy, died in July, 1773, without issue male.

1. " 1773.—Honble. John Tracy, Esquire, dy'd 24th July, and buried August 4th."

2. Will of John Tracy, Esquire, Cursitor Baron of the Exchequer, dated 19th October, 1767, whereby he bequeathed the whole of his real and personal estate to his wife, Katherine Tracy, whom he appointed his sole executrix—" Codicil of me, the Honourable John Tracy, lately " called John Tracy Atkyns, Cursitor Baron of his Majesty's Court of Exchequer," dated 1st August, 1768, whereby he directed his share in certain estate which he had inherited under the Will of Francis Keck, to be sold, and the interest of the money arising from such sale to be paid to his wife, Katherine Tracy, for life, and after her death, the said money was to be divided between his nieces, the Honourable Henrietta Charlotte Keck and Susanna Keck, and his nephews and nieces, the sons and daughters of his late sister, Ann Travell ; and if they died without issue, their share was to be divided among his three other sisters. The said Will and Codicil were proved on the 4th August, 1774.

Note.—The succession of the said daughters of Anthony Keck, to the estates devised by their uncle, Robert Tracy, Esquire, in 1766, proves that the said John Atkyns Tracy died without issue male.

XXVIII. To Prove that FERDINANDO TRACY, third son of John Tracy, died in May, 1729, without issue male.

" 1729.—Maii, Ferdinando filius Johannis Tracy, Armigeri, Sepultus xiii."

Note.—It appears by the Will of Francis Keck, Esquire, dated 29 June, 1728, that Ferdinando Tracy was then the *third* surviving son of John Tracy, Esquire, of Stanway ; and as Anthony Tracy, the fourth son, succeeded to the estates which the said Francis Keck had settled upon him IN DEFAULT *of heirs male of the body of his elder brother Ferdinando,* the said Ferdinando Tracy (who, at the time of his decease, could not have been more than 22 or 23 years of age) must have died without issue male, which agrees with their being no mention of his issue in the settlement of the estates of his brother, Robert Tracy, of Stanway, Esquire, in his Will, dated 16th October, 1766, before referred to.

XXIX. To prove that ANTHONY TRACY, who assumed the name of Keck, died in the year 1767, without issue male.

1. Will of the said Anthony Keck, of Great Tew, in the County of Oxford, Esquire, dated 7th December, 1763, and proved 9th July, 1767, whereby, after bequeathing legacies to his sisters, he devised the whole of his real and personal estate to his *two daughters, Henrietta Charlotte Keck and Susan Keck, whom he appointed* his executrixes.

2. Private Acts of Parliament of the 14 George III, and 58 George III, to enable the said Henrietta Charlotte Keck, afterwards Viscountess Hereford, and the said Susan Keck, afterwards Lady Elcho, to take the name and arms of Tracy, they having severally succeeded to the estates of their uncle, Robert Tracy, pursuant to the settlement thereof by his Will, dated 16th October, 1766, *failing the issue male of his brothers, John Tracy Atkyns, Thomas Tracy, and the said Anthony Keck*

XXX. To prove that THOMAS TRACY, of Sandywell, in the County of Gloucester, died on the 24th of June, 1770, without issue male, his only son, Dodwell Tracy, having died (in his father's lifetime) on the 13th February, 1768, without issue.

1. " 1770.—Thomas Tracy of Sandywell, Esquire, was buried July 2nd."

2. " 1768.—Dodwel, only son and heir of Thomas Tracy, Esquire, and Mary his wife, of Sandywell " was buried February 13th, in the 21st year of his age."

2. Monumental Inscription in the Church of Whittington, in the County of Gloucester.

" To the beloved Memory of Thomas Tracy, Esquire, of Sandywell, in Gloucestershire, youngest son of John Tracy, Esquire, of Stanway, in the said County, who deceased June 24th, 1770, aged 53. This excellent man was distinguished in private life by an uncommon sweetness of temper and benevolence of heart, and possessed in an eminent degree those social and amiable virtues which not only procured him the love of his relations and intimate friends, but the universal esteem of all his acquaintance. He was unanimously chosen by this county in two succeeding Parliaments, to represent the County of Gloucester, which important trust he discharged with the strictest integrity and disinterested zeal.

" He married Mary, only daughter and heiress of Sir William Dodwell, Kt., and had by her one only son, Dodwell Tracy, a youth (from his amiable disposition and distinguished parts) of the most promising hopes, but these alas were blasted, when in the flower of his age he was snatched from the arms of his afflicted parents and friends, January 11th, 1768, at Paris, on his return from his travels in the 21st year of his age. Mary, their lamenting wife and mother, placed this mournful testimony of her tenderest affection to her dear husband and her beloved son. Their remains are deposited in the Tracy vault at Stanway."

4. The succession of the daughters of Anthony Keck, to the estates devised by the Will of Robert Tracy, Esquire, dated October, 1776, proves that the said Thomas Tracy died without issue male.

XXXI. To Prove that ROBERT TRACY became a Judge of the Court of Common Pleas ; that he married Ann Dowdeswell, and had issue three sons ; viz. Robert Tracy, Richard Tracy, and William Tracy ; and died on the 11th September, 1735, aged 80.

1. Will of Robert 2nd Viscount Tracy, dated 3rd May, 1632, wherein he mentions *his sons, Robert and Benjamin,* and their mother Dorothy.

2. Will of Sir John Tracy, of Stanway, dated 12th June, 1673, whereby, after divers limitations, he bequeathed the reversion of his estates " *to Robert Tracy, the first sonne of the Right Honourable* " *Robert, Lord Viscount Tracy father of the said John, Lord Viscount Tracy, by his the said* " *Robert, Lord Viscount Tracy's last wife,* for and during the natural life of the said Robert " Tracy," and to the heirs male of his body, whom failing, " to the use and behoofe of *Benjamin* " Tracy, *second sonne of the said Robert, Lord Viscount Tracy, by his said last wife.*"

3. Entry in the books of the Society of the Middle Temple of the admission of the said Robert Tracy.

" Aprilis 15th, 1673. Robertus Tracy, armiger filius quintus Roberti Vicecomitis Tracy, de Tod- " dington, in Com. Gloucestriæ, admissus est in Societatem Medii Templi, specialiter et obligatur " una cum . . . . Et dat. pro fine, 04=00=00."

4. Will of Richard Dwdeswell, of Poole Court, in the County of Worcester, Esquire, dated 6th April, 1708, and proved 23rd January, 1711, wherein he made a devise " *unto my dear brother,* " *Robert Tracy, Esq., of Serjeant's Inn, in. Fleet Street,* one of Her Majesty's Justices *of the* " *Court of Common Pleas at Westminster.*"

5. Will of Robert Tracy, of Coscomb, in the Parish of Didbrook, in the County of Gloucester, Esq., " late one of the Justices of the Court of Common Pleas at Westminster," dated 15th December, 1732, and proved 4th October, 1735, whereby he devised his estates to his *grandson, Robert Tracy :* and besides other relations, mentions his *daughter-in-law, Mrs. Margaret Tracy, his*

Arthur Walter Tracy.

nephew, John Tracy, of Stanway, Esq., the Right Honourable the Lord Viscount Tracy, and describes his said daughter-in-law as the *mother of his said grandson, Robert Tracy.*

6. Ths Honourable Robert Tracy was buried, September 19th. 1735.   Register of Didbrook.

7. Monumental inscription to the said Mr. Justice Tracy; in Didbrook Church :
   " Near this place lies interred the body of the Honourable Robert Tracy, Esq., son of the Right
   " Honourable Robert, late Lord Viscount Tracy, of Toddington.
   " He was a Judge twenty-six years in the Courts of Westminster, but being struck with a palsy
   " in the year 1726, resigned a commission which he had so long executed with the greatest
   " knowledge, moderation, and integrity to the honour of his Prince, and universal satisfaction of
   " his fellow-subjects.

   Obiit 11° Sept., Anno 1735,
   Ætat. 60,
   Benefacere magis quam conspici."

8. Admission of Robert Tracy (son of Mr. Justice Tracy), into the Society of the Middle Temple, 9th
   November, 1700 ;
   " Novembris 9°. 1700, Magister Robertus Tracy, filius et hæres apparens, Roberti Tracy, Armigeri
   " servientis ad legem, admissus est in Societatem Medii Templi specialiter et obltgatur una cum.
   " Et dat pro fine—nil."

9. Admission of Richard Tracy into the Society of the Middle Temple, on the 24th January, 1708 ;
   " Januarii 24°, 1708, Magister Ricardus Tracy, filius secundus honorabilis Roberti Tracy, unius
   " Justiciariorum de Communi Banco admissus est in Societatem Medii Templi specialiter et
   " obligatur una cum.   Et dat pro fine—nil."

10. Entry of the baptism of William, son of Robert Tracy, Esq., and Ann, in Took's Court, 22nd
    February, 1692 ;
    " 1692.   February.   Wm son of Robert Tracy, Esqre., Ann, in Tuck's Court, was baptd 22nd."   Register of St. Andrew's Holborn.

    Note—The following statement respecting the issue of Mr. Justice Tracy, in the " Baronetage
    of England, by Arthur Collins," published in 1720, shews that Mr. Justice Tracy's three
    sons, Robert, Richard, and William, *were living at that time :* and as Collins refers, in
    another part of his account of the Tracy family, to a " M.S. hujus tam penes Mr. Justice
    Tracy," it may be presumed that he derived his information from Mr. Justice Tracy
    himself.

    " Robert, Viscount Tracy, who had two wives, from his first marriage descends Thomas Charles
    " the present Viscount Tracy, and from his Lordship's second marriage is descended Mr. Justice
    " Tracy, deservedly made one of the Court of Common Pleas by his Majesty King William, and
    " continued by our present Sovereign King George, who hath now living (by Ann his wife,
    " eldest daughter of William Dowdeswell, of Pool Court, in the County of Worcester, Esq.) three
    " sons ; Robert, Richard, and William, and two daughters, Ann, married to Charles Dowdeswell,
    " of Forthampton Court, in the County of Gloucester, Esq., deceased, and Dorothy, unmarried."

XXXII.   To Prove that ROBERT TRACY, Esq., eldest son of Mr. Justice Tracy, died
unmarried in September, 1732.

1. Letters of Administration granted to the Honble. Robert Tracy, Esq., his father, in
   October, 1732 ;
   " Octobris 1732.   Robertus Tracy, Arm. vicesimo tertio die emt. coms. Hon'li Roberto Tracy, Ar,
   " patri n'rali et l'timo. Roberti Tracy, Ar. nuper de Medio Templo, London, ead' def'ti, h'entis,
   " &c. ad ad'strandum bona jura et credita dicti def'ti de bene, etc. vigore commis Jurat."
   " *Note.*—In the Deposition on which the Administration was granted, the said Robert Tracy is
   described as a bachelor.

2. " Robert Tracy, Esq., a Member of the Middle Temple, was buried in the Middle Temple vault,   Temple Register.
   " on Thursday, the 27th day of September, 1732."

XXXIII.   To Prove that RICHARD TRACY, second son of Mr. Justice Tracy, died before
May. 1734, leaving issue an only son, Robert Tracy.

1. Will of " Richard Tracy, of Coscombe, in the County of Gloucester, Esq.," dated 16th January,
   1731-2, and proved 11th May, 1734, wherein he mentions his " *only son,* who is now very young,"
   and his wife Margaret ; and requests her, and the persons whom he appointed guardians of his
   son (in the event of his widow's death or second marriage), " to advise with my honoured father
   " as long as he lives, and after his death with my worthy friends and Kinsmen *Thomas Charles
   " Lord Viscount Tracy* and *John Tracy of Stanway, Esq.;*" in all things relating to the education
   of his said son.

2. Will of Mr. Justice Tracy, wherein he mentions his *grandson Robert Tracy.*

XXXIV.   To Prove that ROBERT TRACY, died in May, 1756, without issue.

1. " 1756.   Robert Tracy; Esq., of Coscomb, was buried May 30th."   Register of Didbrook.

2. Will of Robert Tracy, of Coscombe, in the County of Gloucester, Esq., dated 14th May, 1756, and
   proved 25th May, 1756, whence it appears that he was a Member of the Temple, that he had
   inherited the estates of Coscombe, and died without issue, as he bequeathed all his estates " to
   " my cousin, Robert Pratt, son of my Aunt Dorothy, daughter of *my late grandfather, the
   " Honourable Mr. Justice Tracy,* deceased."

XXXV. To Prove that WILLIAM TRACY, the third son of Judge Tracy, settled in Ireland, married Miss Mary O'Brien, of Dublin, and was buried in Castlebrack.

    1. Evidence of family reputation in the English branch of the Tracy family. Evidence given March 23rd, 1847, by Mrs. E. B. Lambe, on the claim of James Tracy.

    2. Evidence of reputation in the Treston and O'Brien families.

    3. Inscription on the tombstone.

    4. Oral evidence of persons who have seen that tombstone, many years ago.

    The evidence to sustain this point is fully stated in the case.

XXXVI. To Prove that JOHN TRACY, only son of William Tracy, settled in the county of Mayo, and married Catherine Treston, of Cottage, in that county, and died in 1779.

    Evidence as stated in the case.

XXXVII. To Prove that EDWARD TRACY, the eldest son of the said John Tracy, born in 1735, married, first, Mary, daughter of John Treston, Esq., of Cottage, in the county of Mayo, and had issue by her one son, Luke, better known as John.

    Evidence as stated in the case.

XXXVIII. To Prove that he married, secondly, Margaret, daughter of Martin Mc Hale, of Cloonkeash, in the county of Mayo, and had issue by her his second son, Martin Tracy, born in 1800.

    Evidence as stated in the case.

XXXIX. To Prove that LUKE, better known as JOHN, TRACY died at Greenwich, in 1834, without issue.

    Oral evidence. Registry of his burial.

XL. To Prove that MARTIN TRACY married Catherine, daughter of Matthew Toole, Esq., of Tuam, on the 10th of April, 1826, and had issue by her, Edward, his eldest, and Matthew (the Claimant), his second son.

    Oral evidence of members of the family acquainted with the facts. Certificates of baptism of Edward and Matthew.

XLI. To Prove that the said MARTIN TRACY died in 1847, and was buried in Abney Park Cemetery, Stoke Newington.

    Oral evidence. Registry of his burial.

XLII. To Prove that EDWRD TRACY, his eldest son, was drowned while bathing at Bhooz, in the East Indies, in 1850, unmarried.

    Oral evidence. Certificate of military authorities in the East Indies.

IN THE HOUSE OF LORDS.

CASE on behalf of MATTHEW TRACY, Esquire, claiming to be Heir to the Title of Viscount and Baron Tracy of Rathcoole, in the Kingdom of Ireland.

July, 1862.

MATTHEWS & GREETHAM,
68, LINCOLN'S INN FIELDS.

Check Out More Titles From HardPress Classics Series In this collection we are offering thousands of classic and hard to find books. This series spans a vast array of subjects – so you are bound to find something of interest to enjoy reading and learning about.

Subjects:
Architecture
Art
Biography & Autobiography
Body, Mind &Spirit
Children & Young Adult
Dramas
Education
Fiction
History
Language Arts & Disciplines
Law
Literary Collections
Music
Poetry
Psychology
Science
…and many more.

Visit us at www.hardpress.net

Im The Story
personalised classic books

"Beautiful gift., lovely finish.
My Niece loves it, so precious!"

Helen R Brumfeldon

⭐⭐⭐⭐⭐

UNIQUE GIFT

FOR KIDS, PARTNERS
AND FRIENDS

Timeless books such as:

Alice in Wonderland · The Jungle Book · The Wonderful Wizard of Oz
Peter and Wendy · Robin Hood · The Prince and The Pauper
The Railway Children · Treasure Island · A Christmas Carol

Romeo and Juliet · Dracula

Highly Customizable **Change** Books Title **Replace** Characters Names with you **Upload** Photo the inside pages **Add** Inscriptions

Visit
Im The Story .com
and order yours today!

CPSIA information can be obtained
at www.ICGtesting.com
Printed in the USA
BVHW092248270819
556849BV00015B/2191/P